AF605974

The Plastic Age, by Iris Hauser, 2009.

ReVisions

ReVisions

Speculating in Literature and Film in Canada

EDITED BY WENDY ROY

UNIVERSITY OF TORONTO PRESS
Toronto Buffalo London

Toronto Buffalo London
utppublishing.com
Printed in Canada

ISBN 978-1-4875-6758-3 (cloth)
ISBN 978-1-4875-6760-6 (EPUB)
ISBN 978-1-4875-6759-0 (PDF)

Library and Archives Canada Cataloguing in Publication

Title: ReVisions : speculating in literature and film in Canada / edited by Wendy Roy.
Names: Roy, Wendy, 1957– editor
Description: Includes bibliographical references and index.
Identifiers: Canadiana (print) 20250249367 | Canadiana (ebook) 20250249383 | ISBN 9781487567583 (cloth) | ISBN 9781487567606 (EPUB) | ISBN 9781487567590 (PDF)
Subjects: LCSH: Canadian fiction – 21st century – History and criticism. | LCSH: Speculative fiction, Canadian – History and criticism. | CSH: Speculative fiction, Canadian (English) – History and criticism. | CSH: Canadian fiction (English) – 21st century – History and criticism. | LCSH: Apocalypse in literature. | LCSH: Speculation in literature. | LCSH: Dystopian films – Canada. | LCSH: Apocalypse in motion pictures. | LCSH: Dystopian television programs – Canada. | LCSH: Apocalypse on television. | LCGFT: Literary criticism.
Classification: LCC PS8191.A66 R48 2025 | DDC C813/.609 – dc23

Cover design: John Beadle
Cover image: *The Plastic Age*, by Iris Hauser, 2009

We wish to acknowledge the land on which the University of Toronto Press operates. This land is the traditional territory of the Wendat, the Anishnaabeg, the Haudenosaunee, the Métis, and the Mississaugas of the Credit First Nation.

This book has been published with the help of a grant from the Federation for the Humanities and Social Sciences, through the Awards to Scholarly Publications Program, using funds provided by the Social Sciences and Humanities Research Council of Canada.

University of Toronto Press acknowledges the financial support of the Government of Canada, the Canada Council for the Arts, and the Ontario Arts Council, an agency of the Government of Ontario, for its publishing activities.

Canada Council for the Arts
Conseil des Arts du Canada

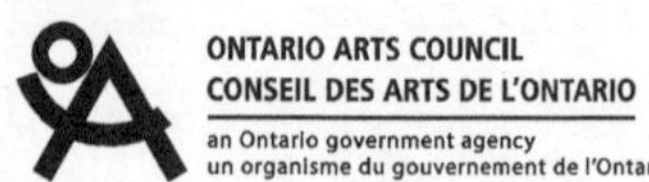

Funded by the Government of Canada
Financé par le gouvernement du Canada
Canada

Contents

Crossing Over: Dystopian and Posthuman Futures for Young People

Interlude

Creating Communities: Consumption and Hunger in Dystopian Cities and Prisons

Interlude

Acknowledgments

I would like to thank the many people and agencies who helped to make this collection possible. First, I acknowledge and thank the Social Sciences and Humanities Research Council of Canada (SSHRC) for Insight and Connections grants that supported my research on apocalyptic and dystopian fiction in Canada, as well as the 20/21 Vision: Speculating in Literature and Film in Canada conference. I also gratefully acknowledge financial assistance for publishing this book from the SSHRC Awards to Scholarly Publications Program. Warm thanks to the University of Saskatchewan, the College of Arts and Science, and the Department of English for financial support for the conference, as well as for scholarly support and sabbatical time that allowed me to conduct research and to complete editing of this book. In particular, I owe a debt of gratitude to my home department for the award of the 2023-2026 Bateman Professorship, which provided research time and funding.

My sincere thanks and appreciation to the many critical and creative contributors to this book and to the conference; without you, the book would never have taken shape. My gratitude especially to emerging scholar Mabiana Camargo, who helped immensely with the project as a research assistant and in many other capacities. Thank you to the professional and helpful staff at University of Toronto Press, including Mark Thompson, Leah Connor, Melissa MacAulay, and Aditi Parikh, as well as indexer Matthew MacLellan, who helped to shepherd this collection through the publication process. I acknowledge that Amy LeBlanc's short story "Someone Is Dead" was previously published in her collection *Homebodies* (2023), by Great Plains Publications. A warm note of appreciation to my friend, Saskatoon artist Iris Hauser, who permitted us to use her spectactular and speculative painting *The Plastic Age* on the cover and as a frontispiece. And finally, my love and thanks to my life partner, Garth Cantrill, for his unfailing support and encouragement.

Wendy Roy

Introduction

ReVisions: Speculating in Literature and Film in Canada

WENDY ROY

In the painting *The Plastic Age* by Iris Hauser that serves as the cover image and frontispiece for this volume, a solitary figure stands on an apocalyptic hillside. Wearing, holding, and surrounded by multiple items of plastic debris – bags, water jugs, plumbing pipe, even a discarded hot water bottle – the person featured demonstrates in a visceral way the destructive force that humans have on the natural environment. At the same time, the rocky, yellow rise and the blue sky streaked by clouds have an eerie beauty, and the figure stands strong and tall, head held high, gazing into the distance. The focus on vision and distance in Hauser's painting is particularly appropriate for this study, because the concepts of the speculative and of speculation, and of envisioning and re-visioning, are at the heart of this collection of essays and creative works.

During the global pandemic that began in late 2019, the value of speculative fiction, film, and television became acutely evident. The health crisis demonstrated that the contemporary world can be a terrifying and isolating place. Through Canadian pandemic novels and television series such as Saleema Nawaz's *Songs for the End of the World* (2020) and the adaptation of Emily St. John Mandel's *Station Eleven* (2021), the crisis also showed that speculative writing and other forms of art can help us to sort out complex uncertainties about ourselves, others, and the world around us in an empathetic and considered way. Works of speculation can provide a humanistic perspective on issues such as health catastrophes, climate change, pollution, and technological innovation that cannot be considered only from scientific perspectives, because they have enormous significance for us all as human beings. Such creations are of value to their audiences for what they illuminate about possible future human experiences. At the same time, these works can be used by their creators to represent and speculate on current and past societal issues, such as relations of class, gender, and race, as well as issues of health, safety, environmental destruction, economic upheaval, and political conflict. For this reason, speculative writing in Canada has become a tool to interrogate colonial systems and histories and to open up spaces for members of often marginalized groups, including women, Indigenous Peoples, and members of LGBTQ2S+ communities. These works can help us to see what is happening in the world around us and, at the same time, to re-envision it, to understand the consequences of our actions, and to imagine revised and perhaps better alternatives.

ReVisions: Speculating in Literature and Film in Canada focuses especially on dystopian and apocalyptic works that speculate about the future and at the same time provide a commentary on the present and the past. This feature of speculative writing has been noted in many other studies; in his 2013 essay on the genre, R.B. Gill argues that "Engaged works of speculative fiction may present other realities, but their alternative worlds will comment on this world – negatively to satirize its shortcomings, or positively to provide a model for emulation" (81). Such works are of vital importance because they ask readers to consider events, developments, and policies in the world today, as well as the impact that these might have on the world of the future. In 1992, critic of Canadian speculative writing David Ketterer called these imagined scenarios "*consequential other worlds*," "linked to the author's present by a sense of putative historical continuity" that influences "the understanding of that supposedly known world" (5). According to his conceptualization, "historical continuity" is significant, but the contemporary world is only "supposedly known" because the work of speculation throws new light on what we perceive and understand about it.

In their analyses, Gill and Ketterer explore and expand on earlier ideas about speculative writing by theorists such as Darko Suvin. Suvin's 1977 concept of the "novum" has become foundational to discussions of science fiction (SF), defined as featuring "*the narrative dominance or hegemony of a fictional 'novum' (novelty, innovation) validated by cognitive logic*" that "deviat[es] from the author's and implied reader's norm of reality" (67, 68). Other than the "totalizing" nature of the novum, key to Suvin's conception of SF is that its "potency" arises from "unalienable historicity" (68) – in other words, its connection of past, to present, to future. As Suvin concludes, "significant SF" is "a way of commenting on the author's collective context" (89), of asking readers and viewers to reflect on what is going on in the present day through an imagining of the future.

SF literary works and films are often presumed to be about imagined scientific or technological innovations, but speculative writing as a broader category includes more open-ended conjecture about the future. The term *speculative fiction* first came into popular use when American writer Robert Heinlein used it in his 1947 essay "On the Writing of Speculative Fiction" to describe "the story of people dealing with contemporary science or technology" (14). While Heinlein's essay referred mainly to human responses to scientific developments, the term has since been used as a suitcase phrase that encompasses science fiction, fantasy, and horror. However, an alternative and perhaps more useful definition, and one related to Heinlein's, is that of well-known Canadian author of dystopian and apocalyptic works Margaret Atwood. In her study *In Other Worlds: SF and the Human Imagination* (2011), Atwood narrows the term, arguing that speculative fiction is different from science fiction in that it is a narrative of the future that does not necessarily focus on scientific developments and does not include "things that could not possibly happen," such as aliens and zombies, but instead centres on "things that really could happen but just hadn't completely happened when the authors wrote the books" (6). While Atwood's ideas have been challenged, notably by well-known SF writer Ursula Le Guin (Atwood, *In Other Worlds* 8), her conception of speculative fiction highlights the genre's focus on human actions and interactions.

Two categories of speculative writing that have become more widespread and more relevant in recent years are apocalyptic/post-apocalyptic and dystopian writing. In contemporary popular usage, the word "apocalypse" is applied to any event that kills a large number of humans, including pandemics, but also nuclear and other global wars, environmental devastation, capitalist excess, and technology gone awry.[1] Marlene Goldman's foundational 2005 study, *Rewriting Apocalypse in Canadian Fiction*, explores the roots of patriarchal apocalyptic thinking in the Christian Bible before analyzing how Canadian writing often resists that originary meaning. As it appears in the Revelation of St. John, apocalypse is the revelation of a purposeful end to the world as we know it through a series of plagues, floods, earthquakes, fires, and other catastrophic events, with the people chosen by God invited into "a new heaven and a new earth" (Rev. 21.1). Goldman points out that rather than focusing on the destruction of the existing world and a joyful future for the elect, Canadian authors, like most contemporary writers, concentrate on the "experience of those barred from paradise" (5) and present "the testimony of apocalypse's traumatized victims" (18). As do many theorists of speculative writing in general, Goldman concludes that such texts help to identify "political and social forces" (17) at work in the contemporary world, through their representations of imagined worlds.[2]

While an apocalyptic event or process may be imagined in such works, often the narrative goes beyond that event to outline a future after the catastrophe. Maximilian Feldner argues that features of the post-apocalyptic genre include "the occurrence of an apocalyptic event, the depiction of post-collapse society, and a narrative structure that connects and interlinks the pre-apocalyptic past with the postapocalyptic present" (167). Susan Watkins, in her critical study of women's post-apocalyptic fiction, takes this argument a step further, arguing that in post-apocalyptic texts there is also a "clear attribution of blame for the apocalyptic disaster" and that such texts focus on "taking the chance to rebuild in a different way" (9–10). As these critics interpret the genre, a linkage of past, present, and future is integral, and indeed this linkage is evident in most post-apocalyptic imaginings in Canada. In addition, most such works place the blame on humans, and many focus on new forms of recovery from a social world in crisis.

Apocalyptic and post-apocalyptic writing goes hand-in-hand with dystopic writing, since an imagined (or real) apocalyptic event can result in a dystopian society, and dystopian elements of a social world can lead to human-caused apocalyptic events. Like apocalyptic writing, dystopic writing is political. Literary and filmic dystopias explore the opposite of the kind of world imagined in Thomas More's *Utopia* (1516): instead of an imagined ideal world or positive utopia (itself likely ironic), such texts represent an imagined nightmare world, again often one that is based on and implicitly criticizes the contemporary social world.

This critique often happens through a focus on language and the power it conveys, as well as through resistance to closure. In their introduction to the 2003 collection *Dark Horizons: Science Fiction and the Dystopian Imagination*, Raffaella Baccolini and Tom Moylan make a distinction between the "*classical*, or canonical, form of dystopia" (1) and the "critical dystopias" that emerged during what they call the "dystopian turn" in the mid-1980s (3). Exemplified by Atwood's *The Handmaid's Tale* (1985), such works "refunctioned dystopia as a critical narrative form" (3) containing both "a narrative of the hegemonic order and a counter-narrative of resistance" (5). Baccolini and Moylan argue that this narrative "most often plays out by way of the social, and anti-social, use of language" (5). The dystopian protagonist, they note, is often forbidden from making use of speech and writing, and thus resistance often entails "the reappropriation of language" (6).

Critical dystopias in particular feature both historical specificity and what Baccolini and Moylan call "a utopian impulse," sometimes evident in a resistance to closure (7). This ambiguity, they argue, "opens a space of contestation and opposition for those collective 'ex-centric' subjects whose class, gender, race, sexuality, and other positions are not empowered by hegemonic rule" (7). As they suggest, dystopic writings, like apocalyptic ones, can be used to illuminate contemporary social and political inequities and struggles and to imagine different futures.

The essays and creative/critical works in this volume focus mainly on dystopian and apocalyptic/post-apocalyptic texts or scenarios, all of them from the Canadian context. As the title of the collection and the cover illustration indicate, most of the contributions also centre on the idea of re-visioning – of looking at Canada and the larger world of the past and future through new lenses, to gain new insights. This can entail adaptation or reinterpretation of a work in a new cultural or historical context, such as the television adaptation of *The Handmaid's Tale*. It can also involve exploration of historical events through a futuristic, speculative lens that asks readers to revise their understandings of past events and current relationships, such as the use by Cherie Dimaline (Métis), Waubgeshig Rice (Anishinaabe), and Jeff Barnaby (Mi'kmaw) of apocalyptic and dystopian scenarios to revisit Canada's history of colonization. *ReVisions: Speculating in Literature and Film in Canada* examines speculative fiction, film, and television, not necessarily set in Canada, but originating from writers of this place and expressing their particular concerns. The critical and creative works in this collection explore and put into practice the re-envisioning of elements of Canadian politics, cultures, and societies, in the process asking important questions about our social world and how we write about it. What do speculative texts tell us about ourselves – our pasts, our presents, and our futures? Which visions of "Canada" do we find in speculative texts? How do these visions reflect our own perceptions of the world? Does this kind of literary and/or cultural imagination offer space for grief, resilience, and hope? Does it help us respond constructively to crises or achieve social or economic change?

Some of these questions are pertinent both to contemporary Canadian fiction and film in general, and to apocalyptic and dystopian writing internationally. Many non-speculative texts published in this country ask readers to reflect on the past and present; these include recent historiographic novels, such as those by Michael Ondaatje and Esi Edugyan, and novels that focus on Indigenous experience, including Tomson Highway's *Kiss of the Fur Queen* (1998), Katherena Vermette's *The Break* (2016) and its sequels, and Michelle Good's *Five Little*

Indians (2020). Speculative works from other countries, such as *Cloud Atlas* by David Mitchell (2004), *The Hunger Games* series by Suzanne Collins (2008–10), *The Power* by Naomi Alderman (2016), *Future Home of the Living God* by Louise Erdrich (Ojibwe; 2017), and *Cloud Cuckoo Land* by Anthony Doerr (2021), may not tell us much about Canada, but they do ask important questions about the planet's past, present, and future.[3] At times, these texts also offer space for hope and resilience.

In Canada, much recent analysis of literary speculations has focused on Atwood's novels, especially *The Handmaid's Tale* and its adaptations and sequel, as well as the *MaddAddam* trilogy (2003, 2009, and 2013). In her speculations about environmental, scientific, and technological change, and how these changes intersect with political, social, and cultural needs and interests, Atwood has tapped into contemporary fears about the end of the current Western social order. As a result, her novels have a sizeable base of atypical readers in both print and electronic form, including those who find compelling the often catastrophizing world views in her fiction. The most recent adaptation of Atwood's 1985 novel has attracted an international viewership that far exceeds the number of readers of her books and at the same time has put her books back on best-seller lists.

Significant for the essays on film and television in this volume are the inroads Canadian speculative narratives have made into contemporary popular culture. Linda Hutcheon argues in *A Theory of Adaptation* that "When stories travel – as they do when they are adapted … across media, time, and place – … [l]ocal particularities become transplanted to new ground, and something new and hybrid results" (150). She devotes a section of her book to the personal, economic, and political motivations of adaptors, including how various aspects of an adapted work become emphasized, excluded, or extended because of particular cultural and political concerns (86–95). Adaptations, and indeed original films and television, help to highlight contemporary environmental, social, and political structures and problems, as is evident in the adaptation of *The Handmaid's Tale*. While the Hulu series was conceived before the 2016 election of Donald Trump to his first term in office in the United States, many commentators have since noted that it seems to comment in a prescient way on the right-wing turn in American politics (see, for example, Somacarrera-Íñigo). As well as being technologically futuristic, because of its production not by mainstream television networks but by an internet streaming site, the continuing series provocatively questions the present and future of social relations in North America. Series creator and writer Bruce Miller used his first Emmy acceptance speech to urge audience members to "go home" and "fight" for the kinds of rights that this show presents as threatened by the contemporary political milieu (Bishop). The eloquent silences of oppressed characters such as Offred/June, played by Elisabeth Moss, take on additional meanings and impacts because of societal concerns forty years after the book was originally published. The Handmaids' confining red robes and white bonnets have become potent visual symbols of protest around the world, including against incursions into reproductive rights, in what has been called "a subversive inversion of [their] association with the oppression of women" (Beaumont and Holpuch).

However, as this collection demonstrates, speculative writing in Canada encompasses much more than works by Atwood or their adaptations, which have been even more critically examined since her public involvement in a series of crises in creative writing and its instruction in Canada.[4] The variety of texts and authors under discussion in this volume attests to this expansiveness. While some of these works can be categorized as genre narratives – zombie films, children's writing, SF space travel stories – a surprising number are by mainstream literary writers who make use of the speculative genre because it allows them to do something that they cannot do with realistic scenarios: as Daniel Heath Justice (Cherokee) notes about writing by Indigenous authors, to "imagine otherwise" (143). Indeed, one of the salient features of Canadian speculative writing is the blurring of boundaries between the popular and the literary. If Phyllis Gotlieb once said that she was a poet in Canada and a writer of SF in the United States (Ketterer 1), the same cannot be said for most of the authors represented in this collection, because distinctions are often no longer made between popular (or genre) and literary writing. Atwood and Mandel can write speculative novels that are literary successes and that also become international hit television series. Dimaline can publish a novel, *The Marrow Thieves*, supposedly for young adults, that crosses over into adult territory after it wins a Governor General's Award. Barnaby can follow some of the conventions of the zombie film in *Blood Quantum* but at the same time pointedly ask readers to consider contemporary and past Indigenous–settler relations in Canada. The fiction and film featured in this collection, then, is not only genre- and boundary-crossing; it is political in that it asks questions about the social world rather than imagining apparently unrelated new worlds or technologies.

Most of these narratives – including the creative works that appear in this volume – focus on human beings in a world irrevocably changed by catastrophic events, whether pandemic or war or environmental degradation caused by human mismanagement, greed, and neglect. However, rather than concentrating on the science or even the physical results of this devastation, these narratives ask readers to consider human relationships and the importance of language and cultural practice to living as a human in such a world.

The differences highlighted and the questions posed by Indigenous speculations are relevant to investigations in this collection. In his 2017 study *Why Indigenous Literatures Matter*, Justice coins the alternative term "wonderworks" to refer to Indigenous fantasy and speculative writing, arguing that the term breaks down "dualistic presumptions of real and unreal" and encompasses "ceremony and ritual" and "dream" as well as "lived encounter and engagement" (152). He reminds readers of the possibilities for speculative writing: to "remind us that other worlds exist; other realities abide alongside and within our own," and, when written by Indigenous authors, to "centre this possibility within Indigenous values and toward Indigenous, decolonial purposes" (153). Justice also quotes American scholar Grace Dillon (Anishinaabe), who wrote in 2012 that "It is almost commonplace to think that Native Apocalypse … has already taken place" (8, qtd. in Justice 166–7). Justice concurs that Indigenous Peoples "have lived" apocalypse: "For populations that faced eighty-percent mortality and higher due to European-inflicted disease, displacement, enslavement, starvation, military action, and internment … the 'end of days' isn't just the stuff of doomsday religionists or science fiction, but of historical memory and lived experience.… And that makes those of us living today the post-apocalypse survivors of world-shaking catastrophes" (167–8). This concept of Indigenous Peoples as living post-apocalypse is evident in several of the texts considered in this collection, including the novels by Rice, Dimaline, and Thomas King (*The Back of the Turtle*) and the film written and directed by Barnaby.[5] The post-apocalyptic worlds imagined in these narratives are not entirely bleak or focused on the past, however; as Justice argues, they acknowledge the importance of ceremony and dream, and they foreground what he calls "Indigenous decolonial purposes."

In compiling and editing this collection, I acknowledge previous key anthologies and studies of speculative writing in Canada. These include the foundational 1979 anthology of historical fantastic and SF works, *Other Canadas*, edited by John Robert Colombo, which was followed by collections including John Bell and Lesley Choyce's 1981 anthology of writing from Atlantic Canada, *Visions from the Edge*, and the Canadian futuristic anthology series *Tesseracts*, beginning with the volume edited by Judith Merril in 1985. More recently, the field has produced Robert J. Sawyer's collection *Distant Early Warnings: Canada's Best Science Fiction* (2009); Neal McLeod's *mitêwâcimowina* (2016), which foregrounds

Indigenous speculative storytelling; and Joshua Whitehead's *Love after the End: An Anthology of Two-Spirit and Indigiqueer Speculative Fiction* (2020). I also acknowledge my debt to two germinal studies of speculative writing in Canada from the 1990s: Ketterer's 1992 monograph *Canadian Science Fiction and Fantasy* and the 1995 essay collection *Out of This World: Canadian Science Fiction and Fantasy Literature*, compiled by Andrea Paradis. Ketterer's study takes a historical approach, exploring early Canadian fantastic writing in both English and French, including works published in pulp magazines and by expatriates; historic and contemporary mythic and fantastic stories; and SF by writers ranging from Gotlieb to William Gibson to Atwood. The collection put together by Paradis originated from the 1995 "Out of This World" exhibit at the National Library of Canada and similarly attempts a comprehensive approach. Its essays include historical overviews of both anglophone and francophone fantastic literatures; explorations of themes such as family and identity; studies of women's writing and genres including magic realism and high fantasy; examinations of fan magazines and children's literature; and analyses of speculative radio, film, and television.

More recent volumes of essays have extended and enriched these foundational investigations. Edited by Allan Weiss, *Perspectives on the Canadian Fantastic* (1998), *Further Perspectives on the Canadian Fantastic* (2005), and *The Canadian Fantastic in Focus: New Perspectives* (2015) present selected proceedings of the biennial Academic Conference on Science Fiction and Fantasy, a gathering that had its origins in the National Library exhibit. Other significant essay collections include *Worlds of Wonder: Readings in Canadian Science Fiction and Fantasy Literature* (2004), edited by Jean-François Leroux and Camille La Bossière, and *Canadian Science Fiction, Fantasy, and Horror: Bridging the Solitudes* (2019), edited by Amy J. Ransom and Dominick Grace. Introductions in the latter two collections take thematic approaches that place science fiction and fantastic writing in the context of Canadian literature in general. Leroux and La Bossière begin with Northrop Frye's famous assertion that Canadian literature is concerned not so much with the question "Who am I?" as the broader locational question "Where is here?" They conclude that while it is impossible "to pinpoint on any map" this theme in SF in Canada (2), it remains a key question. Ransom and Grace focus on another historical theme in Canadian literature and criticism: the two solitudes of French and English Canada and ways in which these solitudes are bridged in Canadian science fiction, horror, and fantasy narratives.[6] The essays in their collection extend the concept of difference to include topics such as geographical borders, gender identities, the species divide, and generic boundaries.

Unlike these two previous anthologies, the theme of this current collection is not related to historic literary criticism in Canada. Instead, it focuses on vision: both visions of the future and acknowledgment and reinterpretation of Canada's historical past. *ReVisions: Speculating in Literature and Film in Canada* builds upon and extends the examinations in previous studies, but also narrows them. Rather than considering historical as well as current examples of speculative writing, this collection emphasizes the contemporary. Rather than grouping SF with fantasy, magic realism, and horror, this collection focuses on a particular type of speculative writing in fiction and film – not primarily technological or scientific and not a portmanteau of other related genres (although these are elements of some of the texts under consideration), but instead speculations about human and posthuman relationships, languages, and cultures. *ReVisions: Speculating in Literature and Film in Canada* narrows the field further by including writing that primarily explores dystopian and apocalyptic/post-apocalyptic worlds, but it also expands the area of study by including speculations in film and television.

Many of the critical essays in this collection focus on a single text or a few related ones, but all acknowledge conversations with broader issues and texts related to speculative writing in Canada. While the choice of which writers to feature reflects, to some extent, the interests of contributors (for example, in the decision not to address all of the speculative writing by Atwood, Lai, or Dimaline), some chapters were solicited in order to ensure that key discussions would be featured. Most of the critical analyses engage with the editorial practices and objectives of close reading – detailed attention to form, language, and interpretation – and to how this focused attention uncovers and underscores meaning. While this approach has often been taken for granted in literary and cultural studies, and has sometimes been criticized, scholars such as Jonathan Culler have more recently emphasized its continuing relevance.[7] Attention to detail, rather than simply to the broad strokes of subject matter or historical context, helps to highlight specific conflicts related to race, class, gender, and colonialism that are critiqued in this collection. In particular, the close attention paid to novels and films by Indigenous authors collectively makes a powerful case for the value of speculative writing in exploring the politics of land, past and future.

As well as the focus on Indigenous experience noted above, speculation on racialization is evident in other texts studied in this volume, including books by Nalo Hopkinson, Larissa Lai, and G.S. Prendergast. A number of essays in *ReVisions* explore primary works that foreground gender: gender relations in novels for young adults, short stories by

Canadian women, novels by Atwood and their adaptations, and the Canadian television series *Killjoys*; and speculations on gender identity and gender diversity in novels by Lai, Kai Cheng Thom, and Nancy Lee. Other chapters pointedly address writing about human-caused environmental degradation, including novels by Dimaline, King, and Monica Hughes, and short stories by P.K. Page and Carol Shields.[8] In many chapters, political and economic strife is explored as an apocalyptic or dystopian catalyst, for example in stories by Atwood and Margaret Laurence and Cold War novels by Lee and Nicolas Dickner. Health crises are also catalysts in some of these narratives, such as pandemics in novels by Mandel and Lai and two of the creative contributions, and a zombie epidemic in *Blood Quantum*. And over-reliance on futuristic technology is examined in works by Lai, Hopkinson, and Atwood, and in the posthumanism of some YA fiction in Canada and the television series *Killjoys*.

Finally, this book crosses the borders between critical and creative writing by including an interview with a writer of fiction and three speculative creative/critical contributions by Canadian residents, set in imagined dystopian and apocalyptic worlds. These "interludes" intersect in unique and constructive ways with the academic analyses in this volume, focusing as they do on theories of Indigenous speculative fiction, interfaces with the imagined dystopian city, and the potential for future apocalyptic pandemics that highlight issues of class and gender. Each provides a commentary or lead-in to one section in the collection or acts as a connective link between two distinct parts.

This book is divided into five sections. The first, "Connecting Past to Future," investigates the ways in which futuristic fiction is often also about the past. The section opens with an essay by Gage Karahkwí:io Diabo on Waubgeshig Rice's *Moon of the Crusted Snow*. Diabo argues that Rice's novel examines the "weight of the past and present that bears upon how we decide to achieve our collective future" (25); their chapter focuses on the novel's exploration of the horrific consequences of capitalistic development in the North, and on the counteracting forces of Anishinaabe knowledge. The second paper in this section, by Alicia Fahey, analyzes the affective aspects of archives in Thomas King's *The Back of the Turtle* and Larissa Lai's *The Tiger Flu*. Fahey argues that these speculative archives help to envision the past, present, and future in new ways; she concludes that the focus on "embodied knowledge and communal responsibility" offers the foundation for alternative modes of "being together in the world" (46). The third chapter in this section, by Matthew Cormier, investigates representations of an apocalyptic historical time period – the Cold War – in Nicolas Dickner's *Apocalypse for Beginners* (*Tarmac*, in the original French) and Nancy Lee's *The Age*. Cormier concludes that these works allow speculative fiction and historiographic metafiction (Linda Hutcheon's term) "to confront and challenge one another" (68) and in the process to create space for "alternative, anti-apocalyptic possibilities" (73).

The book's second section, "Crossing Over," focuses on fiction by and about young people in Canada, an important and expanding subset of the speculative genre. The preamble to the section is an interlude interview by Mabiana Camargo with cross-over writer Cherie Dimaline, in which Dimaline speaks about writing speculative fiction as a Métis author, including using youthful protagonists and imagining alternate realities such as "who we could have been without colonization" (86). The interview leads into a scholarly essay by Gwen Rose, who discusses resistance and resurgence in Dimaline's *The Marrow Thieves* and its sequel, *Hunting by Stars*. Rose argues that the trappings of dystopian fiction, including "the ruined setting," play a secondary role to the "resurgent Indigenous practices" in both novels (96); such resistance is not a counter-narrative, Rose contends, but instead the main narrative, in the way that characters share and depend on Indigenous world views, stories, and languages. Next are two essays about female characters in apocalyptic fiction for young people. Alena Cicholewski examines how Erin Bow's *Prisoners of Peace* and G.S. Prendergast's *Nahx Invasion* duologies, both set on the Canadian prairies, imagine a posthuman future for their protagonists. She concludes that despite the novels' attempts to question gendered stereotypes, a common trope of some YA fiction, "the empowering potential" of each is "constricted by heteropatriarchal social structures" (118). The chapter by William Thompson that concludes this section focuses on how climate change is addressed in children's literature. In particular, it examines the ways three novels by Monica Hughes, *The Keeper of the Isis Light*, *Ring-Rise Ring-Set*, and *The Crystal Drop*, "frame environmental devastation in terms of girls and girls' bodies" and at the same time demonstrate that fiction for young adults had addressed the climate crisis years before its "current imperative" (140).

The third section, "Creating Communities," investigates speculation related to urban spaces that are marked by racialization and gender, and by individual and collective actions and impulses such as eating and hunger. Introducing the section is a critical-creative interlude by Sheheryar Sheikh that explores the concept of *othering* in Nalo

Hopkinson's apocalyptic, Toronto-centred *Brown Girl in the Ring*; the critical reflection then interjects Sheikh's short story "Brown Boy under the Cape" in order to support the concept that there can be a subaltern version of the SF novum that includes the spiritual. Following is an essay by Jessica McDonald on urban place-making in Hopkinson's story collection *Skin Folk*. McDonald argues that these speculative stories show that individuals have the power to shape urban spaces, even those that appear to be beyond their influence, through activities such as eating, working, and travelling. The next chapter, by Shelley Boyd, explores the dystopian prison/town space of Margaret Atwood's *The Heart Goes Last*. Boyd argues that food in the novel serves to replicate the capitalist system, to enforce compliance, and to objectify inmates/residents, but at the same time serves as a mode of resistance. The final chapter in this section, by Kai McKenzie, examines Kai Cheng Thom's *Fierce Femmes and Notorious Liars*. The Chinese mythological figure of the hungry ghost, McKenzie argues, represents how ciscentric society haunts the novel's trans protagonist, even after she has moved to a city where she is able to forge community.

The interlude at this point is a short story by Amy LeBlanc, "Someone Is Dead," that focuses on a microcosmic world of interpersonal relationships, including death and new life, during a pandemic. LeBlanc's story prefaces the next section, "Apocalyptic World-Making," which begins with Jasmine Redford's analysis of the world-building in Emily St. John Mandel's pandemic novel *Station Eleven* through an embedded comic book series. Redford argues that "so-called disposable media and art forms," such as comics, become the basis for personal and cultural identities as characters move into the imagined future (263). Next is an essay by Mabiana Camargo on Atwood's *MaddAddam* trilogy. Camargo refers to theories of space and gender to argue that the novels' imagined future dystopian society highlights contemporary oppressive gender relations through the literal and figurative confinement of three main female characters. The third chapter in the section, by Wendy Roy, investigates the world-building potential of little-studied speculative short stories. Roy argues that the key characteristic of uncertainty allows well-known Canadian authors Margaret Laurence, Margaret Atwood, P.K. Page, and Carol Shields to explore fears about nuclear war and climate change, focusing in particular on human and gendered communication during crisis times.

The final interlude moves from the speculative into the science fictional, with a powerful and imaginative story by Cynthea Masson about human interactions through time, as related to a future engineered religious apocalypse. The story is followed by a final section, "Gender and Indigeneity," on apocalyptic and dystopian film and television in Canada, beginning with June Scudeler's chapter about Jeff Barnaby's *Blood Quantum*. Scudeler argues that Barnaby makes creative use of the conventional zombie movie format to explore the combined negative effects of colonization and toxic masculinity; she concludes that the survival of specific characters suggests a way forward beyond "colonially imposed ideas of Indigeneity and masculinity" (346). The second paper in this section, by MacKenzie Read, examines *The Handmaid's Tale* and its film and television adaptations to analyze who is looking and who is looked at. Read concludes that how these acts are presented encourages audiences either to conspire with the female main character against the oppressive regime in which she is trapped, or to endorse its surveillance of her. The book concludes with an essay by Heather Snell on the television series *Killjoys*. Snell investigates changes in how "tough women" have been represented in film and television over the four decades that separate *Killjoys* from the first *Alien* film, pointing to new post-feminist sensibilities in how action heroines are portrayed.

This volume had its origins in a conference held virtually in 2021, and while some of the contributions reflect on the circumstances around that gathering, they go far beyond what occurred there. Called 20/21 Vision: Speculating in Literature in Film in Canada, the conference was postponed from 2020 (when it was to be called 20/20 Vision and held in person at the University of Saskatchewan) and moved online, as a direct result of the COVID-19 pandemic. An ongoing contemporary, worldwide health catastrophe had an enormous effect on the conference and the kinds of exchanges and collaborations that it could encompass. The results were not all negative, since while we could not come together in person to exchange ideas, scholars and writers from a much wider geographical area were able to attend and participate, including Canadian practitioners of speculative writing such as Dimaline, Nawaz, Goldman, and Wayde Compton. The interchanges that resulted were productive, exciting, and yet limited to what could be expressed through a videoconferencing platform. The interview with Dimaline that is featured in this collection was conducted after the conference but was inspired by some of the concepts and interchanges in her keynote address, especially her argument that Indigenous speculative writing works "to reveal, to interrupt, and to recentre" complex events, processes, and peoples in the past and present ("From Where We Stand"). Several of the essays and creative works in this volume are revised and expanded versions of papers presented at the conference, but others were conceived and written specifically for the collection.

While the global pandemic fundamentally altered the nature of the conference, it also helped to underscore the goals of both the conference and this volume. Occurring shortly after the 2021 uncovering of unmarked graves of Indigenous children at former Residential Schools, which had been known of but not located for decades, the conference and its keynote address highlighted the fundamental importance of speculative writing by Indigenous authors that both reveals the past and reimagines the future. It emphasized, as does this collection, the ways that speculative writing can help to recentre and re-envision broader histories and futures in or relating to Canada. It helped us to see that, as we stand on a metaphoric, dystopian hillside that reveals the devastating impact of our relationships and activities, we can still look into the distance with purpose, hope, and conviction, in a way that exposes and critiques colonial and gendered power structures and at the same time celebrates the power of diversity and collaboration.

NOTES

1 See Andrew Tate's *Apocalyptic Fiction* for a full discussion of the various events and developments that can be considered apocalyptic (14, 18).
2 Allan Weiss argues in "The Canadian Apocalypse" that apocalyptic fiction "speaks out of and to its historical context. By portraying the end, apocalyptic literature reveals much about a culture's concept of time, and about how it sees its relationship to the universe" (35). Weiss's essay thus underscores the historicity of such works of fiction.
3 A number of these texts are equally well-known for their television and film adaptations, not just the internationally popular *Hunger Games* series (2012–15), but also the films *The English Patient* (1996) and *Cloud Atlas* (2012) and the miniseries *The Power* (2023).
4 For information about and discussions of part of this controversy, see the archived UBC Accountable website, Atwood's essay "Am I a Bad Feminist?," and the essays in *Refuse: CanLit in Ruins*, edited by Hannah McGregor, Julie Rak, and Erin Wunker.
5 Goldman noted in her 2005 study that the end of the world as some know it had already happened in a number of Canadian novels published before that date, including Thomas King's *Green Grass, Running Water* and Joy Kogawa's *Obasan*.
6 The phrase is the title of a 1945 book by Hugh MacLennan, set in Quebec, which in turn comes from a 1904 letter by Rainer Maria Rilke, in which he discusses human love.

7 Culler defines "close reading" as "attention to how meaning is produced or conveyed, to what sorts of literary and rhetorical strategies and techniques are deployed to achieve what the reader takes to be the effects of the work or passage" (22).

8 Had this book been conceived after 2020, it likely would have included study of one or more recent Canadian novels about climate change, including Catherine Bush's *Blaze Island* (2020), Michael Christie's *Greenwood* (2020), Rebecca Campbell's *Arboreality* (2022), and Thomas Wharton's *The Book of Rain* (2023). Similarly, had there been space, studies of fiction by Canadian writers about speculative economic and political upheaval, such as Omar El Akkad's *American War* (2017), Claudia Casper's *The Mercy Journals* (2016), M G. Vassanji's *Nostalgia* (2016), and Madeline Ashby's *Company Town* (2016), might have been included. The collection could also have featured additional studies of speculative film and television: for instance, *Orphan Black* (2013–17), a televised alternate history about cloning, and Danis Goulet's *Night Raiders* (2021), which revisits Residential Schools in a dystopian future torn apart by war.

WORKS CITED

Alderman, Naomi. *The Power*. Little, Brown, 2016.

Ashby, Madeline. *Company Town*. Tor, 2016.

Atwood, Margaret. "Am I a Bad Feminist?" *Globe and Mail* online, 13 Jan. 2018, https://www.theglobeandmail.com/opinion/am-i-a-bad-feminist/article 37591823/.

– *The Handmaid's Tale*. McClelland & Stewart, 1985.

– *The Heart Goes Last*. McClelland & Stewart, 2015.

– *In Other Worlds: SF and the Human Imagination*. McClelland & Stewart, 2011.

– *MaddAddam*. 2013. Vintage Canada, 2014.

– *Oryx and Crake*. 2003. Vintage Canada, 2009.

– *The Year of the Flood*. 2009. Vintage Canada, 2010.

Baccolini, Raffaella, and Tom Moylan. "Introduction: Dystopia and Histories." *Dark Horizons: Science Fiction and the Dystopian Imagination*, edited by Raffaella Baccolini and Tom Moylan, Routledge, 2003, pp. 1–12.

Barnaby, Jeff, writer and director. *Blood Quantum*. Prospector Films, 2019.

Beaumont, Peter, and Amanda Holpuch. "How *The Handmaid's Tale* Dressed Protests Across the World." *The Guardian*, 3 Aug. 2018, https://www .theguardian.com/world/2018/aug/ 03/how-the-handmaids-tale -dressed-protests-across-the-world.

Bell, John, and Lesley Choyce, editors. *Visions from the Edge: An Anthology of Atlantic Canadian Science Fiction and Fantasy*. Pottersfield Press, 1981.

The Bible. Authorized King James Version, Oxford UP, 1998.

Bishop, Bryan. "*The Handmaid's Tale* Wins Outstanding Drama at the Emmys." *The Verge*, 17 Sept. 2017, https://www.theverge.com/2017/9/17/16323354 /the-handmaids-tale-emmys-2017-outstanding-drama-series-winner.

Bow, Erin. *The Scorpion Rules*. Margaret K. McElderry Books, 2015.

– *The Swan Riders*. Margaret K. McElderry Books, 2016.

Bush, Catherine. *Blaze Island*. Goose Lane, 2020.

Campbell, Rebecca. *Arboreality*. Stelliform Press, 2022.

Casper, Claudia. *The Mercy Journals*. Arsenal Pulp Press, 2016.

Christie, Michael. *Greenwood*. McClelland & Stewart, 2020.

Cloud Atlas, film. Written and directed by Tom Wykwer, Lana Wachowski, and Lilly Wachowski. Warner Bros., 2012.

Collins, Suzanne. *Catching Fire*. Scholastic Press, 2009.

– *The Hunger Games*. Scholastic Press, 2008.

– *Mockingjay*. Scholastic Press, 2010.

Colombo, John Robert, editor. *Other Canadas: An Anthology of Science Fiction and Fantasy*. McGraw-Hill, 1979.

Culler, Jonathan. "The Closeness of Close Reading." *ADE Bulletin*, no. 149, 2012, pp. 21–5.

Dickner, Nicolas. *Apocalypse for Beginners*. Published in French as *Tarmac*, 2000. Translated by Lazer Lederhendler, Vintage Canada, 2010.

Dillon, Grace. "Imagining Indigenous Futurisms." Introduction to *Walking the Clouds: An Anthology of Indigenous Science Fiction*, U of Arizona P, 2012, pp. 1–12.

Dimaline, Cherie. "From Where We Stand: Nuance and Perspective in Speculative Literature." Keynote address, 20/21 Vision conference, U of Saskatchewan, via videoconference, 16 Aug. 2021.

– *The Marrow Thieves*. Dancing Cat Books, 2017.

Doerr, Anthony. *Cloud Cuckoo Land*. Scribner, 2021

Edugyan, Esi. *Half-Blood Blues*. Serpent's Tail, 2011.

– *Washington Black*. HarperCollins, 2018.

El Akkad, Omar. *American War*. McClelland & Stewart, 2017.

The English Patient, film. Written and directed by Anthony Minghella. Tiger Moth, 1996.

Erdrich, Louise. *Future Home of the Living God*. Harper Perennial, 2017.

Feldner, Maximilian. "'Survival Is Insufficient': The Postapocalyptic Imagination of Emily St. John Mandel's *Station Eleven*." *ANGLICA: An International Journal of English Studies*, vol. 27, no. 1, 2018, pp. 165–79.

Gill, R.B. "The Uses of Genre and the Classification of Speculative Fiction." *Mosaic: An Interdisciplinary Critical Journal*, vol. 46, no. 2, 2013, pp. 71–85.

Goldman, Marlene. *Rewriting Apocalypse in Canadian Fiction*. McGill-Queen's UP, 2005.

Good, Michelle. *Five Little Indians*. Harper Perennial, 2020.

Goulet, Danis, writer and director. *Night Raiders*. Elevation Pictures, 2021.
The Handmaid's Tale, television series. Bruce Miller, showrunner, Hulu, 2017–25.
Hauser, Iris. *The Plastic Age*, painting, oil on canvas, 2009.
Heinlein, Robert A. "On the Writing of Speculative Fiction." *Of Worlds Beyond: The Science of Science Fiction Writing*, edited by Lloyd Arthur Eshbach, Fantasy Press, 1947, pp. 11–17.
Highway, Tomson. *Kiss of the Fur Queen*. Anchor Canada, 1998.
Hopkinson, Nalo. *Skin Folk*. Warner Books, 2001.
The Hunger Games, film series. Color Force/Lionsgate, 2012–15.
Hutcheon, Linda. *A Theory of Adaptation*. Routledge, 2006.
Justice, Daniel Heath. *Why Indigenous Literatures Matter*. Wilfrid Laurier UP, 2018.
Ketterer, David. *Canadian Science Fiction and Fantasy*. Indiana UP, 1992.
Killjoys, television series. Written and produced by Michelle Lovretta. Temple Street Productions, 2015–19.
King, Thomas. *The Back of the Turtle*. HarperCollins, 2014.
Lai, Larissa. *The Tiger Flu*. Arsenal Pulp Press, 2018.
Lee, Nancy. *The Age*. McClelland & Stewart, 2014.
Leroux, Jean-François, and Camille R. La Bossière, editors. *Worlds of Wonder: Readings in Canadian Science Fiction and Fantasy Literature*. U of Ottawa P, 2004.
MacLennan, Hugh. *Two Solitudes*. Macmillan, 1945.
Mandel, Emily St. John. *Station Eleven*. 2014. Harper Perennial, 2017.
McGregor, Hannah, Julie Rak, and Erin Wunker, editors. *Refuse: CanLit in Ruins*. BookHug, 2018.
McLeod, Neal. *mitêwâcimowina: Indigenous Science Fiction and Speculative Storytelling*. Theytus Books, 2016.
Merril, Judith, editor. *Tesseracts*. Press Porcépic, 1985.
Mitchell, David. *Cloud Atlas*. Vintage Canada, 2004.
More, Thomas. *Utopia*. 1516. Broadview Press, 2010.
Nawaz, Saleema. *Songs for the End of the World*. McClelland & Stewart, 2020.
Ondaatje, Michael. *The English Patient*. Knopf, 1992.
– *In the Skin of a Lion*. Knopf, 1987.
Orphan Black, television series. Space Canada, 2013–17.
Paradis, Andrea, compiler. *Out of This World: Canadian Science Fiction and Fantasy Literature*. Quarry Press and National Library of Canada, 1995.
The Power, television series. Amazon Prime Video, 31 March–12 May 2023.
Ransom, Amy J., and Dominick Grace, editors. *Canadian Science Fiction, Fantasy, and Horror: Bridging the Solitudes*. Palgrave Macmillan, 2019.
Rice, Waubgeshig. *Moon of the Crusted Snow*. ECW Press, 2018.
– *Moon of the Turning Leaves*. Random House, 2023.

Sawyer, Robert, editor. *Distant Early Warnings: Canada's Best Science Fiction*. Red Deer Press, 2009.

Somacarrera-Íñigo, Pilar. "'Thank You for Creating this World for All of Us': Globality and the Reception of Margaret Atwood's *The Handmaid's Tale* after Its Television Adaptation." *Revista Canaria de Estudios Ingleses*, no. 78, 2019, pp. 83–96.

Station Eleven, miniseries. HBO Max, December 2021-January 2022.

Suvin, Darko. "Science Fiction and the Novum." *Defined by a Hollow: Essays on Utopia, Science Fiction and Political Epistemology*, Peter Lang, 2010, pp. 67–92.

Tate, Andrew. *Apocalyptic Fiction*. Bloomsbury, 2017.

Thom, Kai Cheng. *Fierce Femmes and Notorious Liars: A Dangerous Trans Girl's Confabulous Memoir*. Metonymy Press, 2016.

"UBC Accountable: An Open Letter to UBC," archived 28 Mar. 2018, http://www.ubcaccountable.com/open-letter/steven-galloway-ubc/.

Vassanji, M.G. *Nostalgia*. Anchor Canada, 2016.

Vermette, Katherena. *The Break*. Penguin Canada, 2016.

– *The Circle*. Penguin Canada, 2023

– *The Strangers*. Penguin Canada, 2021.

Watkins, Susan. *Contemporary Women's Post-Apocalyptic Fiction*. Palgrave Macmillan, 2020.

Weiss, Allan. "The Canadian Apocalypse." Leroux and La Bossière, pp. 35–45.

–, editor. *The Canadian Fantastic in Focus: New Perspectives*. McFarland and Company, 2015.

–, editor. *Further Perspectives on the Canadian Fantastic*. Academic Conference on Canadian Science Fiction and Fantasy, 2005.

–, editor. *Perspectives on the Canadian Fantastic*. Academic Conference on Canadian Science Fiction and Fantasy, 1998.

Wharton, Thomas. *The Book of Rain*. Random House Canada, 2023.

Whitehead, Joshua, editor. *Love after the End: An Anthology of Two-Spirit and Indigiqueer Speculative Fiction*, Arsenal Pulp Press, 2020.

Sawyer, Robert, editor. *Distant Early Warnings: Canada's Best Science Fiction*. Red Deer Press, 2009.

Sorensen, [illegible]. "[illegible] This Wonderful All [illegible]." [illegible], pp. 33–54.

Station Eleven, miniseries. HBO Max, December 2021–January 2022.

Suvin, Darko. "Science Fiction and the Novum." *Defined by a Hollow: Essays on Utopia, Science Fiction and Political Epistemology*, Peter Lang, 2010, pp. 67–92.

Tate, Andrew. *Apocalyptic Fiction*. Bloomsbury, 2017.

Thom, Kai Cheng. *Fierce Femmes and Notorious Liars: A Dangerous Trans Girl's Confabulous Memoir*. Metonymy Press, 2016.

UBC Accountable. "An Open Letter to UBC." archived 28 Mar. [illegible], http://www.ubcaccountable.com/open-letter/steven-galloway-ubc/.

Vassanji, M.G. *Nostalgia*. Doubleday Canada, 2016.

Vermette, Katherena. *The Break*. House of Anansi, 2016.

---. *The Circle*. Penguin Canada, 2023.

---. *The Strangers*. Penguin Canada, 2021.

Wilkins, [illegible]. *[illegible]*. Macmillan, [illegible].

Weiss, Allan. "[illegible] Canada [illegible]." [illegible], pp. 3–18.

---, editor. *The Canadian Fantastic in Focus: New Perspectives*. McFarland and Company, 2015.

---, editor. *Further Perspectives on the Canadian Fantastic: Proceedings of the [illegible] Academic Conference on Canadian Science Fiction and Fantasy*. [illegible], 2005.

---, editor. *Perspectives on the Canadian Fantastic: Proceedings of the [illegible] Academic Conference on Canadian Science Fiction and Fantasy*. [illegible], 1998.

Wharton, Thomas. *The Book of Rain*. Random House Canada, 2023.

Whitehead, Joshua, editor. *Love after the End: An Anthology of Two-Spirit and Indigiqueer Speculative Fiction*. Arsenal Pulp Press, 2020.

Connecting Past to Future: Anishinaabe Knowledge, Archives, and the Cold War

Horrors of Northern Development: (Anti-)Capitalist Infrastructure and Anishinaabe Knowledge in *Moon of the Crusted Snow*

GAGE KARAHKWÍ:IO DIABO

The structures they were leaving behind would likely stand for a few more generations. The homes were perfectly viable shelters from the cold and rain. The band office, the shop, and all the other community buildings would probably last even longer. And all the infrastructure was most likely still functional. But there was no use for any of it.

– Moon of the Crusted Snow 211

From this vantage point on the western edge of town, most of the structures had been visible in the time before. But the reclamation of these ruins by the land was nearly complete.

– Moon of the Turning Leaves 55

In Waubgeshig Rice's *Moon of the Crusted Snow* (2018), the future is a scary but not impossible thing to imagine. The novel's titular imagery, of lunar cyclicality on one hand and of snow frozen over to form a delicate walkable surface on the other, suggests that the future for Indigenous Peoples is not necessarily a topic of inevitable dread. The crusted snow, symptomatic of the coldest stretch of winter right before the spring thaw, is a precarious scenario that comes around every year; it may feel like we as First Peoples are weighed down and liable to collapse through the crust at any moment, yet we and our peoples have also been through this a thousand times before. Cree-Métis-Saulteaux author Jas M. Morgan wrote in 2016 that "Despite dystopic realities, the possibilities of love and kinship as resurgence in the face of ecological disaster are a visceral narrative for Indigenous peoples" ("Visual Cultures"). What makes Rice's novel so viscerally scary yet hopeful is not the uncertain future, but the compounding weight of the past and present that bears upon how we decide to achieve our collective future. That weight – that intangible force threatening to drag us down through the snow – goes by several names: colonization, dispossession, extraction, assimilation, industrialization, atomization, proletarianization, alienation, subjection, and many more rhyming words belonging to that genealogy of processes known broadly as capitalism.

The purpose of this chapter is not to name and thereby thwart the monster that threatens the Anishinaabe people depicted in Rice's novel. Although the novel does have a clear villain with a very legible flaw (namely, the non-Indigenous interloper named Justin Scott who seduces the community with promises of capitalist abundance that give way to cannibalistic hunger), its central conflict concerning the future of the Anishinaabe people is not so easily reducible to a simple opposition of us versus them, bourgeois versus proletariat, or colonizer versus colonized. Rice's protagonist, the town worker Evan Whitesky, is key to establishing this complexity. Rice characterizes Evan as a strong, upright hero: a humble, working-class father who cares for his family and provides for his community according to traditional Anishinaabe ways. For the most part, Evan behaves with a selfless, level head and all-around competency in spite of the desperation that overtakes the reserve following the blackout that severs all contact between Gaawaandagkoong and the rest of the world. Evan is what we might call a model citizen – the exact type of ally you would want to have in the event of an apocalyptic catastrophe. Yet, crucially to the novel's horror, Evan is just as fallible and vulnerable to the aforementioned monster of many names as you and I or even Justin Scott.[1] Anishinaabe legal scholar John Borrows affirms the stakes thusly: "Humans are monstrous: they are figures of destruction and dissolution. They are metamorphic, in both meanings of the term. Humans can also be beautiful, gentle, and nurturing.… Any legal tradition worth its salt must deal with the worst excesses of human nature. It must deal with its monsters" ("Heroes, Tricksters" 834–5). In Evan and Gaawaandagkoong's case, to deal with one's monsters is to contend with one's inheritances – namely, the unwitting inheritances of capital infrastructures, both material and metaphysical.

On the subject of what we inherit, this chapter starts from the premise that imperial capitalism and industry are two of the greatest existential threats to Indigenous life and, by metonymic extension, to all life on Turtle Island. This claim itself is not new. What is unique about Waubgeshig Rice's approach to this premise is how he projects it into a post-apocalyptic future in which the exigencies of Indigenous resurgence have become a matter of life and death. In *Moon of the Crusted Snow*, Rice applies Anishinaabe knowledge in a speculative and cautionary narrative about the growing pains of decolonization and anti-capitalism.

When it comes to analyzing the role of inherited infrastructure in Rice's novel, Anishinaabe knowledge (courtesy of scholars like Basil Johnston, John Borrows, and Leanne Betasamosake Simpson) is naturally an indispensable framework that centres relationality and responsibility as the foundation of a sustainable future with Turtle Island. While Marxian anti-capitalist analysis post-dates and is external to Anishinaabe knowledge, I include it in this context because this framework provides us with the tools and vocabulary to parse capital as a *settler* institution. Rather than to conflate or hierarchically juxtapose these strands of anti-capitalism, I seek to enable these multiple frameworks to complement one another, at least insofar as the social dilemmas dramatized in Rice's novel likewise straddle capitalist and ancestral Anishinaabe ways of being.

Capitalism and its infrastructure are not the novel's only inheritances. Rice cites Ojibway author and knowledge keeper Basil H. Johnston's monograph *The Manitous* as an influence on *Moon of the Crusted Snow* and its adaptations of Anishinaabe oral tradition, with a particular debt to Johnston's interpretation of ancestral "windigo tales" in the final chapter of *The Manitous* (*Moon of the Crusted Snow* 217). Rice clarifies that the windigo is at most "a looming, often implicit figure in this story. The figure is hinted at, but its image doesn't emerge until closer to the end." He adds, "The dream image of the creature written here is also an homage to legendary storyteller Basil Johnston," which would seem to limit Johnston's direct influence on the novel to Evan's terrifying vision of the beast during the nightmare sequence in chapter 27 (217). I would argue, though, that Johnston informs *Moon of the Crusted Snow*'s windigo narrative at a more fundamental level than mere physical description.[2] Johnston's likening of the windigo's hunger to all-consuming capitalist growth is key to how the novel dramatizes the agonizing process of decolonization.

For Johnston, the windigo's greatest threat is as a negative horizon for the Anishinaabe people and their relationship with the land. The windigo embodies the opposite of Anishinaabe knowledge and kinship responsibilities as established by their leading practitioner, Nanabush. Whereas Nanabush teaches the Anishinaabe people through both positive and negative example to behave with care, respect, and reciprocity and to avoid exploiting or harming those with whom we share the earth (Simpson 56–57), the windigo serves as a fearsome cautionary example of the worst that can happen when those teachings are ignored. Johnston emphasizes this symmetry of extremes by organizing *The Manitous* so that the book begins with a chapter on Nanabush, who is the original student and model of Anishinaabe epistemology from time immemorial, and ends with a chapter on the windigo,[3] which represents current-day threats not just to Anishinaabe life, but to all forms of kinship between humans and the natural world.

As Johnston describes it, the windigo is a monstrous being who has rejected the obligations of mutual respect that bind societies and ecosystems together. Although it is known primarily as a cannibalistic beast (especially through its various pop cultural misappropriations over the years), it might be more accurate to describe the being as the embodiment of anti-social irresponsibility. According to Johnston, it represents "the worst that a human can do to another human being and ultimately to himself or herself" and receives its name from the Anishinaabe terms *ween dagoh*, meaning "solely for self," and *weenin n'd'igooh*, meaning "fat or excess" (222).[4] In the latter etymology, we glimpse the inherent self-destructive contradiction of the windigo's condition. Despite possessing superhuman strength and size, the beast is also emaciated and always hungry; no excess can meet its insatiable need for *more*. This irrational and boundless need for personal enrichment, whether caloric or monetary, enables and is enabled by the windigo's selfish disregard for the social bonds of mutual responsibility. A downward spiral of abuses – of one's self, of fellow beings, and of the land to which we all belong – ensues.

In these ways, the windigo's path of destruction is a threat of a planetary scale analogous only to capitalist extractivism, which Naomi Klein defines as a "non-reciprocal, dominance-based relationship with the earth, one of profound taking" (169). Indeed, Johnston gestures towards the philosophical and ecological challenges facing the Anishinaabe people today by likening the windigo's characteristic failure to honour its human and more-than-human kin to the exploitative mechanisms of capitalism. At one point in the people's history, Nanabush's teachings had in fact "driven [the windigo] from their place in Anishinaabe traditions and culture and ostracized [them] by disbelief and skepticism" (Johnston 235). While Anishinaabe knowledge still stands as a powerful safeguard against the re-emergence of the windigo, Johnston stresses the need for caution insofar as its hunger can be seen as reflected in the extractivism of modern industry:

> Actually, the Weendigoes did not die out or disappear; they have only been assimilated and reincarnated as corporations, conglomerates, and multinationals. They've even taken on new names, acquired polished manners, and renounced their cravings for human flesh in return for more refined viands. But their cupidity is no less insatiable than that of their ancestors. (235)

Johnston's mention of assimilation in this passage is a reminder that the windigo is no mere folkloric boogeyman, but instead a real and present danger to Turtle Island. Borrows, citing this same passage from Johnston, reiterates the danger that these monsters "might even consume entire environments through their greed, lust, and desires for money, power, or prestige" ("Heroes, Tricksters" 836–7). Short of that darkest outcome, the greatest risk in assimilating to settler ways of being, as Johnston warns, is that we will systematically unlearn all of the values, wisdom, and responsibilities that we need in order to sustain not just ourselves, but the environment that sustains and precedes us.

This unlearning process begins at the level of language, as a transformation of the terms by which we name our relationships. Michi Saagig Nishnaabeg scholar Leanne Simpson points to a comment from Nipissing elder Glenna Beaucage on Ryan McMahon's *Redman Laughing* podcast that emphasizes precisely this linguistic interference:

> When the treaty came, it turned the word creation into resources, and resources are to be exploited. To me creation is to be respected, but when we say resources, now we can exploit them. We got mixed up. I heard an old man tell me we've become capitalists. Even with our fishing and hunting we've become capitalist. We see money. (qtd. in Simpson 76)

Simpson puts it even more succinctly: "'Capital' in our reality isn't capital. We have no such thing as capital. We have relatives. We have clans. We have treaty partners. We do not have resources or capital. Resources and capital, in fact, are fundamental mistakes within Nishnaabeg thought" (77). Simpson and Beaucage both point to the "mistake" that is introduced into Anishinaabe kinship through a process of mistranslation. The land is an honoured living relative with rights, feelings, and dignity; it is not a resource to be hoarded or traded. Once that first devastating error of translation is introduced into the people's cultural vocabulary, the entire chain of signification is put in jeopardy. If a human being can bring themself to mistreat a family member to the extent of capital exploitation, then there is no foreseeable end to where that abuse will lead or who will remain unaffected.

As the events of Rice's novel make clear, the initial "mistake" of transposing one's relationship to the land into that of owner and property is likely to infect all of one's most treasured relationships, including brothers, sisters, fathers, mothers, and children, at the levels of both immediate filiation and expanded kinship networks. An oblique yet fitting example of how the effects of mistranslation ripple across time appears in Rice's 2023 sequel, *Moon of the Turning Leaves*, when

Evan and his daughter, Nangohns, revisit the abandoned site of the fictional Gaawaandagkoong First Nation, where the events of *Moon of the Crusted Snow* had taken place twelve years prior. "Human life had all but vanished from the place by then," the narrator notes of the former reserve. "On this return, the place felt even more like a graveyard, and Evan realized that he was wearing the black nylon shorts of one of the dead or missing – he couldn't remember who" (*Moon of the Turning Leaves* 56). A sense of elegiac cyclicality – or perhaps a lack thereof – creeps into this passage by virtue of the adverbial phrase "even more." Evan's return trips to the old reserve in the years between the two novels reveal to him that the rhythms of life that had once animated and have since faded away from Gaawaandagkoong were always marked by precarity. In hindsight, the reserve was always akin to a graveyard, even before its buildings began to pile up with corpses during the long winter without electricity. The Anishinaabe people were never meant to survive their displacement into the frozen north; had the genocidal project of settler-colonialism unfolded as intended, Gaawaandagkoong First Nation as a territorial construct would have been a death sentence for Evan's people.

Instead, death insinuated itself into the community gradually, offset only by the people's resilience and ingenuity. Death and expendability nevertheless cling to the material residue of the former reserve, to objects like abandoned buildings, motor vehicles, and Evan's hand-me-down shorts. The black nylon shorts are a remnant of an economy built on the production of synthetic fibres derived from crude oil. They are cheap and durable; they are also damaging to (and, by design, several degrees removed from) the natural environment that provided its raw materials. On one hand, this means that the recycled shorts have outlived both the economy that produced them and the individual who first owned them. Rather than being thrown away like so many other non-biodegradable commodities of old, they have found a new life and purpose alongside Evan's. They enable one another's survival. On the other hand, though, this also means that the shorts, like the fungible nylon material from which they are made, are susceptible to the kind of commodity fetishism that would allow Evan to forget which "dead or missing" relative previously wore them. The shorts, in other words, are demoted from the status of a life-bringing inheritance and a memorial to a departed family member (styled in funereal black, no less) to that of a nameless, lifeless resource. The fact that Evan is jolted into recognizing the alternately morbid and life-affirming provenance of his hand-me-downs upon witnessing the dilapidation of the old Gaawaandagkoong reserve suggests that Rice wants his readers to attend to a similar continuity between materiality, economy, inheritance, and kinship across the two novels.

Included in this windigo-borne mistranslation of living into dead – of kin into kindling, if you will – is the vexed status of material infrastructure like tools, housing, and utility power. This level of inherited mistranslation has pervasive implications for *Moon of the Crusted Snow* (and *Moon of the Turning Leaves*, which informs but mostly lies beyond the scope of this chapter). Broadly speaking, both novels detail a northern reserve's efforts to turn the late capitalist infrastructure it has inherited from Canadian settlement into a liveable home for future generations of Anishinaabe people. Readers learn that Gaawaandagkoong First Nation exists in its current form by virtue of two overlapping colonial processes: removal and development. Forcibly displaced from their ancestral home and left to die in an inhospitable environment, the people of Gaawaandagkoong nevertheless find ways to adapt and survive, oftentimes off the detritus of industry that Canadian settlers have imported into and likewise abandoned in the north. In an example of Rice's impeccable world-building (ironically, a dramatization of world-ending), the novel offers the following description of the reserve's decidedly post-colonial infrastructure:

> Like most of the homes that had been built or brought in pre-fabricated in the last decade, theirs relied heavily on electric appliances. When Evan was a child, his home's stove and fridge had been fuelled by propane – handy in case the diesel delivery didn't come through. With a lighter demand and smaller storage tanks, propane didn't have to be trucked in as regularly.
>
> But the hydro lines from the massive dam to the east now powered homes here, and there were plans to decommission the band's diesel generators and sell them. There was still diesel in them for contingencies, but the upcoming winter was to be the last that the band paid for trucks to bring in the fuel. (29–30)

The home, its machinery, and its fuels are the grammatical subjects of the first four sentences, albeit passive ones. More than just to establish a synecdochic substitutability between the people and the material environment of the house, Rice's choice of subject terms puts the onus on the materials themselves to generate not just electrical power, but also entire networks of demand, consumption, and dependence. As with most details in Rice's novel, we can read this subjectification of machinery in two directions, one informed by anti-capitalism and one informed by Anishinaabe kinship. A Marxian interpretation might zero in on the foregrounding of the technology as a locus, if not an agent, of capitalist need because it does not serve the material needs of its human occupants but exists as a consumer in its own right, a living embodiment of sunk cost. An interpretation drawn from kinship responsibilities might look to the same quirks – the agential home and its interchangeability with the people – as evidence of a new kind of extended family including members both human and machine. In that respect, people and infrastructure serve one another, reciprocally. It only makes sense, then, that Rice should afford a degree of agency and dignified urgency to what capitalism (and, in a further irony, anti-capitalism) would have us see as non-living resources. They and their constitutive elements aren't resources at all; wood, metal, stone, and fossil fuel are nothing if not borrowed pieces of the living body of the land – the latter two elements in particular being the residue of life that has broken down and incorporated back into the earth across scales of time that we as humans can scarcely grasp.

This gesture to identify *Moon of the Crusted Snow*'s post-capital housing and machinery as a form of kin is far from the end of the story, though. Rather, the truth lies somewhere between Karl Marx's paranoia and Anishinaabe epistemology's emphasis on balanced reciprocity. If industrial machines and infrastructures are to be embraced as kin in the extended family of Anishinaabe peoplehood, then the quality of that relationship still needs to be assessed and renewed on that qualified basis. On this cautionary note, Marx and Johnston are much aligned in their critiques of the function of machinery under capitalism, where the bulk of the risk lies. When Johnston describes the present-day windigos of industry at the end of *The Manitous*, he points to how mechanized labour accelerates the pace and volume at which capitalist production can cannibalize the land. For Johnston, nowhere is that more apparent than in the practice of clear-cutting forests:

> One breed subsists entirely on forests. When this particular breed beheld forests, its collective cupidity was bestirred as it looked on an endless, boundless sea of green.... The demands for more speed and more pulp, more timber, and more logs were met. Axes, saws, and woodsmen, sleighs, horses, and teamsters were replaced, and their calls no longer rang in the forest. Instead, chainsaws whined, and Caterpillar tractors with jagged blades bulled and battered their way through the forest.... (Johnston 235–6)[5]

All of the capitalist windigo's disavowals of kinship responsibilities are reflected in this passage: the repetition of "more"; the quiet slip from subsistence to "endless, boundless" accumulation; the harmony of people and forest "replaced" with the cacophony of demolition; the name "caterpillar" graduating from a tiny animal to a massive machine branded with a capital "C." The net outcome of this transformation is a collective loss, not just of the material substance of the forest but of the ecological balance that was previously upheld with slow and careful labour. This ancestral form of labour, bounded by human limitation and a tangible sense of kinship with the land, is warped into violent, proletarianized labour that makes monsters of human and machine alike. Once again, the machines do not satisfy demand – the windigo's hunger knows no satisfaction – but generate more of it.

How, then, does *Moon of the Crusted Snow* contend with monstrosity and its compulsions? The answer has everything to do with Anishinaabe law, as handed down in the people's oral traditions. Borrows, drawing from Hadley Friedland's Nehiyaw-informed discussion of windigo law, outlines how the ancestral law would deal with a scenario like that in Gaawaandagkoong:

> Some of the legal steps for dealing with Windigos include: (1) recognizing warning signs related to harm, such as when people shun human contact, display a lack of self-care, hide their actions, and engage in supernatural obsessions; (2) observing the developing or transpired behaviour by gathering evidence to determine whether someone fits the category; and (3) determining appropriate responses to harm by carefully calibrating responses to fit the circumstances. These responses can be organized along a spectrum of increasingly harsh treatment, which includes kindness, care, questioning, healing, separation, supervision, banishment, and death. ("Heroes, Tricksters" 837)

In *Drawing Out Law*, Borrows cites a story that details the harshest possible outcome for dealing with a known windigo. There, the community gathers in council and decides as a collective that the accused's closest friend must take responsibility for slaying the monster. The friend carries out the task, the community offers gifts to console the monster's grieving human father, and eventually a balance is restored (Borrows 224–5). To restore balance, Borrows insists, is key.

Across this spectrum of legal possibilities, we might recognize the contrasting fates of *Moon of the Crusted Snow*'s ostensible protagonist and antagonist: Evan Whitesky and Justin Scott, respectively. Scott's defeat is a messier affair than those outlined by Friedland and Borrows. Evan and his friends Isaiah and Tyler confront Scott and his crew almost immediately upon concluding that he has stolen a corpse from the town's makeshift mausoleum. Their authority to intervene is derived not from communal consensus, but from a smaller coalition. When the confrontation erupts into a gunfight, Scott is shot down by Meghan Connor, a member of the group of white refugees that arrives to seek asylum in Gaawaandagkoong First Nation shortly after Scott's introduction – not a close friend per se, but a figure of proximate outsider status at least (203). Evan, meanwhile, flirts for a while with antisociality but ultimately does not succumb to the desperate hunger of a windigo. To use Borrows's terms, Evan is canny enough to recognize the early warning signs in his own behaviour, namely, of seeking to shun human contact as a means of self-preservation. Reuben Martens labels those warning signs as symptoms of "petromelancholia" (after Stephanie LeMenager): "an expression of the conditions of grief that we experience when hydrocarbon *resources* start to dwindle, the feeling that we are slowly but surely losing access to cheap energy" (Martens 195; emphasis added). As Simpson and Beaucage might again point out, this grief is tied to a mistaken premise that the land is a "resource." If it is a symptom, it is a learned one, meaning that Evan's ultimate survival depends on recognizing and *un*learning it before it can overtake him.

Evan would seem at first glance to be selfless to a fault: a rock whose stability puts him in an oddly synecdochic relationship with the very infrastructure of the town. Those small instances where he appears to betray his selflessness stand out insofar as they seem uncharacteristic. At the beginning of the novel, Evan briefly betrays the mentality that there is a substantive, albeit unspoken difference between his "work" and his "job." The tasks that he describes as "work" involve subsistence hunting to provide for his immediate family and align with ancestral values. His "work," as detailed in the opening scene in which Evan shoots, gives thanks to, and butchers a moose, is elective and serves as its own reward: "It was harder than buying store-bought meat but it was more economical and rewarding. Most importantly, hunting, fishing, and living on the land was Anishinaabe custom, and Evan was trying to live in harmony with the traditional ways" (6). Meanwhile, his "job responsibilities," as determined by his employers at the local band council, consist of performing routine maintenance tasks for the reserve and tend to "chang[e] season to season" (32). The difference between the responsibilities associated with "work" and with a "job," at least prior to the blackout, is a matter of who benefits from that labour. "Work" seems to be tied to the nuclear family, extending only as far as the grandparents and maybe an especially close brother or aunt, whereas a "job" is tied to the population of the town, towards whom a private citizen like Evan might owe conceivably little were he not being paid for his time.

The closest that Evan comes to remarking or insisting actively upon this difference is when he reacts with annoyance to Isaiah's knocking at his door with a town emergency on a weekend:

> "Terry wants everyone in public works over at the band office right away. He pounded at my door just about fifteen minutes ago. My job was to round you up."
>
> "It's Saturday, damn it!" [says Evan.]
>
> "Yeah, well, he says it's an emergency. He's talking about firing up the generator. No one knows what's going on with the hydro."
>
> The chief calling an emergency meeting on a Saturday morning was serious. Evan snapped awake. (36)

The organization of the week into working and non-working days – a tacit legacy of nineteenth-century industrialization and labour movements – means that Isaiah's entry into Evan's private time and space for public "job" purposes is the crossing of a rather sacred line. Part of the irony, which becomes clear only as the blackout persists, is that Evan, Isaiah, and even Terry's "jobs" are about to lose their transactional quality. For lack of electrical or purchasing power, the band council will not be able to keep up its payroll system, effectively demoting the public labourers to volunteers. Their "job," as it were, becomes synonymous with the "work" that Evan implicitly associates with his immediate family; remuneration is replaced by communal goodwill and a sense of inherent responsibility towards the people as a whole. In a way, this synonymy eventually brings Evan's concern with maintaining Anishinaabe traditions full circle, since the "work" of providing for his kin now grows to encompass a duty towards the expansive whole of Gaawaangadkoong First Nation and the land on which it subsists.

The imbrication of "jobs" (the definition of which lies somewhere between a sense of "vocation" and what Marx called "labour") and ways of relating to others nevertheless stays on Evan's radar as the last remnants of settler institutions in Gaawaandagkoong, including the band council that employs him, fade from relevancy with the blackout. Chapter 22, which opens the section of the novel titled "Part Two: Biboon – Winter," is emblematic of Rice's command of tone, shifting between moods of hope, elegy, humour, numbness, and horror in the context of Evan's daily duties around town. The former affects come largely thanks to Auntie Aileen. Time is of utmost concern in these passages. As an elder in her eighties, Aileen is best equipped to comprehend the scope of the changes that her community is now facing; it also means that her time is limited and therefore precious. The simple but fleeting assurance of her presence and safety are therefore comforting to Evan, who observes that "The smoke coming from her chimney put him at ease," since it meant that "She would be okay for another day" (150). Aileen, it needs to be said, is not a resource by virtue of her wisdom. She has value not as a scarce commodity, but as an elder family member. The honorific of "Auntie" refers not to filiation but instead to the love and respect she commands from the entire community. The fact that it is so easy to conflate these multiple ways of relating – as kin, as resource, as ranked progenitor – speaks to the complexity of the internal dilemma Evan is navigating.

Given that Auntie Aileen's oft-quoted dialogue with Evan about the term "apocalypse" commands perhaps the most attention, it is easy to forget that the long chapter begins with reference to Aileen's late husband, a former military man who goes unnamed. While rummaging for recyclable fabrics in Aileen's closet, Evan comes across the old man's military blazer, with wool that is "faded" and "thin" and brass buttons – once mistaken for gold – that "no longer shone. They never did, really" (146). These observations put the shifting status of public institutions at the forefront of the chapter in ways that reflect Evan's disillusionment with where he stands as a representative of now-obsolete power structures. Like the Remembrance Day ceremonies for which the old man used to stand tall and proud in his blazer, the institution of the national armed forces is now a thing of the past – a collection of obsolete rituals, relics, and relations of domination. The old man, too, seems to have faded from relevance, having retained neither his given name, his military rank, nor even the familial title of "uncle" to match Auntie Aileen's. Whatever function the military may have served in terms of the Anishinaabe people, whether as a dependable source of income and pride (that is, a "job") for members of the remote community or as a guarantor of Canadian state power on the international stage,[6] is now insubstantial, at least in comparison to the functions performed by teachers like Aileen and infrastructural maintenance workers like Evan. Still, the old man's story resonates with Evan as a creeping suspicion that the version of the community that once employed him is, on the one hand, defunct and powerless, yet, on the other, still damaging as a philosophical legacy of colonialism.

Evan's conflicted feelings of suspicion and gratitude logically extend towards the community's surviving material infrastructure as well. Rice makes frequent mention of the presence of duplex housing in Gaawaandagkoong First Nation in order to emphasize its growing incongruity with the community's needs both before and after the blackout. The shifting status of the duplexes is emblematic of the novel's misgivings concerning the socio-economics of place and infrastructure in Gaawaandagkoong. The duplex as a hybrid housing model is an odd although not uncommon phenomenon on the rez. Commercially speaking, the benefit of duplexes is that they combine the geometry and aesthetics of the aspirational single-family suburban house with the urban spatial economy and recurring profitability of the apartment and high-rise models. As with the latter two housing models, the duplex presumes that city land is a precious, scarce resource and that it therefore must concentrate the population onto smaller individual surface areas.[7]

The seeming paradox of the rez duplex foregrounds conflicting ways of organizing people on the land. By taking the single-family house as its implicit model, the duplex meets bourgeois expectations of individual privacy and patrifocal sovereignty that have been handed down as aspirational since the model of the conjugal family home took (house) hold in eighteenth-century Europe at the dawn of imperial industry.[8] That being said, if we think beyond the cynical commercial context, then we cannot discount the practical virtues of the duplex model entirely. Part of what Rice suggests in *Moon of the Crusted Snow* is that the duplex, upon being vacated of bourgeois settler commercial interests, can be repurposed to function, if not as a fully communal structure, then at least as a semi-public housing model.[9] Evan's younger brother, Cam, lives in one of the duplexes. Evan directly associates his brother's chosen home environment with what he sees as Cam's profligacy, namely, his refusal to embrace traditional ways of subsisting on the land. Cam and the duplexes are introduced in tandem. Evan notes that "Only two years separated the brothers, but somehow Evan had landed on his feet in adulthood while Cam hadn't yet. When Evan had been out on the land learning real survival skills with his father and uncles as a teenager, Cam had chosen to stay behind, learning simulated ones in video games" (34). The symmetry of Evan's remark that Cam had not "landed on his feet" in adulthood and had actively refused a traditional education "out on the land" emphasizes that Cam's problem is no mere personality flaw, but instead a product of bad relations, starting with that between land and people.

Readers are encouraged to connect the dots back to just a few lines earlier, where Rice explains that Cam rented an "apartment he shared with this girlfriend, Sydney, and their son, Jordan. They lived in the cluster of duplex buildings originally built for hydro workers, but after the men from the South left, the housing was made available to band members. It was temporary housing for the southerners but, like so much on the rez, it stayed up and got used" (33). A key detail is nearly tossed aside here: the duplexes are another legacy of northern development, having been erected for the use of transient hydroelectric workers and subsequently abandoned. The current Anishinaabe tenants have been grandfathered into the duplexes, effectively repurposing them as low-income housing for families. A complex stigma attaches itself to this transferal. To inhabit the hydro developers' sloppy seconds, as it were, is beheld as a sign of Cam's failure as a provider (with echoes of the racialized and gendered vilification of "welfare queens") and as an Anishinaabe person (in the sense of selling out to the comforts and aspirations of private urban living). Yet Evan's misgivings towards Cam and the duplexes are not entirely unfounded. After all, Cam turns out to be the one who welcomes Justin Scott, like a vampire, onto the premises (132). Later, Cam is complicit in stealing and butchering corpses for Scott's cannibalistic "experiment" (202). Save for Evan's two brief references to them, Cam's partner and child are almost completely absent from both *Moon of the Crusted Snow* and *Moon of the Turning Leaves*; Cam abandons them and flees the community following Scott's death (*Moon of the Turning Leaves* 59). The combination of their father figure's ineptitude and their isolation in the duplexes appears to separate Sydney and Jordan from the community's support network.

By the aforementioned chapter of *Moon of the Crusted Snow*, the cycle of tenancy has begun anew. The duplexes have been vacated and reclaimed yet again, this time by another wave of non-Indigenous settlers. Evan remarks that Scott "and his cronies lived in the duplexes that had been abandoned when families began consolidating as the blackout wore on" (156). The cause of the exodus of Gaawaandagkoong families from the location can be traced to the grief spiral that began with the deaths of Jenna and Tara Jones, who froze to death by the side of the road after leaving a party in Cam's unit. Rice explains that the guilt of having allowed the women to venture home alone at night has since led two cousins, Jacob and Dion McCloud, to commit suicide, adding that "One suicide often led to another among the young people, and the compounding tragedies squeezed the stammering heart of the reserve" (156). Affectively, the grief and guilt surrounding these deaths is enough to transform the duplexes from places of living to sites associated only with tragedy.[10] Socially, the functionality of the duplexes also falls by the wayside. It becomes clear that these compartmentalized, single-family lodgings only made sense within a social and economic system that enabled, if not demanded, individuals to fend for themselves by tapping into the steady flow of capital, namely by virtue of working supply chains that would offer paid access to food, fuel, and other commodities. With those taps shut off, the single-family household and the convenience of individualized commodities become impractical. It makes more sense, as Rice points out, to turn instead towards consolidated, communal living, where spaces and materials can be shared. If the infrastructure itself seemed to beget a certain style of living centred untenably on the sovereignty of the westernized conjugal family, then its second wave of abandonment speaks only further to the obsolescence, associated with Scott and his cronies' descent into cannibalism, and the impossibility (partly by design, considering the Anishinaabe were led here to die) of that segmented way of life in these environmental circumstances.

While the vacating of the duplexes is indicative of a broader shift back towards community, Evan begins to move in the opposite direction, with his selflessness giving way to a paranoid spirit of isolation and hoarding. On the eve of the discovery that Scott has stolen corpses for food, Evan is alone at work on an "experiment" of his own: a "secret project" consisting of "a shelter in the bush that he had begun the day after the food brawl. A backup, in case he and his family needed refuge from whatever turmoil might eventually consume his community" (184). The shelter takes the ironic form of a tipi, which Evan recognizes as not being "characteristic of the Anishinaabeg. But he learned how to build one from a how-to guide in a hunting magazine of all places. He and Isaiah experimented with different sizes on random excursions into the bush over the years. Right now, it was the easiest, most reliable thing he could build in the middle of the winter in a power crisis" (186). The current "experiment" arises from tensions concerning the administration of the communal food cache, which in turn harken to deeper divisions between the traditionalist and the more Westernized segment of the reserve's population. It is not a scarcity of food itself that scares Evan into solitude; it is the selfishness of his own people amid a relative abundance of free (albeit low-quality) food that pushes him over the edge. In this sense, Evan is merely reading the writing on the wall and proactively compensating for the deterioration of social order in Gaawaandagkoong First Nation. Still, his recourse to isolating with his immediate family is a disturbing change of heart for Evan. The status of Anishinaabe cultural resurgence is so precarious at this point in the community's history that Evan's only option in this scenario is to trade one illusory way of life for another by hopping from his electrified single-family house to a lonely whitewashed faux-Indian tipi in the bush. This is no back-to-the-land initiative. This is a flirtation with anti-sociality, albeit a short-lived one.

Surely enough, Evan goes to sleep in his tipi that night and dreams of meeting a windigo face-to-face. The dream has the aura of a premonition insofar as Evan identifies his vision as "the beast Scott had become" *before* the discovery of the missing bodies and the revelation of Scott's cannibalism. Let us not forget, though, that the dream occurs *in proximity* with Scott's villainous reveal, whereas it occurs directly *inside* the "secret project" of the isolation tent. The coincidence of the latter with Evan's windigo vision raises the possibility that the monster in Evan's dream is not necessarily an external threat, but perhaps an internal threat along the lines of a capitalistic paranoia over resources. Once again, the monster has many faces and names. Capitalism and Justin Scott are two of them. Evan Whitesky, himself a rock upon which the community's goodwill is built, nearly becomes one. In heroic fashion, however, he rises above his lowest point to thwart the monsters inside. And by disburdening himself of the weight of those monsters, he avoids collapsing through the crusted snow, at least for another winter.

Twelve years separate the events of Rice's *Moon of the Crusted Snow* and *Moon of the Turning Leaves* – enough time for the earlier novel's guarded optimism towards the sustainability of the town's infrastructure to evaporate with the epochal changes that face the Anishinaabe people of the fictional Gaawaandagkoong First Nation. When Evan and Nangohns return to the site of the former reserve with a search party in *Moon of the Turning Leaves*, the modern infrastructure which had been "visible in the time before" has given way to "the reclamation of these ruins by the land" (55). The prefab buildings and fuel-burning machines that had previously "stayed up and got used," partly out of necessity and partly out of what Martens calls petromelancholic attachment to a dying way of life, crumble along with the political economy of capital that once animated them. The old question of the chicken or the egg persists: was it the infrastructure that sustained the people or the people that sustained the infrastructure? In either case, infrastructure, unlike the land on which it sits, cannot regenerate itself independently of the people. If infrastructure is kin, then it is indeed up to the people to choose to maintain or to refuse it.

It is hard to overstate just how timely and even prophetic Rice's *Moon* novels can appear in our various present moments of mid- and post-COVID-19 paranoia, global war, and collapsing ecosystems. Jared Hickman, in his playfully self-effacing essay on *Moon of the Crusted Snow*, goes as far as to conclude from the novel that "the geological epoch called the Anthropocene might be recast as a theo-geo-political dispensation called the Americocene in which Native ways of being-at-home are thrown into relief as that without which planetary apocalypse ensues" – his eerie reference to "being-at-home" having been written somehow *before* the pandemic lockdowns (24). Hyperbole and America-fixation aside, Hickman is dead right in reaffirming the stakes of Rice's novel as a question of planetary survival. Befitting of its title, *Moon of the Crusted Snow* reads like a play-by-play guide to a changing of the seasons for which many of us, Anishinaabe or otherwise, are woefully underprepared.

NOTES

1 See June Scudeler's essay in this volume for a discussion of monstrous masculinity in another work by an Indigenous writer, Jeff Barnaby's film *Blood Quantum*.

2 Kirsten Bussière adds that, beyond his debt to Johnston, "Rice is thus drawing on a common trope in contemporary Indigenous art, present in popular works such as [Daniel David] Moses's play *Brébeuf's Ghost* (2000) and Armand Garnet Ruffo's film, *A Windigo Tale* (2010), where white colonialism is figured as a windigo as a means to demonstrate the cannibalistic nature of a colonial presence" (53–4).

3 Borrows, who also writes extensively on the legal applications of Anishinaabe wendigo stories, organizes his monograph *Drawing Out Law* in a similar way by including a brief chapter on wendigo law at the end of the book.

4 The complexities of present-day food culture, generational trauma, and fatphobia on Turtle Island make this etymology difficult to contend with. For one, the old stereotype of the corpulent bourgeoisie doesn't quite match up with the current reality in which Western foodways and income inequality have made it so that the poor and racialized are now the ones most vulnerable to obesity, not the wealthy. In a fitting irony, then, the present-day beneficiaries of capitalist wealth – those with access to nutritious foods and free time for physical exercise – circle back to resembling the paradoxically hulking yet emaciated figure of Johnston's windigo.

5 Johnston's reference to the chainsaw as a noisy, almost pestilential harbinger of destruction is evocative, even more so in light of Blackfoot author Stephen Graham Jones's reclamation of the instrument in the title of his metafictional horror novel, *My Heart Is a Chainsaw*. For me, the chainsaw imagery also recalls one of the most chilling pieces of media to circulate in recent years: the video footage recorded in November 2021 by film-maker Michael Toledano from inside a Wet'suwet'en land defenders' camp that shows officers of the Royal Canadian Mounted Police tearing

through their front door with a chainsaw, one of several occasions in which the RCMP has used the tool to intimidate Indigenous protestors.

6 Recall too that, prior to Indian Act reforms following the world wars, Indigenous men lost their Indian status and became enfranchised as Canadian citizens once they acquired official roles in public institutions, including the armed forces and universities.

7 Not to mention the concentration of capital itself, in all its idealizing flavours: economic (access to jobs, markets, supply chains), sociopolitical (access to power and influence), cultural (access to knowledge and arts), and temporal (access to a future). Hence the (un)easy conflation of *polis* with place, to which we're all vulnerable.

8 See chapter 6 of Jurgen Habermas's *The Structural Transformation of the Public Sphere*, which details this period in bourgeois public history.

9 We see this in my home community of Kahnawake, where affordable public housing manifests as a small concentration of duplexes that are administered by the housing branch of our band council.

10 By the end of the novel, the same goes for the reserve itself: "Along with half the people who had lived here, the fledgling spirit they had been trying to nourish in this place had died. There was no use staying somewhere that had become too tragic. The bad memories and the sadness had smothered the good so many people had worked so hard to sustain, even in the wake of the darkness that befell them" (*Moon of the Crusted Snow* 212).

WORKS CITED

Borrows, John. *Drawing Out Law: A Spirit's Guide*. U of Toronto P, 2010.

– "Heroes, Tricksters, Monsters, and Caretakers: Indigenous Law and Legal Education." *McGill Journal of Law*, vol. 61, no. 4, 2016, pp. 795–846.

Bussière, Kirsten. "Beginning at the End: Indigenous Survivance in *Moon of the Crusted Snow*." *Foundation*, vol. 49, no. 136, 2020, pp. 47–58.

Habermas, Jurgen. *The Structural Transformation of the Public Sphere: An Inquiry into a Category of Bourgeois Society*. 1961. Translated by Thomas Burger, MIT Press, 1991.

Hickman, Jared. "The Apocalypse of Settler Colonialism and the Case for the Americocene." *Apocalypse in American Literature and Culture*, edited by John Hay, Cambridge UP, 2020, pp. 17–29.

Johnston, Basil H. *The Manitous: The Spiritual World of the Ojibway*. Key Porter Books, 1995.

Jones, Stephen Graham. *My Heart Is a Chainsaw*. Saga Press, 2021.

Klein, Naomi. *This Changes Everything: Capitalism vs. the Climate*. Knopf, 2014.

Martens, Reuben. "Petromelancholia and the Energopolitical Violence of Settler Colonialism in Waubgeshig Rice's *Moon of the Crusted Snow*." *American Imago*, vol. 77, no. 1, 2020, pp. 193–211.

Marx, Karl. *Capital: A Critique of Political Economy*, vol. 1. 1867. Translated by Ben Fowkes, Penguin Books, 1976.

Morgan, Jas M. "Visual Cultures of Indigenous Futurisms." *Guts*, no. 6 (*Futures*), 20 May 2016.

Rice, Waubgeshig. *Moon of the Crusted Snow*. ECW Press, 2018.

– *Moon of the Turning Leaves*. Random House, 2023.

Simpson, Leanne Betasamosake. *As We Have Always Done: Indigenous Freedom through Radical Resistance*. U of Minnesota P, 2017.

Speculative Archives in Novels by Thomas King and Larissa Lai: Hope in the Midst of Crisis

ALICIA FAHEY

Archives proliferate in Canadian speculative fiction, but little analysis has been done on their centrality to these works, thus raising the following question: what can Canadian speculative fiction teach us about archives? The archives featured in Thomas King's *The Back of the Turtle* and Larissa Lai's *The Tiger Flu*, like archives everywhere, are about origins. They fall under Antoinette Burton's definition of archives as "traces of the past collected either intentionally or haphazardly as 'evidence'" (3). The books' fictive archives include both institutional, state-sanctioned documents and alternative forms of archival memory, such as painted portraits and a tower built from detritus found along the shoreline of the beach.[1]

Speculative fiction imagines alternatives to the present by defamiliarizing the very structures that undergird the social and political milieux. As Mark Rifkin points out, "futurist narratives allow us to see divergent ways of conceiving and perceiving, variable frames of reference through which to understand how things work in the world" (7). Speculative fiction's openness to a "plurality of truths" leads Rifkin to understand it as "less a specific genre … than a mode of relation" (8). Similarly, Larissa Lai writes that "literature, specifically speculative fiction, has something to show us in relation to the work of eruption, or what John Rajchman (via Deleuze) has called the 'knock at the door,' a moment of contingent arrival, not a teleological end, but a double-edged sword that crystallizes hope for an instant, or offers a sign of wonder" ("Insurgent" 94).[2] Indeed, the qualities of relationality and emergence that Rifkin and Lai identify underly the potential of speculative fiction to imagine the world differently. In order to access these "variable frames of reference," speculative fictions, and in particular apocalyptic fictions, are characterized by crisis. Pandemic, contentious technological or political wagers, and/or environmental collapse produce a state of uncertainty whereby the characters must either adapt to survive the broken system or establish alternative modes for living. As Matthew Cormier points out in his essay in this collection, the temporal markers of beginnings and endings are central to the apocalyptic genre (69). Whereas Cormier focuses on the generative potential of the intersections of historiographic metafiction and speculative fiction to interrupt what he calls the "paradoxical momentum" (69) of apocalyptic narratives, this essay focuses on the momentum of beginnings and endings afforded by the archival impulse at work in the speculative novel.[3] In both cases, although this potential to imagine the world differently is not restricted to speculative fiction, the genre is especially suited to imagine futures that can transcend the impasse of ongoing crisis in the present because it is not limited by the same mimetic conventions as realist fiction. The distance from reality affords suspension of disbelief, making alternative realities more plausible. As both Cormier and I observe in our respective texts, the alternative realities that emerge from the coexistence of apocalyptic endings and speculative futures demonstrate a tendency for hope to prevail amidst the crises, leaving readers with lessons of care and support as opposed to violence.

In this essay, I take my cue from growing scholarship about the affective and embodied dimensions of the archive, with a focus on Diana Taylor's distinction between the archive and the repertoire. I argue that manifestations of the archive/repertoire in *The Back of the Turtle* and *The Tiger Flu* demonstrate how archives can facilitate opportunities to overcome the good life fantasies that, to borrow Lauren Berlant's term, enforce a protracted state of "crisis ordinariness." Put differently, speculative archives illustrate how attention to the embodied, performative aspects of the archive can encourage alternative lenses through which to view the past, present, and future. The future-orientation of King's and Lai's novels, combined with the emphasis on embodied knowledge and communal responsibility, offer an emergent sense of hope – hope for that contingent, relational knock at the door that leads to alternative ways of being together in the world.

In *The Back of the Turtle* and *The Tiger Flu*, efforts to rebuild the world depend on knowledge of previous events that prompted the crises in the first place. This knowledge is accessed via the archive. The setting of *The Back of the Turtle* oscillates between Toronto, Ontario, and the fictional community of Samaritan Bay and nearby Smoke River Reserve in British Columbia. Samaritan Bay is living in a sustained state of crisis after The Ruin, an event during which the Toronto-based company Domidion mistakenly deployed copious amounts of a toxic chemical as a defoliant in a pipeline project. The toxic product, named

GreenSweep, "carved a path of destruction all the way to the coast.... It had destroyed all life in the bay and pushed the kill zone out into the ocean some twenty kilometres" (324). In addition to environmental destruction, the chemical killed 137 people and landed more than 300 in hospital (426). Having yet to recover from the tragic events of The Ruin, the remaining inhabitants of Samaritan Bay have become accustomed to the crisis ordinariness of their present – until the protagonist, Gabriel Quinn, arrives, bearing with him a plethora of files obtained from Domidion's archives.

Also set in the future, *The Tiger Flu* takes place during Gregorian year 2145 (and onward) in the "time after oil." This cyberpunk saga chronicles a competition for world domination among a tiny elite in the midst of a threat from out-of-control satellites.[4] The novel revolves around two protagonists who form an unlikely partnership: fifteen-year-old Kora Ko, a resident of Saltwater Flats (an urban area located in the first "quarantine ring" that partially resembles Vancouver, British Columbia), and Kirilow Groundsel, a doctor belonging to the Grist Sisterhood, a community of clones who reside in Grist Village, located in the fourth quarantine ring. The crisis ordinariness of the novel is triggered largely by the Caspian tiger flu pandemic, which infects the majority of the male population but does not discriminate according to wealth, gender, or class. The tiger flu propels the plot when it is brought to Grist Village and kills the last starfish (a Grist Sister who can reproduce organs which are then harvested as transplants for the sisterhood), thus threatening the Grist community with extinction and forcing Kirilow to leave the community in search of a new starfish. Knowledge of the past is essential for preserving the future of the Grist Sisters. Through accessing different forms of memory, archival and other, the novel explores alternatives to the desolate existence of the post-pandemic world of the novel. By invoking the archive as a major player in the potential transformation of society, both King and Lai invite a reconsideration of the form and function of archives.

The Archive and the Repertoire: Approximate Proximity

Insofar as speculative fiction reimagines present systems and institutions, it also reimagines the archive. The "archival turn" of the 1990s has been well-documented by scholars such as Marika Cifor and Anne Gilliland, who identify the "affective turn" in archival scholarship as an alternative to the psychoanalytic approach.[5] In *Moving Archives*, Linda Morra draws on Sara Ahmed's concept of "affective economies" to explain how the affective dimensions of archives are shaped by "the effects of encounter" that produce "reorientation(s) between subject and object" (2). Morra observes that "archives are created as an expression of longing, what Derrida referred to as a desire for origins, but one that is *paradoxically projected into the future*" (3).[6] Significantly, Morra's statement draws attention to the ways in which archives impact the future. The future orientation of the archive is enhanced by its presence in the futurist vision of speculative fiction. Knowledge of the past is crucial for moving forward and summoning the knock at the door that can present alternative ways of being. In these speculative fictions, the archive plays a significant role in upholding – and/or potentially upending – dominant social systems and their vectors of power.

The archives in King's and Lai's novels emphasize embodied, relational ways of knowing. These archives resemble Taylor's definition of the repertoire as embodied practice/knowledge that requires presence ("Archive and Repertoire" 19–20). Whereas the archive is composed of "supposedly enduring materials" such as "texts, documents, buildings, bones," the repertoire consists of "spoken language, dance, sports, ritual" (19). Contrary to the archive, which, according to Taylor, requires objects of analysis that are *external* to or separate from the knower, "[t]he repertoire, this often overlooked system of storage, makes these resources of the past available, useable over time, both through annual repetitions and in moments of crisis. Performances reactivate historical scenarios that provide contemporary solutions" ("Performance and/as History" 72). I am most interested in the ways in which speculative archives in *The Back of the Turtle* and *The Tiger Flu* facilitate a moment of recognition – what Amitav Ghosh describes as a "passage from ignorance to knowledge" (4) – in a way that generates contemporary solutions to the crises of each novel's present.[7]

Taylor maintains that the archive and the repertoire, though distinct, do not constitute a binary relationship. In both novels, archive and repertoire come into contact through "approximate proximity," a term used by Erin Manning to denote "an alliance with thought-in-the-making, an engagement with the edges of how thinking itself does its work" (1). Manning's definition allows the archive and the repertoire to exist in tandem while maintaining their distinctive properties in a way that "would not reduce one to the other, but generate a complementarity" (1–2). Edges figure prominently in contemporary Canadian speculative fiction; the narratives often focus on marginalized voices, spaces, and places. Thus, adapting the supposedly "fixed" materials of the archives to the embodied episteme of the repertoire permits a shift in perspective that promotes an emergence of alternative modes of engagement, ones that hold out hope for transcending the limitations of existing social structures that have failed the characters in the present.

Speculative fictions in general, and King's and Lai's novels in particular, are characterized by crisis. I am compelled by Berlant's claim to read crisis not as a unique event, but rather as an ongoing state perpetuated by the desire for fantasies of the good life.[8] In Berlant's words, we should "turn towards thinking about the ordinary as an impasse shaped by crisis in which people find themselves developing skills for adjusting to newly proliferating pressures to scramble for modes of living on" (8). This quotidian conceptualization of crisis means that "[c]risis is not exceptional to history or consciousness but a process embedded in the ordinary that unfolds in stories about navigating what's overwhelming" (10). This distinction is important because the ordinary becomes a space for "inventing new rhythms for living that could, at any time, congeal into norms, forms, and institutions" (9). Crisis ordinariness is fuelled by what Berlant calls "cruel optimism," which has two central premises: first, a relation of cruel optimism exists when something you desire is actually an obstacle to your flourishing; second, all attachment is optimistic (1). Thus the cycle of attachment and desire that perpetuates cruel optimism necessitates a rethinking of crisis as something ordinary and structural rather than something exceptional. Speculative fiction can draw our attention to the emergent possibilities that arise from ordinary spaces occupied by ordinary people. Is it possible to resist absorption into the system of cruel optimism? What lies in excess of the system? How can the archive and the repertoire converge to facilitate a dissolution of the impasse in the speculative universe, and is it possible to translate this message to the extradiegetic world, the world that the reader occupies outside the text? Through their respective engagements with the speculative archive, both King and Lai underscore the potential of embodied memory to bridge past, present, and future beyond the capitalist systems that fuel the fantasies of cruel optimism. This potential for inventing new rhythms for living reaches its pinnacle when the repertoire is brought into approximate proximity with the archive.

Performing the Repertoire in *The Back of the Turtle*

Amazing how the past could find its way back to the present.

– The Back of the Turtle 319

The Back of the Turtle begins with a series of liminalities. The time is dawn (a period between darkness and light); the location is a beach (where water meets land); the atmosphere includes fog and shadows

(King 1). Chapter 1 begins, "The man stood at the boundary of the beach…." (3). He observes a neon sign, its eroding letters making "the sign undependable" (3), and he recites aloud the logical fallacy *post hoc ergo propter hoc*, a flaw in the reasoning of causation (4). From its beginnings, King is establishing *The Back of the Turtle* as a story of emergence, as Gabriel literally "emerge[s] from the trees" and makes his way down to the beach (1). The signs are unreliable, the logic is flawed, and readers enter into the novel from a place of uncertainty. Samaritan Bay is awaiting the knock at the door that will disrupt the stagnation of the impasse caused by The Ruin.

Gabriel's unwavering faith in science is the fantasy that becomes an obstacle to his flourishing. The cruel optimism of his scientific pursuits are driven by his belief that "Science was supposed to have been the answer. World hunger. Disease. Energy. Security. Commerce. Biology would save the world. Geology would fuel the future. Physics would make sense of the universe. At one time, science had been Gabriel's answer to everything" (446). Later, he realizes the fatal flaw in his reasoning:

> How had he come to such a fantasy, that there was a benign purity in scientific inquiry? He had mistaken the enterprise completely, had seen only the questions and ignored the obvious answers.
>
> What was the proper goal of research?
>
> Profit.
>
> What was the proper use of knowledge?
>
> Power.
>
> He could see his errors now, could see his illusions in stark relief. Too late, of course. Very much too late. (446–7)

Gabriel's shift of perspective is provoked by his realization that he, the architect of GreenSweep, facilitated The Ruin that killed his sister and nephew, among many others, in the quest of the Domidion company for profit and power. This recognition of his complicity in the tragedy forces Gabriel to confront the impasse of cruel optimism. Recognition marks Gabriel's passage from ignorance to knowledge and mobilizes him, prompting him to leave his job at the Toronto-based agri-business company where he works as Head of Biological Oversight and travel to the source of the event.

A pivotal moment of recognition that reveals the cruel optimism of the capitalist enterprise never occurs for Dorian Asher, CEO of Domidion. The company is responsible for numerous global catastrophes, and Dorian goes to great lengths to suppress evidence of its culpability. He attempts to bury archival evidence and manipulate media coverage of

Domidion's ethically bankrupt activities. When the GreenSweep calamity is on the verge of being exposed, Dorian reflects, "Corporate malfeasance or international conspiracy. The trick was to control how the matter was read" (449). Ana María Fraile-Marcos appositely describes what is at stake in Dorian's reasoning: "If a precondition for post-truth politics is a conscious detachment from the reality upon which the post truth discourse is applied, Domidion strategically detaches itself from the dire consequences of the multiple disasters the corporation creates as a result of its biased embrace of the neo-liberal narrative of modern progress" (477). Indeed, Dorian's corporate "ethics" are driven by profit, and in order to continue making profit, Dorian must conceal the truth of the atrocities for which his company is liable. In other words, crisis ordinariness preserves the status quo that allows Domidion to continue turning a profit. Upon discovering that Gabriel spent his vacation in the Domidion archives, Dorian protests, "Access to archives is restricted" (41). Insofar as Dorian is motivated to silence the archive, the archive becomes a site of resistance because of the incriminating evidence it contains.

Despite Dorian's efforts, Gabriel collects records of site reports, risk assessments, confidential memos, requisition records, newspaper articles, photographs, eyewitness accounts, and obituaries (398). He then compiles the documents into a file he names "The Woman Who Fell From the Sky," which alludes to the Haudenosaunee creation story about the world being formed through the collective efforts of animals and humans when a curious, pregnant woman digs a hole to the other side of the world, falls into the hole, tumbles through the sky towards a world consisting entirely of water, and is caught by birds who lower her on to the back of a turtle. The water animals take turns diving to the bottom of the water, eventually recovering mud, which they apply to the back of the turtle in order to create land upon which the woman can live. She gives birth to her twins; the right-handed twin creates order and the left-handed twin brings chaos (King, *Truth* 10–20).

The Sky Woman story is alluded to throughout the novel, including a memorable performance by the exuberant Nicholas Crisp, one of the residents of Samaritan Bay, at his birthday celebration. As Sean Rhoads has argued, Crisp "serves as an analogue for several mythic figures, most predominantly the classical Roman deity Neptune (or Poseidon in Greece), the god of freshwater and the seas" (122). Rhoads asserts that these "multi-mythic parallels" reinforce King's broader message of communal responsibility in the novel (122). Building on Rhoads, I argue that Crisp's embodiment of these mythologies exemplifies the community-building power of bringing the archive into approximate proximity with the repertoire. His enactment of the Sky Woman story constitutes a form of repertoire: an ephemeral, embodied performance that reactivates prior knowledge and makes the past available to the present. Crisp explains that the residents of Samaritan Bay tell the story annually at his birthday celebration "As a reminder" (222). The communal telling of the story, among Crisp, Mara (a friend of Gabriel's late sister who becomes his love interest), and Gabriel mirrors the message of community that is communicated through the story itself.

The Back of the Turtle is not the only book in which King references Sky Woman. In his rendition of the Sky Woman story in the Massey Lecture series *The Truth About Stories*, King contrasts the Indigenous creation story with the biblical story of Genesis. He concludes, "So here are our choices: a world in which creation is a solitary, individual act or a world in which creation is a shared activity; a world that begins in harmony and slides toward chaos or a world that begins in chaos and moves toward harmony; a world marked by competition or a world determined by cooperation" (24–5). King's conclusion echoes his message in *The Back of the Turtle*: humans must choose between the capitalist, individualistic system (epitomized by Dorian and his corporation) and a system of cooperation and communal responsibility (an emergent possibility that exists among the inhabitants of Samaritan Bay). The former will perpetuate the impasse of crisis ordinariness, as exemplified by Dorian's inability to satiate his desires with material wealth; the latter, as exemplified by the Sky Woman story, has the potential to invent new rhythms for living.

Like the left-handed twin, Gabriel Quinn brings chaos to the world with GreenSweep.[9] He returns to Samaritan Bay to bear witness to the consequences of his scientific endeavours. The destruction of the land and people is an impasse from which Gabriel cannot fathom moving forward. Unable to navigate what is overwhelming, he resigns himself to self-annihilation. Each day Gabriel travels to the beach, resolving to drown himself in the incoming tide. Each day he finds a reason to continue living. In the meantime, by writing lists of environmental disasters caused by humans onto the deck of his trailer, Gabriel repurposes the archival evidence that he removed from its institutional safeguarding at Domidion, repeating the ritual he performed on the walls of his rental house prior to his departure from Samaritan Bay. This performative aspect of bearing witness brings the archive into proximity with the repertoire, activating evidence that had previously been hidden.

Gabriel's declaration of human hubris is diametrically opposed to the approach of Domidion executives, who attempt to conceal indicting evidence from public view. Interestingly, the novel begins with several disappearances: Gabriel Quinn, the turtle in Domidion's fish tank, the *Anguis* (a heavy-capacity barge carrying GreenSweep toxic waste that, unable to find a port of call that would allow it to dump its contents, sails aimlessly until it vanishes in a subtropical storm), the Taiwanese families of sailors who emerge from the water of the bay. As the story progresses, what has disappeared becomes visible through performative activations of the archive. Gabriel thus performs a kind of "historical ontology," which Ann Laura Stoler, drawing on Ian Hacking, denotes as "what comes into existence with the historical dynamics of naming" (4). Publicly naming these events radically reorients Gabriel's relationship to the archive and brings the archive into approximate proximity with the repertoire. His actions perform a conciliatory gesture of recognition that welcomes a new, albeit contingent and emergent, mode of relation to Samaritan Bay. When Crisp observes Gabriel's practice of naming, Gabriel says, "I should stop doing that," to which Crisp replies, "No, no ... for it's well and proper to write what must be seen and speak what must be heard" (143). The ritual of bearing witness is the first step in overcoming the cycle of crisis ordinariness and the cruel optimism that drives it. Gabriel's return to Samaritan Bay, in conjunction with his engagement with the archive, prompts a new rhythm for living that resists the cruel optimism underlying blind faith in science or neoliberal corporate greed.

By abandoning the capitalist enterprise of Domidion and turning to the collective, Gabriel chooses community over profit, thus breaking the cycle of crisis ordinariness with his efforts to begin anew. Significantly, the archive alone will not restore Samaritan Bay. The Ruin, as well as the many other environmental disasters Gabriel writes about, are caused by human intervention with nature. Nevertheless, humans are a requisite part of the community and need to find harmony with their non-human counterparts to restore balance to the world. Thus, in *The Back of the Turtle*, hope lies in the possibilities that emerge from communal responsibility. This hope becomes most pronounced at the end of the novel with Sonny's tower. From his idiosyncratic third-person point of view, Sonny, a boy who has been left behind after The Ruin, thinks of the tower's function as "A beacon. A tower beacon. A lighthouse. More or less. A symbol of hope. A guiding light. A monument to perseverance. That's what Sonny will build. Right here on the beach. A tower. A bright tower that will stand against the dark sky and bring the turtles home" (268).[10] At the end of the novel, the characters gather on the beach, alongside Sonny's tower, to welcome home the turtles. Rhoads interprets Sonny's tower as "a sort of anti-Tower of Babel on the beach of Samaritan Bay [built] out of the animal remains and detritus left in the wake of 'The Ruin.' Unlike the original edifice, Sonny's brings diverse people together for a common cause, rather than tearing them apart" (135). Rhoads's reading underscores the performative aspect of the tower as a testament to the past and a promise of a new beginning. Composed, among other things, of the bones of animals who perished in The Ruin, Sonny's repurposing activates the past in a way that is useful for the present. His actions bring the archive into approximate proximity with the repertoire, which initiates the possibility of alternative ways of being that resist the impasse of crisis ordinariness caused by The Ruin.

Indeed, Rhoads's reading of communal responsibility is further illustrated by the characters' collective efforts to return the *Anguis* to sea after it arrives on the beach in Samaritan Bay. Fraile-Marcos contextualizes this moment as an incarnation of the Sky Woman story. She writes, "Rather than the second coming of Christ," the appearance of the *Anguis* accompanies "the second coming of the turtles" (King 104) foreseen by Sonny, "that marks nature's rebirth, reinforcing the Sky Woman story's ethos by showing that salvation lies in the recognition of human and non-human interdependence" (Fraile-Marcos 483). The interplay of the biblical and Indigenous creation stories is evident here, as Fraile-Marcos points out, in the allusion to the second coming. More broadly, the second coming parallels a recurring theme of the novel: the return home. As Crisp sagely states, "Everyone comes home.... Trust an old traveller on that. In the end, we all comes home" (King 108). Both Gabriel and Mara find their way to the reserve; animals and other non-humans return to Samaritan Bay; and the *Anguis* has begun its journey home to its maker. Susie O'Brien reminds us that return is precipitated by the responsibility of bearing witness. She explains, "In *The Back of the Turtle*, storytelling helps to create the conditions for living on in the years to come, which start with the responsibility inhabiting the devastation of the present. It offers a vision of resilience strikingly different from the dominant conception, held by Dorian, which combines devotion to self-preservation with conviction in the inevitability of capitalist resource exploitation" (50–1). In the end, all that has been hidden in the dark is brought to light and, through the approximate proximity of the archive and the repertoire, the characters in the novel will bear witness to the consequences of their actions. The journey is not an easy one, but the return to origins offers the hope of starting over, the emergent possibility to begin again.

Embodied Knowledge and Cooperative Futures in *The Tiger Flu*

The old world is long gone, and in this brave new one we must make up everything all over again. – The Tiger Flu *79*

The possibility of beginning again is also fundamental to Lai's *The Tiger Flu*. The flu pandemic and environmental crises have created an impasse that has rendered current modes of living unsustainable. The cruel optimism underlying *The Tiger Flu* is the fantasy of Isabelle Chow, inventor and CEO of HöST Light Industries, that one can "cure" the mind of the body, in theory immortalizing the human race through disembodiment. This fantasy of immortality materializes through Chow's LïFT Technology, which transports the disembodied subjects to Chang, a satellite planet that orbits Earth. Chang's settlement, Quay Sera, is marketed to those infected with the tiger flu and to fearful elites who have the financial means to pre-emptively transport themselves to the new world. Later, Chow is betrayed by two leaders: Marcus Traskin, lord and CEO of the Pacific Pearl Parkade, where he reigns over one hundred resident men who have been infected with the flu, and Elzbieta Kruk, high Priestess of the New Origins Archive in the third quarantine ring. When Chow realizes that her collaborators are no longer allies, she moves her settlement to Chang's backup mainframe, Eng. Donna McCormack points out what is at stake with Chow's illusory promises of mind and body separation. She notes, "The technology is not perfected yet, and thus Isabelle Chow's promises are not only illusory, but also capture one of the main issues of the novel: that the separation of the mind from the body is central to the violence to which international, neoliberal corporations invite consumers to subject themselves" (399). McCormack illustrates the capitalist underpinnings of Chow's project. The philosophical dilemma of separating the mind from the body is expanded upon by the Grist Sisters, who oppose this theoretical premise. Early in the novel, Kirilow narrates the significance of the mind/body connection to history and memory:

> I dance the dance of nuclear fission, of oil, of coal, of wood and straw. I dance for wheels and automobiles, when they were like living creatures drunk on the rotted bodies of species long dead. I dance for the tiger flu, for Ebola, for AIDS, smallpox, measles, tuberculosis, Black Plague, and death. I dance for stem cells, devilled eggs, cloning, and mutation. All the long path of chance and science, money and murder that Old Glorybind taught me was my messy legacy. Although I can't say I understand it, I know its songs, its oranges and lemons, its ring around the rosy. My body knows something that my mind can't refuse. (70–1)

The intergenerational knowledge of Kirilow's "messy legacy" is transmitted through her body in a dance that is evocative of Taylor's classification of repertoire as embodied ritual. Dance and memory are also connected through the Cordova Girls, who are Grist Sister kin. According to Marina Klimenko, the school in which the Cordova Girls live "offers a kind of community – one based on shared knowledge and memory rather than genetic, bodily, or gender purity" (168). Klimenko's observations are cemented when Myra, leader of the dancing girls, reiterates headmistress Madame Dearborne's message that "In order to survive in the world that is coming, we need to know our history" (Lai 86). The novel demonstrates the impossibility of building alternative futures without knowledge of the past. Access to information creates the possibility of recognition (in Ghosh's sense of the term), enabling the passage from ignorance to knowledge. This passage is how Kora comes to recognize her familial lineage in relation to both the tiger flu and the Grist Sisterhood. In essence, the Grist Sisters' embodied understanding of self depicts an alternative mode of relation that operates in direct opposition to the Cartesian dualism underlying Chow's enterprise. Further, the repertoire of knowledge embodied by the Grist Sisters and Cordova Girls protects information that is otherwise hoarded by the wealthy elite.

In contrast to the capitalist culture of competition illustrated by Chow, Traskin, and Kruk, the Grist Sisters operate through a culture of cooperation, each having roles that contribute to the symbiotic balance of the community. The intergenerational transmission of knowledge that is experienced as embodied memory provides motivation to perform these social roles. Specifically, memory cultivates a sense of duty among the Sisters: duty to each other, duty to the rituals, and duty to one's social position. Glorybind Groundsel, a Grist elder, appeals to this obligation when she compels Kirilow to embark on a journey to save the Sisterhood. She says, "You've also got duty, Kirilow. Don't forget duty" (89). Similarly, Uncle Wai imports a sense of communal responsibility when he explains to Kora why she must live with the Cordova Dancing Girls. He says, "In times like these we put aside our individual desires, Kora. In favour of the larger collective. In favour of survival. You are fifteen now. Old enough to accept when duty calls you" (76). Duty becomes another optimistic fantasy, one that allows the characters to negotiate the crisis ordinariness of their time triggered by the tiger flu. Duty is also what brings Kora and Kirilow into partnership as they attempt to supersede the impasse by building an alternative future to the statist and capitalist systems that oppress them in the present.

Despite (or, perhaps because of) its emphasis on memory, *The Tiger Flu* is preoccupied with forgetting. Residents of Saltwater City implant memory scales in their brains by plugging them into a "halo" they wear on their heads. The primary purpose of the scales, which can be removed and interchanged with other scales in order to accumulate knowledge, is to provide access to privileged information, ranging from an explanation of the phases of the moon, to music, to secret messages about public figures. In essence, the memory scales disseminate information "in a desperate attempt to know and so fix the broken world" (41), reinforcing the notion that memory of the past is essential to imagining alternative futures. Nevertheless, the purveyors of memory must contend with N-Lite, a drug harvested from the Grist Sisters' forget-me-do. In the Grist community, this tonic is primarily used to minimize pain during surgical procedures, specifically the ritual of harvesting and transplanting organs. According to Kirilow, through the use of forget-me-do, "we cultivate what we remember and what we forget in order to make Grist history" (43). Kirilow's statement reveals what is at stake in the dynamics of memory and forgetting: that memory is always constructed, contingent, and incomplete. As demonstrated later in the novel, the construction of memory is tantamount to power. This power dynamic is evidenced by Traskin's and Kruk's use of N-Lite to hold Kora and Kirilow captive. Thus, despite the intentions of its creators, when used for economic profit, forget-me-do, like Gabriel's GreenSweep, inflicts harm. Kirilow's statement that "Forget-me-do makes you feel pain as pleasure" and "takes away all memory and feeling of pain, leaves nothing but a craving to be cut again," explains its potential as a drug that can be sold for profit (21). Ultimately, by putting pain and pleasure on the same continuum, the Grist Sisters are able to ensure the continuation of their species, but the effects of forgetting, when used for less benign purposes, have dire consequences.

Those consequences become especially apparent in part 4 of the novel, set at the New Origins Archive. The NOA is a living architecture with a pulsating surface that "looks like a brain coral, a really enormous one.... Its structure looks like a stack of vertebrae for some prehistoric gargantua, spine diving deep into the ground" (265). The archive is thus a living entity; the blue tendril scales (a more refined version of the memory scales worn by Kora and others) that emanate from the structure "wave gracefully" like seaweed, but also "snatch a little sparrow out of the sky and yank it down into the hungry folds of the archive's pulsing surface" (265). The description of the archive as a sentient being is significant, as is its ability to both create and destroy; the former and the latter are reminders of the archival erasures that occur as a result of the archive's complicated relationship to power. As Erin Wunker explains, archives "represent a series of choices that are inextricably linked to access – or restricted access – to power" (66). In response to Michel Foucault's definition of the archive as that which is enunciable, Wunker asks, "So, what if you're not deemed 'enunciable' by the system? What if, in other words, you are unintelligible? What then?" (66). Indeed, as Kora and Kirilow respond to literal knocks at the door (271, 282) that drive them into the depths of the archive, they are confronted with an absence of answers as language is rendered increasingly incomprehensible the farther they descend. The protagonists express frustration and concern at the diminishment of language, prompting Kirilow to ponder, "Why is it she [Mother Glorybind] can speak but not answer my questions?" (288). Like Wunker, Carolyn Steedman also draws on Foucault in her archival analysis. In particular, Steedman asserts that the archive obscures as much as it reveals (6). In *The Tiger Flu*, the impetus to obscure is illustrated in the Deep Baths of the NOA when Kora and Kirilow, disoriented by N-Lite, arrive at the portal to Eng. N-Lite contradicts the preservation function of the archive by obscuring memory. Those who control the NOA (Kruk and her attendants) use N-Lite to render knowledge unintelligible. Moreover, disembodied knowledge on Eng keeps everything in literal darkness, prohibiting enunciability and characterizing the archive by its limits – what cannot be said – thereby circumventing the possibility of bringing the archive into approximate proximity with the repertoire. Thus, in the Dark Baths, performativity is denied by the absence of enunciability.

Lai's rendering of the building as a prehistoric species is a reminder of the archive's connection to origins. Kora's mother, Charlotte, describes the NOA as "a good place, a place of memory. It holds the blueprints for everything animal, vegetable, and mineral that lived in the time before" (276). The reference to "a good place" gestures to the etymology of utopia as "no place." Lai has described her interest in an "insurgent utopia," which involves "placing worlds in interaction with one another to seek eruptions of the unexpected" ("Familiarizing" 23). These interactions call us "To think of the new utopianism as a kind of insurgent thought … as the combined action of idealistic thought, critical thought, and narrative experiment" (Lai, "Insurgent" 97). There is certainly a utopic element to the NOA, with its ability to restore what has been lost, including bringing back species that have gone extinct, such as the Caspian tiger. This restorative power affirms the archive's connection to origins. However, Lai also shows readers that the restorative dimension, when driven by capitalist intentions, propagates the unequal distribution of, and unequal access to, resources, a point further evidenced by the trade partnerships that support NOA. Limiting access to knowledge is one of the many ways the archive obscures. As Kirilow states while trying to escape the Dark Baths, "This is not a good place, not a good place at all" (294). Although she is tempted by the utopic promise of a reunion with her mother double, Kirilow recognizes that Isabelle Chow's mission exploits individual desire; the promise of immortality is illusory at best.

Despite housing the blueprints to revitalize the planet with all that has been lost since the time after oil, the archive itself does not contain Grist Sister DNA, which Chow needs to achieve verisimilitude on Eng's settlement, Quay d'Espoir. In Taylor's archive/repertoire framework, disembodiment precludes the possibilities of bringing the archive into approximate proximity with the repertoire. Here lies the fundamental issue with Chow's undertaking. Chow believes she can resolve this problem of causal interaction through a biopolitical wager: converting the Grist Sisters into a resource that will augment her project. The desire to use the Grist Sisters to enhance verisimilitude on Eng perpetuates the violence inflicted on the Grist Sisterhood since their original exile from Saltwater City in the time before. Chow's settlement does, however, survive, and the novel ends with Kirilow observing Eng in its thousand-year orbit, implying that espoir, or hope, lives on, at least for another thousand years (330). This optimistic fantasy of immortality on Eng provides a counterpoint to the alternative modes of relation that exist in the New Grist Village.

The Grist Sisters create a counter-public sphere in the village. Like the characters in *The Back of the Turtle* who find new modes of relation through cooperation rather than competition, the Grist system depends on communal responsibility from all its members. Importantly, these contributions are not limited to reproduction; not all Grist Sisters are doublers and the future of New Grist Village is not dependent solely on children. The land and its fruits are essential for the perpetuation of the Sisterhood, thus continuing the legacy of land stewardship integral to the Grist world view.

That reproduction is only one of many social functions needed to sustain the community is evidenced by Kora's transformation into a Starfish Tree, a sentient tree that produces organs as fruit. Kora is one of many Starfish Trees that grow in an orchard in New Grist Village. The Trees help to ensure future generations of Grist Sisters by prolonging the Sisters' lifespans. As a Starfish Tree, Kora's knowledge of the past is shared with the Grist Sisters through a community gathering where stories are disseminated through vibrational communication; audience members receive the messages through their bodies and internalize the memories and affects that the stories relay. This form of knowledge-sharing opposes the institutional power of the NOA. In her storytelling, Kora describes the knowledge systems of the time before as "a time of information blackout. Everything they knew in the time before was stuck on Chang and Eng, and only the elites had access. Even now, our wisest Grist scholars don't know everything they knew" (328). The opposing forms of knowledge distribution are further observed by Klimenko: "Unlike the threatened memory that Kirilow identifies at the beginning of the novel, the memories on which the new queer extended Grist family is founded are shared rather than stolen. The Kora tree insists that the Grist sisters remember her pain when they pluck replacement hearts and livers from her branches, a very bodily activity. It is embodied memory that transcends ethnic, genealogical, or even species-based connection and allows the Grist sisters to form their new more-than-human community" (177). Rather than an unequal distribution of resources, the Grist system is designed for the greater good of the community. Instead of obscuring pain, the relational transmission of pain among the Sisters is a form of communal responsibility. This reorientation between subjects, permitted by the approximate proximity of the archive and the repertoire, promotes an intersubjective understanding of otherness that reveals instead of obscures. Lai's depiction of this exchange through vibrations also expands the notion of enunciability; the redistribution of power in the Grist community renders both knowledge and the individual inhabitants legible. The Kora Tree's ritual of storytelling to share intergenerational knowledge through an embodied method that celebrates the synergy of mind, body, and spirit is grounded in a system that disperses material wealth (in the form of organs) for communal profit rather than individual consumption and power. As with *The Back of the Turtle*, the underlying message of *The Tiger Flu* is a shift away from the capitalist system towards a model that does not depend on the nation/state to fulfil its desires.

Conclusion

In her analysis of *The Back of the Turtle*, O'Brien draws on Haudenosaunee and Anishinaabe scholar Vanessa Watts to explain that the damaging consequences King explores in his novel result from the separation of epistemology from ontology (482–3). In her article "Indigenous Place-Thought and Agency Amongst Humans and Non-Humans," Watts describes place-thought as "a theoretical understanding of the world via a physical embodiment" (20). She continues, "Place-thought is based upon the premise that land is alive and thinking and that humans and non-humans derive agency through the extensions of these thoughts" (20). The negative consequences of bifurcating epistemology and ontology are further emphasized in *The Tiger Flu* and its explorations of the limitations of Cartesian dualism. In an adjacent manner, Taylor reminds us that performance is *both* ontology and epistemology ("Archive and Repertoire" 2–3). A synergistic relationship between these ways of knowing is achieved in the two novels through the approximation of proximity between archive and repertoire. This approximation of proximity is where the hope of overcoming the impasse of crisis ordinariness lies, thus illustrating the potential of speculative fiction to rethink the form and function of the archive through a reorientation of subjects and objects.

Berlant argues that all attachment is optimistic, but is all optimism necessarily cruel? A closer look at Steedman's description of the archive may offer insight into this question. Steedman portrays the ways in which the archive can potentially perpetuate the fantasies that drive cruel optimism. She writes, "The archive is this kind of place, a place that is to do with longing and appropriation. It is to do with wanting things that are put together, collected, collated, named in lists and indices; a place where a whole world, a social order, may be imagined by the recurrence of a name in a register, through a scrap of paper, or some other little piece of flotsam" (76). Steedman's description of longing and appropriation characterizes the archive as an emergent site of world-building. Both King and Lai draw on the archive to build their worlds. Both novels suggest it is possible to supersede the impasse of crisis ordinariness if people detach their desires from a structure of competition and find alternative modes for living that are based on communal responsibility and sustainability. Thus, it is not necessarily desire or longing that present an obstacle to one's flourishing, but rather the systems in which desire and longing are produced and the systems in which they can (or cannot) be realized that can feed the cycle of cruel optimism.

Stoler also writes about the archive in a way that resists falling into "The Ruin" or "the Dark Baths" of cruel optimism. She advocates for a moderate reading of "archival events more as moments that disrupt (if only provisionally) a field of force, that challenge (if only slightly) what can be said and done, that question (if only quietly) epistemic warrant; that realign the certainties of the probable more than they mark the wholesale reversals of direction" (51). Stoler's cautionary approach is warranted. Nevertheless, if wholesale reversals of direction *are* possible, I argue that speculative fiction is where this opportunity arises. The conventions of the genre that allow for this extreme form of imagining can facilitate a reimagining of our world in the present. We do not know what the future holds for the characters in *The Back of the Turtle* or *The Tiger Flu*. King imagines a second coming, not of Christianity, but of turtles, that signals human and non-human interdependence as a mode of relation to disrupt the capitalist quagmire. Lai imagines a queer futurity of reproductive alterity that circumvents patriarchal governance. Both novels end in a moment of contingent arrival with a future that is unscripted, yet hopeful.

Contemporary Canadian speculative fictions depict archives as emergent sites of resistance when they are brought into approximate proximity with the repertoire. Ultimately, the intersection of archive and repertoire stimulates modes of relation that favour community over individualism. It is no coincidence that the stories in *The Back of the Turtle* and *The Tiger Flu* are delivered by multiple focalizers, thus offering multiple points of view that individually are limited, but when brought together create excess. The structure complements the content; in short, it is through the collective that we sustain ourselves, and it is through cooperation rather than competition that we find hope.

NOTES

1 Other examples of fictive archives in Canadian speculative fiction incorporate both forms of archival memory. These include the official documents (course outlines, presidential address, historical excerpts) in Omar El Akkad's *American War*, in conjunction with a shoebox filled with postcards stored in an oil drum; the Bloodlines Genealogical Archive in Margaret Atwood's *The Testaments*, described by Aunt Lydia as "the beating heart of Ardua Hall" (35); and the interview transcripts, graphic novel excerpts, and airport museum in Emily St. John Mandel's *Station Eleven*.

2 See also Dědinová et al., who argue that "Speculative fiction is one of the most potent media for analyzing the condition of [sic] contemporary world because it can explore the causes and consequences of the Anthropocene in ways inaccessible to other fields" (12), and Jennifer Wagner-Lawlor, who notes that "Contemporary speculative fictions have proven themselves powerful tools for revis(ion)ing the shape of history and revaluing the role of imagination" (2).

3 Historical knowledge is imperative for the characters' survival in *The Back of the Turtle* and *The Tiger Flu*, but some of the historical events that inform the speculative present are fictional and thus do not qualify as historiographic metafiction in the same ways as the texts under consideration in Cormier's essay.

4 Fittingly, as I wrote the first version of this paper in 2021, stories of rival billionaires Elon Musk and Jeff Bezos facing off in a race to launch internet satellite service in space dominated the news.

5 Another example of the affective turn occurs in Kate Eichhorn's queer and feminist analysis of archives, in which she notes the importance of understanding archival spaces as repositories of not only *affects* but also *order* (3). Focusing on institutionally based archives and drawing examples from seminal works by Carolyn Steedman, Ann Laura Stoler, and Ann Cvetkovich, Eichhorn encourages a reading of the archive "as an apparatus to legitimize new forms of knowledge and cultural production in an economically and politically precarious present" (4).

6 Katherine Biber and Trish Luker also consider the future orientation of the archive and its effect on the subject/object relationship. According to Biber and Luker, "Records anticipate a future archival user, somebody who might be interested in the information they contain, and the context from which they emerged" (6).

7 In *The Great Derangement*, Ghosh explains, "The most important element of the word *recognition* lies in its first syllable, which harks back to something prior, an already existing awareness that makes possible the passage from ignorance to knowledge: a moment of recognition occurs when a prior awareness flashes before us, effecting an instant change in our understanding of that which is beheld" (4–5).

8 Berlant's examples of good life fantasies include upward mobility, job security, political and social equality, lively and durable intimacy, and meritocracy (3).

9 Based on King's penchant for word play and humour, I'd wager the rhyming of "Quinn" with "twin" is intentional.

10 Mara's portraits of Smoke River Reserve inhabitants who succumbed to The Ruin are another iteration of the repertoire. Mara realizes the connection between the past, present, and future in her artistic process: "Life. There it was. Standing at the easel, looking at what she had created, Mara realized that she might have found a purpose, something that would help her push past the numbing sorrow, something that would help her make the world whole again" (King 127).

WORKS CITED

Atwood, Margaret. *The Testaments*. McClelland & Stewart, 2019.

Berlant, Lauren. *Cruel Optimism*. Duke UP, 2011.

Biber, Katherine, and Trish Luker. "Evidence and the Archive: Ethics, Aesthetics, and Emotion." *Australian Feminist Law Journal*, vol. 40, no. 1, 2014, pp. 1–14.

Burton, Antoinette. *Archive Stories: Facts, Fictions, and the Writing of History.* Duke UP, 2005.

Cifor, Marika, and Anne Gilliland. "Affect and the Archive, Archives and their Affects: An Introduction to the Special Issue." *Archival Science*, vol. 16, no. 1, 2016, pp. 1–6.

Cormier, Matthew. "Speculative Fiction and Historiographic Metafiction: The Cold War in Contemporary Apocalyptic Literary Canada, Coast to Coast." *ReVisions: Speculating in Literature and Film in Canada*, edited by Wendy Roy, U of Toronto P, 2025, pp. 67–82.

Dědinová, Tereza, et al. *Images of the Anthropocene in Speculative Fiction: Narrating the Future*. Lexington Books, 2021.

Eichhorn, Kate. *The Archival Turn in Feminism*. Temple UP, 2013.

El Akkad, Omar. *American War*. Emblem, 2017.

Fraile-Marcos, Ana María. "Precarity and the Stories We Tell: Post-Truth Discourse and Indigenous Epistemologies in Thomas King's *The Back of the Turtle*." *Journal of Postcolonial Writing*, vol. 56, no. 4, 2020, pp. 473–87.

Ghosh, Amitav. *The Great Derangement: Climate Change and the Unthinkable*. Chicago UP, 2016.

Gilliland, Anne, and Michelle Caswell. "Records and their Imaginaries: Imagining the Impossible, Making Possible the Imagined." *Archival Science*, vol. 16, no. 1, 2016, pp. 53–7.

King, Thomas. *The Back of the Turtle*. Harper Perennial, 2014.

– *The Truth About Stories: A Native Narrative*. Anansi, 2003.

Klimenko, Marina. "The Last Doubler: Reproductive Futurism and the Politics of Care in Larissa Lai's *The Tiger Flu*." *Studies in Canadian Literature*, vol. 45, no. 2, 2020, pp. 161–80.

LaCapra, Dominick. *Writing History, Writing Trauma*. Johns Hopkins UP, 2001.

Lai, Larissa. "Familiarizing Grist Village: Why I Write Speculative Fiction." *Canadian Literature*, no. 240, 2020, pp. 20–39.

– "Insurgent Utopias: How to Recognize the Knock at the Door." *Exploring the Fantastic: Genre, Ideology, and Popular Culture*, edited by Ina Batzke et al., Columbia UP, 2018, pp. 91–113.

– *The Tiger Flu*. Arsenal Pulp Press, 2018.

Mandel, Emily St. John. *Station Eleven*. HarperCollins, 2014.

Manning, Erin. *For a Pragmatics of the Useless*. Duke UP, 2020.

McCormack, Donna. "The Times and Spaces of Transplantation: Queercrip Histories as Futures." *Medical Humanities*, vol. 47, 2021, pp. 397–406.

Morra, Linda. *Moving Archives*. Wilfrid Laurier UP, 2020.

O'Brien, Susie. "'The Story You Don't Want to Tell': Decolonial Resistance in Thomas King's *The Back of the Turtle*." *Glocal Narratives of Resilience*, edited by Ana María Fraile-Marcos, Routledge, 2019, pp. 39–55.

Rhoads, Sean. "The Inestimable Nicholas Crisp: Reimagined Mythology and Environmental Renewal in Thomas King's *The Back of the Turtle.*" *Studies in Canadian Literature*, vol. 44, no. 1, 2019, pp. 122–40.

Rifkin, Mark. *Fictions of Land and Flesh: Blackness, Indigeneity, Speculation.* Duke UP, 2019.

Steedman, Carolyn. *Dust.* Manchester UP, 2001.

Stoler, Ann Laura. *Along the Archival Grain: Epistemic Anxieties and Colonial Common Sense.* Princeton UP, 2009.

Taylor, Diana. *The Archive and the Repertoire: Performing Cultural Memory in the Americas.* Duke UP, 2003.

– "Performance and/as History." *TDR: The Drama Review*, vol. 50, no. 1, 2006, pp. 67–86.

Wagner-Lawlor, Jennifer. *Postmodern Utopias and Feminist Fictions.* Cambridge UP, 2013.

Watts, Vanessa. "Indigenous Place-Thought and Agency Amongst Humans and Non-Humans (First Woman and Sky Woman Go on a European World Tour!)." *Decolonization: Indigeneity, Education and Society*, vol. 2, no. 1, 2013, pp. 20–34.

Wunker, Erin. "Archives Undone: Towards a Poethics of Feminist Archival Disruptions." *Journal of Canadian Literary and Cultural Studies*, vol. 8, 2019, pp. 62–73.

Speculative Fiction and Historiographic Metafiction: The Cold War in Contemporary Apocalyptic Literary Canada, Coast to Coast

MATTHEW CORMIER

In the current theoretical-critical moment, speculative fiction as a creative framework to construct literary representations of potential futures is enjoying a resurgence, especially in Canada. While the term "speculative fiction" has circulated since the mid-twentieth century,[1] its current revival is in no small part due to well-documented definitions and endorsements from writers such as Margaret Atwood, who – not without some difficulty – describes the genre in her work of creative non-fiction, *In Other Worlds*, as one consisting of "plots that descend from Jules Verne's books about submarines and balloon travel and such – things that really could happen but just hadn't happened when the authors wrote the books" (6). "It's not me making it up," she once said, "it's just math" ("Margaret Atwood & Ursula K. Le Guin"), referring to the inevitability that such speculations would become realities given enough time or in quasi-identical universes parallel to our own. Yet, the assuredness of such claims aside, scholars in Canada have been probing the directionality of speculative fiction for some time now. Perhaps most notably, the late, renowned Canadianist Herb Wyile, in his book *Speculative Fictions: Contemporary Canadian Novelists and the Writing of History*, explains that "Speculative fiction is not an objective, detached, authentic glimpse into the future, but rather usually a very purposeful, subjective, and rhetorical extrapolation from present circumstances, and the same might be said of historical fiction" (xii). Wyile's work on speculative fiction is undoubtedly indebted to Linda Hutcheon's well-known conceptualization of "historiographic metafiction," which refers to fictionalizations of historical narratives that "often [point] to the fact by using the paratextual conventions of historiography to both inscribe and undermine the authority and objectivity of historical sources and explanations" (*Canadian*

Postmodern, 122–3). The arguments by both of these scholars are captivating in two senses: first, because of their evident critical soundness in the midst of the difficult-to-pin-down intersection of memory, history, experience, and imagination, but second, due to the literary eras that they capture. Hutcheon, for instance, grounds her arguments within the peak period of literary postmodernism in Canada by reading texts published through the 1970s and 1980s, while Wyile builds his case by relying on the aftermath of postmodernist fiction in the decade that follows. And so, the recent rise of speculative fiction, specifically regarding its current preoccupation with imagined futures, comes at a crucial time. It coincides with the ongoing break from the formal and political interrogation of history that was central to literary postmodernism in Canada during the latter half of the twentieth century in favour of the present preoccupation with reframing our perspective of the world – even the past – through an apocalyptic gaze informed by unknown, but affective, imminent threats induced by an uncertain future at a time marked by various crises.

Yet, even in the face of these anticipatory, apocalyptic concerns, some twenty-first-century fiction in Canada makes space for speculative fiction and historiographic metafiction to confront and challenge one another. In this respect, Nicolas Dickner's *Apocalypse for Beginners* (2010; first published in French as *Tarmac* in 2009) and Nancy Lee's *The Age* (2014) constitute an intriguing point of comparison. Both contemporary novels fictionalize narratives taking place towards the end of the Cold War. Dickner's book, which plays out in coastal Eastern Canada, was written in French by a white man born and raised in Quebec, while Lee's novel, set in coastal Western Canada, was written in English by a woman of Chinese and Indian descent who was born in Wales and lived in England before immigrating to Canada. Dickner's and Lee's texts complicate themes of vulnerability, insecurity, and anxiety during this tense historical moment through their primary characters, who are navigating their adolescence, identity, and sexuality. Additionally, the novels contrast the formal aesthetics that honour and renew those of past postmodernist writers in Canada – those writing strategies indebted to the pivotal baton-pass between historiographic metafiction and the present ascent of futuristic speculative fiction. This chapter compares Dickner's *Apocalypse for Beginners* and Lee's *The Age* to shed light on the different ways in which, and reasons why, historiographic metafiction persists in these novels during the currently ongoing speculative turn that chiefly focuses on future scenarios. In doing so, it underscores the work that such texts do to inform or warn readers about humanity's course in the twenty-first century.

Situating and Facing "The End": Markers, Responses, and Approaches

Whether in writing or reading the past or the future, in adapting the frameworks of historiographic metafiction or speculative fiction in all of their intricacies, the temporal markers of "ends" and "beginnings" are of importance. The apocalyptic genre is especially instructive in understanding temporal markers: the biblical apocalypse is a prophesied event that is supposed to bring about the end of the world to make way for a new one, yet the time of arrival of the apocalypse, of its "coming," is unknown, sealed away. As I have written elsewhere, the apocalyptic paradigm is thus powerfully, cyclically affective in this arena of real or perceived temporality: with only the end of *a* world, but never that of *the* world, to guide us, we are perpetually braced for the coming of the forewarned, definitive judgment day, locked in a compromising state of anxiety that, meanwhile, increasingly struggles under the cumulative pressures of ceaseless waves of micro-apocalypses.[2] "Apocalypse," religious studies scholar Tina Pippin suggests, "is an uncertain certainty, a dreaded hope, an endless end. Apocalypse scares and scars" (xii). The Cold War, in which both Dickner's and Lee's narratives are situated, is one such era defined by the fear of an imminent apocalypse, and one that both "scared and scarred." The impending nuclear end of *the* world threatened to destroy nations and incited mass paranoia. Both instigated and justified wars and countless brutalities and hostilities never came to pass, but *a* world did end with the dissolution of the Soviet Union and, with it, the Cold War. The narratives of both *Apocalypse for Beginners* and *The Age* engage in intriguing work in that they are apprehensively speculative about a looming, catastrophic future that readers know does not in fact come to pass. The Cold War in the novels becomes a functional temporal marker – a compass pointing to an end, but also a beginning – and the protagonists in each text parallel this paradoxical momentum even as they are tied to it and respond to it.

Set mostly on the east coast and in Rivière-du-Loup, Quebec, as well as partly in Japan, *Apocalypse for Beginners* chiefly revolves around the aptly named Mary Hope Juliet Randall – Hope to those few who know her – and her family's apocalyptic legacy. The coastal settings in the novel appear to function implicitly as apocalyptic, geographical markers of their own. Ever since coming to the coast of Nova Scotia during colonial times, generations of the Randall family have endured their respective, cursed visions of the apocalypse – cursed precisely because, just as with the biblical apocalypse, none ever come to fruition. Moreover, Hope's breakthrough regarding her own apocalypse at the conclusion of the narrative takes place in another coastal setting: Japan, where nuclear bombs were detonated during the Second World War, a major apocalyptic event. Hope is the youngest member of the Randall family, which has suffered greatly; as the narrator notes, "the Randall family tree could be used in a course on the history of psychiatry in North America over the past one hundred and fifty years" (9). Hope's first and middle names allude to well-known literary characters: "Mary," of course, is a reference to the biblical Virgin Mary and her immaculate conception of Jesus, for the Randall women always receive their apocalyptic visions upon first menstruating, an event that is delayed in Hope's case and that she does not experience until the very end of the novel. Meanwhile, "Juliet" recalls Shakespeare's young and tragic heroine, whose story is set in August, which is also when the narrative of *Apocalypse for Beginners* begins. As her chosen name implies, Hope persists throughout the narrative in her attempts to solve and break the apocalyptic cycle that has tormented the Randalls all the way from France to Canada during colonial times, and then to the United States, and finally Japan at the turn of the twentieth century.

When her frenetic mother takes her to a new town in Quebec to await her predicted apocalypse, Hope makes a new friend in Mickey, who narrates much of the novel. Mickey is both fascinated by and committed to helping Hope with her dilemma. In fact, the thoughtfulness, rationality, and genuine care for Hope that he demonstrates through his narration ultimately work to prolong the reader's suspension of disbelief in the face of situations that sometimes border the absurd; they help readers to empathize with the paranoid state of mind that pervaded the Cold War context in which the narrative is mostly set. Mickey's account traces the teenagers' experiences and relationship as they grow together while bridging apocalyptic markers from the past. His narrative begins towards the end of the Cold War and extends to the turn of the millennium and the growing fears surrounding "Y2K" and the collapse of technology as we knew it, even referencing the Gulf War.

Dickner's world, defined by these apocalyptic, historical markers that have already come and gone, represents a generative intersection between speculative fiction and historiographic metafiction. In this respect, and as critic Marie-Hélène Voyer proposes, "the author exhibits the precarious character of notions of memory, permanence, progress, and the linearity of time" (49; my translation). Voyer goes even further, arguing that, in Dickner's literary universe, the theme and aesthetics of "ruins" – of waste, debris, and leftovers – play especially important roles. Rather than pointing to mourning or melancholia, however, Dickner's use of ruins "is a pretext for all sorts of ironic condensations, playful reversals, surprising overlaps, and joyful anticipations that celebrate both the virtues of oblivion and the highly narrative potential of remnants, debris, remains, and slag" (50; my translation). In numerous instances, Dickner subverts the gravity of the apocalyptic implications that are proposed in the narrative. For example, Mickey speaks of his family's business, a materials company built through generations, explaining that "concrete wasn't just a business; it was a matter of civilization, a mission to be passed on from father to son. We were builders of worlds" (41). Afterwards, he witnesses the collapse of the Berlin Wall on television, observing the "debris" left over from this once powerful symbol of national, global, and ideological divides, and noting how "it was toppling over, and with mind-boggling ease. So a nudge from a bulldozer is all it took to dispose of this shameful structure?" (44).[3] *Apocalypse for Beginners* thus repeatedly faces the end of the world with humour, making a reclamation project of the discarded, the forgotten, and the ruins left behind with each "apocalypse" to look lightheartedly towards hopeful futures.

Coming out of and set in western Canada, Nancy Lee's *The Age* takes a completely different approach in its speculation on the futurity of the Cold War. Often, Lee's novel indulges in fantasies of destruction conjured from the circulation of images and news in popular media; the company that the protagonist, Gerry, keeps; and her vivid imagination. Lee's coastal setting seems to operate implicitly in the background of the novel to evoke a feeling of vulnerability, of defencelessness against the imminent threat of nuclear attack, and this feeling mirrors the insecurities and anxieties of the protagonist. In particular, the attention paid in the narrative to Soviet submarines and their movements subtly works to present the coast as an unsafe area during this period, providing Gerry with inspiration for her apocalyptic fantasies. In an especially poignant speculative scene, a nuclear bomb detonates over a city, and a young boy – Gerry, having swapped genders in the scenario – and a woman hold each other in their final moment:

> It is not the present, he wants to tell her, but the future, that should frighten her. The coming illness: strangers spewing their liquidous insides, loose teeth giving way to bloody gums that gnash at mouldy breadcrusts, rotten crabapples and, later, insects, dog flesh. The almost-dead pleading for food, desperate and crazed, burnt skin torn away in sheets, the blackened pits of open wounds. The tyranny of the well and capacitated. The marvel that many who survive will be without intelligence or compassion. Eternal night, invisible sun, perpetual cold. Thirst so maddening it will make people cry and foam, hysterical with the need to quench the body's heat.

> Girls who continue to have babies, who parade inflated bodies on swollen, blistered feet, who beg for extra food and water. Those who miscarry left to bury puddles of bloody tissue in hidden corners. (50)

This vivid vision, contrary to those that Dickner entertains, is one lacking in any hope whatsoever; the ruins, here, unlike in *Apocalypse for Beginners*, chiefly play out in repercussive, post-nuclear-Armageddon nightmare scenarios rather than being used in a hopeful, playful reclamation project.

Dickner and Lee thus speculate in their respective Cold War narratives by using different strategies, to seemingly disparate ends. That being said, their common practice of combining literary conventions of speculative fiction and historical metafiction produces a similar potentiality. Of this potentiality, this moment of possibility, fellow speculative author Larissa Lai writes that her own "speculative fiction practice combines the work of re-subjectivation with the work of insurgent genealogy. As such, the work is not so much purely oppositional as it is a kind of hybrid genealogical/oppositional/imaginative outward petalling, full of possibilities for rupture or emergence" (23). She goes on to explain that she is "interested in that moment in [her] own speculative fictions when the speculative fiction metaphor [that she has] set up breaks down, and the story has to address the problems attached to the representation rather than the represented" (23). The "metaphor" that Lai references, by which she means the opening created by realistic imagined futures, can be persuasive and informative in the work that it undertakes, forcing readers to confront certain ideologies and subjectivities in new, defamiliarized ways. Yet the potency of speculating on similar realities and subjectivities in familiar scenarios cannot be understated. In her keynote address to the 20/21 Vision: Speculating in Literature and Film in Canada conference, for example, author of the acclaimed novel *The Marrow Thieves* Cherie Dimaline speaks to speculative fiction's power to reveal, interrupt, and recentre, in a similar fashion to Lai, but also makes the important observation that time is not linear; moreover, as a strong example, she points to the post-apocalyptic experiences of Indigenous Peoples ever since the beginning of colonization, and the need to acknowledge such realities and to maintain an informed mindset when reading speculative fiction.

The potentiality of speculative fiction, then, in concert with the contextual familiarity that historical metafiction offers, might present significant opportunities to provoke profound critical reflection. Speculative fiction set in the past rather than the future, when it can be grounded in well-known historical contexts and read with informed mindsets, shows special promise. "Historiographic metafiction works to situate itself within historical discourse without surrendering its autonomy as fiction," Hutcheon tells us. "And it is a kind of seriously ironic parody that effects both aims: the intertexts of history and fiction take on parallel (though not equal) status in the parodic reworking of the textual past of both the 'world' and literature" ("Historiographic Metafiction" 4). Hutcheon further argues that "[h]istoriographic metafiction manages to satisfy such a desire for 'worldly' grounding while at the same time querying the very basis of the authority of that grounding" (5). Yet, when speculative fiction meets historiographic metafiction, such as with Dickner's *Apocalypse for Beginners* and Lee's *The Age*, this "'worldly' grounding" takes on a different purpose than to query authority; instead, it functions to recall a familiar historical backdrop upon which to propose anti-apocalyptic alternative futures. In the case of these two novels, adolescents going through a tumultuous period of their lives between "markers" – from childhood to adulthood – during a reflectively transitional historical period face the apocalyptic threat of the Cold War all the while progressing towards a more hopeful future. This particular juxtaposition of speculative fiction and historiographic metafiction thus, through different approaches, creates space for alternative, anti-apocalyptic possibilities.[4]

"The Future Ain't What It Used to Be": Cold War Adolescence and the Anti-Apocalyptic

In the words of New York Yankees' legend Yogi Berra, and as quoted as an epigraph to *Apocalypse for Beginners*, "The future ain't what it used to be." Time is slippery between apocalypse, speculative fiction, and historiographic metafiction. The "in-between" areas – those liminal spaces or times between markers of importance – can be instructive. As a biographical point of departure to this section, both Dickner (b. 1972) and Lee (b. 1970) experienced the winding down of the Cold War during their teenage years, and, perhaps consequently, *Apocalypse for Beginners* and *The Age* demonstrate what seems to be an intimate understanding of some of the challenges of that transitional period in one's life within the uncertain, often apocalyptic historical climate of the time. Each novel is certainly a *bildungsroman* in its attempt to put into context certain difficulties and pressures that adolescent girls and young women face, through the perspectives of their protagonists, Hope and Gerry. As such, the differences between the novels and how they grapple with the Cold War and beyond as temporal, apocalyptic markers extend to their characters and the relationships that they develop during this time.

In *Apocalypse for Beginners*, Hope and Mickey are two loners who come together to support one another. In particular, the instability of the mental health of Hope's mother, as the date of her predicted apocalypse comes and goes without incident, leads Hope to adopt Mickey's family as a substitute support system until she leaves him to travel to Japan on her own to try to solve the mystery of her apocalyptic compulsion. In Hope's case, the apocalyptic visions that plague her family are intrinsically tied to puberty, as if one rite of passage made way for the other: "So, at puberty, every Randall was supernaturally made privy to the details of the end of the world – the date, the time, the exact form it would take" (8). Hope's mother, Ann, had received her vision when she was thirteen years old after the institutionalization of her mother:

> On September 1, 1966, at dawn, after two days of cramps and migraines, Ann Randall, still shaken by her mother's confinement, woke up sweating so profusely that the sheets clung to her body. Off Yarmouth, the rumbling of a storm could be heard.
>
> From that moment Ann knew – and would never for an instant forget – that the end of the world would take place in the summer of 1989. (11–12)

What is especially gendered in the case of the Randall family's affliction, however, is that, for the women, their apocalyptic visions begin only after their first menstruation. Upon witnessing her prophecy, Ann "became aware of another event – one that was wet, sticky, and unmistakable. She slid three fingers down her thighs and they came back stained with brownish blood. Her Spell from Hell was sealed" (12).

In tying the Randall women's apocalyptic curse to menstruation, Dickner not only attempts to emphasize the pressures on adolescent women, but also adds a particularly cruel marker for Hope to think about alongside the potential end of the world in a hostile, late Cold War era. Throughout the novel, as Hope progresses through her teenage years, she seeks her own apocalyptic date, an urgency that grows once the summer of 1989 comes and goes without fulfilling her mother's vision, with her mother then becoming even more detached from reality. Without the appearance of a date, however, Hope does not begin to menstruate – which is an added, gendered pressure to her pursuit of her own prophecy as well as her identity as she is becoming a young adult. Hope persists, however, and shows a strong sense of character even as external events evolve: as she and Mickey watch the developments of the new apocalyptic threat in the Gulf War, Mickey observes that the footage "[l]ooks like the end of the world," to which Hope replies, "[o]r the beginning of a new one" (130). Hope's search takes her away from Mickey and to New York and then to Japan; despite her hardships and the pressures surrounding her, she never loses hope, through sheer determination, and finds her date: 18 July 2001.

Hope's pursuit of her apocalyptic date is a solitary and nomadic one, as she leaves behind the only stability that she had ever known in Mickey and, by extension, his family. Perhaps not surprisingly, as I have discussed elsewhere (Cormier, "Destruction" 19), Hope's actions throughout the narrative align with the reaching and surmounting of important temporal markers and the contexts that defined them, especially the Cold War. For instance, much of Hope and Mickey's relationship involves them living with a "bunker mentality," stowed away in the latter's basement – nicknamed "the Bunker" – and watching fearmongering news on television. Hope's mother had fuelled this mentality herself for years by purchasing immense quantities of non-perishable foods in anticipation of her predicted apocalypse; however, the event that takes place in the summer of 1989 is simply the passing of another temporal marker, the end of just one world, in the collapse of the Berlin Wall, and, within two years, the end of the Cold War. Once the Cold War ends, so too does the hold that the bunker mentality had on Hope, and she decides to venture out on her own to chase down the clues that she has gathered regarding her own apocalyptic prophecy. The morning after a party, Mickey wakes up with Hope nowhere to be found. On a hunch, he checks under the couch cushion, where she had kept all of her savings: "There could be no mistake: instead of a thick envelope stuffed with money, my hand found nothing but springs, foam rubber and unidentified crumbs. Hope had closed her secret account" (138). With the ending of the Cold War, so too comes the end of Hope's self-confinement: she empties "the Bunker" of all that she had financially saved and rationed and leaves it for what would be the final time.

On Hope's date of the supposed apocalypse, Mickey waits in suspense, but the day passes by without cataclysm, and without word from Hope. Then, a piece of mail from Tokyo:

> Sanitary napkins.
>
> More specifically (based on my recently acquired expertise), these were extra-thin, hypoallergenic napkins with NanoNikki™ micropores and super-leaky-proof-yet-ultrasoft wings. A model made for today's active young Japanese woman.
>
> Hope Randall was no longer a medical mystery. (252)

Hope not only survives beyond her apocalyptic date, but also various markers, including the end of the Cold War, the Gulf War, and Y2K, along with the cultural ideologies they perpetuated. In doing so, she overcomes accompanying strain to her mental and physical health, and she does so without the help of her family or of a man. Unbeknownst to the protagonists, however, the world-ending (for some) events of 9/11 are to take place in just a couple of months. Nevertheless, once Hope has overcome these challenges on her own, the novel ends on a hopeful note with Mickey leaving for Tokyo to find her, having now received a symbolic invitation to do so: "Things were so much better now that the end of the world was behind us," he exclaims (254). Through this intersection of speculative fiction and historiographic metafiction, *Apocalypse for Beginners* allows anti-apocalyptic optimism to prevail.

Lee's *The Age* focuses not only on the interruptive visions of destruction of the young teenage protagonist, Gerry, but also on the gang of slightly older anarchists with whom she surrounds herself and who are planning a terrorist act in protest of the threat of nuclear attacks during the Cold War. Because she has an unstable home and is upset at a father who abandoned her for a new family, this cast of characters becomes a new surrogate family to her, one that will help her strike back at her father. While Gerry, like Hope, has an unstable background, her response to it is radically different. If we could classify Hope's initial state as conservative or defensive in terms of her well-established bunker mentality, we can think of Gerry's as offensive or combative. As scholar Annika Rosanowski observes, Gerry's "last name, Cross, defines her character: she is constantly cross with everyone, lashing out whenever she feels insecure or hurt" (121). As mentioned earlier, much of Gerry's antagonism is tied to her parents' divorce and her subsequent sensations of abandonment and resentment. Gerry persists in a downward spiral with the anarchist group, until their terrorist act goes wrong, one of her friends is killed, and she finally reconciles with her mother and testifies against them at the end of the novel. Throughout the narrative, as suggested by her name, her anger and sadness often coincide with the confused feelings towards her fluid gender and sexuality that seem to consume her, frequently alongside her relationships with others and their influences on her. The outset of the novel demonstrates one of the ways in which she links these feelings to her anger: "Always, it seems, Gerry's mind is full of them, girls, flitting and hovering. At school, they swarm beside lockers, drawn to one another but not to her. She scolds herself to ignore them. When they see her face on the evening news, that's when their gaping mouths will be worth imagining" (2–3). Despite her anger and cynicism, however, Gerry remains persistent and curious, even though her curiosity most often ends up hurting her.

In most instances, when Gerry follows her curiosity, she is punished for it in some way. The first punishment occurs when she goes to meet her anarchist group. She arrives at Megan's house and climbs up to her window, where she sees her engaging in a sexual act with Ian, whom Gerry has known since she was a child:

> Megan moves her hips in slow underwater circles that make Gerry shudder.
>
> She mimics Megan's hips with her own, tosses her head as she imagines Megan doing. Low in Gerry's belly, secret muscles twitch and tense. The grit under her sneaker shifts with her rocking. Her foot starts a slow, easy slip. She steps back to steady herself but finds only soft, yielding air. As she tips, her fingers snatch at the ledge, her hands flail out, a sting catches her wrist. The ground slams up against her back. (3–4)

In trying to indulge her curiosity, Gerry hurts herself and feels further humiliated; later that night, in yet another painful moment, she gets jumped in the park and beaten up by a group of boys until one of them realizes, "*It's a fucking girl*" (13). The hardships that Gerry faces are constant and perhaps more painful because of the fantasies in which she indulges. In an act of defiance in response to being jumped, she asks Megan to help her shave her head. While Megan cuts her hair, they talk, and Megan tells her why she likes Ian, to which Gerry replies, "'Like brother and sister?' Gerry tries not to think of Megan having sex with Ian. The idea, matched with her own nakedness, starts a low, syrupy heat inside of her" (37). After this brief embarrassment, the conversation continues and turns to a security guard that Megan was supposed to meet to receive a code to be used in their terrorist attack. When Megan tells her that the meeting was a waste of time, Gerry asks,

> "Did you still have sex with him?"
>
> The clippers clack off. Gerry scoops a fistful of dead hair, rolls it between her fingers, waits, then turns, curious why Megan has stopped. Megan's face is still but tense, as if she's trying to solve a math problem in her head. "What makes you think I had sex with him?"
>
> Gerry worries she's gotten it wrong, that she's about to look stupid. (38)

As this passage indicates, Gerry is constantly bombarded with moments of tension, of micro-anxieties that feed her insecurities, shame, and, consequently, her anger and violent tendencies. Her fantasies thus become a form of speculative escapism to which she increasingly turns, especially due to the effects of the Cold War climate and the anarchist actors that surround her.

In fact, Gerry's own speculative, post-apocalyptic imaginings borrow elements from the developing Cold War as she learns them through the incessant flow of news. The reports that she views on television are particularly influential, not only providing her with details of escalating tensions between the United States and the Soviet Union, but also with imagery: "A routine Soviet dispatch balloons into a full-blown naval occupation of the north Atlantic, one hundred and forty warships and submarines hulking in the waters between Greenland, Norway, and Scotland's Shetland Islands. Gerry scratches at her hands as she watches the news.... Missiles awake in their underwater chambers. On sea-soaked decks of aircraft carriers, jet engines whine, bellies full of nuclear payload" (82). Her constant exposure to reporting on intensifying Cold War tensions legitimizes and thus strengthens her post-apocalyptic fantasies and the hold that they have on her. Gerry imagines this speculative apocalyptic narrative – which seems to her very possible, given the Cold War conflict – because it is a means of ending her current world to make way for a new one in which she has what she feels is missing from her current life. In this fantasy, Gerry is a boy who survives the nuclear apocalypse resulting from the Cold War and locates a group of survivors. He finds a father figure in Dan, who leads the group of survivors; the boy also feels a sense of belonging and family with respect to his group of survivors. He has a loving partner, with whom he experiences sexual intimacy; she becomes pregnant and miraculously gives birth to a healthy child in this post-apocalyptic wasteland. And so, while Gerry's Cold War–inspired reveries present a number of horrors, they also allow for a new life, one in which the protagonist can make up for the absent relationships in their life: a relationship with their father, a supportive family structure, a romantic partner. Moreover, the post-apocalyptic setting in the wake of a speculated nuclear end to the Cold War serves to dramatize and accentuate the importance of these relationships to Gerry even when they should undermine the possibility of the fantasy becoming reality.

The closer the date of the act of terrorism that Gerry's anarchist group has planned, the more that Cold War paranoia appears to ensnare Gerry. She panics when she hears air raid sirens, only to learn that they warn of an electrical storm in the area (151–2). She worries at the news that President Reagan is always considering the threat of nuclear action (153). Yet her fantasies remain strong: even in reading her group's terrorist manifesto, which explains why they are about to detonate a bomb, Gerry does not grasp the reality of what she is about to do (160). Of course, it is too late in the day of the act when Ian attempts to abort the mission and flee with the bomb, only to have it explode and kill him. Grief brings Gerry to a harsh, overwhelming reality: "Her mind is full of Ian, the bony rectangle of his shoulders, the smell of his shaving cream, sea water and astringent, his smile when he teased, the way his voice got wistful and gravelly late at night. The swarm of him, so real and immediate, forces her to her hands and knees. Her jaw aches as her mouth stretches wide. She clutches her head and howls" (248). The breaking of the fantasy into this cruel reality is too much for Gerry to handle, and she attempts to take her own life; however, her mother manages to resuscitate her. The aftermath of Ian's death leaves Gerry in semi-state of purgatory in the form of a deep depression, one from which Ian's memory, paradoxically, saves her. In part because Gerry wants the truth to come out about Ian, that he was not deranged or suicidal, she decides to come forward.

Gerry confesses to the crime and her part in it to her mother, and then to the police. When she threatens to break down in front of them, "[d]etails are what break the spell.... Her voice settles in her body, a vessel of shame and guilt" (273). Despite this challenge, however, Gerry's grounding in reality in this passage, as well as the more significant acknowledgment of reality that represents her confession to the police, speak to her growth. Afterwards, her lawyer tells her that they should remain positive; Gerry, in turn, "imagines her mom before she was married, gentle and optimistic, smart enough to study chemistry, certain and secure. She touches her mom's fingers, traces the divot left by her wedding ring" (274). Her mom replies to her touch by saying, "I always wore that thing too tight" (274). It is here that the anti-apocalyptic moment opens up – not outside of the apocalyptic cycle, but at a denouement that allows for a brief, but significant reflection and maturation. *The Age* proposes hope in this conclusion; as Rosanowski explains, "Gerry's understanding of care as something mutual and therefore not a weakness functions anti-apocalyptically in that it helps construct a future by meeting needs: here in the form of emotional support and protection, rather than focusing on violent retaliation. The apocalyptic metaphors are missing from the ending, enabling an optimistic reading of her future, in which she is walking toward her mother" (123). Gerry and her mother can let go of the man who abandoned them both and recognize the support and love that they have in each other – the care, in Rosanowski's terms. This resolution becomes concretized during the final scene of the novel, in which they attend the funeral of Gerry's paternal grandfather. The two wait with apprehension to see if Gerry's father will appear; when he does not, "Gerry leans against her [mother], relieved for a moment not to hold herself straight" (280). While both novels differ greatly in their strategies and tone, their shared "anti-apocalyptic" resolutions, to echo Rosanowski's assessment of *The Age*, represent their most compelling interventions, made possible by the tensions between speculative fiction and historiographic metafiction in relation to temporal markers of ends and beginnings.

Conclusion

Both of these *bildungsromane*, Nicolas Dickner's *Apocalypse for Beginners* and Nancy Lee's *The Age*, focus on similar themes – the challenges of adolescence for young women from difficult or unstable domestic situations – and are set towards the end of the Cold War, which influences to various degrees the narratives of their protagonists, Hope and Gerry. The comparisons and contrasts between them, from the light and playful characteristics of Dickner's novel to the darker and at times more destructively fantastical elements of Lee's, are compelling because of the profoundly different perspectives from which they were written. Lee's positionality is much more marginalized and vulnerable than Dickner's, perhaps explaining to some degree the sombre introspection that defines *The Age* by contrast to the whimsical set of narrative constraints that *Apocalypse for Beginners* entertains.

Nonetheless, the common, innovative intersection of generic conventions that both authors employ, evoking speculative fiction and historiographic metafiction, adds to the potential for comparative analysis. Each novel presents a speculative narrative within the context of a familiar historical period that brings with it well-known – and now better understood – cultural and ideological influences, pressures, and anxieties. Through this intersection, both authors draw upon the cyclical potency of the apocalyptic genre, with its temporal markers, to create various opportunities for growth and learning. The combination of speculative fiction and historiographic metafiction makes space for a moment of anti-apocalyptic denouement in these novels as Hope and Gerry become young adults. Evidently, this denouement, within the apocalyptic cycle, is a respite and cannot last. In *Apocalypse for Beginners*, a narrative significantly dominated by global apocalyptic events, the terrorist attacks of 9/11 are on the horizon; in *The Age*, we do not know at the end of the narrative precisely what the consequences are for Gerry regarding her participation in the terrorist plot. That being said, both novels offer hope to these protagonists and lessons to readers that can be taken and applied as we face our own set of apocalyptic markers in the twenty-first century – both happening now and in speculated futures.

NOTES

1 The origin of the term is often attributed to American writer Robert A. Heinlein and his 1947 essay "On the Writing of Speculative Fiction."

2 I have also investigated this conceptualization of apocalypse with respect to its affective potential ("Theorizing the Apocalyptic Turn") and in relation to nationalism and the Canadian nation-state ("Emergent Critical Strategies Against the Nation-Trap" and "The Destruction of Nationalism").

3 While not referring to it as a thematic of ruins, I discuss this particular motif in Dickner's novel with the cycle of construction and destruction in my article "The Destruction of Nationalism."

4 For an additional, insightful reading of the potential for hopeful futures or anti-apocalyptic possibilities in speculative fiction in Canada, against what theorist Lauren Berlant calls "cruel optimism," see Alicia Fahey's chapter in this volume, "Speculative Archives in Novels by Thomas King and Larissa Lai: Hope in the Midst of Crisis" (49).

WORKS CITED

Atwood, Margaret. *In Other Worlds: SF and the Human Imagination.* McClelland & Stewart, 2011.

Atwood, Margaret, and Ursula K. Le Guin. "Margaret Atwood & Ursula K. Le Guin (Rebroadcast)." *Portland Arts and Lectures*, 23 Sept. 2010, https://literary-arts.org/archive/ursula-le-guin-margaret-atwood-rebroadcast/.

Cormier, Matthew. "The Destruction of Nationalism in Twenty-First-Century Canadian Apocalyptic Fiction." *American, British and Canadian Studies*, no. 35, 2020, pp. 9–26.

– "Emergent Critical Strategies Against the Nation-Trap: The Digitization of Literary Apocalyptic Affects and Larissa Lai's *The Tiger Flu.*" *Canada and Beyond: A Journal of Canadian Literary and Cultural Studies*, no. 11, 2022 pp. 167–82.

– "Theorizing the Apocalyptic Turn in the Literatures of Canada: Un/Veiling the Apocalyptic Direction in Affect Studies." *All the Feels/Tous les sens: Affect and Writing in Canada/Affect et écriture au Canada*, edited by Marie Carrière, Kit Dobson, and Ursula Moser, U of Alberta P, 2020, pp. 3–22.

Dickner, Nicolas. *Apocalypse for Beginners.* Published in French as *Tarmac*, 2000. Translated by Lazer Lederhendler, Vintage Canada, 2010.

Dimaline, Cherie. "From Where We Stand: Nuance and Perspective in Speculative Literature." 20/21 Vision conference, 16 Aug. 2021, U of Saskatchewan, Saskatoon, via videoconference. Keynote address.

– *The Marrow Thieves*. Dancing Cat Books, 2017.

Fahey, Alicia. "Speculative Archives in Novels by Thomas King and Larissa Lai: Hope in the Midst of Crisis." *ReVisions: Speculating in Film and Literature in Canada*, edited by Wendy Roy, U of Toronto P, 2025, pp. 45–65.

Heinlein, Robert A. "On the Writing of Speculative Fiction." 1947. *Writing Science Fiction & Fantasy: 20 Dynamic Essays by the Field's Top Professionals*, edited by Gardner Dozois et al., St. Martin's Griffin Press, 1993, pp. 5–11.

Hutcheon, Linda. *The Canadian Postmodern: A Study of Contemporary English-Canadian Fiction*. Oxford UP, 1988.

– "Historiographic Metafiction Parody and the Intertextuality of History." *Intertextuality and Contemporary American Fiction*, edited by Patrick O'Donnell and Robert Con Davis, Johns Hopkins UP, 1989, pp. 3–32.

Lai, Larissa. "Familiarizing Grist Village: Why I Write Speculative Fiction." *Canadian Literature*, no. 240, 2020, pp. 20–39.

Lee, Nancy. *The Age*. McClelland & Stewart, 2014.

Rosanowski, Annika. "Post-Apocalyptic Fiction in Canada after 9/11: A Future Based on Care." *Apocalyptic Chic: Visions of the Apocalypse and Post-Apocalypse in Literature and Visual Arts*, Fairleigh Dickinson UP, 2017, pp. 118–31.

Voyer, Marie-Hélène. "Nicolas Dickner et le charme discret des ruines." *Études françaises*, vol. 56, no. 1, 2020, pp. 49–64.

Wyile, Herb. *Speculative Fictions: Contemporary Canadian Novelists and the Writing of History*. McGill-Queens UP, 2002.

Interlude

Interrupting the Fire with Story: An Interview with Cherie Dimaline

MABIANA CAMARGO

Cherie Dimaline is a writer, activist, and member of the Georgian Bay Métis Community in Ontario. Her best-selling novel *The Marrow Thieves* (2017) won several prizes, including the Governor General's Literary Award for Young People's Literature, the Kirkus Prize for Young Readers' Literature, the Amy Mathers Teen Book Award, and the Burt Award for First Nations, Métis, and Inuit Literature. *The Marrow Thieves* has been translated into a number of languages and remained on national bestseller lists for years after its publication. The novel focuses on a young Métis protagonist and his created family in a near-future dystopian Canada; it reimagines Canadian Residential Schools as part of a terrifying future in which Indigenous Peoples are hunted so that their dreams can be harvested.

The follow-up to *The Marrow Thieves, Hunting by Stars* (2021), was an American Indian Library Association Honor Book. It continues the story of seventeen-year-old Frenchie but is also a meditation on hope, human connectedness, and the links between generations. Dimaline's 2019 novel *Empire of Wild,* which focuses on the Métis mythological figure of the Rogarou, and *VenCo*, her 2023 novel about present-day witches, both appeared at the top of Canadian best-seller lists. She won the 2025 NSK Neustadt Prize for Children's and Young Adult Literature.

Dimaline's speculative fiction has been influential in how readers and writers think about speculative writing and about literature focused on Indigenous characters and youth. She uses speculative fiction to rethink social organization and to question systemic oppression. Despite being aimed at younger audiences, her writing is appreciated by an adult audience because of its power to dismantle white Western colonial ways of being and values while reasserting Indigenous ones.

This interview was sparked by conversations and presentations at the 20/21 Vision: Speculating in Literature and Film conference in

August 2021 and was conducted via email by Mabiana Camargo, a researcher and writer from Brazil who is completing a dissertation on women's apocalyptic and dystopian fiction in Canada.

MABIANA CAMARGO: I want to start by asking about your keynote address to the 20/21 Vision: Speculating in Literature and Film conference. You argued in that talk that speculative fiction must include *perspective* and *nuance*, which enables it not only to reframe colonialist contexts and sets of assumptions about how the world works, but also to become an active manifestation of other ways of thinking and being. And the way perspective and nuance are brought to the genre is through three key concepts: "to reveal, to interrupt, and to recentre." Can you talk more about these three functions of speculative fiction and how they contribute to the idea that stories can "interrupt the fire," or interrupt ongoing colonial oppression and its agenda?

CHERIE DIMALINE: Mohawk poet and publisher Janet Rogers once remarked how the work we create today as writers will help shape culture tomorrow. How terrifying, but also something that we need to think about when we are creating and putting text out into the world for consumption. Every time we tell our stories we are changing the way the world moves. Speculative fiction is such an effective tool in this process. It reveals our perspective on the world and reveals who we are – which is especially important for writers who are not white, male, straight, and cisgender, a group that has been over-represented in published literature.

Speculative fiction also allows us to imagine alternate realities – who we could have been without colonization, how we could have gotten there, for example. This then allows us room to have profound joy. It also gives us a window into potential ways of living and thinking.

Finally, spec fic allows us to take the old stories we have ingested as a society (or societies) and provide intimate and informed points of view outside of the original narrative, which as any scientist or researcher knows, is necessary to uncovering truth. We need new ways of thinking about our roles and responsibilities (which may actually be very old ways) if we are going to survive. Speculative fiction is a way of widening the lens on how we can do this, but only when it is as it should be – nuanced and informed by perspective.

MABIANA CAMARGO: Why did you decide to write in this genre, and what does it allow you as an Indigenous writer? What were the problems you encountered while writing your speculative novels, and what did you most enjoy about writing in this genre?

CHERIE DIMALINE: I stumbled into speculative fiction with a story idea. I had no idea I was going to be entering the genre and kind of went in blind. Of course, once I realized where I was going, I turned to the greats – people like Octavia Butler and Nalo Hopkinson – to learn the ropes. It was so liberating to develop a brand new world, taking as much or as little of the baggage and beauty from the "real world" as necessary.

The one thing that was brand new to me when writing these books was the amount of research that would have to be blended into the process. Other kinds of story, of course, require research, but not at this level. What are the impacts of climate change? How will we live if certain scenarios play out? What actually happens when we dream and when we do not? I needed these pieces to be as factual as possible so that I could build the fantastical and fictional in a way that at least had some base in the truth. After all, I was asking people to suspend their disbelief for hours at a time, I had to at least get them half-way there.

MABIANA CAMARGO: Your 2017 novel *The Marrow Thieves* was published to great acclaim, and not only won the Governor General's Award for fiction for young people but also was a finalist for CBC's Canada Reads competition. Why did you decide to write a sequel to *The Marrow Thieves*? Did your reasons or goals change during the writing process because of the pandemic caused by COVID-19?

CHERIE DIMALINE: The honest answer is I wrote the sequel because readers asked for it. When I wrote the last lines of *The Marrow Thieves*, I had no intention of there being a sequel until it was requested – again and again, at almost every event I went to. At first, this made me feel bad, like I had forgotten something or hadn't given the readers enough of a story for them to carry onward. But then a teacher reminded me that this was an amazing position to have – to be the person telling a story that young people are excited to read. Which is also a very scary place to be since young readers get involved and pay very close attention – you can't get away with a thing.

The second part of why I wrote the sequel is because I realized that I had carried on the story for myself, in my mind. I knew what happened next. I knew where the characters were going to go in their journeys, so why not share that? Especially for Indigenous youth who are always doing such heavy lifting of bringing us back home.

Writing *Hunting by Stars* during the pandemic was actually a bright spot for me. The world I had created on the page was horrible and the world outside my office window was terrifying, but at least in the manuscript, I had some control. I had built characters I knew were strong and resourceful. I had complete faith in them and so moving them towards their own individual growth and successes, even through such a tough landscape and structures, was an act of comfort.

MABIANA CAMARGO: I am curious about the representation of Story in your speculative writing. *The Marrow Thieves* and *Hunting by Stars* use Story (with a capital "S") to retell the past by directing readers back to the Residential School system, and to look to the future by inviting them to learn about Indigenous cultural figures and practices. Both novels have chapters entitled "Coming-to" stories that refer to the life events of different main characters. In *Hunting by Stars*, you write, "Story is a home, it's where we live, it's where we hold everything we'll need to truly survive – our languages, our people, our land" (21). Can you comment on the centrality of Story to your novels? How do you envision individual stories as components of communal ones?

CHERIE DIMALINE: In the books, the characters are responsible for telling their own coming-to stories. This is a direct representation of the idea that no one can tell you who you are, no one can toss you into a category – we identify ourselves using our own words and stories. The characters use the stories to introduce who they are – who they *really* are – at that moment. They can also choose to share who they have been, and how they have arrived to be at that moment.

Story to me is everything: it's where we carry what is important to us and make sure it can be transmitted and walk into the future. Writing about community and from that perspective is such a gift. There is so much celebration that happens when you write your community, or your communities, the people to whom you belong. It is the biggest act of self-love, a reminder of everything you are, an honouring of your family and ancestors, and sometimes an act of planning a way forward. In the *Marrow Thieves* books, Story is the framework of community made portable so that our characters can always carry their hope with them, no matter what.

MABIANA CAMARGO: That's a beautiful way of defining Story. Your speculative novels draw on the importance of community, kinship, and friendship. Your characters are able to fight against oppression only if they have other people as kin and as allies, but also if the link between the generations is maintained and respected. In *The Marrow Thieves*, the protagonist, Frenchie, encounters other Indigenous Peoples who become his family, with Minerva and Miigwans as elder and leader. In *Empire of Wild*, a novel that borders the speculative genre, Joan can only succeed in her mission of finding and saving her husband with the help of the young Zeus and the elder Ajean. Can you talk about the links between different generations and among community members as a whole in these novels? How did these links affect your decision to choose young people as main characters, such as Frenchie and Rose in *The Marrow Thieves* and *Hunting by Stars* and Zeus in *Empire of Wild*?

CHERIE DIMALINE: I was raised in my community – an amazing privilege and also a loud place to be. Loud with voice, music, story, and the physicality of it all. My family still hunts, still harvests, still fishes the Georgian Bay as we have for hundreds of years. Silence is a full sound here. I have always been a small part of a large web that, at all times, includes multiple generations. (At our last family get-together, the oldest was ninety and the youngest was one.) For me, because I am so lucky, any successful gathering is only a success when there are old stories being told and little kids running around. It's this beautiful combination of strong links to our past and quick movements into our future. It's an aesthetic that appears in my stories because it is my own experience.

Having a chosen family is so important to so many communities – kin-making. The larger our families are, the more people there are to hold us when we need it and also the fewer strangers there are to harm us.

Young people in my books are always central because I am continuously impressed with the ways in which they move in the world, how they are the very best of us and everyone who came before them, and still manage to be their own people even carrying so much of the "before." If we, as families and communities, are constellations, then the young people are a kind of North Star.

MABIANA CAMARGO: I am struck by the development of your characters in *Hunting by Stars*. Frenchie has to perform unethical actions to attempt an ethical approach to life and to his community, and Rose, who becomes extraordinarily powerful and resilient, also has to make hard decisions. Why did you give these young characters so much responsibility despite their young age?

CHERIE DIMALINE: Young people are remarkable – truly. They adapt, create, push through, break boundaries, and revive truths every day. I needed the characters to reflect the hard work and incredible genius of the youth I know, which is always evolving. They are also in a terrifying world in the books and I needed to make sure they were resilient enough to survive it. Especially considering they will be a part of how their world moves forward by the end of Book 3....

MABIANA CAMARGO: It's great to hear that there may be a third book in the series! In *The Marrow Thieves*, Frenchie and his friends and family head north to escape the "schools" and their "recruiters," but then in *Hunting by Stars*, the North is not a safe place anymore. Instead, the characters head south because of the promise of a better life in the United States. Is the shift in the representations of North and South deliberately intended to deconstruct the stereotype of American politics in what was then a post-Trump era?

CHERIE DIMALINE: I definitely wanted to play with stereotypes and what it means to "be safe" in the narratives. Having North as the first location of assumed safety and then taking it away was a viewpoint into the relentless development of the North. Giving the United States a more progressive leader and to be the direction the group heads in *Hunting by Stars* was my small attempt to provide a thin balm to our southern neighbours (it was written at the height of the first Trump madness). It was a reminder that change can and must happen.

Of course, any cardinal direction in this story is going to play out only so far since colonialism and capitalism are everywhere and the direction they need to head is inward – the spot between soaring upwards and digging in deeper.

MABIANA CAMARGO: *The Marrow Thieves* and *Hunting by Stars* explicitly use bones and their marrow to symbolize the boundaries that divide individuals into different social and cultural groups, and, at the same time, to reclaim Indigenous beauty that was suppressed in the colonizing process. In *Empire of Wild*, the Rogarou can be eliminated – or reset – only through the power of bones. Can you discuss your choice to use bone and marrow as powerful imagery in your novels?

CHERIE DIMALINE: For me, it all comes back to the day I realized that the land in my community most certainly held the remains of generations of my family. I was quite young when it occurred to me, and became somewhat of an obsession over the years – that intimate belonging through matter, that connection of the landscapes of body and place. It seems like instinct to build bones and belonging into stories, which are largely about the same feeling of home.

Then, years later, when I saw what marrow looks like under a high-powered microscope – like a galaxy of stars – well, that drove it deeper for me, expanding that connection from body to soil to the entire expanse of the universe.

MABIANA CAMARGO: Please give us a glimpse into the proposed television adaptation of *The Marrow Thieves*. And can you also tell us about the adaptation of *Empire of Wild*, in which you are also involved? What is it like writing or being part of adaptations of your work for other media?

CHERIE DIMALINE: COVID-19 put a pause on *The Marrow Thieves* development, but we will be resuming talks soon. *Empire of Wild* is being adapted into an opera by Ian Cusson, a Métis composer from my community in Penetanguishene who has brought so many beautiful Indigenous stories to the stage. Rights to the book have also been optioned for a television series and I am developing those pages with some wonderful producers.

As primarily a novelist, it is so much fun to adapt my work in a new playground where I get to use sound and light, colour and actors to build and expand. Screenwriting is a very different kind of craft that stretches new muscles and uses new language (like stage direction and soundtrack), and I am uncovering more about my stories through it.

MABIANA CAMARGO: You've mentioned a third book in *The Marrow Thieves* trilogy, probably focusing on the characters Miigwans and Isaac. Do you know exactly where you want to go with this novel? Will the book end *The Marrow Thieves* saga? I would appreciate it if you could share your perspectives on this upcoming novel to satisfy our curiosity!

CHERIE DIMALINE: The third book will be the conclusion of our group's main story. Of course, there are a thousand ways they and their world could go after we leave them, but the trilogy will culminate in one possible way forward. I am playing around with different narrators as I quite loved bringing in a femme voice for half of *Hunting by Stars* (through Rose). The spotlight is still up for grabs!

MABIANA CAMARGO: As a final question, do you have any predictions about how speculative fiction in Canada might evolve in the decades to come?

CHERIE DIMALINE: I sincerely hope that speculative fiction will become hopeful – more utopian than dystopian in setting, at least. Good fiction requires drama and conflict, but maybe we can at least have them play out in a better future. We have had so much turmoil over the past few years (okay, when have we not?), and artists are always eager to reshape and build. I am especially excited to read what young writers are going to give us in the coming years, those who lived through the pandemic and came out of it with stories to shape our collective culture.

WORKS CITED

Dimaline, Cherie. *Empire of Wild*. Random House Canada, 2019.

– "From Where We Stand: Nuance and Perspective in Speculative Literature." 20/21 Vision conference, 16 Aug. 2021, U of Saskatchewan, Saskatoon, via videoconference. Keynote address.

– *Hunting by Stars*. Penguin, 2021.

– *The Marrow Thieves*. Dancing Cat Books, 2017.

Crossing Over: Dystopian and Posthuman Futures for Young People

Indigenous Resurgence and Resistance in Cherie Dimaline's *The Marrow Thieves* and *Hunting by Stars*

GWEN ROSE

Cherie Dimaline's *The Marrow Thieves* (2017) and its sequel, *Hunting by Stars* (2021), in addition to being intended for a young-adult audience, are often classified as works of speculative fiction. The novels are, of course, also works of Indigenous fiction, not simply because Dimaline is Métis, but also because the plot of both novels explicitly centres on Indigenous characters navigating a dystopian near-future world otherwise much like our own. Given this setting, the novels can also be classified as dystopian fiction, somewhat more specific than the broader category of speculative fiction. Raffaella Baccolini and Tom Moylan argue that dystopian fiction is often "built around the construction of a narrative of the hegemonic order and a counter-narrative of resistance" (4). In Dimaline's novels, the hegemonic order is settler-colonialism, responsible for the environmental degradation of the world.[1] This degradation is implicated in the loss of dreaming for settler people, and finally, in the continued – and heightened – oppression of Indigenous Peoples. The dreamless settlers notice that members of Indigenous communities have retained their ability to dream, and they become hunted by the settlers for their marrow, which is thought to contain their ability to dream.

Dimaline's imagined world contains a myriad of ties to our own past and present. Her political commentary comes into focus via what is perhaps a rejection of generic categories in favour of foregrounding Indigenous perspectives. Cherokee scholar Daniel Heath Justice highlights the limits of generic labels for Indigenous works of speculative fiction, noting that standard "terms and concepts … don't take seriously or leave legitimate space for other meaningful ways of experiencing this and other worlds – through lived encounter and engagement, through ceremony and ritual, through dream" (152). Justice instead calls works of Indigenous speculative fiction "wonderworks," which emphasize Indigenous "epistemologies, politics, and relationships" (152). Other Indigenous scholars and scholars of Indigenous literatures agree; the editors of *Read, Listen, Tell: Indigenous Stories from Turtle Island* note that "genre is secondary to the transmission of knowledge. As such, a strict application of genre categories is not always relevant to Indigenous writing" (McCall et al. 326). Similarly, Chickasaw scholar Jodi Byrd describes "the limits that non-Native popular genres inflict on the stories that Native literary imaginings seek to tell" (354), while Chippewa scholar Danika Medak-Saltzman suggests that "Indigenous futurist works do not simply 'include' Native people as part of the narrative; rather, they are generated by and inspirational *for* Native peoples" (143). Byrd asserts that Indigenous speculative fiction "challenges readers with transgeneric aesthetics that seek means to heal the ruptures of colonialism at the exact moment colonialism begins to fall apart" (354). In *The Marrow Thieves*, the trappings of speculative or dystopian fiction – the ruined setting, the future world – are secondary to the resurgent Indigenous practices that represent a different form altogether.

Collectively, Indigenous cultural, political, and spiritual forms of resistance and renewal are termed "resurgence" by Nishnaabeg scholar Leanne Betasamosake Simpson in *As We Have Always Done*. Resurgence provides an alternate, and perhaps more appropriate, approach to reading and interpreting *The Marrow Thieves* and *Hunting by Stars* than the divisions and definitions of traditional generic categories. The settler-colonial forces that antagonize the main character, Francis Dusome, often called French or Frenchie, and his family throughout the two novels manifest in a variety of ways, reflecting different facets of settler-colonial life and individualistic philosophy. In contrast to these aspects of the novel, which often feel like the last gasp of an already broken machine, is *resurgence*, which Simpson defines in relation to her own community as "all of the Nishnaabeg practices and ethical processes that make us Nishnaabeg – including story or theory, language learning, ceremony, hunting, fishing, ricing, sugar making, medicine making, politics, and governance.... [It is] *how* we live, *how* we organize, *how* we engage in the world – the process" (19). In Dimaline's fictional world, the resistant and defiant Indigenous characters who refuse to capitulate to settler-colonial pressures do so in large part by leaning on their traditional values, cultures, world views, stories, traditions, and languages, and also by sharing what they can with one another in acknowledgment of the cultural devastation that has already occurred. As Dimaline notes, this sharing is a response to "colonialism and capitalism," which are all around; her characters thus face "inward – the spot between soaring upwards and digging in deeper" ("Interrupting the Fire" 90). The ecological destruction of the novel's world is portrayed as stemming from present-day ecological crises, all by-products of colonial industry, and the hunt for Indigenous people within the novels, who are placed within what are termed "schools," literally echoes the significant and long-term abuse of the Indigenous Peoples of Turtle Island through the Residential School systems in Canada and the United States. This hegemonic order, in keeping with the genre of dystopian fiction, is the backdrop for a narrative of resistance. Rather than portraying resistance as a counter-narrative, however, the thread of resistance running through *The Marrow Thieves* and *Hunting by Stars* is in every way the main narrative. In contrast, the hegemonic forces of settler-colonialism and the dystopian world they have created for Dimaline's protagonist and the novels' other main characters, who are all Indigenous, provide both the setting and the connection to the real world that the novels draw upon.

While the resurgent Indigenous practices within Dimaline's work are constant and consistent between each novel, distinct aspects of settler-colonial life are explored in each of the novels. In *The Marrow Thieves,* technology is a spectre within the shadow of the schools, and the bone marrow extraction process remains shrouded in mystery. Science and industry, implicated in both the destruction of the world and the murder of Indigenous people via marrow extraction, is contrasted with the power of Indigenous cultures to defeat the technological processes that are used in the extractions. *Hunting by Stars* opts to explore the inner workings of the schools in detail, as French is captured into one, and his narrative perspective offers a longer look at the psychological pressures that settler-colonial agents exert on the Indigenous prisoners within. The selfishness of the settler government and its agents, who lack empathy and dehumanize the Indigenous human beings they have power over, is brought into sharp focus. Resurgence is presented as a healthy and vibrant collectivism, in opposition to the inherent self-centredness of settler-colonialism, embodied in the Agents, and even in the way Dimaline addresses the difficult topic of Indigenous people who internalize colonialism and effectively become settlers themselves. Throughout both novels, resurgent Indigenous practices offer an alternative to settler-colonialist greed. These practices within the novels reaffirm Indigenous values and cultures, consequently constituting political statements in the real world that reflect on the current reality for Indigenous Peoples and the importance of continuing to uplift and support Indigenous cultures and diversity. Ultimately, an acknowledgement of Indigenous resurgence is far more important than any generic categorization of Dimaline's work, since it helps her protagonists overcome repeated and varied instances of settler oppression.

Resurgence through Story, Language, and Practice in *The Marrow Thieves*

In *The Marrow Thieves*, the role of settler-colonialism in creating the novel's dystopian setting is established early on. Dimaline essentially imagines what would happen if some of the documented effects of our own world's changing climate caused by industrial activity were left unmitigated, positing that rapid destruction of the natural world as we know it could take place in the very near future.[2] The first-person narrator throughout much of the novel, French, describes "the industry-plundered Great Lakes" (11), which are now "grey and thick like porridge" (24), possibly the result of a catastrophic bursting of an oil pipeline in the Great Lakes. David Schwab notes that in a "worst-case discharge [of Enbridge's Line 5 pipeline] … 1,000 km of Lake Huron-Michigan shoreline and specific islands are potentially vulnerable" (10). In the novel, French's mentor, Miigwans, reports that California has been "swallowed … by the ocean" (24), referring to rising sea levels, "one of the most significant effects of climate change" (Mimura 281). French's remark that the natural world he lives in suffers from a "lack of pollinators" (*Marrow Thieves* 8) reflects the potential effects of pesticide use; researchers have "found fewer wild bees and observed reduced growth rate and reproduction of bumblebee colonies" in treated fields (Raine and Gill 39). Pollution, global warming, and pesticides are by-products of settler-colonial capitalism. Miigwans, the leader of French's created "family" group, explicitly blames the United States of America, a settler nation-state, for exacerbating the situation in the speculative future of *The Marrow Thieves*: "America reached up and started sipping on our lakes with a great metal straw" (24). Pipelines, too – which Ranjan Datta and Margot A. Hurlbert identify as a having an outsized impact on Indigenous communities (1) and which Indigenous Nations have often protested ("Indigenous Pipeline Blockades") – "snapped like icicles and spewed bile over forests, into lakes, drowning whole reserves and towns" (*Marrow Thieves* 87). The ecological destruction of the world of *The Marrow Thieves* and *Hunting by Stars* is, in effect, a direct product of Western industrialization.

The foreboding "Recruiters" who capture Indigenous people before placing them in "schools" are the darkest elements in the novel and are inherently connected to settler-colonialism, from both Dimaline's (and our own) very real past and the imagined, speculative future world of *The Marrow Thieves*. Miigwans describes "the first residential schools: where they were, what happened there, when they closed" (25) to the young people in his group. The RCMP's historic role in seizing Indigenous children from their families in order to forcibly place them in Residential Schools, outlined in 2011 by Marcel-Éugène LeBeuf, is echoed in Miigwans's description of "the new residential schools" (*Marrow Thieves* 89) that the family must contend with, with the RCMP replaced by the militaristic Recruiters. The Recruiters and schools fulfil a horrific purpose: to satiate the desires of settlers who have "stopped dreaming" (26) to regain something they have lost, even at the cost of the lives and well-being of innocent Indigenous people. Miigwans tells his family, "We go to the schools and they leach the dreams from where our ancestors hid them, in the honeycombs of slushy marrow buried in our bones" (90). The process of extracting bone marrow in the real world causes "physical symptoms, including pain, fatigue, and nausea" (Garcia et al. 1046) at the best of times, but in Dimaline's world, those who run the schools take things even further: beyond inflicting pain on unwilling Indigenous donors, in *Hunting by Stars*, French's brother, Mitch, tells him that "the inability to heal without bone marrow" will kill the victims after "a month, maybe two" (74). The Recruiters, schools, and technological extraction process are, after the past ecological destruction that has set the stage for their damaged world and loss of dreaming, the manifestation of settler-colonial forces within the present-time setting of *The Marrow Thieves*. The world of the novel is hell for the Indigenous individuals who populate its pages because the predominant ways in which the futuristic setting differs from our own world are portrayed as extensions into a speculative future of existing settler-colonial selfishness and its effects on Indigenous people in the real world.

Resurgence offers French, Miigwans, and the rest of their family an avenue towards resistance, towards the possibility of a different future than the present they occupy in the novel. In the pan-Indigenous world of *The Marrow Thieves*, where isolated members of different nations band together over shared Indigeneity, the efforts of characters to regain and rebuild Indigenous ways of life reflect the practices of resurgence. Simpson states that for Indigenous Peoples, "it is in relationship to each other that we can enact and renew our political and governing practices" (194). The personal relationships that French and his family have with one another and learn to build with the community they eventually join are pivotal to their resurgent practices.

For the family members, this begins with "Story." Simpson writes that "stories throughout time have always been a renunciation of dominance, tragedy, and victimry.... [There is no] division between 'tribal' and 'new'" (196). This is true for Dimaline's characters: the stories Miigwans tells them are not new, nor old; they simply are. Yet they are important: French says, "We needed to remember Story. It was [Miigwans's] job to set the memory in perpetuity.... [I]t was imperative that we know. He said it was the only way to make the kinds of changes that were necessary to really survive" (25). To "really survive" is for members of the community to regain themselves, who they are, and Miigwans and Simpson are not the only people to speak of the importance of stories in this respect. Pueblo author Leslie Silko writes that "story constructs our identity.... [Through it] we know who we are" (238). For French's family, Story ranges from "a hundred years in one long narrative ... sometimes ... focused on one area, like the first residential schools.... Sometimes we gathered for an hour so [Miigwans] could explain treaties, and others it was ten minutes to list the earthquakes in the sequence that they occurred, peeling the edges off the continents like diseased gums" (*Marrow Thieves* 25). Story, always appearing the novel's text with a capital S, explains who they are, where they have come from, and the situation they face in the moment. It is "imperative that [they] know" Story because storytelling is a resurgent practice that leads to both a renewal and a rebirth of their identities as Indigenous people, separately and together as a group, and to resistance against the forces of settler-colonialism that loom in the background.

Small, commonplace resurgent practices abound in Dimaline's novel as well – what Simpson calls "everyday acts of Resurgence" (195). Minerva, the family's Elder, cups the smoke from Miigwans's tobacco and pulls it over her head, "making prayers out of ashes and smoke" (19). She is smudging, making do with the materials and situation at hand, keeping traditional practices alive despite the circumstances, and Miigwans shares this practice, "taking extra-long hauls [on his smoke] so she could smudge herself" (149). Family member Wab also smudges before sharing what is called her "Coming-to Story" (79), and when the small family group discovers an Indigenous community near Espanola, they are elated to recognize "Tobacco. Cedar ... [and] sweetgrass" by smell alone as they approach (168). These traditional herbs, alongside sage, are used to smudge, and with the stability afforded by a less nomadic life, the community has also established a sweat lodge and a Council (168). The words "sweat lodge" and "Council" are enough to send French's mind racing; it is clear how much he, and the others, value traditional practices in any form.

The community is re-establishing resurgent practices one step at a time, through ceremony, governance, hunting, crops, and more. They are finding themselves again, becoming more than just a group of hunted people on the run, and in the process remembering who they were and where they are from. Clarence, an adult member of the community, says he is from the "middle grounds" "where the bomb landed and the poison's leeched [sic] into the banks" (193); however, this tragic past does not stop him from telling French that "All we need is the safety to return to our homelands.... [W]e can start healing the land. We have the knowledge, kept through the first round of these blasted schools, from before that.... When we heal our land, we are healed also.... We'll get there. Maybe not soon, but eventually" (193). Resurgence is also resilience, resistance, and hope for the future – so powerful in a novel where it may otherwise seem absent, particularly to French's family who have been fleeing the Recruiters for years. A connection to traditional lands and territories that refuses to fade, even in the face of the destruction imposed by settler-colonialism upon that land, demarcates a way forward for the future, a sign that resurgent practices extend from the present as well.

The label of "family" that members of French's group apply to themselves, none related, many from different Indigenous Nations, is also a nod to Indigenous definitions of family and kinship that are very different from settler views. Settler scholar Jo-Anne Fiske has documented the positive effects of Indigenous kinship networks, including "collective labour and mutual support" and "collective responsibility for child care" (344). While many of these networks were composed of those related by blood, this was not universally the case; as in *The Marrow Thieves*, Indigenous communities historically thrived when kinship ties were extended to those without family, who otherwise "suffered greater alienation and hardship" (346). French was nearly dead, without food or the skills necessary to acquire it, when Miigwans and the family group first found him (*Marrow Thieves* 14). What Fiske calls "the pains of autonomy," which "were rendered more problematic by ... the Indian Act" (346), highlighting the historical role of settler-colonialism in disrupting Indigenous ways of living, is also present in the novel, as French narrates how he lost first his father (7), then mother (12), and finally brother (4), all because of settler persecution via the Recruiters, before drifting into the wilderness where Miigwans and his new family find him. Incorporating him into their family is itself an act of resurgence, a traditional Indigenous practice that refutes the individualism that dominates settler world views, but also an opportunity for him to learn more resurgent practices in the future, including the hunting and tracking skills that could enable him to survive similar scenarios.

Resurgence is part of French's character growth and his development as a person in these moments of learning from his Elders, as he goes through the early stages of adolescence. This development ranges from the simple to the complex, even within the space of a single scene. For example, when French has a chance to kill a moose while out hunting, he first patiently waits for the right shot: "always go for the sure target. Miig had taught us that on one of my first hunts, and I listen to my Elders" (49). Then he makes an even more mature decision, but one that is also rooted in the resurgent teachings of his Elders. He asks himself, "could we travel with this meat before it rotted? No. And could we smoke and dry it? No, Miig wouldn't let us set up camp for that long, especially not with a steady thread of smoke reaching above the trees" (49). French has also learned from his Elders to value animal life, and since they "would be leaving half, at least half, behind to rot" (49), he sees killing this moose as wasteful: not worth the animal's sacrifice. He imagines the moose "being here through it all" – that is, the dystopian events of the previous decades, "the wars, the sickness, the earthquakes, the schools – only to come to this?" (49). If the family could use the moose's whole body, "[h]ide and sinew to stitch together for tarps, blankets, ponchos ... bone for pegs and chisels" (49), perhaps it would be worth it. Here, in French's thoughts, traditional, resurgent knowledge is reflected, but also the maturity to make the right choice, one that reflects a growing appreciation for these collective practices.

Indigenous languages, finally, play a pivotal role in the resurgent practices of both groups in the novel, French's family and the larger community by Espanola. In *The Marrow Thieves*, given that many of the characters come from different Indigenous Nations, they have no single language, but choose to uphold the value of all of them, referring to them as "the language" or "language" at times, but also acknowledging the unique and diverse nature of each language and group of attached cultural traditions. Family member Rose tells French that Minerva has been teaching her and the other "homesteaders" (the family's name for those who stay behind at camp during hunting outings) "just a little of the language" (38) – in this case, Anishinaabemowin. Rose's own development as a young Indigenous person includes learning the lessons that Minerva can teach: to keep camp, identify herbs and medicines, and speak Anishinaabemowin. Hearing about "the language" is all French needs to become intensely jealous, although he had previously derided the choice of remaining at camp; he yanks his braid out of his shirt as if to compensate, but nothing can make up for the importance of language. Although Dimaline does not suggest pan-Indigeneity as a solution to reduced Indigenous populations, the Indigenous characters of the novel do recognize that any words or stories, in any Indigenous language, will have value in a world where many of them lack this knowledge. When French and the others join the community near Espanola, French describes how "The Council spent a lot of time piecing together the few words and images each of us carried: hello and goodbye in Cree, a story about a girl named Sedna whose fingers made all the animals of the North" (214). Here, language is connected to stories, and sharing words, stories, and languages is a communal activity that brings members of the group together. They know that their connections are tenuous, that they have only small links to a diverse number of cultures (scattered words in Cree, but an Inuit story, for example), but they focus on sharing what they have: "They wrote what they could, drew pictures, and made the camp recite what was known for sure" (214). All is of incredible importance to them, described by French as "keys" that will help them "give shape" to themselves (214).

Language first reaches the teenagers of the family through Minerva, so it is fitting that it is through her that the undercurrent of resistance that exists in *The Marrow Thieves* boils to a point where explicit action, against the Recruiters, the schools, and settler-colonialism, is taken. Minerva is the family's link to a traditional world and someone whom they haul around on a cart rather than leave behind. Much as Mitch sacrificed himself to the Recruiters to save French, Minerva gives herself up intentionally to cover for her family. After French declares, "I'm going after Minerva" (153), no more will the group run away. Chi-Boy's words speak for them all, and for Minerva's actions, too: "Sometimes you risk everything for a life worth living, even if you're not the one that'll be alive to live it" (152). Here, when he talks about "risk," he is commenting on the jingles Minerva has crafted in secret and carried for miles, even though the group must be silent at all times – they are "worth living" for, because of the cultural importance of jingles, used on the dress for the Jingle dance, a "medicine dance to help heal afflicted people" (Turningrobe). Minerva values the language, culture, and practices of her people above all else; this is what she is always trying to pass on to the group, and the jingles, along with her star blanket, are what she leaves behind knowing she will be captured. Minerva's resurgent practices – her language lessons, her jingles, her knowledge of plants and animals, and more – remind the family of who they are. Consequently, Chi-Boy is also echoing French's words in asserting that some things are worth living – and fighting – for. Their resistance, previously defined largely by their will to pass on their traditions and culture in the form of various resurgent practices, will become an active one.

It is Minerva who strikes the pivotal blow against the novel's settler-colonial forces, reaffirming language's place as perhaps the most important of all resurgent practices, at least in the novel's imagined world. Technology, with its distinctly settler-colonial associations, is defeated by language and song. French and his family learn through a double-agent that Minerva was taken to a school. She is portrayed in the retelling as having been "humming and drumming out an old song on her flannel thighs," her link to the traditional world present as always, her spirit unflappable. Then Minerva "called on her blood memory, her teachings, her ancestors. That's when she brought the whole thing down" (172). Language is linked to her ability to do so; when French relates that, "As it turns out, every dream Minerva had ever dreamed was in the language. It was her gift, her secret, her plan" (172), he implies that, because Minerva speaks Anishinaabemowin as a native speaker, the extractive technology not only had no power to steal her dreams, but the language within them destroyed the settler machines entirely. Just as she has diligently collected the materials for her jingles, Minerva has "collected" dreams, "every day" until the day she destroys the school (172–3). Contrasting with the powerful image of Minerva, resurgent, drumming and singing "words in the language that the conductor couldn't process, words the wires couldn't transfer" (172), the technological apparatus of "the wires … the probes" (173) fails completely. The school, "a fallacy of glass and steel," becomes "nothing more than one storey, maybe two, of jagged edges, melted computer parts, and chewed-up bricks" (173). The images of manufactured goods – glass, steel, bricks, and computer parts – typical of settler-colonial society, on one hand, and Minerva's unadorned singing, on the other hand, is a powerful nod to the potency of the latter's resurgent practices.

Yet Dimaline's evocations of resurgence do not begin and end with Minerva. The Indigenous community's attempt to rescue Minerva from a van, as she is transported after destroying the school, fails when she is killed in a last-ditch effort by the settler driver to prevent her resurgent power from being allowed to carry on and overthrow their system. Miigwans sings her song for her as her voice fails, "to make sure she left with the dreams so she'd have all the magic she needed" for the afterlife (211). Song and language were Minerva's most powerful tools, the key to her resurgent practice, and Miigwans gifts them in turn to her as she dies. Honouring the dead is thus also part of how the Indigenous people of *The Marrow Thieves* retain their humanity. They are devastated at first, feeling that their efforts to resist have now faded: "get the Elder, [get] the key" (202), they had told themselves, believing that they have now lost that key (213). When a new group of travellers appears, among them a fluent Cree speaker, they realize the truth: "The key doesn't have to be old, the language already is" (227). This man, later revealed to be Miigwans's lost husband, Isaac, "dream[s] in Cree." Along with their dreams, the resurgent practices of the community, piecing together the language that they have, painstakingly restoring traditions and ceremonies, have always been the key. They are already doing what they need to do to "really survive."

In *The Marrow Thieves*, Indigenous resurgence enables resistance to the forces of settler-colonialism, whether they manifest as technologically driven ecological destruction, or the settler Recruiters who are willing to hunt down other human beings for their own needs. Yet resurgence also represents far more than just resistance; it is never defined by its opposition to settler perspectives or ways of living, but valued because of what it brings to Indigenous Peoples on its own. It represents renewal, restoration, the way forward that Clarence speaks of. Resurgence is a dream itself, a dream of the future in which the world of the novel can be, has been, healed. Positing resistance while critiquing the past, *The Marrow Thieves* is itself a work of Indigenous resurgence, Dimaline's own nod in the real world to the vitality of Indigenous ways of knowing, speaking, living. As French says at the novel's close, "I understood just what we would do for each other, just what we would do for the ebb and pull of the dream, the bigger dream that held us all. Anything. Everything" (231). French is echoing Chi-Boy and Wab from earlier in the novel (55) and affirming yet again the importance of community and connection, as well as their hope for the future, which remains resurgent despite the many challenges they have faced.

Challenging Internalized Racism through Resurgent Community in *Hunting by Stars*

The core themes of *The Marrow Thieves* – the downfall of the Western world and resulting loss of dreams for settler people, and the opposing idea that Indigenous resurgence posits not just survival for now openly hunted Indigenous people, but also renewal and success – are both reiterated and expanded upon in *Hunting by Stars*, published in 2021. The greed and selfishness of settler-colonialism and the accompanying implication of technology in damaging the natural world is revisited, but the latter quickly recedes into the background as the psychological implications of the post-disaster hunt of Indigenous individuals by settlers becomes a focal point. The sequel picks up immediately following the closing lines of *The Marrow Thieves*, with French kidnapped by Recruiters at night following the relaxed vigilance of the group given their elation at finding Isaac. Placing the protagonist and the main narrator of *The Marrow Thieves* inside a school allows for the aforementioned increase in narrative focus on the psychology of the school's "Agents," who mastermind the plans for marrow extraction, and, later, everyday settler people who demonstrate a similarly selfish loss of compassion for the shared humanity of Indigenous Peoples. Internalized racism also becomes a theme in *Hunting by Stars*, exploring the complex and heartbreaking experience of the choice – foreshadowed and also present to a less in-depth extent in *The Marrow Thieves* – of some Indigenous people to side with the settler-colonial government, schools, and Agents, for their own self-interest. Dimaline's stylistic choice to incorporate multiple narrators in *Hunting by Stars*, however, also allows the novel to retain the core focus of *The Marrow Thieves* – largely through Rose, who is also French's love interest – on the power of Indigenous resurgence via both a sense of community and relationships with the natural world. A more nuanced and complex novel emerges, which still emphasizes "Indigenous resurgence as a set of practices through which the regeneration and reestablishment of Indigenous nations could be achieved" (Simpson 16), in opposition to the dystopian devastation of Dimaline's fictional setting that yet echoes the form of incorporating real-world concerns and all-too-possible catastrophes, as in *The Marrow Thieves*.

French awakens a captive in one of the schools, but his dreams serve to connect his style of narration back to that of *The Marrow Thieves* and reintroduce for Dimaline's readers, after a four-year gap in publication time in the real world, the importance of Story, simultaneously connecting *Hunting by Stars* to the real world. In French's dream, Miigwans, the sharer of Story, reiterates the role of settler-colonial technology in the devastation of the natural environment, again incorporating real-world technology that has already been flagged by experts as potentially environmentally devastating. He tells of the devastation caused by "[e]arthquakes in fracked landscapes" (*Hunting* 22), a possibility corroborated by Xuewei Bao and David W. Eaton, who note that "The rate of earthquakes induced by fluid injection from oil and gas operations in parts of North America has surged in recent years" (1406). Miigwans's description of "[t]sunamis across poisoned waters" (*Hunting* 22) seems to reference the 2011 Fukushima nuclear disaster, which "brought long-lasting damage to Japan" (Behling et al. 411). Dimaline even addresses our world's most recent events, including the COVID-19 pandemic that was not – and could not have been – referenced in *The Marrow*

Thieves, but which is evoked in this novel's more detailed descriptions of the epidemic of dreamlessness. Miigwans relates that "sicknesses were released. A virus, a pandemic of plague, a cure, and then another would step up to replace it" (22). His words link *these* pandemics to the mysterious disappearance of dreaming that is the final affliction for Dimaline's fictional world, and to its persecution of Indigenous people who can still dream.

If resurgence comes, as Simpson writes, "from within Indigenous thought systems, intelligence systems that are continually generated in relationship to place" (16), then relationship to place can allow French to overcome his physical dislocation in the school, an artificial, unnatural surrounding that evokes settler-colonialism. The fact that he retains the power to dream allows him to connect with Miigwans and his "family," despite their physical separation, and even to connect with his mother, whom he knows to be dead. Dreams are a link to resurgence for French when nothing else can be, and also allow Dimaline as an author to highlight the dichotomy between the holistic, compassionate, and connected web of Indigenous beliefs and practices that make up resurgence and the unfeeling nature of the schools French now finds himself in. Without dreams, his mother tells him, "we're just machines, … [a]nd you can't reason with machines" (10), which echoes Miigwans in *The Marrow Thieves* when he says that "a man without dreams is just a meaty machine with a broken gauge" (88). Dimaline's repetition of the metaphor of settler people – the architects of modern technology – literally becoming machine-like in their dreamless state is a pivotal part of the expanded treatment in *Hunting by Stars* of the struggle between Indigenous world views and settler-colonial hegemony. Though the entire family will have to face off against a group of unempathetic settlers in the novel's climax, it is French who must reckon most with the robotic, unfeeling, and unreasoning attitude of settlers in this sequel. Worse yet, he first encounters this attitude in someone who was once close to him, who should understand Indigenous resurgence and not be espousing the settler philosophy of self-preservation: his older brother, Mitch.

Mitch was last seen in the early pages of *The Marrow Thieves*, surrendering himself to the Recruiters so that French could escape. Now, in the school, French encounters a Mitch who long since surrendered himself again, seemingly more voluntarily, to the nebulous "Program" meant to indoctrinate Indigenous residents of the schools. While it might mean their survival, it also means turning on each other, becoming pawns of the white operatives within the schools and being pressured to police one another. French quickly realizes that Mitch is "not being Mitch" (86) at all – that is, his attitudes have changed so drastically as to make him unrecognizable. Now a lower-rung operative of the schools, Mitch himself can no longer see French's "tells" (86), the subtle signs of his emotions written on his face. French reflects that his adopted family knows him better than his own brother, not because of the time they have spent apart, but because Mitch has aspired to become one of the Agents. He suffers from, to use a phrase defined by Mi'kmaw scholar Cyndy Baskin, "internalized colonialism" (2083). Baskin utilizes the phrase in relation to contemporary issues facing Indigenous women stemming from colonial behaviours and hierarchies that have infiltrated some Indigenous communities (2083–4). Mitch's situation is more in line with a broader term, "internalized racism," which Stuart Hall defines as "the 'subjection' of the victims of racism to the mystifications of the very racist ideologies which imprison and define them" (27). Mitch and other Indigenous people within the school who have capitulated to "the Program" internalize and then repeat on their own the dialogue of white operatives.

Talking to French, Mitch reduces Indigenous lives to "part of the solution," including what he blithely refers to as "supply[ing] medicine to the population," which French knows full well is a reference to the horrific process of extracting marrow (73). He describes the opportunity for Indigenous people, trapped in the schools, "to join in the meaningful work once they've proven themselves," further stating, "we all work together like a well-oiled machine" (72). He evokes the dehumanizing language of Western industrialism and science – cogs in a wheel, gears in the machine – and calmly corrects French about the details of the extraction process: "it's not the extraction that kills a patient. It's the inability to heal without bone marrow. Basic science" (74). Having internalized this logic, having accepted the supremacy of "basic science" over any emotional response to the murder of Indigenous individuals, he apologizes to French for leaving him behind when the Recruiters came for them: "If I could take it all back and make sure you went with me, I would" (84). French is appalled, telling Mitch, "You saved me!" (84), but this new version of Mitch has fully bought into the narrative the Agents and the Program have drilled into him. Mitch's description of the schools as "for the well-being of all the people" (84) is telling; the racially specific sacrifice that he supports parrots the language of utilitarianism in highlighting only the "greater good" (Kahane et al. 194). Yet researchers such as Guy Kahane and his team have demonstrated that this philosophy is most often deployed as a logical device in scenarios where some "sacrifice" is concerned, and particularly when participants must rationalize the sacrifice of someone or some ones other than themselves; while people are often ready to formulate "a 'utilitarian' bias in the context of sacrificial dilemmas[, this] may not carry over to other contexts, casting doubt on the assumption that it is driven by a general concern with maximizing the good" (194). Even in Western academic circles, then, utilitarianism has been exposed as a philosophy employed by those who lack empathy, employing it only when it is convenient for them.

Mitch's willingness to buy into this philosophy as a former prisoner, to betray his own people and his own family, is weaponized against French, as – despite French's horror at who and what Mitch has become – Mitch offers him, through the Program, what he knows is his only chance to escape the school himself. Dimaline offers a strong contrast between Mitch's internalized racism, the idea that the lives of his own people are an acceptable sacrifice, and French's continued Indigenous resurgence: his internal acknowledgement of the importance of language, culture, and the natural world outside the school's whitewashed walls. Yet French must at least pretend to acquiesce to the strictures of the Program, must fool both Mitch and Mitch's white superiors. In this fashion, Dimaline introduces, in a painful twist, additional trauma into French's life, a psychological exploration of the depths settler-colonial people have sunk to, and a commentary on the manipulation of Indigenous people into betraying each other, which is to a lesser extent manifested in the real world of the internalized colonialism Baskin explores.

Hunting by Stars works within a multiple-narrative form in order to reinforce the alternative resurgence offers to the schools, most often through Rose as she travels cross-country with Derrick, the man whom French considered his romantic rival in *The Marrow Thieves*, in an attempt to find and then free French. They, too, are waylaid – Derrick is injured in a bear trap – but Rose refuses to leave him behind. This too is resurgent behaviour within the context of an unforgiving world. Defined in so many different and yet related and equally compelling ways by Simpson, resurgence is "a flight out of the structure of settler colonialism and into the processes and relationships of freedom and self-determination" (17). Rose cares for Derrick even after this horrifying and debilitating injury: despite her strong desire to find French as soon as possible, "She had nothing but concern: no pity, no annoyance, no urge to cut him loose and leave him" (103). Settler people may leave one another behind, but Rose makes the choice to do otherwise of her own free will and self-determination. The solidarity she displays, and which she and French's family group have always displayed, including their attempt to rescue Minerva in *The Marrow Thieves*, is in contrast to the isolating and sabotaging behaviours forced onto French in the Program.

To survive the schools, even to get a chance at escape, French must forego contact with the other Indigenous people in the school, as well as suffer the Program's attempts to deprive him of his own humanity. Unlike Rose, French *must* betray his family and other Indigenous individuals, in ways small and large, if he is ever to escape. He meets Agent Mellin, the white Agent who is Mitch's superior and who, like all the employees of the school, treats Indigenous people – including even Mitch, who does not notice – as subhuman. They are referred to as "occupants," "residents," or, when cooperative, "helpers" – but never as people, language that comes from Mitch but which he has clearly internalized from his now-superiors (139). When French refuses to disclose details about his family, Agent Mellin orders him taken to "the Correction Room," a room of mirrors, lights, and sirens (111). When he has disclosed enough information to gain her trust, he is given a job policing other inmates. He had briefly travelled through a common area before, an open area remarkably like the central room of a correctional unit – as of course, the schools really are. But now, as a member of the Program, French realizes that he "can't hang out in the common room with everyone else" (140). He calls these other Indigenous people "inmates," a fairly accurate description for them in their current situation, but Mitch insists on labelling them "residents" and does not understand French's desire to spend time with them: "why would you want to? Those people have no hope of moving into the system.... We ... are the now, the future.... We're going to make sure future generations will be safe and well and whole" (140).[3] Despite joining this "system" for a chance to escape, French hears what Mitch is really saying, asking, "Whose future generations?" (140). Mitch ignores the question, refusing to acknowledge the implication that it is settler-colonial children, specifically, who will be safe – saved by the sacrifice of Indigenous children. French must cease his questioning, however, and play along. Despite the fact that he realizes as soon as he begins the role of "helper" that he "was not one of them anymore" (142), displaying solidarity with "those people," that is, the other Indigenous people in the common room, those who continue to actively resist, will only extend his stay in the school.

Like Rose, French values Indigenous world views and resurgent practices, including community and solidarity. He finds these where he can, as Dimaline uses French's position in the school and the moral quandaries to which he is subjected to highlight how even prisoners take risks in order to offer solace to each other, even in the darkest of days. French is able to grasp at some small gestures of resurgent solidarity: he is tasked with delivering meals to the inmates whose marrow is about to be extracted, this world's exclusively Indigenous version of Death Row, but without any crimes committed or any trial, fair or otherwise. He speaks to these people in whispers, defying orders, as Dimaline evokes the language of resurgent practices: "Saying [their] names felt like medicine, felt healing and precious.... Saying them felt like resistance" (165). Then they pass him written messages, small offers of humanity or communication to the outside world from people who know they are doomed. The writers surely know that French can do nothing with them, but the messages offer hope, increase their sense of humanity. French does everything he can for these people, as Dimaline incorporates resistance to settler-colonialism even in this difficult experience for French and difficult part of the narrative. These "individual everyday acts of resurgence" (Simpson 194) are small and yet significant connections between Indigenous people, and these acts allow them to share one another's humanity in dire circumstances.

As French remains committed to resurgence despite the moral challenge he is facing, Rose is presented with a similar situation as Dimaline highlights the harsh reality of internalized colonialism: that it can take place anywhere, even without prompting. Rose and Derrick find a house in the woods, and upon learning that two Indigenous people dwell there, believe they might find solidarity and community, such as they have found elsewhere amongst Indigenous individuals who have gathered together to ward off settler-colonial hunters. While they build such a bond with the younger of the two, Nam, Nam's uncle, known only as "the Chief," seems to have internalized colonial power structures. The Chief keeps a harem of white women, promising a cure to their dreamlessness borne out of his Indigeneity. Nam reveals to Rose and Derrick, however, that the Chief himself no longer dreams (184). They can only form theories about why, but Nam thinks that he has been deprived of dreams in a fashion befitting a would-be-settler because, before the dream-sickness, the Chief "was just plain old corrupt Chief Henry Williams, a stereotype. He had the biggest house on the rez and two brand-new boats. He was in tight with the oil dudes, living a good life with the consultation money meant for the band" (184). The Chief tells his group of women fake dreams, stories from "Maria Campbell and Waub Rice ... and some are just [Nam's] dreams" (184). Rose, Derrick, and Nam – who will join them when they leave – must grapple with escaping from an Indigenous man who upholds none of the resurgent practices they have learned; for example, the Chief scorns Rose's advice that his group must tend their garden more carefully. Rose has traditional advice, the "specific teachings" of the Creator – that "[t]he three sisters," corn, beans, and squash, should be planted close together (158), for example – but the Chief ignores this suggestion as he has ignored tradition. Dimaline is making a pointed example of the Chief; just as Nam has pointed out that the "corrupt chief" is a stereotype in our world, Indigenous authors have been at pains to challenge what âpihtawikosisân (Chelsea Vowel) calls the "perception out there among many Canadians, that First Nations bands are based on traditional Indigenous governance systems." As she emphasizes in her blog, the majority of band-council structures are organized around colonial governing practices: they "do not reflect traditional governance systems at all." Not all such chiefs are corrupt, but – as with many settler-colonial elected officials – such instances do occur, frequently enough to have become what both Dimaline and âpihtawikosisân refer to as a stereotype.

In *Hunting by Stars*, Dimaline implies that such individuals, more connected to settler-colonial ways of life than to resurgent practices, will struggle when settler-colonial people suffer. The Chief is no longer connected to the natural world, as are Rose, French, and the majority of Dimaline's Indigenous characters; correspondingly, he, too, has lost the ability to dream. The encounter is harrowing for Rose and Derrick, as the Chief begins to drain Derrick's blood for his group's consumption. While he can tell them that he is "not some colonial monster" because he is "not stealing marrow" but "simply borrowing blood" (163), he has internalized settler-colonial attitudes. Almost equally monstrous as stealing marrow is his plan to keep Derrick a prisoner and an unwilling, continual blood donor. Rose and Derrick escape, and they and their family gain a new member, Nam. Just as French manages to care for others and build and maintain human connections in the dire circumstances of the school, so too do Rose and Derrick even as they must also look to self-preservation long enough to escape the Chief's distorted home.

French faces a similar quandary with Mitch, and to his credit he tries to save his brother, to reinvigorate in Mitch an appreciation for resurgent practices and who he was before he was indoctrinated by the Program. His desperation to save Mitch stems not only from their tie as siblings, but from the way he sees Agent Mellin mock Mitch, "thinking my brother was an idiot," and Mitch respond as a "kiss-ass" (222). The power structure is uneven, and always will be. The Agents will never fully trust or empower Mitch; his only real chance at a future is to regain an Indigenous identity and world view. The alternative is the despair French experiences when the Agents force him to betray and capture Indigenous strangers as a "test." He feels "a weight I wasn't sure anyone could bear," and connects it to who they want him to be, how they want him to behave, and who they are and how they act: "How did people move underneath it? Maybe the Recruiters' steps were so clunky out in the woods because they couldn't bend their knees under the buckle. Maybe the schools' structures were so bland because why bother with design when the people no longer look up?" (223). French comes perilously close to the edge, but he follows through with the test, in order to have the opportunity to rejoin his family, ostensibly as a spy and traitor. The final problem for French is not that Mitch is sent with him on this second mission; it is that Mitch, like the Chief, is irredeemably steeped in settler-colonial ideology.

French and Mitch join his family, and he has one final opportunity to convince Mitch, but his brother rejects him. When he tells Mitch that Rose is in danger, having gone to the school to find French, Mitch responds, "So she's going to the school. Isn't that just perfect?" (265). Mitch no longer fits in outside the school, "snapping branches and sliding around in the mud-soaked peat like a real amateur" (257), "in such a hurry to collect that he was missing the beauty" (258). French does what Nam, unbeknown to Rose or Derrick, has done earlier: he kills a blood relative who has fallen victim to internalized colonialism, in order to save adopted family members who represent resurgent hope, community, and love. In tasking French with this impossible burden, Dimaline highlights the intense difficulties of her imagined world. However, shared humanity shines through in the end, through Miigwans's understanding of what French has done with Mitch and what he would have had to do in order for the Agents to trust him. Miigwans knows, and forgives, telling French, "you only did what you had to do to get to us, to keep us safe" (379). They discuss French keeping and memorizing the notes given to him by the inmates; his role and "responsibility" is as a carrier of their messages and his debt is to those he "brought in" (381). Ultimately, *Hunting by Stars* ends with solidarity and with acceptance of the fact that it is the settler people who have burdened French with this weight, having created for him an impossible moral choice. Resurgence, again embodied in community and love, endures in Miigwans. French knows that "even now, now that he knew everything, all of it, he was still there" (381).

Conclusion

The two novels, published four years apart and with the sequel not initially planned by Dimaline, might be expected to show some disparity, despite the events of their respective plots being separated by only a day. This disparity exists largely in the more mature issues that *Hunting by Stars* addresses, but the second novel builds on the framework that Dimaline has already established in *The Marrow Thieves*. Settler-colonialism – represented through non-Indigenous characters' use of technology in the novels, their philosophical outlook, and their rampant abuse of power – remains the antagonizing force throughout, but it does not dominate the novels. Indigenous resurgent practices and the growth of the novels' Indigenous characters are more important. In *The Marrow Thieves*, language, storytelling, and the land take precedence, while in *Hunting by Stars*, community and solidarity take centre stage, in keeping with this novel's increased focus on the psychological impacts of settler-colonialism. Resurgence runs through the texts like a thread of renewal, rebirth, and resistance. Dimaline's novels reflect the real-world implications of settler-colonialism in her and her readers' time. The history of Indigenous Peoples on Turtle Island, such as that of Residential Schools, is mixed with their present experiences of environmental degradation and their voices going unheard, while the novel suggests a speculative future that seems only too possible. The novels themselves constitute works of resurgence, arguing for decentralizing colonial practices and philosophies and respect for Indigenous ways of knowing and living. In connecting Dimaline's work to Simpson's, I argue that this resurgent resistance is already taking place, in the form of these literary works, and in many other aspects of our real-world life. As a settler myself, I can only hope that we listen. If not now, these novels ask, then when?

NOTES

1 The impact of hegemonic capitalism on Indigenous Peoples and/or the world at large is also a theme of Waubgeshig Rice's *Moon of the Crusted Snow*, as explored in Gage Karahkwí:io Diabo's "Horrors of Northern Development: (Anti-)Capitalist Infrastructure and Anishinaabe Knowledge in *Moon of the Crusted Snow*," and of the film *Blood Quantum*, explored in June Scudeler's "What If the Natives Were Immune? Dismembering Colonial Masculinity in Jeff Barnaby's *Blood Quantum*." Both essays are in this volume.

2 As Dimaline herself notes, this imagining was very much by design: "The one thing that was brand new to me when writing these books was the amount of research that would have to be blended into the process.… What are the impacts of climate change? How will we live if certain scenarios play out? What actually happens when we dream and when we do not? I needed these pieces to be as factual as possible so that I could build the

fantastical and fictional in a way that at least had some base in the truth" ("Interrupting the Fire" 87).

3 As mentioned earlier, this utilitarian perspective is a science-fiction trope, but also a goal of settler-colonial governance concerning the Indigenous Peoples of Turtle Island: they can assimilate into mainstream society or be discarded, and the "future generations" their oppressors care about are only those that look, talk, and act like them. Canada's Residential School System began in 1883 under the leadership of Prime Minister John A. Macdonald with the intent of "assimilate[ing] Canada's indigenous people into European culture" – at the expense of their own cultures (Kennedy).

WORKS CITED

âpihtawikosisân (Chelsea Vowel). "The Myth of the Corrupt Chief and Band Council (Part I)." *Stories. Language. Futurisms*, 15 Feb. 2016, https://apihtawikosisan.com/2016/02/the-myth-of-the-corrupt-chief-and-band-council-part-i/.

Baccolini, Raffaella, and Tom Moylan. "Introduction: Dystopia and Histories." *Dark Horizons: Science Fiction and the Dystopian Imagination*, edited by Baccolini and Moylan, 2013, pp. 1–12.

Bao, Xuewei, and David W. Eaton. "Fault Activation by Hydraulic Fracturing in Western Canada." *Science*, vol. 354, no. 6318, 2016, pp. 1406–9.

Baskin, Cyndy. "Contemporary Indigenous Women's Roles: Traditional Teachings or Internalized Colonialism?" *Violence against Women*, vol. 26, no. 15–16, 2020, pp. 2083-101, https://doi.org/10.1177/1077801219888024.

Behling, Noriko, et al. "Aftermath of Fukushima: Avoiding Another Major Nuclear Disaster." *Energy Policy*, vol. 126, 2019, pp. 411–20, https://doi.org/10.1016/j.enpol.2018.11.038.

Byrd, Jodi. "Red Dead Conventions: American Indian Transgeneric Fictions." *The Oxford Handbook of Indigenous American Literatures*, edited by James H. Cox and Daniel Heath Justice, Oxford UP, 2014, pp. 344–58.

Datta, Ranjan, and Margot A. Hurlbert. "Pipeline Spills and Indigenous Energy Justice." *Sustainability*, vol. 12, no. 1, 2020, pp. 1–9, https://doi.org/10.3390/su12010047.

Dimaline, Cherie. *Hunting by Stars*. Penguin, 2021.

– "Interrupting the Fire with Story: An Interview with Cherie Dimaline." Interview by Mabiana Camargo. *ReVisions: Speculating in Literature and Film in Canada*, edited by Wendy Roy, U of Toronto P, 2025, pp. 85–91.

– *The Marrow Thieves*. Dancing Cat Books, 2017.

Fiske, Jo-Anne G. "Political Status of Native Indian Women." *In the Days of Our Grandmothers: A Reader in Aboriginal Women's History in Canada*, edited by Mary-Ellen Kelm and Lorna Townsend, U of Toronto P, 2006, pp. 336–66.

Garcia, Maria, et al. "Motivations, Experiences, and Perspectives of Bone Marrow and Peripheral Blood Stem Cell Donors: Thematic Synthesis of Qualitative Studies." *Biology of Blood and Marrow Transplantation*, vol. 19, no. 7, 2013, pp. 1046–58, https://doi.org/10.1016/j.bbmt.2013.04.012.

Hall, Stuart. "Gramsci's Relevance for the Study of Race and Ethnicity." *The Journal of Communication Inquiry*, vol. 10, no. 2, 1986, pp. 5–27.

"Indigenous Pipeline Blockades Spark Canada-wide Protests." *BBC*, 11 Feb. 2020, https://www.bbc.com/news/world-us-canada-51452217.

Justice, Daniel Heath. *Why Indigenous Literatures Matter*. Wilfrid Laurier UP, 2018.

Kahane, Guy, et al. "Utilitarian' Judgments in Sacrificial Moral Dilemmas Do Not Reflect Impartial Concern for the Greater Good." *Cognition*, vol. 134, 2015, pp. 193–209, https://doi.org/10.1016/j.cognition.2014.10.005.

Kennedy, Mark. "'Simply a Savage': How the Residential Schools Came to Be." *Ottawa Citizen*, 22 May 2015, https://ottawacitizen.com/news/politics/simply-a-savage-how-the-residential-schools-came-to-be.

LeBeuf, Marcel-Eugène. "The Role of the Royal Canadian Mounted Police during the Indian Residential School System." *The Royal Canadian Mounted Police*, 2011, http://resolve.library.ubc.ca/cgi-bin/catsearch?bid=5796564.

McCall, Sophie, et al., editors. *Read, Listen, Tell: Indigenous Stories from Turtle Island*. Wilfrid Laurier UP, 2017.

Medak-Saltzman, Danika. "Coming to You from the Indigenous Future: Native Women, Speculative Film Shorts, and the Art of the Possible." *Studies in American Indian Literatures*, vol. 29, no. 1 2017, pp. 139–71.

Mimura, Nobuo. "Sea-level Rise Caused by Climate Change and Its Implications for Society." *Proceedings of the Japan Academy: Series B, Physical and Biological Sciences*, vol. 89, no. 7, 2013, pp. 281–301. https://doi.org/10.2183/pjab.89.281.

Raine, Nigel, and Richard Gill. "Tasteless Pesticides Affect Bees in the Field." *Nature*, vol. 521, 2015, pp. 38–40, https://doi.org/10.1038/nature14391.

Schwab, David J. "Statistical Analysis of Straits of Mackinac Line 5: Worst Case Spill Scenarios." University of Michigan, Ann Arbor, March 2016.

Silko, Leslie. "Language and Literature from a Pueblo Indian Perspective." McCall et al., pp. 236–43.

Simpson, Leanne Betasamosake. *As We Have Always Done: Indigenous Freedom through Radical Resistance*. U of Minnesota P, 2017.

Turningrobe, Sophia. "The Healing Dance: Native American Jingle Dress." *Sister Sky*, 14 July 2020, https://sistersky.com/blogs/sister-sky/the-healing-dance-native-american-jingle-dress.

Posthuman Girlhoods in Canadian Young Adult Science Fiction

ALENA CICHOLEWSKI

Apocalyptic and dystopian visions of the future continue to be popular with readers of young adult fiction. In Canada, adolescent literature duologies such as Erin Bow's *Prisoners of Peace* (2015, 2016) and G.S. Prendergast's *Nahx Invasion* (2017, 2019) position their teenage protagonists in post-apocalyptic and distinctly Canadian settings.[1] Whereas Bow's Greta is held hostage by an artificial intelligence in Saskatchewan, Prendergast's Raven tries to survive a (supposed) alien invasion in rural Alberta. During their adventures, both Greta and Raven must transform their bodies to cope with the demands that an increasingly hostile environment makes of them: Greta becomes an artificial intelligence and Raven is turned into a human/alien hybrid.

The posthuman transformations of both protagonists, in Victoria Flanagan's words, can be read as "problematis[ing] the act of feminine subject formation, questioning what it means to be female (and, indeed, even human) in worlds that have undergone major social transformations" (105). Such representations of posthuman female bodies/minds can subvert established notions of girlhood, but the texts in question can also simply adhere to the standard of "dystopian YA [that] often favors traditional girlhood" (Green-Barteet and Coste 83). The Canadian setting is important in each primary text, as the protagonist's confrontation with hostile environments influences her embodiment. In both cases, this happens mostly through depictions of natural landscapes as potentially dangerous, be it the prairies of Saskatchewan in Bow's novels, with the climate crisis in full swing, or the winterly forests of rural Alberta in Prendergast's books. A particular focus is on the implications of the futures envisioned by both series. While the novels imagine a diverse future Canadian society, including the presence of people of colour and from LGBTQ2S+ communities, in both duologies the female protagonists must dramatically change their bodies to be able to protect their loved ones, turning them into self-sacrificing and distinctly female saviour figures. I argue that despite the novels' attempts to question and/or destabilize conventional notions of girlhood and the gendered stereotypes that go along with them, the empowering potential of the posthuman Canadian girlhoods envisioned by both Bow and Prendergast ultimately remains constricted by heteropatriarchal social structures.

Contexts: Female Embodiment in Dystopian Settings

Dystopian and apocalyptic fiction for young adults reached its prime between 2008 and 2012, with Suzanne Collins's *Hunger Games* series as its most prominent representative (Trites 115).[2] Canadian writers continue to participate in this global trend: Catherine Knutsson's *Shadows Cast by Stars* (2012), Maureen McGowan's *Dust Chronicles* trilogy (2012–14), and Cherie Dimaline's *The Marrow Thieves* novels (2017–21) are all well-known examples of dystopian young adult novels by Canadian authors.[3] Often, these books or series focus on a female protagonist and feature a Canadian/Canada-inspired setting.

My focus is on how the respective female teenage protagonists of Bow's *Prisoners of Peace* and Prendergast's *Nahx Invasion* duologies undergo a process of posthuman transformation that optimizes the capabilities of their bodies/minds. My analysis is informed by the works of Donna Haraway, N. Katherine Hayles, and Elizabeth Grosz, as well as by the novels' reception in young adult fiction criticism. Haraway's seminal *Cyborg Manifesto* conceptualizes the cyborg as a binary-disrupting, liminal, and empowering way of (self-)positioning (Haraway 154), and provides a theoretical background against which to read the respective protagonists' development towards increasingly hybridized identities. Building on and expanding Haraway's line of thinking, Hayles draws attention to the "intensely ambiguous" implications of becoming a cyborg that, on the one hand, "contribute to liberatory projects," but on the other hand, run the danger of increasing social injustice by setting up hierarchies between those who can afford to use cybernetic technologies to their advantage and those who cannot (174–5). As the respective protagonists' changing physicality is an important part of their subject formation in both book series, Grosz's work, which explains how philosophical ideas such as the Cartesian mind/body dualism have been used to marginalize women on account of their physicality, is particularly relevant for this chapter (3–4). What unites Haraway, Hayles, and Grosz's ideas is their emphasis on questioning dichotomous patterns of thought to subvert patriarchal social structures.

Roberta Seelinger Trites and Victoria Flanagan have shown how work by Grosz, Haraway, and Hayles can be productive in the analysis of young adult fiction. Trites's book uses concepts of posthumanism in addition to material feminism (as defined by Alaimo and Hekman) to examine "twenty-first century feminism in adolescent literature" (Trites 115), and Flanagan's *Technology and Identity in Young Adult Fiction* connects posthumanism to representations of technology. In her eco-feminist analysis of representations of female embodiment in American young adult dystopias, Trites observes that they "frequently investigate what it means to inhabit a human body; dystopias and other speculative fictions often track how turmoil in the body politic effects subsequent turmoil of the human body itself" (115). In a similar vein, Flanagan argues that "posthuman YA fiction … centres on the processes of identity formation as experienced by female subjects, and how technology can affect such processes" (106). Both Trites and Flanagan recognize the importance of embodiment for practices of posthuman becoming, especially in novels with female protagonists.

Trites warns against considering twenty-first-century YA dystopias as feminist by default, simply by virtue of their employment of the *strong female protagonist* trope. She outlines how those novels often fail in implementing their ostensible feminist agendas by "objectify[ing] the female body so badly that even the female protagonists objectify their own bodies, participating as objects of exchange in male homosocial love triangles" (148). In contrast to Trites, Flanagan is more optimistic about "posthuman YA fiction" and its potential to "pose complex questions about the relationship between mind, body, selfhood and identity" (106). My analysis of Bow's Greta and Prendergast's Raven explores how far their posthuman becoming subverts common stereotypes of girlhood while being mindful of inherent contradictions that concern, on the one hand, the empowering qualities of the protagonist's transformations and, on the other hand, the prominent role of male characters in the protagonists' personal growth. These issues potentially undermine the feminist connotations of both novels, in line with Trites's insight that "female friendships in YA dystopias are subordinated to heterosexual attractions" (121), although that is less true for the bisexual protagonist of Bow's first book in the duology, *The Scorpion Rules*.

As noted above, also relevant for my analysis of Bow's and Prendergast's novels is their representation of the Canadian environment. In contrast to American dystopian young adult fiction that tends to represent what Megan McDonough and Katherine A. Wagner identify as "nature as refuge" for the female protagonist (158), and which often "suggest[s] that a female protagonist's awakening is catalysed by her experiences within nature and that these experiences shape nature into a place ideal for claiming her agency" (157), the two Canadian duologies at hand formulate a hostile role of nature for the plot. Instead of functioning as an idealized alternative to the "unchanging daily grind of … urban environments," as American YA typically represents nature (McDonough and Wagner 159), Bow's windswept and drought-ridden Saskatchewan prairies and Prendergast's freezing cold Alberta forests are more in line with representations of wildlife and landscapes that have long permeated Canadian children's and adolescent literature (cf. Alter 163), and indeed many examples of literature for adults in Canada in which nature is endowed with "sinister and terrible elements" (Frye 357) or "seen as dead, or alive and indifferent, or alive and actively hostile towards men" (Atwood 65–6). In the book series by Bow and Prendergast, the threatening natural environments become another obstacle for the protagonists to overcome on their paths towards personal growth and serve to remind them of the physical limitations that persist despite their posthuman transformation. In these ways, novels by both authors avoid the problem of reducing the body to "a politicized object, rather than [it] being regarded as a material reality that interplays through discourse with environmental factors to support and enhance a self-defined identity" (Trites 122). My close readings in this chapter will focus particularly on passages that concern the interplay between the protagonists' bodies and social and environmental factors.

Becoming an Artificial Intelligence in Bow's *Prisoners of Peace* Duology

In her *Prisoners of Peace* duology, American-born Canadian author Erin Bow takes her readers 400 years into the future. An artificial intelligence called Talis has gained world domination, ostensibly to save humanity from fighting wars over increasingly scarce resources and to prevent further environmental degradation.[4] To blackmail national leaders into keeping the peace, Talis has installed a hostage system that forces each head of state to send a close family member, either their offspring or a grandchild, to a so-called Precepture school. There, in an implicit reference to the Residential School system in Canada, the children are educated exclusively in English by robots of various quality and perform compulsory manual labour, mostly fruit and vegetable cultivation and livestock farming. Hostages at the Preceptures who rebel against the system are punished; depending on the gravity of their misconduct, the robotic Precepture leaders might reduce access to food, water, and air conditioning/heating for the whole cohort of the offender and/or subject the rebellious prisoner to physical abuse.[5] Similarly, if a head of state refuses to send a close relative to the Precepture, Talis uses his orbital weapons to destroy whole cities of the nation in question. If a nation declares war on another, the hostages of both nations are killed.

The Scorpion Rules (2015), the first book of the series, is set in a Precepture in rural Saskatchewan. The plot follows sixteen-year-old Greta Gustafson Stuart, "Duchess of Halifax and Crown Princess of the Pan Polar Confederacy" (8), who serves as an extradiegetic, homodiegetic narrator for most of the novel. When readers encounter her for the first time at the beginning of the book, Greta appears to be a dutiful and obedient hostage and takes her responsibilities as heir to the throne of the Pan Polar Confederacy seriously: "I was born to a crown. I was born to a fate defined by my bloodline and by the forces of history. I was born to a duty that I did not choose, and cannot set aside" (31). Greta has accepted her (presumed) duty to behave well at the Precepture School and to aspire to a dynastic marriage with offspring to continue her family line after she is released on her eighteenth birthday. She seeks solace in stoic philosophy to cope with the constant threat of being killed in retribution for her nation's and her mother's warmongering. Not only does Greta's attitude conform to traditional ideals of femininity, but so does her external appearance, most strikingly her long red hair: "In Halifax, I had two maids to fuss over my hair, and they amused themselves (if not me) by doing elaborate things with it. Here I merely put it in two thick braids, which I coil around my head, out of the way" (57). Although Greta consents to adapt her outward appearance to conventional ideals of beauty, as this passage suggests, she is not entirely comfortable playing the role of the exceedingly feminine princess.

Greta's outlook on life changes when she meets Elián Palnik, the hostage from the Cumberland Alliance, a small republic bordering the Pan Polar Confederacy at Lake Ontario. In contrast to the other hostages, most of whom grew up in noble families and were prepared for their duty their whole lives, Elián spent his childhood and youth on a farm and was surprised when he was taken to the Precepture, because his grandmother, General Wilma Armenteros, had recently been appointed secretary of strategic decisions in the newly founded Cumberland Alliance. Due to his upbringing, Elián does not accept his fate as a hostage and rebels against the system, even if that leads to physical punishment. From her first meeting with Elián, Greta is fascinated by the new boy: "Elián had come into my life the way comets had once come to medieval skies.... He'd come like a portent of doom" (77). At the root of Greta's scepticism is the ongoing political conflict between Elián's home country and her motherland for access to Lake Ontario's quickly decreasing water levels, which could get them both killed if war is declared. While Greta at first perceives Elián's continued resistance as foolish, witnessing how he is tortured repeatedly by the Precepture's robots raises doubts in her concerning the Precepture system. According to Miranda Green-Barteet and Jill Coste in "Non-Normative Bodies, Queer Identities: Marginalizing Queer Girls in YA Dystopian Literature," this plot development exemplifies "the way romance in YA dystopia leads a protagonist to question the status quo" (86). Green-Barteet and Coste contrast Greta's attraction to Elián with her slowly awakening romantic feelings towards her female roommate, Da-Xia; they suggest that Greta's "queer romance in *The Scorpion Rules* prompts not just rebellion but a character's growing self-awareness of identity and subjectivity" (87). However, Greta and Da-Xia's budding romance is cut short by the Cumberland Alliance's attack on the Precepture and their attempt to use Greta to blackmail the Pan Polar Confederacy into giving them access to Lake Ontario.

Although artificial intelligence Talis (in a female human body that he has borrowed for this purpose) manages to reconquer the Precepture, the war-like activities between Elián's and Greta's nations are supposed to lead to their deaths. However, Greta manages to negotiate a treaty with Talis. In exchange for Elián's life, she volunteers to become an artificial intelligence, despite the mortal danger that the transformation process poses: "For so long I had thought that I had no choices. *I choose....* I choose not to die.... I choose to let my mind be unspooled slowly, so that it may be copied. I choose upload. I choose to become AI" (295). This passage demonstrates that Greta perceives her choice as potentially empowering, as suggested by her repeated and emphatic use of the word "choose." Greta's transformation can thus be read as exemplifying what Hayles conceptualizes as "[cybernetic] liberatory projects that seek to bring traditional dichotomies and hierarchies into question" (174–5), as Greta's negotiation is successful despite the power imbalance between her and Talis. However, it should be noted that this questioning of hierarchies is limited to Greta changing Talis's mind and does not amount to a general critique of AI supremacy (or even a rethinking of monarchy as form of government or settler-colonialism more generally). In contrast to other young adult novels that feature motifs of posthuman becoming and that often characterize their adolescent protagonists as "uninvolved in the decision-making process" and thus tend to represent them as "victims of circumstance, rather than empowered advocates of technological progress" (Flanagan 17), Bow's novel endows protagonist Greta with the agency not only to make her own decision but also to negotiate a way out of a hopeless situation in the face of certain death. The positive representation in *The Scorpion Rules* of its protagonist's transformation is in line with a trend that Flanagan observes in twenty-first-century young adult fiction that "represent[s] technology as both enabling and empowering for female subjects, and in doing so endorse[s] the posthuman conceptualisation of subjectivity as fragmented and plural, with a focus on the processes of becoming (rather than being)" (127). While Greta initially struggles with reconciling her new AI abilities with her body's physical demands and her human memories, she eventually finds a balance. Her at times painful experience of posthuman becoming proves to be beneficial in the long term as it enables her to empathize with her human subjects and simultaneously gives her the power to initiate large-scale political change.

Green-Barteet and Coste argue that Greta's choice to become an artificial intelligence "diminishes queerness through a posthuman saving-the-world trope" (88), but I am hesitant to agree with them, particularly considering the events unfolding in *The Scorpion Rules'* sequel, *The Swan Riders* (2016). While Greta's transformation forecloses any physical intimacy with Da-Xia, at least for the foreseeable future, it also constitutes a way for her to break free from the heteronormative structures constricting noblewomen in the novel's diegetic world. Greta gives up her status as the legitimate successor to the throne of the Pan Polar Confederacy to become a cyborg – a being whom Haraway conceptualizes as "the illegitimate offspring of militarism and patriarchal capitalism" (151). Haraway's description resonates in Greta's transformation as it is a result of a military conflict, and the novel gives this process certain anti-patriarchal undertones. Instead of aiming for an advantageous dynastic marriage and early motherhood, posthuman Greta is free to advocate for changes within the oppressive AI supremacist system, a project with which she starts to succeed by the end of the second book in the series. Green-Barteet and Coste's conclusion that "Greta's saving-the-world narrative reaffirms the status quo" (89) is accurate for the end of *The Scorpion Rules* and the first half of *The Swan Riders*, but by the end of the second book, Greta has transformed how artificial intelligences relate to the human bodies they temporarily inhabit, and she eventually manages to destroy the orbital weapons system that Talis uses to blackmail humanity into obedience, with his consent.

Directly after Greta's transformation, she relishes her newly improved data processing powers: "Oh, it was glorious, feeling my new intelligences flipping through the memory of every time I'd seen her [Da-Xia's] face, building the database, gaining mastery. I *liked* mastery" (*Scorpion Rules* 356). However, Greta's survival of the process of transforming into AI is threatened by her difficulties with bringing her bodily human memories in alignment with her new capabilities of evaluating those situations in a purely rational, disembodied way. Particularly strong emotional memories that are related to intense physical sensations tend to run in loops, causing sensory overload in Greta: "I was overloading. Inside, outside, again and again. How can one person be two things? How can two things be one person? I was turned inside out so many times that I had no outside" (368–9). Greta's struggles in reconciling her new and improved AI mind with her human body amount to what Flanagan conceptualizes as a "critique [of] the Cartesian concept of mind/body separation" (104). Greta's human body is more than just an empty husk for her mind to fill; it has not only physical needs but also memories of its own and as such is an essential factor in Greta's subject formation.

At first, Greta perceives her human body primarily as a liability, which is particularly visible when she and Talis travel on horseback toward the AI headquarters. Due to a global scarcity of resources, horses have replaced other modes of transportation and are the most practical means of transport. Because Greta is unused to riding, her legs become so sore that she can hardly move, illustrating that even as an AI, physical matters remain of concern. The post–climate-crisis setting of the Saskatchewan prairies exacerbates the toll that the journey takes on Greta's body as the heat in combination with the lack of water and vegetation accelerates the rate of her bodily exhaustion. The harshness of the environment works to show that despite her optimized mental capacities, Greta's human body remains a limiting factor in her travels. Although Greta's datastore provides her with the procedure for riding, her theoretical knowledge fails to prepare her for the actual experience: "There are some things only bodies can know, and one of them is how to stay on top of a running horse" (15). The demands of simultaneously navigating the challenging environment and coming to terms with her new identity as an AI burden Greta. Thus, Bow's book series engages with earlier traditions concerning the representation of nature in Canadian adolescent fiction in which "the individual's struggle against hostile nature" is a recurring motif (Alter 163).

Rather than just using the harsh natural setting as an obstacle for the protagonist to overcome on her way towards personal growth, the novel also explains how greed and ruthless exploitation of resources have led to this situation. The responsibility for environmental degradation is placed firmly in the human sphere as temporary narrator Talis clarifies in the prologue of *The Scorpion Rules*: "It started when the ice caps melted. We saw it coming, and were braced for the long catastrophe, but in the end it came unbelievably fast.... The water reserves gave out, the food supplies collapsed, and everybody caught these exciting new diseases, which is one of those fun side effects of climate shift that we didn't pay enough attention to" (1–2). Anthropogenic climate change and its consequences are the justification that Talis gives for his world domination. By pointing out humanity's failure to conserve nature, he presents his intervention as ultimately beneficial for both humanity and wildlife. Within the duology, the premise of AI supremacy as justified due to human incompetence remains unchallenged; even those characters who resist the Precepture system mostly criticize *how* Talis is ruling the world and do not question *whether* he should do so. This also applies to Greta, who is convinced that her becoming an AI is the most effective way of creating a benign kind of AI hegemony that treats human subjects in a more benevolent way than Talis's absolutist approach.

Greta's transformation changes not just her way of thinking, but also her body. When she first learns that for the process to succeed, a datastore device will need to be implanted in her chest, Greta is appalled: "It was so biological, such a mishmash, a horror" (*Scorpion Rules* 320). Greta did not understand AIs to be so involved in corporeal matters, and this passage is another instance in which the novel disrupts Cartesian ideas of a mind/body duality. While the AIs themselves are pure data, they still require a host, either a human body or a robotic one, to exist. Greta's line of thought that moves from the neutral term "biological" to a colloquial "mishmash" before admitting her "horror" shows that her upcoming hybridity has mostly negative connotations for Greta. Her expectations concerning the empowering implications of her transformation have given way to scepticism, so that right after the completion of the transformation, Greta even calls herself a "monster" (354). However, throughout the second book of the series, Greta learns to reconcile her self-image with the "mishmash" that constitutes her posthuman becoming, and by the end of the duology, the empowering qualities of the transformation prevail.

The datastore is not the only modification that marks Greta's posthuman body: the most striking change in her outward appearance is the loss of her long hair, which had to be shaved off before her AI transformation procedure. Although it is tempting to equate Greta's extremely short hairstyle with a conscious abandonment of her femininity and to read her formerly long hair as representative of the human past that she has left behind, I argue that posthuman Greta's behaviour is still influenced by her previous experiences and socialization as a human girl. This applies particularly to her ability to empathize with marginalized characters through remembering her own feelings of powerlessness as a hostage.

This skill is the key to resolving the major conflict in *The Swan Riders*, a rebellion of the so-called Swan Riders, humans who volunteer to provide their bodies to AIs for temporary possession. As inhabitation by an AI causes severe nerve damage in human hosts, Swan Riders whose bodies have been used by AIs suffer from a disease called Rider's Palsy, which leads to seizures and eventually kills the affected person. While the human volunteers, mostly impoverished people for whom serving a higher purpose appears more attractive than starving to death, are aware of the risk, the AIs' casual disregard of their sacrifice is a cause of resentment. While Talis's proposed solution for the problem is limited to violence, Greta approaches the issue from a different point of view: she endeavours to understand the rebellious Swan Riders' motivations and eventually manages to find a compromise. It is precisely the interplay of Greta's originally human capacity for compassion, her bodily memories of suffering at the hands of entities more powerful than her, and her improved intellectual power that ultimately leads to a peaceful conflict resolution. Greta develops a technique that allows the Swan Riders' minds to have an impact on the AIs inhabiting them, thereby strengthening the bond between AI and Swan Rider to honour the latter's sacrifice.

Bow's *Prisoners of Peace* duology explores questions concerning female subject formation in relation to technological enhancement through its protagonist, Greta. While Greta's struggle with her new posthuman identity is resolved at the end of the second instalment, when she grows into her new power, the books also reproduce certain generic conventions of YA dystopias that leave Greta stuck in traditional stereotypes of girlhood. These include the fact that important stages of Greta's development are initiated by male characters, be it Elián nudging her towards open rebellion or Talis's control over her AI transformation. Although the AIs can inhabit bodies of any gender, which to a certain extent disconnects gender identification from bodily features, Bow's diegetic setting is a far stretch from the postgender world that Haraway imagines in her *Cyborg Manifesto*. Despite Greta's rejection of her predetermined trajectory from hostage to wife to mother to queen, the characters in the book remain caught up in a constricting patriarchal and heteronormative framework. Although her posthuman transformation is represented as empowering on a personal basis for Greta, large-scale social change that improves the living conditions of wider sections of the population is only hinted at near the ending of the second book.

Becoming Alien in Prendergast's *Nahx Invasion* Duology

In contrast to Bow's dutiful Greta, Prendergast's Raven Bailey is introduced to readers as a troublemaker. At the beginning of the first novel, *Zero Repeat Forever* (2017), sixteen-year-old Raven is at a summer camp somewhere in the forests of Alberta, where she performs court-ordered community service as a camp counsellor. Reflecting on her name, extra- and homodiegetic narrator Raven explains, "Raven doesn't suit me.... Rave suits me, like a party, but only some of the time. Not right now. Rage would be a better name right now. My karate instructors used to joke that Rage could be my fighter name, in between telling me that anger needs to be controlled, especially in martial arts" (15). Raven explicitly connects her outbursts to her insecurities concerning her cultural identity: "Black mom, long-gone white dad. Does that make me mixed?... Adding all that to my mom's posh English, my stepfather Jack's Michif, and the French they taught me at school, makes me feel like about ten people at once" (15). In contrast to the generally positive representations of multiculturalism in Canadian young adult literature (cf. Alter 167),[6] Raven experiences her multicultural upbringing as at times overwhelming. By having a female teenager of colour as a protagonist, the *Nahx Invasion* duology differs from the majority of young adult dystopian novels that tend to focus on the experiences of white girls (cf. Thompson 148). Raven's racialization is not a mere superficial gesture of inclusion, but is addressed on the diegetic level multiple times and is thus relevant to the plot of the book series.

Raven's anger issues worry her parents, who fear that Raven as a person of colour cannot expect leniency from the Canadian court system. Raven's rebelliousness also leads to her friends getting into trouble, such as her seventeen-year-old boyfriend, Tucker Derkach, and his twin brother, Topher. At first, Raven considers herself lucky that she and Tucker are in the woods when presumed extraterrestrials called the Nahx invade Earth and destroy all large cities (including Raven's hometown, Calgary). The summer camp becomes an idyllic refuge for Raven and her fellow campers, whose excellent hunting and gathering skills make them self-reliant. However, eventually the dwindling resources and the imminent beginning of winter motivate the camp inhabitants to venture outwards looking for housing and food. When Tucker is supposedly killed by the Nahx during such a mission, Raven is devastated. Still, she and the remaining camp counsellors desperately need supplies, so they continue to explore the surrounding area. After several such expeditions during which Raven's group finds shelter at a hidden secret military base, Raven is severely injured in a fight with Nahx forces, but is saved by the second protagonist of the novel, a Nahx soldier called Eighth who has fallen in love with Raven at first sight. In a turn of events that Sarah Sawler has described in her online review of the book in *Quill and Quire* as "unsettling" and bordering on a romanticizing of domestic abuse, Eighth takes Raven to an abandoned hotel where he nurses her back to health, despite her resistance. Their time together is shaped by misunderstandings and conflicts, and after Raven has recovered from her injuries, Eighth – whom Raven has renamed August after misunderstanding the hand signs with which he communicates due to his muteness – takes Raven back to the military base. While experiencing racist micro-aggressions and other conflicts at the base, Raven starts to realize that she misses August and, when her housemates manage to take him captive, she frees him and flees with him. However, they are pursued by her former acquaintances from the base who shoot at them and hit Raven.

Because Raven is close to death, August offers her the poison in the darts with which the Nahx shoot humans, and she agrees for it to be used on her. While the Nahx substance is transforming Raven's body, her mind starts to grapple with the consequences of her choice: "I feel the beginnings of disdain for my own weak, imperfect species. This is how we become perfect. This is how we live forever" (323). This suggestion of becoming perfect through posthuman transformation has clear transhumanist connotations and stands in contrast to the epigraph from Edgar Allan Poe, "I have no faith in human perfectibility," that prefaces the novel. Both books of the series contain intertextual references to canonic horror authors: in *Zero Repeat Forever*, each part of the book is introduced by an epigraph from Poe, whereas its sequel, *Cold Falling White* (2019), quotes Mary Shelley's *Frankenstein*. Works of those authors also appear on the diegetic level of Prendergast's novels. *Zero Repeat Forever*'s male protagonist, August, reads a copy of Poe's *The Raven* because the title reminds him of his love interest, and the title of Prendergast's book is taken from Poe's line "Nevermore," which in August's sign language consists of a combination of the words "zero," "repeat," and "forever." *Cold Falling White*'s male protagonist, Xander, who is a friend of Raven, reads Shelley's *Frankenstein*, but the novel does not play such a prominent role on the diegetic level compared to the extent that Poe's *The Raven* is present in *Zero Repeat Forever*. The novels' intertextual nods to classics of horror fiction are an act of self-positioning within the horror genre. However, due to intratextual features such as the alien invasion plot and Raven's posthuman transformation, I regard the novels as science fiction rather than horror as the books seem more designed to encourage readers to speculate about the extraterrestrial threat and the consequences of Raven's posthuman becoming than to evoke strong emotions of fear, dread, or disgust.

The full implications of Raven's decision to accept the Nahx poison are explained to readers in *Cold Falling White*. At the beginning of the novel, Raven as narrator shares how she experiences the transformation process:

> I am as weightless as a thought, as a shadow underwater. The only thing that gives me substance is the sense of filling up with … something. Something thick and powerful and inhuman, unearthly. I want to squirm away from it but there is nothing to squirm with. All I am is a selection of verbs: to fill, to grow, to change, to perfect. It's as though I'm being rebuilt from scratch.… I'm being entwined in something, as though my nerves are unraveling and tangling into some idea of … I can't see it. I can't hear it or smell it or taste it. It's nothing, a void, like the space left behind when something is lost. I can feel its emptiness, feel it trying to consume me, to ensnare me. But there's something else resisting it, something stubborn and intractable, something *human*. (6; first and last ellipses in original)

Raven's mind feels disconnected from her body – it is "weightless as a thought" and "there is nothing to squirm with." The resulting void is filled by what readers know to be the Nahx substance, which she characterizes as "thick, and powerful and inhuman, unearthly," thereby evoking sensations of being threatened and overwhelmed. However, Raven's human side resists the transformation through key character traits that have already been established in the originary book: her stubbornness and her intractability. Whereas the Nahx poison is designed to turn its victims into marionettes with no will of their own, Raven's transformation remains incomplete. She benefits from the advantages of being turned into a human/alien hybrid with a physically stronger body, improved healing abilities, and sharper mental capacities, but she does not suffer from the unconditional obedience that usually accompanies this enhancement of the human body/mind. Visually, a metallic pallor appears on Raven's skin that marks her as *other*. Somewhat ironically, Raven's (pre-transformation) skin colour has been described as "golden" in *Zero Repeat Forever*, which makes her eventual human/

alien hybrid look appear as a logical progression; the golden shimmer of Raven's skin has become more pronounced, but this time, she perceives the change as positive rather than as a burden, which was the case for her previous racialization as a person of colour.

During her transformative trance, Raven has apocalyptic visions that are later revealed as pointing to a threat of global proportions that eventually turns out to be the reason for the creation of the Nahx. After her transformation, Raven wakes up at a Nahx army base from which she manages to escape. Whereas the harsh environment of the wintery Alberta forests constituted an existential threat to Raven before her transformation, her alien/human hybrid body is unaffected by the cold and able to cover long distances quickly. This forms a sharp contrast to Bow's book series in which protagonist Greta's body struggles to cope with the hostile environment as her mental capacities have been enhanced but not her physical prowess. While the focus of Bow's *The Swan Riders* is on Greta's efforts to reconcile the demands of her AI mind with the needs of her human body, Prendergast's novels do not explore such matters. Raven quickly acclimatizes to her new abilities and prioritizes her quest of reuniting with her love interest (and her other friends) over self-reflection. Thus, Raven's transformation is represented as unambiguously empowering for her: for the first time in her life, she can perceive her own culturally hybridized identity as an asset rather than a burden. In this sense, Raven is shown to find "pleasure in the confusion of boundaries," as Haraway suggests regarding cyborgs more generally (2). Still, this transgression of boundaries is limited to Raven's embodiment that combines human and extraterrestrial features. In the course of *Cold Falling White*, Raven turns her newly acquired power into an instrument to maintain the status quo, a plot point to which I will come back later.

Searching for her friends, Raven meets a Métis girl. The novel uses this encounter to reference real-world Canadian history. While Raven is worried about the young woman who is in hostile Nahx territory, the girl herself immediately identifies Raven as alien and thus a potential enemy, and points her gun at her, as the following dialogue ensues:

> [RAVEN:] "Have you been up here since the invasion?"
> [GIRL:] "We've always been here, freak." …
> [RAVEN:] "You don't need to be scared. I'm not going to hurt you or anyone. I just need some information."
> [GIRL:] "I'm not telling you anything. *Shipwaytay* [Michif for *leave*]. Get off our land." (84)

In this passage, *Cold Falling White* contextualizes the Nahx attack as another foreign invasion of what is thought of as Canadian territory. Although Raven's question clearly refers to the recent Nahx invasion, the Métis girl's answer makes clear that she sees the Nahx occupation of the territory as just the latest event in a series of imperialist interventions. By referring to her people as those who have "always been here" and by calling the territory on which the meeting takes place "our land," the girl asserts her people's claim to the land in question. Her use of the Michif language, which is left untranslated in the novel because the chapter is told from the perspective of Raven, who can speak Michif due to her Métis stepfather, works to emphasize her rootedness in Métis culture. The novel's casual inclusion of Indigenous characters highlights their enduring presence in the face of challenging circumstances; this is not only true for the unnamed girl, but also for Raven's stepfather, Jack, who manages to survive the Nahx invasion and, together with Raven's mother, escapes to Quadra Island where they find refuge in an Indigenous community. The novel not only highlights solidarity between different Indigenous groups but also extends this notion to others when Jack offers Raven's Chinese-Canadian friend Xander shelter.

Human/alien hybrid Raven is also keen on making connections with others and finding allies. After befriending Blue, who belongs to a species that looks like flickering blue fireflies and whose members are united through collective consciousness, Raven and the readers finally learn about the ulterior motives behind the Nahx invasion. Blue's species, which has existed on Earth since long before there were humans, created the Nahx from human DNA to fend off an unspecified extraterrestrial threat to Earth that will invade at sites where nuclear testing has taken place. However, the Nahx did not meet their expectations, which is why they developed the Nahx poison to turn humans into supersoldiers. As soon as Raven understands the reasons behind her creation, she chooses to fight and is willing to sacrifice herself for the benefit of all life on Earth. In contrast to *Zero Repeat Forever*, in which Raven spent most of the plot obsessing over her love interests (first Tucker, then August), in *Cold Falling White* she has become more altruistic. Even more so than in Bow's *Prisoners of Peace*, in what Green-Barteet and Coste would call a "saving-the-world move to posthumanism [that] underscores the traditions of her world" (88), Raven eventually submits to the role that other, more powerful entities have designed for her, adopting the identity of a self-sacrificing saviour figure. Earlier in the book, the reanimated alien/human hybrid Tucker forms a love triangle with August and Raven, a trope that has become a generic convention for YA dystopias (cf. Trites 150). While Raven's posthuman body has the potential to question conventional gender boundaries, this potential is never further explored, and instead Raven is re-feminized by being cast as "the object of exchange between men" (Trites 121). The situation is resolved through Tucker's self-sacrifice to protect Raven, once again forcing her into the role of a damsel in distress and giving Tucker the opportunity to become her knight in shining armour. In the latter part of the book, however, Raven comes to regard herself as August's protector. August's somewhat naive personality makes their exchanges of affection read more like a mother-son relationship than a romantic partnership. In the final chapters, Raven persuades August not to join the fight and makes her way to the battlefield in Saskatchewan's Athabasca sand dunes on her own, finding solace in the fact that her sacrifice might save the lives of her loved ones.

Raven's transformation in Prendergast's *Nahx Invasion* duology is represented as a significant step towards personal growth and self-empowerment. The hardships Raven experiences enable her to become more mature and to develop from a boy-obsessed teenager with anger issues to an altruistic alien/human hybrid who uses her newly won powers for the good of all life on Earth. However, similarly to Bow's Greta, the empowering qualities of Raven's transformation are undermined by her dependency on male characters throughout both books and by her eventual acceptance of a role that others have designed for her. Although Prendergast's books feature representations of queerness, as in Raven's friend Xander who starts a love affair with another human male character, or by including Nahx side characters who engage in polyamorous relationships, the protagonist, Raven, remains firmly situated within a heteronormative framework.

Conclusion: Posthuman Female Empowerment and Its Limits

Both Bow's *Prisoners of Peace* and Prendergast's *Nahx Invasion* use heroines whose characterization is in line with the established trope of the strong female protagonist to negotiate female identity formation in the face of global crises. Reading the book series' protagonists and their development alongside posthuman theorizing enables me to focus on how the entanglements among gendered stereotypes, settler-colonial histories, and specifically Canadian environments influence the protagonists' posthuman embodiment. My analysis draws attention to the limits that the books in question set on the liberatory potential of posthuman transformation.

Bow's and Prendergast's novels emphasize their protagonists' individual experiences and only hint at how human enhancement might change (Canadian) society at large; Greta and Raven choose to engage in processes of posthuman becoming to cope with challenging circumstances and to escape impending death. During their transformations, their already strong bodies are enhanced with superhuman abilities, and their brain functions are optimized. Greta's and Raven's posthuman becoming is represented as necessary to survive in an increasingly hostile world. Although both girls at first struggle to come to terms with their posthuman bodies/minds, they perceive their transformation as ultimately empowering. For them, it is particularly rewarding to use their new powers for the benefit of their fellow human and more-than-human life forms: Greta heralds a new era of a more benign AI supremacy, whereas Raven fights to defend Earth against an extraterrestrial threat. While a didactic message that endorses socially desirable behaviour is to be expected of young adult fiction, it also risks reducing the protagonists from independent girls to self-sacrificing saviour figures who put their own interests last. Readers might also react with a slight uneasiness witnessing how both marginalized protagonists (Greta as a queer person and Raven as a person of colour) start out seeking to dismantle oppressive systems only to revert to fighting for maintaining the status quo once their posthuman transformation has positioned them closer to the ruling powers. This development can also be tied back to the interconnections between the generic conventions of the *bildungsromane* that have long influenced young adult fiction and that often take the form of protagonists first rebelling against social norms before eventually submitting to them, which is then presented as a sign of personal growth.[7]

If both book series fall short of letting their protagonists not only question but also change the status quo, can the representation of their heroines' posthuman transformation as empowering still be considered feminist? As my analysis has shown, the novels' questioning of traditional gender stereotypes remains on a rather superficial level with their employment of a prototypical strong female protagonist. A closer look reveals that in both duologies, all important steps towards the protagonists' personal development are initiated by male characters. In *Prisoners of Peace*, Elián constitutes the inspiration for Greta's rebellion (and also works as her love interest, before she realizes her romantic feelings for her female roommate), and Talis remains in control of Greta's choices as an AI. In *Nahx Invasion*, Raven's decisions are heavily influenced by her two male love interests, Tucker and August. Thus, despite the empowering qualities of their posthuman bodies/minds, the agency of both Greta and Raven remains limited by the patriarchal, heteronormative structures that surround them.

My intention is not to malign Bow's *Prisoners of Peace* and Prendergast's *Nahx Invasion* series or to lament the dearth of feminist young adult fiction. Instead, my chapter seeks to continue ongoing conversations about the wider implications of representations of posthuman transformation in adolescent literature. Combining posthuman theorizing with considerations of gendered stereotypes, environmental aspects, and settler-colonial histories can open up new and fascinating perspectives on Canadian young adult science fiction. To what extent those insights are transferable to other genres and/or other national literatures remains to be seen.

NOTES

1 It is common for young adult dystopias to combine both (post-)apocalyptic and dystopian elements, according to Ruediger Heinze, who states that the setting of anglophone young adult dystopian novels "is often apocalyptic or post-apocalyptic as an explanation for the dystopian state of affairs" (34).

2 While young adult dystopias became particularly popular in the late 2000s and early 2010s, there are a few earlier examples of adolescent literature with dystopian settings, such as the three young adult novels by Monica Hughes published in the 1980s and 1990s that are discussed in William Thompson's chapter in this collection.

3 Further examples of young adult dystopian fiction by Canadian authors include Carrie Mac's *Triskelia* trilogy (2006–8), Cory Doctorow's *Little Brother* series (2008–20), Catherine Austen's *All Good Children* (2011), Jo Treggiari's *Ashes, Ashes* (2011), Moira Young's *Dustlands* trilogy (2011–14), Hugh MacDonald's *The Last Wild Boy* trilogy (2013–21), Eric Walters's *The Rule of Three* series (2014–18), Kate Blair's *Transferral* (2015), L.E. Sterling's *True Born* series (2016–18), Colleen Nelson and Nancy Chappell-Pollack's *Pulse Point* duology (2018–20), and Jerri Chisholm's *Eleven* trilogy (2020–22).

4 Throughout the books, Talis is consistently referred to by male pronouns, even when he is inhabiting human women's bodies, because Talis used to be a human man before he was turned into an artificial intelligence. As an AI, he continues to identify as male, indicated by his use of male pronouns for himself.

5 The description of Preceptures in the novel evokes associations with real-world Canadian Residential Schools, especially in that children are forcibly separated from their families because of their heritage and then put into boarding schools in remote areas where they are forced to perform manual labor under the threat of physical abuse and where

every form of instruction takes place exclusively in English, although each Precepture hosts prisoners from different nations. The hostages killed at the Preceptures are also buried on school grounds. *The Scorpion Rules* indicates that the Precepture is located in a building that used to belong to the Catholic Church, and the AI that serves as principal of the Precepture calls himself "the Abbot."

Despite this implicit reference to real-world Canadian history, the novel does not include any explicit references to Indigenous Peoples, their histories, and/or cultures. While this omission might be read as an erasure of Indigenous Peoples, the novel's association of the Catholic Church with the Preceptures might also point at transnational legacies of child abuse perpetrated at Catholic institutions worldwide; examples from the twentieth century include the homes for children of unmarried mothers in Ireland (e.g., the Bon Secours Mother and Baby Home) or the Catholic missions involved in the forced removal of Indigenous Australian children from their families (e.g., the Garden Point Mission). Thus, rather than reading the omission of Indigenous Peoples in the novel as a perpetuation of settler-colonialist thinking – an obvious conclusion considering that the diegetic future Canada of the books is a monarchy ruled by a Scottish-Canadian queen – one might also consider the implied references to real-world Canadian histories as a gesture towards transnational solidarity or rather what Michael Rothberg has termed multidirectional memory, with the Preceptures serving as a starting point for the exploration of diverse histories of victimization through the Catholic Church. Disentangling those interconnected threads is beyond the scope of this chapter but might be explored in future publications.

6 Based on the premise "that the political and historical development of multiculturalism in Canada and Canadian literature for young readers have been closely intertwined" (166), Grit Alter argues that "since the 1990s some publishers have increasingly included multicultural works in their programs which present multicultural children as members of Canadian society and not merely and exclusively as strugglers who try to fit in" (167). Regarding newer (twenty-first-century) Canadian young adult fiction, Alter observes that "a look at recently published multicultural literature for young readers shows that an approach to depicting cultural otherness beyond victim vs. perpetrator and immigrant vs. native dichotomies is recognizable. The respective books pay tribute to cultural heritages, and allow young readers to see beyond ethnic and national boundaries and to perceive and appreciate the other for who they are as humans" (167).

7 For more details on the generic entanglements between young adult fiction and *bildungsromane*, see Šárka Bubíková's "Transformations of the Bildungsroman in in Young Adult Literature in English."

WORKS CITED

Alaimo, Stacy, and Susan Hekman. *Material Feminism*. Indiana UP, 2008.

Alter, Grit. *Inter- and Transcultural Learning in the Context of Canadian Young Adult Fiction*. LIT Verlag, 2015.

Atwood, Margaret. *Survival: A Thematic Guide to Canadian Literature*. 1972. McClelland & Stewart, 2004.

Austen, Catherine. *All Good Children*. Orca Book Publishers, 2011.

Blair, Kate. *Transferral*. Dancing Cat Books, 2015.

Bow, Erin. *The Scorpion Rules*. Margaret K. McElderry Books, 2015.

– *The Swan Riders*. Margaret K. McElderry Books, 2016.

Bubíková, Šárka. "Transformations of the Bildungsroman in Young Adult Literature in English." *The Borders of Fantasia*, edited by Antonella Cagnolati, FahrenHouse, 2015, pp. 83–97.

Chisholm, Jerri. *Ending Eleven*. Entangled Publishing, 2022.

– *Escaping Eleven*. Entangled Publishing, 2020.

– *Unraveling Eleven*. Entangled Publishing, 2021.

Dimaline, Cherie. *Hunting by Stars*. Penguin, 2021.

– *The Marrow Thieves*. Dancing Cat Books, 2017.

Doctorow, Cory. *Attack Surface*. Tor Books, 2020.

– *Homeland*. Tor Books, 2013.

– *Little Brother*. Tor Books, 2008.

Flanagan, Victoria. *Technology and Identity in Young Adult Fiction: The Posthuman Subject*. Palgrave Macmillan, 2014.

Frye, Northrop. "Conclusion." *Literary History of Canada: Canadian Literature in English*, 2nd edition, vol. 2, edited by Carl Klinck, Alfred Bailey, Claude Bissell, Roy Daniells, Northrop Frye, and Desmond Pacey, U of Toronto P, 1976, pp. 333–64.

Green-Barteet, Miranda A., and Jill Coste. "Non-Normative Bodies, Queer Identities: Marginalizing Queer Girls in YA Dystopian Literature." *Girlhood Studies*, vol. 12, no. 1, 2019, pp. 82–97. *Berghahn Journals*, https://doi.org/10.3167/ghs.2019.120108.

Grosz, Elizabeth. *Volatile Bodies: Toward a Corporeal Feminism*. Indiana UP, 1994.

Haraway, Donna J. "A Cyborg Manifesto: Science, Technology, and Socialist-Feminism in the Late Twentieth Century." *Simians, Cyborgs, and Women: The Reinvention of Nature*, Routledge, 1991, pp. 149–81.

Hayles, N. Katherine. "The Seductions of Cyberspace." *Rethinking Technologies*, edited by Verena Andermatt Conley on behalf of the Miami Theory Collective, U of Minnesota P, 1993, pp. 173–90.

Heinze, Ruediger. "Through a Glass, Darkly: Contemporary Young Adult Dystopias." *"Tell Freedom I Said Hello": Issues in Contemporary Young Adult Dystopian Fiction*, edited by Christian Ludwig and Nicole Maruo-Schroeder, Universitaetsverlag Winter Heidelberg, 2018, pp. 27–46.

Knutsson, Catherine. *Shadows Cast by Stars*. Atheneum, 2012.
Mac, Carrie. *The Droughtlanders*. Puffin Canada, 2006.
– *Retribution*. Puffin Canada, 2007.
– *Storm*. Puffin Canada, 2008.
MacDonald, Hugh. *And All the Stars Shall Fall*. Acorn Press, 2018.
– *The Last Wild Boy*. Acorn Press, 2013.
– *Our Rock and Our Salvation*. Acorn Press, 2021.
McDonough, Megan, and Katherine A. Wagner. "Rebellious Natures: The Role of Nature in Young Adult Dystopian Female Protagonists' Awakenings and Agency." *Female Rebellion in Young Adult Dystopian Fiction*, edited by Sara K. Day, Miranda A. Green-Barteet, and Amy L. Montz, Ashgate, 2014, pp. 157–70.
McGowan, Maureen. *Compliance*. Skyscape, 2013.
– *Deviants*. Skyscape, 2012.
– *Glory*. Skyscape, 2014.
Nelson, Colleen, and Nancy Chappell-Pollack. *Pulse Point*. Yellow Dog, 2018.
– *Underland*. Yellow Dog, 2020.
Prendergast, G.S. *Cold Falling White*. Simon & Schuster, 2019.
– *Zero Repeat Forever*. Simon & Schuster, 2017.
Rothberg, Michael. *Multidirectional Memory: Remembering the Holocaust in the Age of Decolonization*. Stanford UP, 2009.
Sawler, Sarah. Review of *Zero Repeat Forever*. *Quill & Quire*, https://quillandquire.com/review/zero-repeat-forever.
Sterling, L.E. *True Born*. Entangled Publishing, 2016.
– *True North*. Entangled Publishing, 2017.
– *True Storm*. Entangled Publishing, 2018.
Thompson, William. "Climate Change and the Girl Body: Hope and the Dystopian Future in Three Novels by Monica Hughes." *ReVisions: Speculating in Literature and Film in Canada*, edited by Wendy Roy, U of Toronto P, 2025, pp. 139–57.
Treggiari, Jo. *Ashes, Ashes*. Scholastic Press, 2011.
Trites, Roberta Seelinger. *Twenty-First-Century Feminisms in Children's and Adolescent Literature*. UP of Mississippi, 2018.
Walters, Eric. *Fight for Power*. Farrar, Straus and Giroux, 2015.
– *Fourth Dimension*. Penguin, 2018.
– *The Rule of Three*. Farrar, Straus and Giroux, 2014.
– *Will to Survive*. Farrar, Straus and Giroux, 2016.
Young, Moira. *Blood Red Road*. Margaret K. McElderry Books, 2011.
– *Raging Star*. Margaret K. McElderry Books, 2014.
– *Rebel Heart*. Margaret K. McElderry Books, 2012.

Climate Change and the Girl Body: Hope and the Dystopian Future in Three Novels by Monica Hughes

WILLIAM THOMPSON

Climate change fiction is one of the fastest growing genres for children and young adults in the twenty-first century. Young activists such as Greta Thunberg have provided a voice for children and young adults in response to climate change, reframing the conversation both politically and economically, particularly for those young people who will inherit the environmental damage of the last three centuries. Climate fiction, or cli-fi, as coined by journalist Dan Bloom in 2007 (Crace), has its roots in the fiction emerging from the environmental movement of the twentieth century. For children and young adults, cli-fi has a more direct connection to the science fiction and dystopian literature of the late twentieth and early twenty-first centuries. Since 2000, cli-fi for young adults has found a fuller expression in novels such as *The Carbon Diaries* duology (2008, 2010) by Saci Lloyd and *Pacifica* (2018) by Kristen Simmons, which depict a world altered by climate change. The increasing popularity of such texts speaks to the growing awareness among young adults of the political and economic impact of environmental devastation on a planetary scale.

Broadly speaking, cli-fi is a loosely defined category of fiction that describes the human impact on the environment. According to Adam Trexler, "Climate fiction is not the result of a literary 'school' of related authors. No singular influence or unitary 'idea' connects all climate fiction. Climate change itself is a remarkably broad series of phenomena in the nonhuman world, politics, and the media" (10–11). Climate fiction for young adults has emerged gradually, refocusing earlier genres and framing a growing awareness of environmental issues for young adults. In their introduction to *The Lion and the Unicorn*'s issue dedicated to climate change in 2021, Marek Oziewicz and Lara Saguisag emphasize the urgency of the current crisis: "Climate change calls for a transformation of our economic, energy, food, social, and other systems on a scale more rapid and radical than any historical mobilizations executed by human societies. No less important, climate change poses a challenge that is at once psychologically traumatizing and conceptually daunting" (vi). Oziewicz and Saguisag's introduction works to situate the scholarship of children's literature in relation to the climate crisis, but it is also a call to action. They ask what children's literature as a genre can do in the face of such a crisis: "Is it not impossible – indeed, extreme childishness – to dream that stories have the power to frame the urgencies of climate change in ways that mobilize action for the unprecedented changes our planet needs?" (viii). One could respond that children's literature is a genre that has been framing and telling the story of climate change in various ways for decades, even if it has lacked the political rhetoric to outline the crisis in its current form.

British-born Canadian science fiction author Monica Hughes is a case in point. Three of Hughes's books, published between 1980 and 1992, serve as a forerunner to twenty-first-century cli-fi for young adults, marking the emergence of the genre long before the term appears in regular use. Both *Ring-Rise Ring-Set* (1982) and *The Crystal Drop* (1992) are set in uniquely Canadian landscapes – the tundra of the Northwest Territories and the drought-stricken prairie of southern Alberta, respectively. These landscapes become a coming-of-age arena for protagonists Liza and Megan. Both characters are displaced from their homes, and each undergoes a coming of age tied to her relationship with the land and the climate crisis. *The Keeper of the Isis Light* (1980), the first in Hughes's *Isis* trilogy, is science fiction rather than dystopian fiction, but Olwen, genetically modified by her robot guardian, is equally tied to her own landscape and must come to terms with the alteration of her planet by settlers from Earth. While the alterations to Olwen's home do not rise to the scale of the climate disasters in *Ring-Rise Ring-Set* or *The Crystal Drop*, Olwen's coming of age is tied as much to the landscape as are Liza's and Megan's. I argue that these books by Hughes represent a forerunner to climate change texts of the twenty-first century; they frame environmental devastation in terms of girls and girls' bodies, but they also demonstrate that texts for children and young adults were already active in a conversation about climate change and the climate crisis long before it reached its current imperative.

With forty-nine books to her name, nearly half of which are science fiction, Hughes has left behind a legacy of other worlds for children and young adults. Many of Hughes's future worlds incorporate some element of dystopia, in which her child protagonists are set in opposition to the authoritarian, and often tyrannical, forces of a frequently techno-centred society. The political and social implications of her dystopic worlds are many and varied, but more poignant are those dystopian works that bring together environmental concerns and female coming of age. *Ring-Rise Ring-Set*, *The Crystal Drop*, and *The Keeper of the Isis Light* all feature young female protagonists whose sexual coming of age becomes inextricably tied to the environment. In these texts, Hughes shifts the focus of the young adult dystopia away from its primary concern with growing social and political awareness and moves it in the direction of something that is both more intimate and more climate based: the girl body in relation to the destruction of the land by a male-dominated, techno-centred society.

Although Hughes's dystopic novels are not all environmentally focused in this way – the social and political dystopia of Hughes's *The Other Place* (1999) being a case in point – these three texts yolk emerging female sexuality, the environment, and a dystopic future. *Ring-Rise Ring-Set* locates fifteen-year-old Liza in a science station on the Canadian tundra, where a group of scientists is attempting to slow the advance of glacial ice caused by a ring of asteroidal dust that has encircled the equator. *The Crystal Drop* has thirteen-year-old Megan Dougal and her younger brother leaving their home on the drought-stricken Alberta prairie, which they must traverse alone following the death of their mother during childbirth. *The Keeper of the Isis Light*, the first of Hughes's *Isis* books, is set on the planet Isis, where sixteen-year-old Olwen is the keeper of the light. Following the arrival of a settler ship from Earth, Olwen witnesses the despoilment of the planet she has come to regard as hers. Although different than the other books in its representation of environmental damage, *The Keeper of the Isis Light* more forcibly ties female sexuality to the landscape. As Olwen has been physically and genetically altered by her robot guardian to adapt her to the unique conditions of the planet, she experiences the damage to Isis like a bodily wound, the emotional pain of which manifests in response to the settlers' rejection of Olwen because of her reptilian appearance. These texts by Hughes embody many of the larger social and political concerns inherent to dystopian fiction; however, such concerns are backgrounded in order to highlight the relationship between the landscapes and their respective main characters.

Climate change fiction for young adults finds a close cousin in earlier dystopian literature of the twentieth and twenty-first centuries, such as Lois Lowry's *The Giver* and Suzanne Collins's *The Hunger Games*. Both are landmarks in the development of dystopian fiction for young adults, and both were adapted into feature films, *The Hunger Games* franchise spanning four films released between 2012 and 2015. Both Lowry and Collins incorporate some degree of environmental damage into their books, but the environment is not the focus. One of the first memories Jonas, the main character of *The Giver*, receives is that of sunshine: "Before Sameness. Before Climate Control" (Lowry 108). In the world of *The Giver*, sameness extends beyond the environment to social order and individual behaviour. Such social control finds a fuller expression in *The Hunger Games*, in which sixteen-year-old Katniss participates in the yearly competition and fight to the death, established by the Capitol as a means of suppressing and manipulating the twelve districts of Panem. It is Peeta Mellark, Katniss's fellow tribute from District 12, who states, "I can't go down without a fight. Only I keep wishing I could think of a way to … to show the Capitol they don't own me. That I'm more than just a piece in their Games" (Collins 142; ellipsis in original). In this way, Peeta's words and the fight against the tyranny of the Capitol become central to both the series and Katniss's arc as a character.

Such governmental tyranny and male-dominated control is a hallmark of young adult dystopian fiction. In their introduction to *Utopian and Dystopian Writing for Children and Young Adults*, Carrie Hintz and Elaine Ostry locate both utopian and dystopian literature within the long tradition of science fiction and fantasy for children and young adults. A central component of such literature, they suggest, is an awareness of social and political organization, yet the genre remains grounded in romantic conceptions of the child and childhood. According to Hintz and Ostry, "To the Romantics and their heirs, children were innocent and pure, close to nature and God, possessing greater imaginative powers than adults. They were emblems of hope and the future, capable of converting adults to a better way of life" (6). This conception of childhood is "one of the most prevalent cultural myths of the Western world" (6), and it persists into the dystopian literature of the twenty-first century, embodied by such characters as Jonas and even Katniss.

Such romantic notions of children and childhood, however, are only part of what feeds into the development of more recent dystopian writing for children and young adults. Kay Sambell draws the connection between dystopic writing for children and that for adults by making the link to such early dystopian texts as Aldous Huxley's *Brave New World* (1932) and George Orwell's *Nineteen Eighty-Four* (1949). Sambell identifies the didactic nature of such texts for adults, finding a similar function in dystopian writing for children. More specifically, she characterizes dystopic writing for children as didactic literature that is both politically and socially motivated with an emphasis on technology in relation to human suffering. She cites Hughes as one of many children's authors who depict a future world in which injustice and governmental tyranny become the normative experience for children. But for Sambell, the involvement of the child reader is equally important in such texts: "The dystopia foregrounds future suffering, then, to force readers to think carefully about where supposed 'ideals' may really lead, underlining the point that these hugely undesirable societies can and will come about, unless we learn to question the authority of those in power, however benign they may appear to be" (248). Placing dystopic texts for children within a larger literary framework emphasizes the social, political, and technological dominance over the individual's ability to act in response to mechanistic or government control. Hintz and Ostry agree that such a pedagogical element exists within children's literature in general, and utopian and dystopian writing in particular. Children's literature specializes in what they call "cross writing" (7), or writing that serves two audiences simultaneously, both the child and the adult: "Most children's literature, no matter how fanciful, contains lessons to be learned. It is an inherently pedagogical genre, and with cross writing, children learn more as they reread at different times in their lives" (7). Hintz and Ostry thus argue that utopian and dystopian writing for children operates in a subversive way to comment on social issues by means of the clear divide between the child and the adult world.

Apart from its didactic function, fixing young adult dystopias into a wider literary, social, and political framework is enough to link Monica Hughes's novels to this larger tradition. To a greater or lesser degree, political and social change is the impetus in her fiction. In her novel *The Other Place*, black-uniformed members of the World Government Police break down the door of the Fairweather apartment in order to arrest the parents of pre-teen Alison for subversive activities. The family is then relocated to a penal colony on another planet, which Alison does not realize until she follows her younger brother Gordie out of the prison dome and into the seemingly uninhabitable desert. Alison eventually learns that the colony, located on a planet parsecs from Earth, is in fact a social experiment to test whether or not a group of children, left to their own devices, can build a new and better society.

Orwellian in its depiction of the future, *The Other Place* represents a society given over to the tyranny of the World Government. The book's dystopic elements are reminiscent of the control of the Thought Police and Big Brother in Orwell's *Nineteen Eighty-Four*. Although most of the book takes place in the prison dome and then the rustic children's settlement in the forest, the book nonetheless uses the basic trope of political tyranny as the means of moving the plot forward. *The Other Place* lacks any focus on environmental concerns and is perhaps less interesting as a depiction of a future dystopia because of its use of standard dystopic tropes; however, the book eventually sets aside such tropes and underscores childhood as holding the seeds of social change. Such a shift both mitigates the bleakness of the dystopian future and identifies the child and childhood as the foundation for hope and a new utopia.

Similarly, in *Ring-Rise*, *Crystal*, and *Keeper*, the dystopian future is as much a vehicle for a message of hope as a warning about climate change. Each book links the coming of age of the main character to a concern for the environment. In each, the main character is further positioned in opposition to the hegemonic, techno-centred forces that represent an environmental threat, and more importantly, the adolescent girl's body is connected to the devastated landscape.

Both *Ring-Rise* and *Crystal* depict an environmental catastrophe, in the Canadian North and West, respectively. In each case, the tension around coming of age and environmental threat, rather than the more typical trope of political tyranny, causes the protagonist to act. In *Ring-Rise*, Liza is acutely aware of the awkwardness of her body and her inability to fit into the social structure of the science station built into the tundra. Unlike Megan in *Crystal*, Liza is at first less concerned with the immediacy of the environmental threat than she is with her role working to find a way to stop the glacial ice from advancing. In the seemingly utopian society of the science station, families no longer exist and genders are divided according to task: the floor mother takes the place of the family, while work is assigned along traditional gender lines. As Liza notes, men do the exciting work of trying to stop the ice, while women cook, clean, and perform domestic tasks that keep the station running. She voices her complaint to Master Bix, the leader of the science station: "Men get to work on the really important things, like how to get rid of the ring and stop glaciers growing before they cover the whole world." Liza's complaint is specifically related to gender. She points out that, unlike women, men get to leave the science station and go on expeditions: "They're not stuck in the City for year after year the way we are. They can go fishing. At the very least girls ought to be allowed to go fishing!" (19). Such a division of labour suggests a troubling step backward for gender equality and gender relations, but more importantly, Liza's recognition of its unfairness sets her apart from the community.

Ostensibly, the artificially imposed social structure of the science station emerges out of necessity, but Liza's inability to fit within such prescribed gender roles is what forces her out onto the tundra. Master Bix explains to Liza that while the division of labour seems unfair and artificial, the station needed a way to work efficiently in its efforts to combat the ice: "you must blame it on the pressure of the times ... this need for a structured society has made us turn back to old-fashioned ideas. Perhaps we *should* make some changes" (19; ellipsis in original). Master Bix appears unopposed to making changes in terms of prescribed roles; however, Liza continues to feel trapped because she lacks the necessary grades to embark on a scientific career. The gender divide is therefore intolerable for Liza, and she forms a plan of escape. It is noteworthy that while *Ring-Rise* presents an environmental catastrophe as the basis for its dystopic vision, it is Liza's resistance to gender restrictions that causes her to hide aboard one of the convoy of snowmobiles journeying north to the edge of the ice.

Once Liza leaves the city, the central tension of the book shifts to the measures the city is prepared to take to halt the advancing ice and the effect those measures have on the Ekoes, the remnant of the Inuit people who still live in the North. The Ekoes, more than half a myth to the logically minded members of the city, remain close to the earth and live a day-to-day relationship with the land. They retain their myths and stories: the ring is the mouth of Paija, "the dreadful spirit who stumps the world on her one great leg, her hair as black as midwinter, her mouth filled with as many teeth as there are stars in the sky" (45), and who swallows the sun in winter, only to spit it out again in the spring. Liza is rescued by the Ekoes, who greet her as Iriook, a daughter returned from the land of the spirits. She is able to find a home as Iriook among the People as she is never able to find a home as Liza in the city: "Liza looked at her family, dirty, stained, their lips crusted with dried blood. For a second she saw them with her City eyes and was revolted. But only for a second. She was one of them now.... They were her family, and she was worthy of being one of them.... She was Iriook" (48). As Iriook, the girl of the People intended for Namoonie, she is able to recognize the more immediate threat of the black snow that comes from the city. The black snow is the city's solution to global cooling, but it poisons the ground and kills the caribou.

Liza returns to the science station after a winter with the People, but she has to make a choice about where she will live. Her choice emphasizes the binary nature of the text: the scientists and the Ekoes, the city and the land. Choosing to remain with the People and helping to protect them and their way of life from the science station and the black snow positions Liza in relation to the People and the land and in opposition to the city and the scientists. The People are part of the land, and in choosing to remain and become the wife of Namoonie, Liza chooses to align herself both spiritually and sexually with that landscape. *Ring-Rise* ends with the possibility of dialogue between the People and the science station, while the hope for a solution lies with Liza's decision to remain with the People.

As a writer of dystopic fiction, Hughes refuses to settle for the bleakness of a dystopian vision that denies any possibility of social and political agency on the part of the child protagonist. In her essay "The Struggle Between Utopia and Dystopia in Writing for Children and Young Adults," Hughes asserts that she has learned as a writer that "You may lead a child into the darkness, but you must never turn out the light" (156). Such a maxim could be read as a way to limit the depiction of a dystopic vision in a children's book; it also speaks to an awareness of and a regard for the child reader of such a text. Hughes's representation of future worlds is grounded in such a concern. Neither do her books shy away from difficult political, social, or environmental issues. She writes, "My stories come not just from my everyday world, but especially from an awareness of the fragility of our modern society and the increasingly degraded environment. As I test each new idea for its possibilities, I soon become aware of the tension between these two often contradictory maxims. Dystopian worlds are exciting! But the end result must never be nihilism and despair" (156). In not wanting to leave her child reader in the dark, Hughes must necessarily work to resolve this tension. Never does one of Hughes's dystopic novels end, as it does for Winston Smith in *Nineteen Eighty-Four*, with "TWO AND TWO MAKE FIVE" (290).

Alexa Weik Von Mossner reinforces the importance of hope as a necessary part of dystopian texts for children and young adults. In her study of Lloyd's *Carbon Diaries* duology, she writes, "scholars and writers tend to agree that in the case of the young adult dystopian text, one cannot in fact do *without* at least a glimmer of hope. The young reader expects – and needs – stories that are gripping but nevertheless offer at least a promise that a better world will be possible" (70). Such a promise of hope is more of an imperative in climate fiction, where the environmental threat is both recognizable and quantifiable on a daily basis. Realities such as ocean acidification, increasing greenhouse gases, and increasing species extinction had become fully part of the environmental conversation by the time Hughes was writing her dystopian novels in the 1980s. Climate change, on the other hand, operates on a much larger scale, involving the interplay of oceanic and atmospheric systems over longer periods of time. Trexler explains that the very nature of climate change as a global phenomenon interferes with many people's ability to grasp its significance. Some authors, according to Trexler, attempt to localize climate disasters in order to make the crisis more real to a reading public: "Climate change literature would seem to concretize global warming by setting narrative where climate change creates floods, storms, wildfires, and droughts, and people suffer from famine, lawlessness, exile, and war. Creating a connection between the reader and characters immersed in disastrous global warming, readers could immediately experience climate change as a threat to their centers of felt value" (76). The difficulty in localizing climate change in this way means that cli-fi sometimes fails to take into account the planetary nature of the problem. Trexler suggests that the more recent inclusion of cityscapes in climate change fiction has helped broaden the discussion to include urban as well as rural spaces, but the difficulty for writers of climate fiction is the same for readers: the sheer complexity of the issue. Trexler writes, "the first hurdle faced by a novelist is to construct a fictional space where climate change presents itself as an immediate problem" (78), a good example of such immediacy being Lloyd's duology. Weik Von Mossner identifies *The Carbon Diaries* as a climate text that uses an "ecological catastrophe to motivate personal, political, and ecological change" (70), which also serves, in part, as a response to the question Oziewicz and Saguisag raise in their introduction to *The Lion and the Unicorn's* special issue. Climate change fiction for young adults may not necessarily do the legwork of political and environmental activism, but it ensures the issue remains present and relevant for young readers.

In *The Carbon Diaries 2015*, the voice that speaks in response to the climate crisis is that of sixteen-year-old Laura Brown. Laura begins a diary on the eve of a massive reduction in carbon emissions for the United Kingdom. As she counts down to the beginning of the new restrictions, Laura notes in her diary entry of Friday, 2 January, "When I got home, my parents were asleep in front of the TV screen, every single light in the house was blazing and Kim was in the bath with the stereo and her bedroom HD on. I don't know what's gonna happen to this family once rationing really kicks in." In the twenty-first century, the teenage girl has become a forceable presence in both popular culture and young adult fiction, and many dystopian and climate change books for young adults make use of such adolescent girls to speak on behalf of the climate crisis. In her 2004 introduction to *All About the Girl*, Anita Harris writes, "young women suddenly seem to be everywhere. They are the new heroes of popular culture, the dominant faces on college campuses and the spokespeople of public education campaigns" (xvii). In young adult fiction, teenage girls are the characters who resist and rebel against hegemonic systems of power and authority; girls such as Laura Brown and Katniss Everdeen explore their limits in terms of who they are and what they desire. After the publication of *The Hunger Games* in

2008, Katniss quickly became the poster girl for teenage rebellion and teenage desire, particularly following the release of the first film in 2012 starring Jennifer Lawrence. However, the position of these girl characters is not without its difficulties. Harris writes, "The category of 'girl' itself has proved to be slippery and problematic. It has been shaped by norms about race, class and ability that have prioritized the white, middle class and non-disabled, and pathologized and/or criminalized the majority outside this category of privilege" (xx). There is no question that white, adolescent girls have dominated the young adult dystopia and climate change novel, which thus far has framed the young adult response to political tyranny and environmental devastation in terms of white, able-bodied adolescent girldom.

It seems unsurprising, then, that in the 1980s and early 1990s Hughes was using white, girl characters to speak both in response to the climate crisis and as the voice of hope. In *The Crystal Drop*, Megan Dougal takes control of what is left of her family in the face of an environmental disaster: a hole in the ozone layer causing drought and global warming. The disaster in this book, much more than *Ring-Rise*, anticipates climate change fiction of the twenty-first century. *Crystal* is set in the second decade of the twenty-first century. Drought has devastated the prairie landscape of southern Alberta, and the book opens with Megan beside the body of her newly dead mother and baby brother. Megan and Ian, her younger brother, are the only two left on the family farm, and the only people still living in the area that is fast becoming a desert. After burying her mother and the baby in the sand of an irrigation canal, Megan determines that the only hope for her and ten-year-old Ian is to journey cross-country to Lundbreck Falls in the Rocky Mountains, where they can join their uncle. He has become part of a community called Gaia (a Greek mythological name for Mother Earth), in which the inhabitants have a new regard for the care and preservation of the planet.

While *Ring-Rise* sees Liza working to forestall the coming climate crisis, *Crystal* has Megan responding to a crisis already underway. Both books employ what Alice Curry refers to as a "tipping point," in which an "apocalyptic motif of a material brink, edge or threshold underscores the urgency of the novels' call for climate action" (21, 22). Such a call forces the coming of age of characters such as Liza and Megan, but it also doubles as a call for readers of such dystopian texts. Curry writes, "For young readers positioned on the brink of adulthood and soon to be called upon to maintain, or reconstitute, existing ontological frameworks, such a brink positions them on a further threshold – or tipping point – preceding entry into adult systems of political and social responsibility. Unlike child readers, whose potential for effective social responses to climate change is limited, young adults await the imminent transgression that will see them affirm, or refute, the social systems that regulate them" (22–3). Megan's act of transgression at the beginning of *Crystal* is to take her and her brother's lives into her own hands and abandon the family farm for a seemingly hopeless quest to find a new community. The promise of this new community enables Megan to act on behalf of herself and her brother, and it gathers mythic proportions for her, reinforced by the picture of Lundbreck Falls on the calendar that her mother hung above the stove.

For Megan, Lundbreck Falls and the community of Gaia represent hope and the new utopia in the West. Megan and Ian get ready to leave the farm, and Megan has the picture of the falls scored into her memory when she returns to the empty house for Ian's hat: "As she crossed the kitchen on her way out, the calendar above the electric stove caught her eye, the water frozen forever falling. 'Soon,' she whispered. 'We're coming'" (27). Even more than the picture, the crystal drop hanging in the window and burning like fire and water becomes for Megan a talisman of hope: "Magic. Good luck, maybe. Impulsively she pulled it free. The nylon thread was long enough to make a loop, and she hung it around her neck, the sunwarmed crystal below her collar bone" (27). The crystal drop connects Megan to her mother and reinforces the promise of the falls and Gaia, which in turn leads Megan through the wilderness toward the Promised Land in the West.

Megan's journey is a quest in the tradition of the hero's journey, a cultural story Margery Hourihan calls "a paradigm of adolescent development, and specifically of male adolescent development" (58). The hero story, according to Hourihan, defines the male hero in opposition to the natural world in important ways, the conceptual centre consisting "of a set of binary oppositions: the qualities ascribed to the hero on the one hand and to his 'wild' opponents on the other" (24). But Megan's quest for Gaia is not couched in such binaries or oppositions. Megan's desire is for family and community in the face of personal loss and an environmental catastrophe. In this way, Megan's relationship with the devastated landscape is fundamentally different from that of many of the male characters she encounters. Hourihan writes, "The environmental movement, like feminism, represents a profound challenge to some aspects of the myth of the hero, and it is significant that in contemporary texts concerned with a woman's search for self, the experience of deep empathy with the natural world is often an important stage in that process of discovery" (33).

Such a process of discovery can be applied to the "search for self" of adolescent girls such as Liza and Megan. *Crystal* outlines a coming of age for Megan, but it is also as much about family as it is about environmental destruction. An orphan herself, Megan immediately assumes the role of a mother to her newly orphaned brother. She thinks constantly about protecting him, admonishing him regularly about wearing his hat, drinking too much water, or acting impulsively. She and Ian journey across the country in stages, seeing with shock and despair the landscape reduced to sand, hard-packed earth, broken fences, and blowing tumbleweeds. The book begins in fire and ends in water. By the time the siblings encounter their first serious trial at the old Head-Smashed-In Buffalo Jump Museum, Megan looks back to see smoke on the horizon, "Almost about to where the farm was. Where the farm would have been. By the time they got back they probably wouldn't have a roof over their heads any more. The whole land was tinder dry and the house was wood" (73). Megan is driven as much by what lies behind as what lies ahead: a burned-out farm or Lethbridge and foster care as opposed to the promise of Lundbreck Falls and Gaia.

As a quest narrative with an environmental connection, Megan's journey also contains overtones of imperialist ideologies and racial stereotypes. Megan and Ian meet a group of teenage Indigenous boys at what is left of the Head-Smashed-In Buffalo Jump Museum; these boys are not quite villains, but they are the first threat the siblings encounter on their journey. Mike Spotted Eagle, the group's leader, introduces Megan to Napi, the trickster figure of the Blackfoot people and the spirit of the buffalo. Mike gives Megan a new way to understand the hole in the ozone and the destruction of the land, beginning with the death of the buffalo: "Tearing up the land for wheat so nothing'd hold it down when the wind come. Draining the good swamp for more land. Moving rivers. Damming them. Chemicals poisoning air and earth and water. Poisoning Napi's good world. Yeah, white man's driven Napi out of his world. Now see what's left. Nothing" (59). Mike sees the death of his world in terms of white domination, white imperialist power, and white technology in a masculine context. Much like the Ekoes in *Ring-Rise,* Mike and his friends are stereotypical in their representation; nonetheless, they have a destabilizing effect on Megan and her quest. Mike shifts the responsibility for the environmental devastation onto settler culture and settler and imperialist ideologies, which, for Megan, works to reframe her understanding of the disaster. Clare Echterling, in her research on so-called classic children's literature, argues that reframing children's texts in terms of a post-colonial, eco-critical lens would mean "refusing to read such texts as apolitical, ahistorical, or ideologically innocent, and instead foregrounding their engagement with, indebtedness to, and perpetuation of attitudes toward nonhuman nature and the environment that are deeply entwined with racism, sexism, speciesism, and imperialism" (95). While racial stereotypes are present in both *Ring-Rise* and *Crystal*, Liza and Megan understand, to varying degrees, the connection between the climate disasters and imperialist, racist attitudes; however, it takes encounters with First Peoples in order for them to make the connection.

The survivalist groups that Megan and Ian encounter after they leave the museum constitute an element of this white, imperialized power that still exists in pockets over the landscape, groups of hoarders who want to control the remaining food and water. Mitch and Sadie, who save Megan after she is shot, see the survivalists for what they are. Sadie comments, "I call them 'firstists.' Meaning they don't believe in the good Lord, only in being first, grabbing the food and water and letting the rest of the world go hang. Badly raised as children, I reckon" (145). Sadie sees what amounts to masculinity gone wrong as the result of bad parenting, and by extension, bad mothering. Sadie is the voice of conservative, Christian values in the text, and while her objection to the survivalists' methods speaks to a Christian ideology based on traditional gender stereotypes, it nonetheless positions her in opposition to the techno-based hegemony that caused the environmental catastrophe.

If Christian in sentiment and ideology, Sadie's comments at the same time reposition the survivalists in relation to eco-feminist values and ideals. Iris Ralph identifies such ideals as "cooperation, negotiation, compromise, nonhierarchical relations, empathy, sharing of space and place, listening, dialogue, and actively endeavoring to mitigate, avoidance [sic], and reduce suffering and violent confrontation" (136). As an approach, "Feminist ecocriticism provides a lens for understanding environmental degradation as a consequence of the patriarchal domination of nature and the attendant and inextricable oppression of women" (Murphy 43). In young adult dystopian fiction, this oppression extends to girls and children. In *Crystal*, these eco-feminist values stand in direct opposition to the survivalists, who are the masculinized remnants of the hegemonic power structures that brought about the climate crisis in the first place.

Mitch and Sadie are a normative, Christian family, but their ability to maintain their farm in the midst of the book's environment crisis is questionable. Megan recognizes that the couple can barely eke out a living on their tiny farm, further suggesting that such a lifestyle will necessarily fail. Survival in this new world relies on eco-feminist ideologies embodied in the goal of Megan's quest, the community of Gaia, which for her constitutes a new utopia. If somewhat idealized, this community has a firmer grounding in eco-feminist ideals than it does Christian ideologies.

Like Liza in *Ring-Rise*, Megan ends her journey in a significantly different place than where she began. Both protagonists are facing womanhood, and both see that womanhood in part in terms of a relationship with a man. Given that men in these texts tend to represent the larger hegemonic structures of male dominance and male authority, any ascension of female power and female selfhood would seem to be undercut by such a coupling. Nonetheless, both Namoonie and Gideon are part of an earth-centred vision of the future, one that aligns with eco-feminist ideals. In Gaia, Megan finds, if not a new utopia, at least a promise for the future and a community in which the land will be cared for and respected.

Both *Ring-Rise* and *Crystal* end with the greater possibility of female power and female autonomy,[1] but such autonomy manifests much more fully in Hughes's earlier novel *The Keeper of the Isis Light*. For the protagonist, Olwen, living alone on the planet Isis with only her robot guardian and the gigantic, dog-like creature called Hobbit for company is something of a utopia. With the arrival of the settler ship from Earth, Olwen's world is disrupted and the valley below the mesa despoiled. From the point of view of the colonists, Isis is a new world, free from the overcrowding and pollutants of Earth. In this way, Isis is a utopia from either perspective – Olwen's and the colonists' – which rapidly begins to change once Olwen begins to interact with the people from the ship.

Olwen's narrative is a coming-of-age story, but it centres on her sexual awakening more than the stories of both Liza and Megan. According to Sara K. Day, "By removing adolescent women to potential dystopian futures, authors complicate the question of sexual awakening as empowerment, as their novels both reflect contemporary Western culture and anticipate futures in which young women's bodies continue to be treated as contested and contestable spaces" (79). Olwen's empowerment literally lies with her body. She has been genetically augmented, allowing her to climb to the heights of Isis, unlike the settlers who are confined to the oxygen-rich valleys. Her robot guardian has radically altered Olwen's physical appearance to protect her from the dangers of the planet, including increasing her bone density and bone structure, changing the pigment of her skin, and giving her greater strength, which in turn changes her relationship with the settlers. In order to hide the changes he has made to Olwen's body, Guardian manufactures a protective suit, complete with an opaque mask that conceals Olwen's face from the newcomers. According to Day, in many dystopian texts "the female protagonist's appearance has been modified or controlled in very literal ways that may not be immediately perceived as harmful" (79). In fashioning her a mask and environmental suit, Olwen's robot guardian is trying to protect her, and Olwen herself is driven by her desire to connect with the newcomers. But Olwen, even more than Megan or Liza, is interested in the opposite gender, in finding someone to talk to and spend time with, and it is this desire that leads to the revelation of her appearance and her decision to separate herself from the settlers.

Mark London is the young man from the ship with whom Olwen falls in love, and he accompanies her to the top of the mesa, keenly aware of her fearlessness as she nimbly climbs ahead of him. Mark begins to understand the impact of the settlers on the planet only after seeing it from the top of the mesa: "it was a shock to see the great dish antenna of the Lighthouse, and beyond it, dizzying depths below, the squat shape of Pegasus Two, standing alien, in an ugly circle of blackened stubble" (48). Only then is Mark able to understand Olwen's position as the former sole inhabitant of the planet: "Around the bridge across Lost Creek he could see from up here the blackish-red stains of mud where the ground had been chewed up by the tracks of the crawlers. It looked as if Isis itself had been wounded and had bled" (48). Mark is able to recognize Olwen's unique position as the keeper of the light and her claim to the planet. He sees the despoilment of Isis as she sees it, but this recognition does not extend to her physical appearance.

The revelation of Olwen's appearance causes a permanent divide between Olwen and the colonists and reinforces their perception of her as other, as monster, as alien. Mark climbs the mesa a second time, and when he arrives at the top, he sees Olwen without her protective suit. The shock of her appearance causes him to step backward over the edge of the cliff. Olwen is able to save Mark's life, but the fact of her physical difference permanently separates her from the settlers.

The interview with Captain Tryon near the end of the novel most acutely reinforces the changes Guardian has wrought in Olwen's appearance, for the Captain has difficulty thinking of Olwen as human. He thinks of her in two ways: as both the keeper of the light on Isis and the daughter of his old friend, Gareth Pendennis. As the keeper of the light, Tryon sees Olwen as alien, something both beautiful and exotic: "There was a dignified symmetry in the wide nose and heavy eyebrows that balanced the weight of glorious red hair cascading down her shoulders. The goldish green of her skin was exotic, and even the nictating membrane, which he saw slide across her eyes in a sudden light reflection, had a strange kind of fascination" (95). However, seeing Olwen as the daughter of his old friend, Tryon cannot repress his revulsion: "she was disgusting. Words like Neanderthal and reptilian sprang to his mind. He thought of Dr Jekyll and Mr Hyde; and the horrifying monster movies of his childhood crowded unbidden into his mind" (95–6). For Captain Tryon, Olwen is the other, both alien and monstrous. He fails to recognize that Olwen's body is perfectly suited to living on Isis. She has become a hybrid, born of human parents but modified to become adapted to the planet, the only one of her kind. Olwen's genetically modified appearance moves the text from the dystopic and the developmental to the posthuman. According to Elaine Ostry, a common trope within young adult fiction is the search for identity, which for a character like Olwen is problematized by the understanding she is no longer entirely human: "In the posthuman young adult science fiction novel, this search takes a particularly sharp turn when the protagonist realizes that he or she is not conventionally human, that many people would consider him or her to be an aberration. The revelation is often the result of much searching: the protagonist acts as a detective to uncover the mystery of his or her identity" (224). Olwen confronts her humanness because of the response of the settlers to her genetically modified appearance, and unlike Lisa and Megan, Olwen's story ends in separation and withdrawal rather than family and community.

Olwen's story is also an adolescent or developmental narrative, and the damage to the planet and her rejection by the colonists creates the element of dystopia that links this text to both *Ring-Rise* and *Crystal*. As Carrie Hintz suggests, the developmental narrative is one wherein protagonists often experience shame and embarrassment as part of their attempt to understand and fit into a larger social and political arena: "The adolescent embarrassment protagonists experience in these young adult novels adds to the dramatic tension and makes their political actions seem uniquely heroic. These adolescents find themselves in harsh environments, or in situations, where they must make difficult – even agonizing – choices" (256). As Hintz states, shame is grounded in the body, and the adolescent's experience of shame becomes intensely intimate. The tension, therefore, is between the intimate space of the emergent adult body and the social arena, which for Olwen is her relationship with Mark and the settlers, and any rejection within that arena becomes a rejection not only of the adolescent but also of the adolescent body. Such a rejection is more poignant for Olwen than it is for Liza and Megan, but all three adolescent girls experience it to one degree or another. All three share an intimate connection to the land, but Olwen's connection manifests as a literal early warning system that tells her of the approaching storms on Isis. She describes it as "a peculiar kind of restlessness, like an itching underneath my skin" (*Keeper* 112). Olwen chooses to leave the mesa and make a new home in the north of Isis, but she also chooses to use her unique connection to the planet to warn the settlers of any approaching storms.

The connection between the adolescent, female body and the environment is Monica Hughes's particular representation of a dystopic future in these three texts. Liza, Megan, and Olwen experience a bond with the land, and all three see themselves and their sense of identity in relation to that land. Questions of identity and sexual awakening are fundamental to the adolescent developmental narrative, but such questions become amplified within dystopic futures wherein girls and girls' bodies are the central focus. *Ring-Rise Ring-Set, The Crystal Drop*, and *The Keeper of the Isis Light* are all dystopic, and the environment plays a primary role in the representation of their future dystopias. More specifically, these texts yolk the girl body to a climate crisis and the destruction of the landscape, which in turn positions these adolescent girls in opposition to the hegemonic power structures that cause the climate crisis and despoilment of the land. Hughes was writing these books as science fiction in the 1980s and early 1990s, but they represent narratives in which young adults respond variously to climate crises. In this way, young adult books have been adding to the narrative of environmental damage for decades. That narrative has now encompassed the climate crisis and reached a critical point in the 2020s. For political and environmental activists like Thunberg, the climate crisis requires both action and a fundamental change to how we interact with the planet. She writes, "It is my genuine belief that the only way we will be able to avoid the worst consequences of this emerging existential crisis is if we create a critical mass of people who demand the changes required. For that to happen, we need to rapidly spread awareness, because the general public still lacks much of the basic knowledge that is necessary to understand the dire situation we are in" (2–3). Young adult fiction has been doing its part to spread that awareness, and authors such as Hughes have been and continue to be part of the conversation that insists on changing the seemingly unavoidable dystopic future we are creating for ourselves into something more equitable and more sustainable.

NOTE

1 See Alena Cicholewski's chapter in this volume for a further discussion of female identity formation in later Canadian YA novels and series, and for a critique of young female protagonists and their ability to resist patriarchal social structures.

WORKS CITED

Collins, Suzanne. *The Hunger Games*. E-book edition, Scholastic Press, 2008. Kindle.

Crace, John. "Global Warning: The Rise of 'Cli-fi.'" *The Guardian* online, 31 May 2013.

Curry, Alice. *Environmental Crisis in Young Adult Fiction: A Poetics of Earth*. Palgrave Macmillan, 2013.

Day, Sara K. "Docile Bodies, Dangerous Bodies: Sexual Awakening and Social Resistance in Young Adult Dystopian Fiction." *Female Rebellion in Young Adult Dystopian Fiction*, edited by Sara K. Day, Miranda A. Green-Barteet, and Amy L. Montz, Ashgate, 2014, pp. 75–93.

Echterling, Clare. "Postcolonial Ecocriticism, Classic Children's Literature, and the Imperial-Environmental Imagination in *The Chronicles of Narnia*." *The Journal of the Midwest Modern Language Association*, vol. 49, no. 1, 2016, pp. 93–117.

Harris, Anita. *All About the Girl: Culture, Power, and Identity*. Routledge, 2004.

Hintz, Carrie, and Elaine Ostry. "Introduction." *Utopian and Dystopian Writing for Children and Young Adults*, edited by Carrie Hintz and Elaine Ostry, Routledge, 2003.

Hintz, Carrie. "Monica Hughes, Lois Lowry, and Young Adult Dystopias." *The Lion and the Unicorn: A Critical Journal of Children's Literature*, vol. 26, no. 2, 2002, pp. 254–64.

Hourihan, Margery. *Deconstructing the Hero: Literary Theory and Children's Literature*. Routledge, 1997.

Hughes, Monica. *The Crystal Drop*. Harper Trophy, 1992.

– *The Keeper of the Isis Light*. Atheneum, 1981.

– *The Other Place*. Harper Collins, 1999.

– *Ring-Rise Ring-Set*. Magnet, 1982.

– "The Struggle between Utopia and Dystopia in Writing for Children and Young Adults." *Utopian and Dystopian Writing for Children and Young Adults*, edited by Carrie Hintz and Elaine Ostry, Routledge, 2003, pp. 155–61.

Huxley, Aldous. *Brave New World*. Digital edition, HarperCollins Publishers, 2021.

Lloyd, Saci. *The Carbon Diaries 2015*. 2008. E-book edition, Hodder, 2011. Kindle.

– *The Carbon Diaries 2017*. 2010. E-book edition, Hodder, 2011. Kindle.

Lowry, Lois. *The Giver*. E-book edition, Houghton Mifflin, 1993. Kindle.

Murphy, Patrick D. "Introduction." *Dystopias and Utopias on Earth and Beyond: Feminist Ecocriticism of Science Fiction*, edited by Douglas A. Vakoch, e-book edition, Routledge, 2021, pp. 41–3. Kindle.

Orwell, George. *Nineteen Eighty-Four*. 1949. Penguin Books, 2008.

Ostry, Elaine. "'Is He Still Human? Are You?': Young Adult Science Fiction in the Posthuman Age." *The Lion and the Unicorn: A Critical Journal of Children's Literature*, vol. 28, no. 2, 2004, pp. 222–46.

Oziewicz, Marek, and Lara Saguisag. "Introduction." *The Lion and the Unicorn: A Critical Journal of Children's Literature*, vol. 45, no. 2, 2021, pp. v–xiv.

Ralph, Iris. "Ecofeminist Climate Fiction: Merlinda Bobis's *Locust Girl*." *Dystopias and Utopias on Earth and Beyond: Feminist Ecocriticism of Science Fiction*, edited by Douglas A. Vakoch, e-book edition, Routledge, 2021, pp. 128–46. Kindle.

Sambell, Kay. "Carnivalizing the Future: A New Approach to Theorizing Childhood and Adulthood in Science Fiction for Young Readers." *The Lion and the Unicorn: A Critical Journal of Children's Literature*, vol. 28, no. 2, 2004, pp. 247–67.

Simmons, Kristen. *Pacifica*. E-book edition, A Tor Teen Book, Tom Doherty Associates, 2018. Kindle.

Thunberg, Greta, compiler. *The Climate Book: The Facts and the Solutions*. Penguin, 2023.

Trexler, Adam. *Anthropocene Fictions: The Novel in a Time of Climate Change*. U of Virginia P, 2015.

Weik Von Mossner, Alexa. "Hope in Dark Times: Climate Change and the World Risk Society in Saci Lloyd's *The Carbon Diaries 2015* and *2017*." *Contemporary Dystopian Fiction for Young Adults: Brave New Teenagers*, edited by Balaka Basu, Katherine R. Broad, and Carrie Hintz, Routledge, 2013, pp. 69–84.

Interlude

Othering ad Infinitum: A Critical-Creative Examination of the Secular and Spiritual in Nalo Hopkinson's *Brown Girl in the Ring*

SHEHERYAR B. SHEIKH

A remarkable thing about Nalo Hopkinson's *Brown Girl in the Ring* is how much it has been embraced by the science fiction–critical community. The novel boasts little in the way of scientific leaps in progress, arguably none sustained throughout the narrative in such a way that any would constitute a traditional SF *novum* (in Darko Suvin's term), and the story is more spiritually driven than it is technologically fortified.[1] While opinions of SF readers are divided on the genre or mode into which the novel fits, it has been nominated for the SF-specific Philip K. Dick Award as well as the SF-or-fantasy James Tiptree Jr. Award, and it has won multiple other awards.

Although Hopkinson is politically and socially aware of her Caribbean-Canadian roots within Toronto's mosaic, her debut novel's central concern does not seem to be the construction of meaning through an approach to issues of racism. Rather, the novel is primarily concerned with the protagonist Ti-Jeanne's coming of age through the process of understanding her spiritual gifts and balancing those with her secular life as a minority citizen of a future derelict Toronto. However, *Brown Girl*'s nuanced layers of commentary on the characters' habitation of place in relation to people around them, the multiple contradictory facets – and faces – of each character, and the decay of Toronto at the hands of the elite class and a Caribbean-Canadian male figure enable the novel's narrator to make a strong argument for spiritual struggle against the crude power politics of neocolonization in a dystopian Toronto.

The novel reads like a *bildungsroman* that is concerned with Ti-Jeanne's coming of age through the acceptance of her spiritual gifts and her role as a mother. She starts out as a single mother of a baby whose father, Tony, she is attracted to but does not trust because of the gangland company he keeps and his drug habit. Ti-Jeanne lives with her grandmother, Gros-Jeanne, whom she considers an eccentric healer with spiritual or magical skills. One of Ti-Jeanne's worries is centred on visions in which she can "see with more than sight" (9), especially about the ways in which people around her will die (16–17). When Ti-Jeanne's paramour is ordered by downtown Toronto's de facto ruler, Rudy, to demobilize Gros-Jeanne so that she can be a donor for a heart transplant, Ti-Jeanne is forced to confront and accept her ability to call on her spiritual guides in order to defeat Rudy and to rid Toronto of his tyranny.

The background storyline and idea of the heart transplant, which begins the novel and aids plot progression until the end, has been termed by Laura Salvini, in "A Heart of Kindness: Nalo Hopkinson's *Brown Girl in the Ring*," as the Suvinian novum, because it gives the novel the scientific plausibility of a novum, literally "new thing," that SF writing requires (183). But the idea of the heart transplant is not the novel's central technological innovation and plays no part in Ti-Jeanne's development at any point. She is neither aware of this development, nor preoccupied with it. Instead, what comes to the fore again and again in the novel is the spiritual pull of her visions. As threat from Rudy escalates, Ti-Jeanne is forced to confront, learn, and then enact and improvise on the processes of calling her spiritual helpers and guides. Each time Ti-Jeanne or Gros-Jeanne perform the ritual, they follow a certain set of actions: call for the spirit guide's help, offer blood and something sweet, and light a cigar or cigarette (91–2, 195). This process-based invocation, which contains spiritual if not scientific logic and the abilities it engenders – such as granting Ti-Jeanne invisibility (105, 197) – is the real novum of the novel, even though it may be an *"[i]nvalidated novum"* because its "ontology is unclear" (Csicsery-Ronay 53). It certainly does not fulfil a central criterion for a novum listed in Istvan Csicsery-Ronay's *The Seven Beauties of Science Fiction* in that it is not "rationally explicable," but it does fulfil the other pivotal criterion of "elicit[ing] a wholesale change in the perception of reality" (6) for the characters in the novel.

Establishing access to the spiritual realm as *Brown Girl*'s novum opens up another dimension to the text. Not only does it allow the creation of another spiritual world within the novel, but also it enables a closer examination of each character's multiple coexistent, often contradictory selves. They are not others in the sense of separate aspects of singular entities. Often, they are separate beings from disparate dimensions occupying the same space and time. Also, an even more subtle aspect of the novel is that *othering,* "the political and sociocultural method of building a hierarchical powerplay between characters"

(Kim 33),[2] works on multiple levels between all the characters, even within the secular dimension. This nuanced layer is uncovered once access to the novum is centralized in the shift between two separate systems of rationality: from scientific logic to spiritual reasoning.

A critical examination of the novel's othering would yield enough wealth to constitute an essay, but it would not be able to demonstrate the subtleties as they exist across the spectrum of minority-based characters in *Brown Girl*. This is where the critical-creative hybrid essay comes in. The creative component of this essay, "Brown Boy under the Cape," is a Sufi short story set within the universe of *Brown Girl*. The story intersects tangentially with the plot of the novel and is used as a tool to understand and demonstrate the idea of a spiritual novum – which is rare in SF, because often the novum is technological – and to create more othering to corroborate how it works in the novel. The short story is an exploration, through a Sufi, Pakistani-Canadian minority member's experience, of the subaltern experience of the same landscape, in the same time frame, and it aids *Brown Girl*'s challenge to the status quo secular, white, Canadian version of SF by adding another set of tiles to the mosaic.

"Brown Boy under the Cape," which is incorporated within this essay, is followed by a commentary on the methods used to write it. The main character, Zaahid, is a Pakistani-Canadian Sufi apprentice at the culmination point of receiving his first enlightenment. He is conflicted, much like Ti-Jeanne, by the pull of spiritual and secular beliefs in seemingly opposing directions. Similarities between the story and the novel include ethnically charged usage of language, conflicting sense of identity, the protagonist coming of age, and othering ad infinitum. In all other aspects as well, especially in the nuances of political and sociocultural othering, the attempt is to mirror the style and commentary generated by the narrator in *Brown Girl*.

Othering in *Brown Girl*

There is considerable difference between hybrid forms and "other" forms contained within a single entity. Otherness exists in contrast to *hybridity*, because the latter focuses on the compatibility between, and even fusion of, two or more aspects of being. The *Oxford English Dictionary* defines a hybrid as "the offspring of two animals or plants of different species" or, in common usage, as a composite made from combining two different elements ("Hybrid"). Homi Bhabha revises the scientific concept further to meaningfully articulate what he calls "Third Space," which is the hybridity formed from the composite of two or more cultures combining via "translation and negotiation," especially through the process of colonization and then decolonization (38).

Hybridity in Hopkinson's novel is most evident in the grandmother, Gros-Jeanne, who is both a traditional "healer, [and] a seer woman" (36). Critics such as Elena Bustamante recognize that "dualities and fragmentations appear throughout the novel," but her judgement that these are signs of "schizophrenia" (14) seems short-sighted. Bustamante fails to descry the subtle othering that Ti-Jeanne projects onto her grandmother's spiritual and religious sides by dismissing them, at least in the beginning of the novel, as obeah (or black magic), and her natural treatments through herbs as mostly ineffective "bush doctor remedies," which are sometimes even harmful (*Brown Girl* 36).

Othering can be distinguished from additional conceptualizations of multiple entities. Uriah Kim, in "The Politics of Othering in North America and in the Book of Judges," writes that "the rhetoric of othering is part of a colonial discourse in which the colonizer's self-identity is confirmed by a construction of the other as the inferior opposite, thereby maintaining the colonizer's superiority as natural and scientific" (33). While at first Ti-Jeanne others her grandmother's spiritual and natural healing sides by undermining them, by the end of the novel, it is the scientific and secular side of her reality that Ti-Jeanne finds to be impotent. In effect, the narrator advocates a socio-political deflation of the othering mechanism by which colonial supremacy is achieved through establishing the scientific as natural and as superior.

In *Brown Girl*, the characters who do not have spiritual gifts are helpless compared to those who hold those gifts. For example, Rudy's henchmen, Jay, Crapaud, and Crack Monkey, as well as Ti-Jeanne's beau, Tony, are unable to reconcile the existence of a spiritual world that has connection to their own. Crapaud mocks Rudy's magic by saying, "duppy bowl, my ass" (113), and Rudy calls the magic "freaky" (110) and is unable to distinguish between positive and negative spiritual acts (118). These instances of what can be termed "secularly locked" characters (indicating how these characters are unable to access any other realm of power with which to influence their sociocultural or political position in society) are important, because by rejecting and even mocking the spiritual realm and its powers of magic, they are in fact perpetuating the colonial othering of a non-Eurocentric set of beliefs and actions.

This is the subtle genius of Hopkinson's novel. The only overt instance of othering (except the spiritual-secular one) appears to be racially motivated, but is quickly diffused as unimportant: when street kids chant the N-word at Ti-Jeanne, she is more concerned about the kids "patting her body, looking for things to steal" than she is about the racist term (31). The power destabilization in this novel is not the development of a means to tackle the politics of the N-word. The project is much larger in scope, and one that destabilizes the narrative structures of colonial othering at its roots. In *Brown Girl*, the narrator legitimizes the spiritual dimension and gives it credence as the counter-colonizing and othering lens through which non-spiritual entities are viewed.

The title of this essay, "Othering ad Infinitum," takes its cue from one specific moment in the text, when Gros-Jeanne others a part of herself. The moment starts with Gros-Jeanne "switching to the more standard English she used when she was speaking to non-Caribbean people" (63). One of the street children, Susie, is injured, and she is hesitant to receive treatment from Gros-Jeanne because she thinks the old woman will "eat" her (63). As Gros-Jeanne attempts to reassure the girl that her culinary inclinations do not include cannibalism, she downplays her ability to inflict harm by showing how the powers are tempered by her intentions: "[T]his is my granddaughter. I didn't eat her.... So that proves I don't eat children" (63). Later in the novel, her former husband is seen as the killer and consumer of human life through his duppy bowl. As that passage indicates, the children are legitimately afraid of Gros-Jeanne's power, and their fears are assuaged only by her statement of her intentions about how to use those powers. While convincing the children, she not only changes the way she speaks but also calls herself "Mistress Hunter," rather than Mami Gros-Jeanne (63), thereby othering an essential part of her identity as Ti-Jeanne, her granddaughter, knows her. In addition, she assures the children that she will perform only conventional healing to the injured member of their party (64). If she is othered by the children and also others a major part of herself, this cycle begins to take on, analogically, something akin to a Droste Effect ("50 Stunning Examples"), an infinite reflection between two facing mirrors in which the original image is lost. The colonizing and counter-colonizing powerplay is put into a mosaic of regressive reflections – an ad infinitum othering – and an apparently neutral state is reached in which the children trust Gros-Jeanne to heal Susie, and they also do not steal anything in her house as payment for the healing (67).

The entirely spiritual entities in *Brown Girl* appear to be in harmony with their multiple selves. As Monica Coleman points out in "Serving the Spirits: The Pan-Caribbean African-Derived Religion in Nalo Hopkinson's *Brown Girl in the Ring*," Eshu "is said to have over 200 manifestations representing the many dimensions of his character" (7).

The process of "combination" or hybridization of disparate selves in the novel happens only among the novel's spiritually inclined human characters. Mami Gros-Jeanne is seen as a hybrid from the beginning (though Ti-Jeanne severely others her spiritual and natural healing aspects), but her spiritually realized self goes through another kind of transformation. At the end of the novel, when Gros-Jeanne's heart is transplanted into Premier Uttley's body, a visceral form of othering occurs. Though Bustamante argues that "[both] Uttley and Gros-Jeanne will benefit from this new hybridized self" (25), the text quite clearly states that Gros-Jeanne's "heart [is] rejecting" Uttley's body and taking over its functions (*Brown Girl* 236). When the body of the premier regains consciousness, the text implies that her decisions and actions will be Gros-Jeanne's.

Ti-Jeanne goes through several stages of othering and being othered before she embraces her multiple identities, including as spiritually gifted Caribbean-Canadian, by improvising the spirit-calling ritual and by calling the spirits to defeat Rudy (*Brown Girl* 195, 221). As Jessica McDonald argues in her "allegorical reading," "the novel's setting [is] a concretization of the fraught politics of genre" (142). McDonald acknowledges that the sci-fi elements in the novel are created out of spiritual and magic dimensions of Ti-Jeanne's access to power, and the most significant outcome of her acknowledgement is the allowance not only for Ti-Jeanne's alternate epistemologies to coexist within the sci-fi universe, but also for Ti-Jeanne to have complete agency over which one she wants to adopt at any given point.

Besides its characters' interplay of othering aspects of spirituality and conventional secular wisdom, the novel itself others the secular, predominantly white SF concept of the novum, even though most critics miss this by trying to find a hybrid space for the novel within the SF realm. McDonald notes that hybridity is denied often to non-white subjects, and they are relegated to (negative) singularities as "black bodies, black epistemologies ... often only allowed to exist under the cover of alienness in science fiction" (141). In her interview with Hopkinson, Dianne Glave calls Hopkinson's novel a "hybrid space of genre-identified science fiction, fantasy and horror, as well as being part of black literary creation" (148–9). But McDonald and Glave fall short of recognizing that the novel asserts one type of vision as dominant over, and even ethically superior to, the other. By ignoring the powerplay between the visions that the novel offers, these critics miss that by putting Gros-Jeanne's heart in charge of Premier Uttley's body and mind (and thereby in charge of Premier Uttley's decisions), the novel others the previously othering elite, and implies that the new

Gros-Jeanne-Uttley entity will come up with a more ethical, grassroots approach to rejuvenating Toronto (*Brown Girl* 240).

A Creative Exploration

An essential question to ask of any critical essay that deviates from standard format is, "why this form?" How does a creative exploration of *Brown Girl in the Ring* enable depth and further insight into the arguments made in the critical component of this essay?

A limited portion of the thesis can be argued without a demonstration that creative explorations allow: the plethora of examples of othering in the novel's universe saturate and support this essay's idea and thesis. But incorporating a creative component does one thing more sci-fi than any analysis can: it boldly goes where no one has gone before in the universe of *Brown Girl in the Ring*. This is not to undermine the possible existence of fan fiction, but it is to assert that no creative-critical hybrid examination of the novel has been made in this exact manner.

The best reason for a critical-creative hybrid has perhaps been provided by the critic Bustamante, who says that "when the ideology of cultural and racial confrontation is challenged, speculative fiction becomes particularly useful in the creation of what Homi Bhabha refers to as counter-narratives" (12). The "ideology of cultural and racial confrontation" has indeed been challenged, and very seriously so, by those Cory Doctorow calls the "Sad Puppies" who "hijacked" the SF-centred Hugo Award for 2015 ("On the Hugo Award"). As Doctorow points out, these people, feeling threatened by what they perceive as "'social justice warriors' bent on excluding white men," tried to rig SF award ballots to feature only those texts that worked with "traditional" SF tropes. As it is more a political movement by this group than a literary one, it seems that, to counter the hegemonic role played by conservative SF consumers, *Brown Girl*'s project of othering those who other minorities must be continued (at least for the present).

Given that this hybrid paper is an examination of powerplay between epistemologies, care has been taken that neither component, creative nor critical, undermines the other, even as they combine to assert the same thesis. The story appears below, starting with the title "Brown Boy under the Cape" and ending with the word *Fin*.

Brown Boy under the Cape

Zaahid opened the tap and started washing his hands and face and arms and feet in the correct order. He didn't feel pure, and he felt unsure about the water helping. But he made the prayers like his Sufi Sheikh had taught him. *Let go of your lower self*, said Zaahid's Sheikh in his head. *Let the water rub out your impure thoughts and drown your ego.* He finished washing his feet and came out of his washroom to stand on the black woollen shawl folded up on the floor, facing Mecca, the holy city. Zaahid, living in the run-down apartment with his brother on Yonge Street in Toronto, had never been to Mecca, or to his father's home in Pakistan, and would likely never leave Canada, now that airplanes had stopped landing in Toronto. He had no passport. And yet, this urge to travel and to know the world had made him itch since he could remember.

Now he closed his eyes and tried to imagine himself as a purified being without any sense of ego. *God, I am here*, he said in his head, and then began reciting the Arabic words of the evening prayer.

Before he knew it, he had finished the prayers and was sitting on the shawl. It was time to complete the ritual and to unfold the shawl. But Zaahid sat there, full of doubt about his life as a Sufi apprentice and his other life as a video-gaming teenager without a college in his future, because colleges had shut down so long ago.

He felt empty of belief, devoid of certainty, and yet without any questions. He felt at rest between two worlds. The first was the world of his brother and their friends and their concerns about the next round of hand-held gaming on the PS VITA they had salvaged from the ransacking of Sony's Toronto headquarters three years ago. Often, Zaahid would start criticizing them, and the criticism would turn into a rant on everything that Zaahid felt was wrong with his friends, with Toronto, the world, and existence in general. Sometimes they would argue back, but mostly they just went on with their lives and gave him the silent treatment until he came back to his senses and played his own round of *Tekken* XX on the VITA.

The other world was his religious one. In the company of his Sheikh, and while performing his meditations and prayers, Zaahid never felt a moment was being wasted. He felt he was doing the right thing when praying or being obedient to the God he could not see, but whose presence he felt like a soft layer between him and the harsh world of the streets outside. The problem with his Sufi life was that it did not spill over into the world outside. Toronto – the world – was living according to its own rhythms, and it seemed impossible to reconcile the soft melody of Sufism with the thrum outside. In the outside world, it was so difficult to believe in his Sheikh's words.

He unfolded the shawl, and it became a long, flat chaadur of wool. Taking it by the edges, Zaahid wrapped the shawl around his shoulders and kept sitting on the floor. This part usually helped. The prayed-upon prayer mat that became shawl and woollen cape had a softness and coolness. It gave Zaahid the feeling that he was protected from the multiple layers of doubt in his head. The Sheikh had told him that the feeling of putting on the woollen shawl was a different one for every adept. *To each, his own required feeling comes*, were the Sheikh's words. The sentence seemed awkward, and Zaahid tried to correct it in his head, but he could not form one that he liked more than the awkward one. It was easy to remember, too.

If he could have articulated what he felt after pulling on the cape, Zaahid would have said that his ego was no longer troubled by being split between two worlds, and having to choose between them. The light black cloth kept out the worries endemic to sensitive teenagers like himself. If he could muster enough courage to abandon all his fears and state plainly the effect of the prayer-mat-woollen-cape, Zaahid would say that it was a device of both magic and logic – that it enabled him to see the exact significance of every moment of his life, and thereby achieve a state of absolute equanimity.

It was with this crystal clarity that he envisioned himself getting up, walking the ten storeys to the ground floor, and going outside, still wearing the woollen cape around his shoulders. It would be the first time Zaahid would leave his apartment with the cloth since his Sheikh had given it to him a year ago. It had not occurred to Zaahid to ever wear it in public. It had always been an unfathomable notion to be seen with it hanging around his shoulders.

But it was not a bizarre thing to think tonight. It seemed strangely appropriate. So, he did it. He walked down the stairs wearing the cape.

It was a busy evening turning into a busier night. The Strip of Yonge Street was thronged with people. Most of them were waiting in lines to get into clubs of all sorts. People of all ages, nearly devoid of clothing, standing around within sweating distance of each other. The scriptural thought entered Zaahid's head: *Judge not lest ye be judged*. He was fanatically overdressed for the Strip. On any other day, in any other garb, he would have been petrified and would have sweated profusely. But tonight, with the cape held around him, he breezed through the crowds and they seemed to take little account of him.

Turns to dust, your ego, in the face of true reality. It was his Sheikh's voice in Zaahid's head, but these were words his Sheikh had never spoken. He thought about it while making his way through the crowd, caped like a foolish superhero. The words that formed in his head didn't seem to come together how he would think in everyday speech. Things seemed loftier, more rhythmic in a religious sense. *Be your true self, Zaahid. Be free of dualities. You are one, like everything is one.* His Sheikh's voice again, loud and resonant in Zaahid's head. He flowed through the crowd in the direction that seemed to him the only right direction in the universe for him to flow. His brother and friends were a few blocks away in the Silver Arcade, and Zaahid would walk up to them in his Sufi garb for the first time in his life. *I am at peace with that because I am one with everything*, he thought.

He kept walking, and the people made way for him, and the garish lights and the bars and the dissonant music coming out of the clubs did not bother him. It seemed like the soundtrack to a multireal world. Who knew how many other Sufis and mystics were on the streets.

He looked across at Yonge's other sidewalk at one point and saw a beautiful Black woman walking in the other direction, and over her head hovered a ball of glowing fire. *Is she Sufi?* was all he thought, as Zaahid kept heading for the rendezvous with his brother and friends. *Sufi is as Sufi does.*

There they stood, outside the Silver Arcade, two of them smoking, a third on the PS VITA, while the rest stood around watching the tiny screen over the player's shoulder. When he reached them, he raised a hand out of the cape, and said, "Salam, folks." Zaahid had never before used the word *Salam* with anyone except his Sheikh.

"Hey, dude," his brother Aziz said. "Nice shawl." It could have been sarcasm, but was it? *Meaning, it's your choice what to take it as*, said Zaahid's Sheikh's voice in his head.

"Thanks, bro," Zaahid said sincerely. No rants came to mind, no thoughts other than that he was with people he had grown up with and had come to call his family. He stood around while they passed around the VITA and smokes from one to the other, not paying him much attention as they commented on their top scores.

Egoless in the cape, forgoing all notions of judging how his brother and friends were spending their time on a video game, Zaahid was able to see the value of this moment better than he could ever have seen it without the cloth around his shoulders. The PS VITA was an excuse. The real worth of this moment was how much these practically orphaned kids were able to bond. He was able to feel the pulse of their friendship as a shield against the scum of Yonge and Toronto at large. His world was safer and more full of goodness because of these people. Ali, Musa, Farid, Rashid, Arif, and Zaahid's brother Aziz.

At length, Ali offered Zaahid the hand-held, and touched the fabric of the cape, saying, "This is ace stuff. I need to get one of these." There was no sarcasm in Ali's voice.

It appeared as though the cape had power to infect others around Zaahid with a peaceful feeling as well. As he pressed each button just at the right time and notched up a series of home runs on *MLB*, topping the high score, the boys looking over his shoulder smiled and patted his back.

And so the time passed, and they kept moving in and out of the Silver Arcade, smoking, laughing, gaming. And for a while, the night was perfect for them all. None of them felt left out. Judging not, and not being judged.

Now it was dark out. From one instant of feeling completely at home, in the next moment Zaahid knew it was time to leave. He was required to be elsewhere. He got up, and said "Salam" once again, and they peacefully let him go even though there was in the air a feeling that the night would not be the same without him. It was as if they also felt the cosmic alignment of things, in a dimension invisible to them, which was dictating Zaahid's need to be elsewhere.

Stepping outside the Silver Arcade, Zaahid felt the first tremors. The crowds outside were all looking in the same direction. He followed their gaze and saw that the CN Tower, Toronto's largest building, was leaning one way, and then swaying the other. People screamed around him, and the tremors shook the ground harder. It was difficult to keep standing, especially as everyone started running around Zaahid. There could have been a stampede.

But just as soon, the ground became still, and so did the CN Tower. Nothing was damaged, though the quake would have been quite high on the Richter scale. This was not a natural quake, though, and Zaahid knew it with a certainty that he could not explain even though he felt it in the core of his self. *Be the truth,* he told himself. *You are one with everything.*

He began to lift off the ground, and hovered and then flew in a gentle arc in the direction of the CN Tower. None of this surprised him. It was as if all this had always been destined, and he was but a player playing his part.

He looked down at the people who were beginning to point up at him, and some of those people were his friends, among them his brother, who had come out of the Silver Arcade. Zaahid waved to them as he flew higher and closer to the CN Tower's highest floor.

The whole sky around the tower seemed filled with people. Among the people were also some other beings. A skeleton-shaped thing, a giant being like an octopus, a group of beautiful translucent women. And so many humans were floating in from all directions. One of them seemed very familiar, just like Zaahid's Sheikh.

And it was the Sheikh.

He came closer and closer to Zaahid, and hovered near him, and said *Salam* inside Zaahid's head rather than with his lips.

Salam, Sheikh, Zaahid found himself replying. *You were right. The cape works.*

It's the cosmic dance, the Sheikh said. *We play our part.*

Some of the spirits were moving into the tower through the closed windows. There was an old, frail man in there, who looked like an ancient version of the city's gang leader, Rudy. There was also a woman, and a spirit standing on its head. Was this the cosmic dance Zaahid's Sheikh had just mentioned? The choreography seemed chaotic, yet meticulously orchestrated, with blood spilling out of bodies posturing right before Zaahid's eyes.

What does this mean, Sheikh? Zaahid asked, calmly turning to his spiritual guide.

For a while, the Sheikh did not answer. He seemed intent on what was going on inside the tower. An elevator door opened, and spirits moved onto the top floor, and they converged on the old man and tore him to pieces. The violence felt like the right thing, even if it was so blatantly one-sided.

At length, there was peace again inside the tower. One by one, the spirits and people hanging in the air around him began to float away or disappear. Zaahid and his Sheikh remained suspended there.

This was the course of justice, son, the Sheikh said. *When one person's ego becomes so big that it upsets the world's order, it takes great violence to restore the balance. God keeps account of all things and never lets the cosmic order stay out of balance for long.*

I understand, Zaahid said, and felt like he was reading a script as he said it.

Your understanding has just begun, said the Sheikh, and began to float away. Zaahid knew the Sheikh was right. There was much to learn, and it appeared that this was only the beginning.

Much later that night, once Zaahid had floated back into his own apartment, he sat on the floor facing Mecca. He knew that taking off the cape would bring the exhilaration of having been part of something enormously significant. But he kept the cape around him all night, and steeped himself like his Sheikh's tea in that covering until morning came.

Fin.

Methodology: Reinforcement of the Othering Power of *Brown Girl*

Many of the world's religions have an overarching deity that uses angels and spirits to carry out cosmic tasks. As Salvini points out, "Gros-Jeanne's words [serving the spirits] stress the tight link among peoples of the African diaspora, and also the connection between Vodou deities and Catholic saints in their role of intermediaries with God" (182). But it is not just the Vodou-Catholic connection that must be made. There is a more universal appeal in Hopkinson's novel, and the connection can apply to Sufism's belief in interceding saints, various forms of angel worship, and many other belief systems that have links to beings in the spiritual realm beyond the secular one. Being a member of the global Sufi community, and knowing that members of this global community also congregate in various groups in Toronto (a simple Google search of "Sufism in Toronto" suffices to demonstrate this fact), the author of this creative-critical work has chosen to write the story from the perspective of a Sufi apprentice coming of age in the same Toronto as the one inhabited by Ti-Jeanne from *Brown Girl*.

Care has been taken to constantly reinforce an othering similar to the novel's. The title of the short story is a play on the title of the novel and also establishes a link of co-relativity between the two protagonists. The name of the story's main character has been chosen as Zaahid (altering the spelling of "Zahid") to showcase the duality of the character being "devoted to God" while also being an "ascetic" ("Zahid"). Zaahid is shown to question his Sheikh's spiritually inclined wisdom just as much as Ti-Jeanne questions Gros-Jeanne's spiritual and healing abilities (*Brown Girl* 36). "Brown Boy" includes no love interest for the protagonist, but he constantly others his friends' secular beliefs. This mirrors Ti-Jeanne constantly challenging Tony's ability to help her raise the baby because of his lack of intelligence and commitment (24, 25, 61, 62, 73, 70, 84). When she sees him naked, she even labels him "The devil!" (79).

Language and sight are other ways in which the story and novel overlap. The story mirrors *Brown Girl*'s othering through the code-switching that Zaahid becomes conscious of. He says "Salam" to his friends rather than using more secular greetings, and he notices that he makes the linguistic switch.[3] Similarly, Gros-Jeanne in *Brown Girl* performs conscious code-switching and self-othering when talking to the street children (63). Both the novel and story also focus on a spiritual dimension that cannot be spied with conventional power of sight (9), and both protagonists are able to see spirit beings, although Zaahid's correspondent ability develops only near the end.

Near the end of both the short story and the novel, the two protagonists are in close proximity to each other. Zaahid from "Brown Boy" is hovering outside the CN Tower and getting instruction from his spiritual guide, his Sheikh. Similarly, Ti-Jeanne is inside the CN Tower, gaining insight on her spiritual gifts while also putting them into effect (221–9).

At the end of both the novel and the short story, Zaahid and Ti-Jeanne are seen to be at peace with their hybridized selves. This is not to say that one of their previous modes of thinking is *not* superior. Quite blatantly, in each, the realm of magic and spiritual belief undermines and others the secular self, while creating the hybrid that is at peace (*Brown Girl* 247). This mirroring effect is the story's attempt to perpetuate the novel's powerplay, while also adding diversity to *Brown Girl*'s universe of spiritual belief systems and giving room to linguistic and ethnic multiplicity that is engendered by othering the dominant, status quo of the mainstream – secular, white Canadian – perspective.

This essay's object is to examine the power-struggle within SF and to lend credence, through means of creative and critical writing, to the subaltern vision of a spiritual SF novum. I have aimed also to challenge what Jessica McDonald calls the "presence of underlying assumptions about the kind of textual universe that is considered viably science fiction" (133). The struggle is made more meaningful by recent conflict over control of the Hugo awards and the refusal to admit variety into the SF canon. This essay and its incorporated short story, "Brown Boy under the Cape," stand with *Brown Girl in the Ring* in refusing to be decentred or othered.

ACKNOWLEDGMENT

Alí Ibu Usmán Hujwírí's *The Kashf Al-Mahjúb: The Oldest Persian Treatise on Sufiism* has informed much of my developing understanding about Sufism and esoteric Islamic practices.

NOTES

1 Darko Suvin, Yugoslavia-born professor emeritus at McGill University, wrote prolifically about science fiction as a genre. He uses the term *novum* to describe a mechanism or object particularly significant to qualifying works that belong in the genre of SF. A novum, or "new thing," is the overarching technology or idea that enables the text to become fundamentally science fictional, but it must be *"based on cognitive logic"* (Suvin 45). The novum can be time travel as in *Back to the Future*, a transporting device as in *Star Trek*, artificial intelligence, or new chemical materials. The details about how new ideas such as time travel operate may vary between texts that use that mechanism as a novum, so stories written after the original story about time travel are not repeating but modifying the novum, and thereby not perpetuating but nuancing it.

2 Here Kim refers to Edward Said's foundational idea of *othering* from *Orientalism* (1978). In the process of othering, according to Said, one cultural group asserts superiority over another by first creating distance between itself and the other and then imagining and applying a hierarchy over the other as (at least) a form of cultural dominance. Said distinguishes between the "Westerners" who have sought benefit from this othering by proliferating an image of themselves as scientific and rational, and the created image of the "Arab-Oriental" as barbaric (49), but of course the term "Arab-Orientals" can be extended and applied to all colonized peoples.

3 Code-switching, or switching between languages or registers of one language, according to Bill Ashcroft, Gareth Griffiths, and Helen Tiffin, is a means of "inscribing alterity" and "installing cultural distinctiveness in the text" (71). I believe the juxtaposition of languages also enables the cultivation of Bhabha's Third Space, creating moments of pause and interrogation by readers about the multiple markers of identity within the characters whose story they are reading.

WORKS CITED

"50 Stunning Examples of the Droste Effect." *Webdesigner Depot RSS*, 29 Sept. 2009, https://www.webdesignerdepot.com/2009/09/50-stunning-examples-of-the-droste-effect/.

Ashcroft, Bill, Gareth Griffiths, and Helen Tiffin. *The Empire Writes Back: Theory and Practice in Post-Colonial Literature*. Routledge, 2002.

Bhabha, Homi. *The Location of Culture*. Routledge, 1994.

Bustamante, Elena C. "Fragments and Crossroads in Nalo Hopkinson's *Brown Girl in the Ring*." *Spaces of Utopia: An Electronic Journal*, no. 4, 2007, pp. 11–30.

Coleman, Monica A. "Serving the Spirits: The Pan-Caribbean African-Derived Religion in Nalo Hopkinson's *Brown Girl in the Ring*." *Journal of Caribbean Literatures*, vol. 6, no. 1, 2009, pp. 1–13.

Csicsery-Ronay, Istvan. *The Seven Beauties of Science Fiction*. Wesleyan UP, 2008.

Doctorow, Cory. "On the Hugo Award Hijacking." *Boing Boing*, 13 Apr. 2015, https://boingboing.net/2015/04/13/on-the-hugo-award-hijacking.html.

Hopkinson, Nalo. *Brown Girl in the Ring*. 1998. Grand Central Publishing, 2012.

– "An Interview with Nalo Hopkinson." Interview by Dianne D. Glave. *Callaloo*, vol. 26, no. 1, 2003, pp. 146–59. *JSTOR*, https://www.jstor.org/stable/3300637.

Hujwírí, Alí Ibu Usmán. *The Kashf Al-Mahjúb: The Oldest Persian Treatise on Sufiism*. Translated by Reynold Alleyne Nicholson, Taj, 1982.

"Hybrid." *Oxford English Dictionary*, https://doi.org/10.1093/OED/8459251414.
Kim, Uriah. "The Politics of Othering in North America and in the Book of Judges." *Postcolonial Theology*, edited by Hille Haker, SCM Press, 2013, pp. 32–40.
McDonald, Jessica. "Beyond Generic Hybridity: Nalo Hopkinson and the Politics of Science Fiction." *Canadian Literature*, no. 228–9, pp. 133–49.
Said, Edward W. *Orientalism*. Vintage, 1979.
Salvini, Laura. "A Heart of Kindness: Nalo Hopkinson's *Brown Girl in the Ring*." Special Issue on Vodou and Créolité, *Journal of Haitian Studies*, vol. 18, no. 2, 2012, pp. 180–93. *JSTOR*, https://www.jstor.org/stable/41949211.
Suvin, Darko. "On What Is and Is Not an SF Narration." *Science Fiction Studies*, vol. 5, no. 1, 1978, pp. 45–57.
"Zahid." *Quranic Names*, https://quranicnames.com/zahid/.

Creating Communities: Consumption and Hunger in Dystopian Cities and Prisons

Small Acts of Urban Place-Making in Nalo Hopkinson's *Skin Folk*

JESSICA MCDONALD

In the foreword to her 2015 short-story collection, *Falling in Love with Hominids*, Nalo Hopkinson writes, "I see the ways in which science fiction is too often used to confirm people's complacency, to reassure them that it's okay for them not to act, because they are not the lone superhero who will fix the world's ills" (3). "And yet," she continues, "humanity as a whole is not satisfied with complacency" (3), nor is humanity changed by it. Hopkinson's foreword tacitly frames the aims of her collection as corrective, directed towards what she envisions as this conundrum of the genre. The relationship between the foreword and the text proper, the problem of complacency and the stories offered in response, are exemplary of Hopkinson's fiction in *Hominids* and beyond. In its keen attention to the small, everyday, individual acts of its characters – despite the global and extraordinary conditions in which those characters live (science fictional, dystopic, or speculatively transformed as their worlds often are) – Hopkinson's writing replaces *complacency* as a familiar and affective readerly output of science fiction with *agency*.

Most crucially, for this chapter, Hopkinson's stories demonstrate the power of individual agency to shape urban space, even – and especially – spaces that seem out of the scope of individuals' influence. The spaces I refer to have been deemed by anthropologist Marc Augé the "non-places" of "supermodernity": shopping malls and chain stores, buses and streets, airports and trains, hotels, banks, food courts, and other sites whose functions depend on the logistics of "transport, transit, commerce, [and] leisure" (94). Augé's foundational *Non-Places: Introduction to an Anthropology of Supermodernity* (translated 1995) theorizes that non-places can be defined in contrast to "places of identity, of relations and of history" (52). Non-places facilitate temporary, transient activity, usually done in solitude. In the non-place, Augé contends, individuals' identities become largely irrelevant because it is primarily their roles as passengers, consumers, or customers that define them, and they are seemingly unmoored from cultural or historical contexts beyond the space. This, he explains, creates a "resulting feeling of 'disorientation'" and a "break or discontinuity between the spectator-traveller" and the non-place itself (84). In a non-place, Augé argues, people all receive the same "instructions for use" (96) that direct their behaviour and movement, which creates similitude among the masses. But, as the masses leave, they become individuals again.

Augé's theory encapsulates popular conceptions of urban space that Hopkinson's speculative fiction complicates. Such conceptions, circulating in public discourse, exemplify how these "[g]eographies of the everyday" are seen as not really places at all, and are "normally undermined" (McKittrick, *Demonic Grounds* 21) – ignored, dismissed, made almost invisible, even if they are ubiquitous. These are sites that can seem so structurally, systemically established that they appear to be an inevitable background of supermodernity, unchangeable by individual hands. But, of course, this understanding, with Augé's theory alongside it, does not account for how individual bodies and identities can yield different experiences of the same space, nor does it leave room for how individuals can and do *produce* (to use Henri Lefebvre's foundational term) these spaces in creative and disruptive ways. Augé's theory thus threatens to disempower the individual space-dweller, and it seems to encourage complacency in the same ways that science fiction does, according to Hopkinson.

By contrast, Hopkinson's speculative fiction advocates for the still-strong possibilities of place-making in contemporary urban geographies many see as ever more "placeless," especially as they are marked by relations of transaction, such as between the shopper and the shop or the passenger and the streetcar. Her writerly commitment to geographical agency is therefore the motivating force of my chapter, which will study these qualities in her debut short-story collection, *Skin Folk* (2001). *Skin Folk* foregrounds the power of the individual, and of relations between individuals, to turn "anonymous" urban spatiality into community, or non-place into place. Three stories provide the focus of my chapter: "A Habit of Waste," "And the Lillies-Them A-Blow," and "Something to Hitch Meat To." All three feature geographies of the non-place, such as streetcars, food courts, banks, and corner stores, and all three spotlight characters who move from being passive to active makers of these spaces. In "A Habit of Waste," urban foraging and other practices of using, making, finding, and recycling are central to one poor Torontonian's life of abundance. For the main character of "And the Lillies-Them A-Blow," chance encounters in downtown Toronto's streets and shops lead to an optimistic desire to forge anew, both literally and figuratively. And in "Something to Hitch Meat To," supernatural powers of visual perception and physical manipulation are used to de-naturalize urban space as a "given" and assert its changeability instead. All three speculative fictions depict small but important "[s]patial acts" (McKittrick, *Demonic Grounds* xix) that Hopkinson's characters undertake as part of their urban navigation. This chapter aims to read those acts within the characters' trajectories to understand how urban place and non-place can be transformed by the ordinary and extraordinary movements of solo city-dwellers.

"Warp the Mirror": Hopkinson's Speculative Fiction

Nalo Hopkinson was born in Kingston, Jamaica, spent her youth in Guyana, Trinidad, and the United States, and then moved to Toronto, Ontario, Canada, where she lived for more than thirty years before moving to California for a decade. In 2021, Hopkinson returned to Canada to take a professorship in creative writing at the University of British Columbia. Her body of work continues to be valued as a robust contribution to Canadian literature. Hopkinson's books are often set in futuristic and fantastical versions of Toronto, and they frequently feature stories of diverse diasporic Caribbean-Canadian experiences. She has become an especially prolific and powerful voice in speculative writing in Canada, winning the Sunburst Award for Canadian Literature of the Fantastic and Canada's Aurora Award, as well as being recognized by national establishments such as Canada Reads, for which she has been both a judge and a competitor, when her debut novel, *Brown Girl in the Ring* (1998), was shortlisted in 2007.

Hopkinson's oeuvre pulls together many threads from the fabric of speculative fiction, such as from science fiction, Afrofuturism, horror, fantasy, and magic realism. Her stories draw on the comedic and the erotic, the peculiar and the everyday, the taboo as well as the banal; they depict passing encounters with the strange, just as they linger on the familiar; they conjure hearsay and rumours, dreams and nightmares, stories of romance and conflict, surprise and whimsy; they feature friends, family, neighbours, strangers, enemies, and more. Her work often incorporates Euro-Western fairy tales (such as Red Riding Hood and Bluebeard, in *Skin Folk*) and Caribbean folklore (including the figures of Anansi and Dry Bone, also in *Skin Folk*). And her stories are embedded in an intertextual index of other works, including

Octavia Butler's science fiction (Brooks 79), "Goblin Market" by Christina Rossetti, and writing by Black feminists such as Toni Morrison (Brooks 79). Hopkinson's is a richly textured and complexly referential body of work.

The World Fantasy Award–winning short-story collection *Skin Folk*, the focus of this chapter, includes fifteen of Hopkinson's stories that explore how "the extraordinary is part of the fabric of day-to-day life" ("*Skin Folk*"). The book encapsulates the tensions I name above, which are both characteristic of Hopkinson's creative capacities and of the Caribbean "worldview," in which what she identifies as "[t]he irrational, the inexplicable, and the mysterious exist side by each with the daily events of life" ("Introduction" xiii). These tensions are also integral to rethinking the non-place, as a geography that reads as too "day-to-day" to be anything touching the extraordinary. Throughout *Skin Folk*, Hopkinson comes up with new technological and social innovations to confront vital topics of contemporary life such as queerness and sexuality, race and gender, capitalism, migration, and abuses both structural and individual. The stories engage with the mutually influencing relationship between macro structures and micro actions: the characters are pulled between recognizing their own power on one hand, and on the other hand, feeling puppeteered by larger forces of fate, spiritual figures, magic, technology, and the logics of "white supremacist capitalist patriarchy" (hooks 170). Consuming – literally (as in, ingesting) and figuratively (as in, buying or acquiring) – is central to these texts: from the basic, such as eating cans of pork and beans or shopping for groceries, to the more unusual, such as enhancing sexual encounters with the purchase of techno-magical SkinSuits.

The collection's narrative moulding of materials from different genres, traditions, and real-world issues into creative forms and figures is fitting for a book titled after transformable and ambiguous beings. Hopkinson explains that "Throughout the Caribbean, under different names, you'll find stories about people who aren't what they seem. Skin gives these skin folk their human shape. When the skin comes off, their true selves emerge. They may be owls. They may be vampiric balls of fire. And always, whatever the burden their skins bear, once they remove them – once they get under their own skins – they can fly. It seemed an apt metaphor for these stories collectively" (*Skin Folk* 1). The title of her collection highlights the possibilities of transformation that emerge from the recognition that things are not always as they seem, including what appear to be the static, inevitable geographies around us. Even the most banal urban environment can reveal itself to be dynamic, changeable, full of possibility: the landscaped garden beds of a Dominion Bank, the food court in a packed shopping centre, or the aisles of the biggest bookstore on the street.

Hopkinson's writing not only represents alternative ways of inhabiting space but also validates for readers that they may partake in the same geographical experimentation. Hopkinson thus centres the act of "making the impossible possible," to use her own words, rather than encouraging in her readers a passive submission to fixed ways of inhabiting the world ("Making the Impossible" 98). In Hopkinson's view, this sense of permissiveness is what makes "[s]peculative fiction" a "great place to warp the mirror" – that is, to "impel the reader to view differently things that they've taken for granted" ("An Interview" 149), such as the seeming rigidity of the built world around us. This idea that urban space is inevitable, or unavoidably *as-is*, can admittedly be "seductive" because, as Katherine McKittrick observes in *Demonic Grounds*, "that which 'just is' not only anchors our selfhood and feet to the ground, it seemingly calibrates and normalizes where, and therefore who, we are" (xi). A stable, legible, fixed geography might hold promise of a stable, legible, fixed self, resulting in tacit acceptance of one's ever-increasing role as a consumer. But the value of speculative fiction, as Hopkinson articulates it and as I take it up in the remainder of this chapter, is that the genre provides a lens through which to critique this internalized attitude that space "just is" and to see more clearly the varieties of ways it can be.

Eating Ornamental Cabbage and Other Acts of Radical Foraging: "A Habit of Waste"

Like much of her fiction, Hopkinson's "A Habit of Waste" takes place in a futuristic, science-fictional Toronto landscape. The story's central technological innovation is a service called MediPerfiction, which allows clients to purchase new bodies, onto which their identities are downloaded. The story's narrator, twenty-eight-year-old Black Torontonian Cynthia, uses MediPerfiction to switch her original body, with "full, tarty-looking lips," "fat thighs," and an "outsize ass" (183), for what the catalogue describes as the "*boyish beauty*" of a thin, white, blond-haired figure with "lithe muscles and small, firm breasts" (184). The story follows Cynthia's life after the body-switch, as she works unenthusiastically at the food bank; manages the reactions of her Trinidadian-Canadian parents after she arrives "on their suburban doorstep" a "white woman with … flippy blond hair" (187); and comes to know Mr. Morris, an elderly, generous, Trinidad-born Torontonian who is a loving widower, a former employee let go from the car plant, and now an urban forager and patron of the food bank at which Cynthia works.

Cynthia begins the story as a character whose movements around the city resemble a kind of somnambulism. She finds herself "nodding off" in the streetcar on her way to and from work (183), a passive traveller rendered so, it seems, by the exhaustion and repetition of her job. There, Cynthia is depicted as robotically dispensing canned goods, or just "the usual," to users of the food bank, alerting them only when prompted by the system if their rations do not meet the prescribed levels of vitamins and carbohydrates (185–6). At home, living alone in a domestic space where she theoretically has more freedom, Cynthia is "sprawled on the sofa," "watching reruns" on her couch (the suggestion: not even original episodes), and "eating pork and beans straight from the can" (without the energy to reheat) (185). Cynthia's life appears shaped by cycles of consumption, or "habits of waste," so much so that even the fundamentals of her job ask that she regulate other people's physical ingestion. Primarily defined by her roles as passive commuter and passive consumer, in both personal and professional dimensions, Cynthia does not seem to have agency according to her life's current script, ghostwritten as it is by consumer-capitalism's ideologies of overwhelming labour, transactional movement, and the pull to consume.

Cynthia's roles as passive traveller and consumer of urban Toronto are depicted in stark contrast to those of Mr. Morris, with whom she forms a reluctant and then fond relationship. Their encounters at the beginning of the story are strained and wooden, informed by their consumer service provider-receiver relationship in the transactional non-place of the food bank. Cynthia's conversations with Mr. Morris and the other patrons feel "artificial" to her and are prompted by the computer's commands (185–6). Her social distance from the people who use the food bank is reinforced by the job's physical set-up, with Mr. Morris's order "stacked ... on the counter between" him and Cynthia (185). This material arrangement marks a separation between the urban space-dwellers: Mr. Morris's provisions, along with the counter, literalize the metaphoric barrier between him and Cynthia, the "disenfranchised" consumer and the "privileged" facilitator of his consumption. Even later, when a co-worker asks Cynthia to deliver Mr. Morris's rations to his apartment and "[c]hat with him a little bit" (189), Cynthia does not want to bring herself in closer proximity to Mr. Morris, a reaction that reveals her wish not to cross the literal, geographic, and metaphoric barriers that separate them. Cynthia wishes, instead, to maintain the naturalized "boundaries" of the food bank as urban non-place, boundaries which divide service provider from service user.

These barriers begin to break down, however, when Cynthia goes to Mr. Morris's place to deliver rations and reluctantly stays to share a Thanksgiving meal with him. Surprised by the "plate after plate of food" (193) he lays in front of her, Cynthia discovers that Mr. Morris forages much of his diet from Toronto's urban landscape, and he uses the food bank only to round out his meals. With a makeshift slingshot, he hunts wild rabbit in the nearby ravine (196); he harvests mulberries and makes jam from other found fruits; and he "dig[s] up chicory root" for his coffee (199), among other acts of urban foraging and finding. Perhaps most unique of his self-resourced spoils, though, is the "ornamental cabbage" that Mr. Morris harvests from the front landscaping of the Dominion Bank on Bathurst and Queen. When Cynthia finds out about the origins of the cabbage, she responds with shock and disgust: "I almost spat the salad out.... 'We're eating ornamental cabbage that you *stole* from the front of a building?'" (194). She is likewise grossed out by the wild rabbit she at first thinks is roasted chicken: "Are you *crazy?* Do you know what's *in* wild food? What kind of diseases it might carry?" (195). Demonstrating her specific sense of "cultural edibility," a set of social scripts that determine what is seen as appropriate to eat (Poe et al. 909), Cynthia cannot fathom that someone could derive nourishing food from the bank's garden beds, or from "off the street" (195), these corners of contemporary geography so public and shared, and yet invisible, unthinkable in their subversive value.

But Mr. Morris embraces his agency as an urban-dweller and refuses to take for granted even the most "non" of places around him. In part, he does this by resignifying his environment with creative and sometimes unpredictable names and ideas about use, and according to new concepts of value and waste. He tells Cynthia there is "plenty to eat, right here in this city, growing wild by the roadside" (198). For him, the greens at the bank are not "ornamental cabbage," but "flowering kale" (194). In this case, Mr. Morris repurposes the corporate, disciplined non-place of the bank so that it becomes a source of nourishment, hospitality, and actual *pleasure*, given how much Cynthia and Mr. Morris enjoy their meal. Much like Ti-Jeanne's "improvisation" to heal the cityscape around her in Hopkinson's *Brown Girl in the Ring* (discussed by Sheheryar B. Sheikh in the interlude before this chapter), Mr. Morris actively negotiates the urban geographies around him, making something different out of what Cynthia experiences as the rise-and-grind culture of a working, commuting, consuming Toronto.

Mr. Morris's actions are charged with more meaning when considered in light of the subversive potential of urban foraging shown by real-world practitioners. Urban foraging, defined by Rachel Black as "the act of searching for and gathering food in the city without exchanging goods or money" (141), can be necessary "to support livelihoods; [to] provide essential foods, medicine, and materials for households; and to create opportunities to connect with nature and maintain social ties" (Poe et al. 902). In "Urban Foraging and the Relational Ecologies of Belonging," Melissa Poe and fellow researchers describe their finding that for many practitioners, urban foraging has the potential to turn the non-place into place, so to speak: "foragers spoke of how through foraging they had created a deeper, more intimate knowledge of the city with layered meanings built up over time" (910). Foraging, in other words, can "root" people to "a new place while bridging their connections to former homes and ways of life" (Poe et al. 910), as Mr. Morris demonstrates in his use of environmental knowledge from his Trinidadian upbringing and from the Toronto public library he visits to find new information on urban sustenance. But these layered meanings can also be more political in character. Urban foraging is one way of rejecting, protesting, or simply ignoring the "institutional regulations, land-use policies, and urban greenspace management practices [that] specify which plants can go where, who may engage with them, and how" (Poe et al. 906). Urban foraging can circumvent the "prescribed" ways of inhabiting cities, however unavoidable those ways may seem, and can encourage experimentation in space-making. As Catherine Bates writes in her essay on foraging in two works of literature, urban foraging can be downright destructive to expected modes of urban space-dwelling, as it is often a way to "disrupt the urban with 'wild' activity" and remake urban space via the praxis of sustainability (191). This "wild" activity can appear "criminal" under the scope of white-supremacist, settler-colonial governmental policy. In "A Habit of Waste," the tension between "normal"/mandated activity and "wild"/criminal activity arises when Mr. Morris tells Cynthia about the ornamental cabbage pulled from the Dominion Bank, "I ain't really stealin' it; I recyclin' it! They does pull it all up and throw it away when the weather turn cold" (194). In the slippage between "stealin'" and "recyclin'," the framework of criminality is tested, for who decides which is which? Moreover, this comment makes clear that Mr. Morris has deep knowledge of the urban practices around him, given his attention to the bank's landscaping schedule and protocols. Mr. Morris's efforts thus show how "[f]oraging becomes a creative living practice" that "refigur[es] the city in terms of what can be found to survive" and "engages with the overlooked and discarded as potential resources" (Bates 195–6). The non-place, in this framing, becomes shared resource for sustenance, even for abundance.

Unlike Cynthia, then, who struggles to acknowledge the worth in the world around her – herself, her work, fellow urban-dwellers and their attendant geographies – and whose passivity is signalled by her unthinking commuting and consumption, Mr. Morris adopts a fresh perspective on familiar features of the cityscape. He perceives the value of the frequently unseen and the disregarded, and he derives nourishment from the discounted bounty around him, not to mention that, as an urban forager, Mr. Morris physically gets his hands dirty and influences, materially, the land around him. His actions literalize that he has embraced his agency as a city-dweller through his adoption of what Rinaldo Walcott and Idil Abdillahi might describe as "modes of unauthorized being" or "self-authored acts": in other words, "the ways in which Black people break 'rules,' authorizing for themselves new ways of being in the world" (69–70). For Mr. Morris, this rule-breaking occurs when he rejects the mandated dietary requirements of the food bank, "steals" from the front landscape of the bank, and uses a slingshot for unlicensed hunting (it seems) in city ravines, among other actions. Abandoned and dismissed by the existing social structures around him, as an aging, widowed Black man with a marginalized position in the established system of sociality and spatiality, Mr. Morris self-authors disruptive and unconventional ways of inhabiting the city.

By the final pages of the story, Mr. Morris's actions seem to have sparked a transformation in Cynthia, too, and opened her to the world of metaphorical and literal foraging as a way out of her "habits of waste." In this spark of transformation from one character to another, herein too lies the story's advocacy for individual agency. It is only these one-on-one encounters with Mr. Morris, the carrying out of community aid, sharing a dinner table, conversing across difference, that seem to ignite agency in Cynthia. The final scene shows Cynthia turning her eye towards the leftover cocoa when she visits her parents. Normally, she would avoid such beverages because of her new figure. But here at the end, she tells her dad, "I just want to finish what's left in the pot.... I mean, you don't want it to go to waste, do you?" (202). The diction reveals a thread drawn between Cynthia and Mr. Morris, the former taking on the latter's habits against waste. The same goes for when Cynthia expresses her intention to "eat everything" her parents serve, and she says she will have to manage the resulting effects on her body: "You've got to work with what you've got" (201). Her language here calls back to Mr. Morris's statement from a previous scene, when he tells her, "You have to learn to make use of what you have" (199). These parallel lines establish that a meaningful and instructive connection between "Old Man Morris" and Cynthia has been made, anonymous food bank patron turned friend and mentor, the differences and distance between them to a degree minimized, as we see in the reverberations of Mr. Morris's teachings in Cynthia's speech. Cynthia's unthinking consumption looks to be replaced by a watchful, deliberate attention to what is around her, including "waste" left in the pot. The story ends with the suggestion that Cynthia, like Mr. Morris, can live in joyful abundance – indeed, can be "so happy" she is "giddy" (201) – in a city that now seems much richer than it did before. Cynthia may literally be warming an old pot of cocoa-tea in the final lines of "A Habit of Waste," but figuratively, she is choosing to make what she can of contemporary geography's left-behind "remains" (201).

From Filing Papers to Forging Metal: "And the Lillies-Them A-Blow"

Much like Cynthia in "A Habit of Waste," Samantha, the Torontonian protagonist of *Skin Folk*'s "And the Lillies-Them A-Blow," moves from passive to active inhabitant of urban space. The story begins with Samantha in a semi-somnambulist state in which events happen to her, but she cannot seem to effect change. In her downtown apartment, a bag of groceries that she "should unpack" sits neglected, and she does not remember what is in it ("hadn't she bought strawberries or something last night?") (204). On her wall, "her mother's intricately patched quilt" hangs "kate-a-corner," and Samantha thinks to herself, "She really should straighten it, brush off the film of dust" covering it (204), but she does not put thoughts into action. The apartment, in general, signals a metaphorical stagnancy: "A bra was draped on the bookshelf," "a dust bunny circled in an unseen draft in the corner," and "[l]ast night's dirty dinner plate sat on top of the TV" (204). Even the "half-eaten carrot stick" and the "congealing butter" become like visual signs of the motionlessness of Samantha's life at the beginning of the story (204).

Her work materials, "three glum sheets of scribbled notes" (204), are buried under these remains of the previous night's dinner, suggesting again Samantha's subdued motivation to act and her disinterest in completing tasks at work as well as home. The report these notes are to become, called "A Chronological History of Provincial Government Support of Neighbourhood Centres in Ontario's North," is "little more than a title," even though it is due that day (204). At work, robotically "pounding at her computer keyboard" the whole shift long, Samantha submits the report by day's end, but she remains behind on the "administration budget" and "overheads for tomorrow's staff meeting," so she expects she will be "working late again" (205), marking this as a common occurrence for her. Samantha's time proceeds according to the directed pace of her employer's deadlines, dictated by the day-to-day of meetings and budgets. Her sleepy dissatisfaction in this office work renders her less like someone who is empowered by the acceptance that a job need only be a job, and more like an instrument worn in and down to meet workplace goals.

Samantha's passivity is amplified by descriptions of her navigating the night-time geographies of downtown Toronto's Yonge Street. The street at first seems conventional in the way it "checks the boxes" of dominant conceptions of non-places, with consumption at its core. Samantha notices, as she passes storefront after storefront, "a record store bray[ing] out the latest dance hits," a "cacophony of flashing lights and bells" bursting from a video arcade, and giant posters of "impossibly thin, impossibly busty women" covering the buildings (206). These are spaces designed to attract customers *en masse*, very much in line with Augé's theorization of the non-place as a site in which individuals become types whose functions are purely transactional. To draw in these street-masses, the stores use trendy music, attention-seeking sensory outputs, and well-known marketing strategies ("sex sells" and the beauty standards of the time). Even the fact that the "[p]eople on the streets moved very slowly," "gawking" and "dawdling" (206) as a group, marks this street as legible through Augé's theory, since the people move together as directed by the signs and signals.

But like other characters studied in this chapter, Samantha experiences unexpected encounters that propel her transformation from passive to active dweller of urban place and non-place. The encounters begin when Samantha is the surprise recipient of a vase of lilies – "[n]asty" flowers, in her eyes – at her doorstep (203). What follows is a series of similar, unexpected "deliveries" of physical and non-physical kinds: in short, snippets of language that pop up, for Samantha, in both oral and textual forms. Hopkinson's introduction to the story explains that these snippets are reprinted verbatim from a real-world interview with Miss Queenie, or Imogene Kennedy, who was a Queen of Kumina, an Afro-Jamaican cultural and religious form practiced in Jamaica.[1] Read together, the fragments of speech and text tell of a profound transformation in Miss Queenie's life, starting with, "*One day, I remember one day I find some lillies, and I plant the lillies-them in a row…*" (203). Like Samantha's, Miss Queenie's transformation begins with the discovery of lilies. From there, the fragments narrate Miss Queenie's real-world recollection of falling at the roots of a cotton tree (205), discovering a grave or tomb around and inside the tree (206), and then having a twenty-one-day communion in which the spirits talk to her and share language and wisdom with her at the cotton tree roots (213). In Hopkinson's fictional world, Samantha gives no signs of following or knowing the story of Miss Queenie's transformation. After some of the story mysteriously appears typed on the screen of her work computer, she thinks, "Who could have typed those words and what the hell did they mean, anyway?" (205). The words continue to be conjured around Samantha in out-of-the-blue circumstances, such as in a downtown street evangelist's sermon as Samantha walks by (206) and in the voice in her head that she hears as she traverses the urban landscape (213).

Taken together with Samantha's somnambulist state at work and home, these mysterious messages at first seem to underscore the story's characterization of Samantha as the passive receiver of actions. But they begin to trigger in Samantha small but important changes. For instance, it is only when the message appears at random on her work computer that Samantha forcefully decides to reject the breathless pace of her office job and leave for the day, despite her looming deadlines and tasks: "Screw this. She was going home early tonight" (205). Later, surprised to hear another of the strange messages coming from the street evangelist, Samantha changes literal direction, and she seeks refuge in a store. It is, in fact, the "World's Biggest Bookstore" (207), a real-world book retailer that opened in 1980 in Toronto, now closed, which was founded by family members of the Coles chain bookstore fame. Here, in this "enormous box-like structure" known for "garish yellow walls" and a "brightly lit" commercial interior (Taylor), Samantha comes into an unexpected state of quiet, deliberate attention. As she walks, she takes her time, "stopping here or there when a book caught her eye" (207). She becomes captivated by one book in particular, and she "ease[s] the large, heavy volume down" and then "ease[s] the book open" to run "her hand slowly down a full-page colour photograph" (207). The repetition of the verb "ease," combined with her relaxed pace, marks Samantha's time at the store as much different from the always-behind, rush-to-the-deadline existence she is caught in at the beginning of the story. The book's physicality seems to demand careful, deliberate handling. It is a "massive essay in photography of the various styles of adornment across the African continent" (207), and it includes photographs of a woman wearing a "billowing robe" and "stylized silver crosses," with "orange-sized balls of amber pinned into her hair" (207).

Samantha buys the book and, at home, becomes absorbed by it. She reads for hours and takes in the complicated hand-crafted adornments featured in its pages: "The master jewelers of Benin had been carving tiny, intricate brass and gold figures through the lost wax method for centuries" (208), and people featured in the book wear "huge brass anklets," "sparkly finery" for "festival days," and kohl makeup (208). The book is all about small and big acts of *making*, and Samantha is inspired by these age-old techniques to shape materials (brass, gold, wax, and minerals that make kohl) into more. Situated as it is within a story about navigating Toronto, the book becomes symbolic in its celebration of making, and it resonates thematically with suggestions of urban place-making found throughout the story and the rest of *Skin Folk*. The carving, glass-blowing, and other forms of craftsmanship highlight the physical effect individuals can have on materials derived from urban surroundings, much like Mr. Morris's hunting, berry-picking, and foraging.

One day after she finds the book, Samantha walks home again through the same streetscape, and the reader is first shown lingering signs of her passivity. She "doze[s] on the subway ride home" and does not "wake up until Dundas, one stop too far south" (211), abstractly signalling a return to her somnambulism from the beginning of the story. The blips of isolated city-dwellers Samantha spots on the street include a few women described as "hookers," and to her, they seem uncharacteristically "lacklustre" in their interactions with one another (211). Otherwise, she sees "straggly knots of people gathered around the various benches under the trees" (211), their physical positions emphasizing their hazy vagueness from Samantha's perspective (under the cover of trees) and the still-present sense of urban individuals as "masses" (they are knotted as if they are hard to tell apart).

But the scene shifts abruptly, and Samantha bursts awake when she trips crossing the street. She stumbles and falls, feels "a sharp pain across the side of her skull as it crack[s] against a root of the tree," and then blacks out momentarily (212). Much like Miss Queenie, Samantha finds herself at the root of a tree, and the fragment that comes to Samantha's mind in her unconsciousness is, again, Miss Queenie's: "*and I inside the cottn tree lay down. And at night-time I see the cottn tree light up with candles and I resting now, put me hand this way and sleeping …*" (212). Slowly coming to, Samantha finds that the women she just observed on the street have come to check on her. They help her to her feet in an act of community care that goes against Samantha's previous sensory experience of the downtown street as an anonymous urban landscape. That the "hookers" Samantha initially dismisses become her helpers is a telling detail of the place-making, or community-making, that happens in the story. While the fall itself can be categorized as another event that happens to Samantha, knocked out by the darkness of the night and unhelped by her metaphoric somnambulism, it sparks community action. The women come to her rescue, physically lift her, and encourage her to go to the hospital, rather than standing by as passive onlookers.

Much like the time spent between Cynthia and Mr. Morris in "A Habit of Waste," this street encounter directs Samantha even more towards change. Indeed, Samantha seems to be "knocked" into clarity and action once she gets home: she takes her health into her own hands and makes *S'wikkidi lango*, sugar water, the idea for which comes to her in one of the Miss Queenie fragments (213). Drinking the hot water for her chills, she returns to the big book of artistry and admires all the "beauty made by hands" (213–14). She looks to the vase that carried her lilies, and "[s]he wonder[s] what she could fill it with" (214), a thought symbolizing her new will to take action, fill the vase, effect change. This will is concretized in the final moment of the story: having experienced a shift in perspective, Samantha decides to tender her resignation, leave office work behind, and sign up for a certificate in goldsmithing. Like Mr. Morris, Samantha makes the choice to use her hands to alter materials around her for sustenance, since this new path will be her source of financial stability, but also for aesthetic and personal reasons. Samantha is attracted to crafting meaningful items out of materials that appear to be scraps, and she seems drawn to *making* as a lineage from her African ancestors, as well as her immediate maternal origins, since her mother is a quilter (210). In this final decision, a career change, the story offers an optimistic step towards the transformation that has developed in Samantha all along. The reader is left to consider: what world might she forge with her new abilities?

Point, Click, Transform: "Something to Hitch Meat To"

At the beginning of "Something to Hitch Meat To," main character Artho is presented as a passive witness to the urban landscapes around him. "Streetcar coming. Artho got on" (24): this simple juxtaposition frames Artho as robot-like, a machine led by the cues of city transit rather than by his own will. Once on the streetcar, the narrator notes, Artho "stared blankly out the window" while "[t]raffic was gridlocked" (24), and he "leaned his head against the streetcar window and dozed" (25). Distractedly daydreaming about his supper, he does not pay attention to the passing stops: "It wasn't until he reached his stop that he realized he really had forgotten to buy the damned avocados" for his meal (25). Even when Artho takes action in these early parts of the story, the actions are minor. He "picked up a bone lying in the street," the bone itself symbolic of lifelessness, and the reader is told he does this for "[n]o reason" at all, "one of those irrational things you do," the words dismissing the bone's significance (23). Later, once he remembers to buy the avocados for his dinner, the ones he picks up are "tired," "wrinkly," and rotten inside, echoing the lifeless chicken bone (25).

Artho's muted impact on his surroundings is paralleled by scenes he witnesses in the non-places of the city. For instance, he spots a line of children walking by him in the street, "chain[ed]" together with "each toddler hanging on dutifully to one of the knots in the rope by which they were being led" (23). Shortly after, Artho is driven – on the streetcar, and thus at the mercy of its movements and schedule – "past a woman struggling with two huge dogs on leashes": "The dogs' handler tugged futilely at their leashes, barely able to keep up" (24). Like the children, Artho seems limited in his ability to actively shape, or even perceive with purpose, the world around. Like the dogs, he seems led along by the machinations of city life that leash him down – gridlock, for example, becoming a metaphor for his disempowerment. And like the dogs' walker, he is unable to get a handle on his own agency.

These sights and scenes amplify Artho's affecting experiences navigating the structural and other forces that shape his city life. Most significantly, Artho deals with racist micro-aggressions from other city-dwellers with such regularity that the story emphasizes racism as a routine experience for Black people, like Artho, who traverse urban geography. For instance, in the first moments of the story, a woman makes flirtatious gestures at Artho, and then whispers to her friend, "God, Latino men are just so hot, don't you think?" (23). Not only a moment of racialized objectification, this comment is also a misreading, as Artho is not Latino: "Latino? What the hell?" he thinks (24). At the corner store, Artho is treated grumpily by the man who "served Artho at least twice a week," the same man who "cheerfully make[s] change" with "old women or guys in suits" (25), an observation that discloses Artho's regularly troubling treatment in commercial non-places as a Black shopper. Artho recalls, too, being made "late for work … because six taxis in a row had refused to stop for him" (37), a reference to racial profiling by taxi drivers. And Artho's boss, Charlie, makes a racist "joke" about Artho's genitals (35). These encounters come at Artho with persistence, so much so that when he is questioned about his mistreatment in the city, Artho says, "it's not like I can do anything about it!" (37), a phrase that suggests his sense of powerlessness.

But much like Samantha's unexpected encounters, Artho experiences random interruptions in perception that spark his movement from passive to active. In particular, he gains a curious ability – indeed, super- or more-than-natural ability – to see the world differently. For example, when he watches the dog walker from the streetcar window, his vision flickers, "like when an old film skips a frame," and "this woman walking on ordinary woman legs" becomes a "being whose natural four-legged stance had been twisted and warped so that all it could manage was this ungainly two-legged jerking from foot to foot" (24–5). Later, the same visual shake-up happens again: Artho is overcome with "a weird unfamiliarity," and the ears of people around him begin to register as "knurls of deformed cartilage," "twisted carbuncles of flesh" (28). Like Mr. Morris's power of resignifying the urban landscape, Artho's new perspective views urban-dwellers in ways that emphasize their materiality, and in these cases their biological and evolutionary lineages. He begins to see people not just as blank, anonymous masses, makers of "formless noise" (28), ghost-like passersby of the non-place, but as human beings with bodies.

Artho's transformation is pushed further when he encounters Anansi in the form of a little girl named Nancy. Anansi, a trickster figure typically in spider-like form from Akan folktale originating in West Africa, features diversely in the stories circulated in the African diaspora. In the originating Asante stories, Anansi "existed halfway between the earth and the sky and had the power to restructure both the world of the divine and the human," bringing "wisdom and stories" while also showing "disregard for the rules of society and community" (Marshall 31–2). It seems no coincidence that Artho meets Anansi, or Nancy, in a food court, another non-place defined by consumption and transactional relations, much like the food bank in "A Habit of Waste." Sights of thoughtless ingestion beckon Artho's attention, including to Nancy's father "hurriedly stuff[ing] a burger into his mouth," causing "[g]reen relish" to "ooz[e] between his fingers" (29). And likewise, Artho notices the food court's passing, superficial encounters, as when he spots an "old man who'd been forced to share the table" with Nancy and her father offer "her a strained nice-little-girl smile" (29), a gesture that implies inauthentic, scripted social interaction more than meaningful community-making.

But within minutes, Artho begins to pay closer attention to Nancy, as well as to his surroundings and the people-as-people (not masses) in the food court. Artho and Nancy lock eyes, a physical manifestation of one-on-one connection, and he finds himself "swaying slightly from side to side" as she sings in his direction and "glar[es] at him from the depths of her specs" (30). In this moment, for Artho, the masses turn individuals, now eye-to-eye and in tune with one another's sounds and movements. Shaken, Artho gets up to leave, but the very next sentences suggest his perception is sharpened: "he suddenly became aware of the movement of his legs: push off with left leg, bending toes for leverage; contract right knee to extend right leg, heel first; shift weight; step onto right foot; bend right knee; repeat on the other side" (30). It is as if the food court encounter makes him cognizant of his own reality as an embodied navigator of space, an individual who has impact.

From here on, Artho's abilities become more concrete. At his job, his agency is bound by the limits of digital space, as he spends his work hours editing the bodies and skin of actors in pornographic videos: he would "point, click, and drag his mouse as he smoothed out the cellulite and firmed up the pecs of the perfect naked models on the screen" (29). His job, essentially, is to change the appearances and materiality of the actors. But this power-to-change becomes more tangible, as Artho first recognizes when he mischievously draws a tattoo on one of the people in the video he is editing: an Adinkra symbol called the Nkyin kyin. Adinkra symbols, originating from Gyaman people in what is now Ghana, are typically used on cloth and other material, and they carry important cultural, spiritual, proverbial, and intellectual meanings. Artho understands the Nkyin kyin in particular as "the West African Adinkra symbol for 'always changing oneself'" (34). After placing the symbol on a man in the video, Artho is flabbergasted when the tattoo magically moves from the screen and settles, temporarily, on his own body: "it came all the way *off* the screen, skidded right across the keyboard, and came to rest on his thigh. Alarmed, he released the mouse. The symbol melted through the cloth into the meat of his leg. 'Shit!' It tingled for a second, then faded" (40–1). This moment is significant not just because Artho's limited agency is moving beyond the digital realm, but because it brings the symbol of change, visualized through the Nkyin kyin, quite literally into Artho's body, marking him as a figure of self-transformation.

This Nkyin kyin moment foreshadows that, in the end, Artho's ability grows to include manipulating the spatial bodies around him. After encountering Anansi, Artho finds he can now "click" and "double-click" to change built landscapes, an iteration of his editing tasks at work. For example, he clicks the door handle of his work building, then its exterior wall, to change the "dull brick" into a more decorative, ornate appearance (41). Literally, then, Artho gains the techno-magical capacity to "edit" buildings, their contours and colours, tones and textures. But figuratively, his ability is a metaphor articulating the city dweller's influence on contemporary space. Through the literal and figurative impacts of his actions, Artho denaturalizes urban geographies, revealing their alterability. And in observing these impacts, he becomes impassioned by agency: his "skin began to prickle" with "hope" (41). In the final moments, he is "almost bouncing" enroute to the streetcar (43), notably the starting point of the story and the place in which Artho seemed most listless and powerless, "staring blankly" (24) as he travelled. But now, he returns, "dancing along in his excitement" about "[a]ll these choices" (43). The active verb marks his vibrant mobility, and the superlative language suggests an abundant future foretold by Artho's newfound agency. He excitedly runs through "where he'd like to plant the Adinkra symbol next" (43). Much like the previous two stories, "Something to Hitch Meat To" depicts an individual who sheds the role of passive observer of the city's changes and embraces the ability to take part instead. While the story does not show the reader what happens beyond the streetcar stop, it concludes with the optimism of Artho's motivation to make change. And in leaving open for speculation the many possible choices Artho may make, the story refuses to foreclose the spatial transformations to come as he navigates the city.

"The very small things": Transformations in the Quotidian

Again and again, Hopkinson's stories return to the power of the individual, and of small-scale, interpersonal relationships, to shape the world. Characters who choose to harness the capacity they have to speak and act, however restricted they may feel, are rewarded, although the results are not always perfect. In "Ganger (Ball Lightning)," about a couple whose sex life is altered by techno-"wetsuits," a simple act of skin-to-skin contact – the touching of hands – defeats the murderous electric monstrosity that the wetsuits become after they charge for too long. The order of the house is restored, the space having been thrown into chaos by the monster-suit's havoc, and the couple is reunited in the wake of this single touch. In "Whose Upward Flight I Love," city trees escape their rooted positions to fly up into the air, and the city workers who try to wrangle the trees into security are not totally successful. Some trees escape. But even in this depiction, the very act of individuals struggling to control the urban landscape physically – first by planting the trees, and then by attempting to lock them in position – becomes a metaphor for the complex relationship between people and the urban geographies they can work to transform. The same complexity inflects "Snake," Hopkinson's stomach-churning story about a paedophilic serial killer who, in the end, is caught by the watchful eyes of birds-turned-city-dwellers who have been paying careful attention to his insidious movements in public space. The killer relies on urban complacency to get away with his acts, but he discovers the city is filled with observant individuals whose choices, like his own, shape the social geography they share.

In putting forth the power of the individual to make space differently, to transform the most seemingly un-transformable of places, Hopkinson's work embeds itself within the "shape-shifting reality of the Caribbean" (Brooks 91) and draws on the speculative features of the eponymous genre of fiction to reaffirm, in particular, Black individuals' and communities' profound abilities to make space. *Skin Folk* represents fictionally the ways that urban geographies have long been transformed by the political, social, and affective movements of Black people. These movements show how city streets, public transit, stores, food courts, and other staples of urban geography are not merely dismissible "backgrounds" but important factors in the relations and experiences produced through them. Take the city street, for example: Walcott and Abdillahi open their book *Blacklife: Post-BLM and the Struggle for Freedom* (2019) by drawing attention to Toronto's Yonge Street as a site for vital histories of Black protests against police violence (11). Walcott reminds his reader of this history in another book, building on the work of Robin Kelley, when he writes, "Black men have remade the street corner as one site of communal gathering that is both labor and pleasure" (*The Long Emancipation* 6). Because transportation racism and mobility inequities have long troubled the experiences of Black commuters in cities, movements of solidarity and protest have formed in response, such as the Montgomery bus boycott of 1955–6 (Crosbye 135) or the Bus Riders' Union formed in Los Angeles, California, in the 1990s (Kelley 152).

Given the inequity and violence built into non-places and other urban landscapes, it is difficult to have faith in the power of individuals to change these spaces. And by foregrounding how Hopkinson's speculative fictions advocate for individual agency, I do not want to repeat what Walcott identifies as a troubling "victim to victor" line of thinking whereby the individual actions of Black people are seen as needing improvement, for example to make urban space more liveable ("Reconstructing Manhood" 76). I am especially concerned not to repeat individual-centred thinking that bolsters, as Kelley puts it, the "self-help" narrative of Black urban poverty that places the blame on individuals who do not act "right" by positioning "black behaviour" as "the source of urban poverty and violence" (91). These ideas have a long and violent history in what Saidiya Hartman describes as "the blameworthiness of the freed individual" that resulted from enslaved Black people gaining "rights" (6), which in practice holds Black individuals responsible for horrific generational outcomes of a brutal Empire, such as for cycles of poverty and the survival mechanisms they generate.

In my reading, Hopkinson's work rejects these troubling possibilities by showcasing the non-normative acts of individuals as makers of urban geography, acts such as covertly pulling food from the garden beds of a big bank, subverting your company's video-editing protocols, or swapping abstract office work for hands-on metal forging. Hopkinson's characters are not mechanically guided by signs and cues, as described by Augé's theory, but instead take actions as varied as the urban topographies they navigate. The stories therefore spotlight "glimpses of Black freedom" (5) that Walcott characterizes as "unscripted, imaginative, and beyond our current modes of intelligibility" (4), made visible "as the Black body configures and reconfigures modes of being in the world, often in the vernacular cultures of Black people's everyday and ordinary lives" (*The Long Emancipation* 5–6). Hopkinson's work reflects this reality in its spirited animation of the "mundane" places that her Black characters navigate, places I too have long navigated and hold dear: the shopping malls, bus stops, and chain stores that were the landscape of my youth. But for a white person living in a nation hostile to People of Colour but stubbornly tolerant of the misbehaviour of people who look like me, my embodied experiences of these places are markedly different from those of Hopkinson's characters. For them, there are the racist micro-aggressions and intensified surveillance by bigoted shopkeepers (in Artho's case), the marginalization and resulting invisibility (in Mr. Morris's), the acute danger felt by Black women walking home on Toronto streets in the dark (in Samantha's), and all the other shades of injustice that influence the characters' engagements with urban space.

Against these social-geographic forces of inequity, the imaginative work of Hopkinson's stories lies again in the individual actions of her characters to manifest what adrienne maree brown theorizes as the principle that "small is all" (41), or it is "the very small things that create the largest shifts in the world" (26). I am not surprised that brown indebts her work explicitly to the speculative fictions of Octavia Butler, which, in brown's words, show the power of the "interpersonal" in their demonstration of "how radical ideas spread through conversation, questions, one to one interactions" (22). From the bus stop, to the mall, to city streets, the geographies of Hopkinson's short fiction also produce small acts of genuine connection and community care, inciting political subversion and solidarity-building, professional fulfilment as much as profound spiritual encounter. This very collection shows the influence of Hopkinson's geographical sensibility on other writers, as seen in Sheikh's "Brown Boy under the Cape," a short story that likewise denaturalizes the anonymity of urban space, such as Toronto's Yonge Street, by depicting the joyful, spiritual, and personally enriching experiences that can unfold in such landscapes. Hopkinson's fiction, not to mention Sheikh's creative response to it, shows that we have a "right to the city," as David Harvey famously phrased it, and a "right to change ourselves by changing the city," one small act at a time.

In the call for papers circulated for this collection, Wendy Roy asks, "Which visions of 'Canada' do we find in speculative texts?" Hopkinson's stories answer this question with pragmatic optimism based on the will and actions of dynamic individuals. Story, as McKittrick writes in *Dear Science and Other Stories* (2021), is essential to Black forms of resistance, subversion, knowledge-making, and knowledge-sharing. "[A]s an interdisciplinary methodology," McKittrick expands, "the story – theoretical, creative, groovy, skilled, action-based, secreted, shared – is a verb-activity that invites engagement, curiosity, collaboration" (9). Considering McKittrick's words alongside Roy's question, I see how Nalo Hopkinson's speculative stories share essential knowledge about Canada's futures. The vision of Canada found in her writing is one in which social, cultural, and material geographies can be transformed, and people along with them. This vision relies on the lift of agency over the drag of complacency; it demands the deliberate practice of awareness, not the fog of inattention. This vision can emerge, astonishingly, from the accumulation of single moments, the touch of hands, a conversation, quiet care for another's safety, meals shared between unexpected companions. Most crucially, this vision is premised on a persistent commitment to small, everyday acts of community-making, because it is these that subtly but powerfully shape our geographic lives.

NOTE

1 For more on Miss Queenie in relation to Kumina, see Olive Lewin's *Rock It Come Over: The Folk Music of Jamaica* (2000) and Maureen Warner-Lewis's "The *Nkuyu*: Spirit Messengers of the Kumina."

WORKS CITED

Augé, Marc. *Non-Places: Introduction to an Anthropology of Supermodernity*. Translated by John Howe, Verso, 1995.

Bates, Catherine. "Sustainable Urban Foragings in the Canadian Metropolis: Rummaging through Rita Wong's *Forage* and Nicholas Dickner's *Nikolski*." *British Journal of Canadian Studies*, vol. 26, no. 2, 2013, pp. 191–212. *EBSCOhost*, https://doi.org/10.3828/bjcs.2013.11.

Black, Rachel. "Eating Garbage: Socially Marginal Food Provisioning Practices." *Consuming the Inedible: Neglected Dimensions of Food Choice*, edited by Jeremy MacClancy, Jeya Henry, and Helen Macbeth, Berghan, 2007, pp. 141–50.

Brooks, Kinitra D. *Searching for Sycorax: Black Women's Hauntings of Contemporary Horror*. Rutgers, 2018.

brown, adrienne maree. *Emergent Strategy: Shaping Change, Changing Worlds*. AK Press, 2017.

Crosbye, Emily. "'Not That Kind of Tired': Rosa Parks and Organizing the Montgomery Bus Boycott." *Understanding and Teaching the Civil Rights Movement*, edited by Hasan Kwame Jeffries, U of Wisconsin P, 2019, pp. 131–43.

Hartman, Saidiya V. *Scenes of Subjection: Terror, Slavery, and Self-Making in Nineteenth-Century America*. Oxford UP, 1997.

Harvey, David. "The Right to the City." *New Left Review*, no. 53, Sept./Oct. 2008, https://newleftreview.org/issues/ii53/articles/david-harvey-the-right-to-the-city.

hooks, bell. *Outlaw Culture: Resisting Representations*. Routledge, 1994.

Hopkinson, Nalo. *Brown Girl in the Ring*. 1998. Grand Central Publishing, 2012.

– *Falling in Love with Hominids*. Tachyon, 2015.

– "An Interview with Nalo Hopkinson." Interview by Dianne D. Glave, *Callaloo*, vol. 26, no. 1, 2003, pp. 146–59. *JSTOR*, https://www.jstor.org/stable/3300637.

– "Introduction." *Whispers from the Cotton Tree Root: Caribbean Fabulist Fiction*, edited by Nalo Hopkinson, Invisible Cities Press, 2000, pp. xi–xiii.

– "'Making the Impossible Possible': An Interview with Nalo Hopkinson." Interview by Alondra Nelson, *Social Text*, vol. 20, no. 2, 2002, pp. 97–113. *Project MUSE*, https://muse.jhu.edu/article/31932.

– *Skin Folk*. Warner Books, 2001.

Kelley, Robin D.G. *Yo' Mama's Disfunktional! Fighting the Culture Wars in Urban America*. Beacon, 1997.

Lefebvre, Henri. *The Production of Space*. 1974. Translated by Donald Nicholson-Smith, Blackwell Publishing, 1991.

Lewin, Olive. *Rock It Come Over: The Folk Music of Jamaica*. U of the West Indies P, 2000.

Marshall, Emily Zobel. "Liminal Anansi: Symbol of Order and Chaos: An Exploration of Anansi's Roots Amongst the Asante of Ghana." *Caribbean*

Quarterly, vol. 53, no. 3, 2007, pp. 30–40. *JSTOR*, https://www.jstor.org/stable/40654609.

McKittrick, Katherine. *Dear Science and Other Stories*. Duke UP, 2021.

– *Demonic Grounds: Black Women and the Cartographies of Struggle*. Minnesota UP, 2006.

Poe, Melissa R., et al. "Urban Foraging and the Relational Ecologies of Belonging." *Social & Cultural Geography*, vol. 15, no. 8, 2014, pp. 901–19. *Taylor & Francis*, https://doi.org/10.1080/14649365.2014.908232.

"Skin Folk." *Publishers Weekly*, 15 Oct. 2001, https://www.publishersweekly.com/9780446678032.

Taylor, Doug. "Toronto's 'World's Biggest Bookstore' (Demolished)." *Historic Toronto: Information on Toronto's History*, 5 Jul. 2016, https://tayloronhistory.com/2016/07/05/torontos-worlds-biggest-book-store-demolished/.

Walcott, Rinaldo, and Idil Abdillahi. *BlackLife: Post-BLM and the Struggle for Freedom*. ARP Books, 2019.

Walcott, Rinaldo. *The Long Emancipation*. Duke UP, 2021.

– "Reconstructing Manhood; Or, the Drag of Black Masculinity." *Small Axe: A Caribbean Journal of Criticism*, vol. 13, no. 1, 2009, pp. 75–89. *Project MUSE*, https://muse.jhu.edu/article/261520.

Warner-Lewis, Maureen. "The *Nkuyu*: Spirit Messengers of the Kumina." *Savacou*, vol. 13, 1977, pp. 57–82.

The Possibilities of Prison Food in Margaret Atwood's *The Heart Goes Last*

SHELLEY BOYD

In her collection of essays on speculative fiction *In Other Worlds: SF and the Human Imagination*, Margaret Atwood argues that because of the twentieth century's many atrocities, "The future societies imagined" by contemporary writers are "more likely to be dark than bright" (84–5). With past failings haunting utopian fiction, Atwood coins the term *ustopia* to reflect her dialectical vision: "you see … within each utopia, a concealed dystopia; within each dystopia, a hidden utopia, if only in the form of the world as it existed before the bad guys took over" (85). This "good versus bad" or "us versus them" model holds especially true for Atwood's 2015 novel *The Heart Goes Last*, which focuses on the global economic collapse of 2008, when large segments of the American population were increasingly divided into the "haves" and the "have-nots." The main characters, Stan and Charmaine, have lost their jobs and home. After living in their car and dumpster-diving for food, the couple signs up for the Positron Project in the gated town of Consilience. They are guaranteed a home, safety, and employment – the middle-class lifestyle they once enjoyed – but every other month they must switch places with their "Alternates" and live segregated in male and female prisons (47). Inside the prison, Stan and Charmaine work for free, and when living on the outside, they earn "Posidollars," which they put towards the purchase of goods "from the internal-network digital catalogue" (42) operating *within* Positron's larger town enclosure. The Positron Project comes with a life sentence, as citizens who join this for-profit social experiment can never leave. The couple thus assumes a slave-like or indentured servant-like existence, forever beholden to the profit-driven corporation.[1]

Within this ustopian context, Positron's foodways function as multifaceted mechanisms of control, underscoring imprisoning capitalist ideologies that have indelibly shaped human experience. Within and beyond the institutional confines of Positron, food serves several key functions in maintaining neoliberal capitalism: the *replication* of the current system; the reward for, or reinforcement of, prisoners' *compliance* within the system; and the *objectification* of prisoners as consumable goods. Yet, despite the seemingly closed, tightly controlled environs of Positron, food also serves as a means of *resistance* – a means of questioning and challenging the status quo. Through her multifaceted food symbolism, then, Atwood crafts an ustopian parable that warns against an unsustainable, dehumanizing neoliberal system focused on consumer desires, while at the same time highlighting the possibilities of free will when used for the greater social good.

When writing *The Heart Goes Last*, Atwood admits to having had in mind at least a few prison-related models tied to both food and capitalist principles. The first was Canada's Prison Farm Program, which began in the 1880s and was cancelled in 2010. When the federal government ceased the program's operations, the rationale behind the decision was "that farming was not a useful [employment] rehabilitation method in today's high-tech society" (Montgomery). At the time of its cancelation, Atwood participated in a protest in Kingston, Ontario, in front of the regional head office of Correctional Services Canada; in her speech at the rally, Atwood extolled the virtues of farming as opposed to the government's focus on finances: "Money is an entirely human invention – a mental construct that has value only if we think it does, and that can therefore vanish in a flash when the systems it serves melt down.... The body can survive without money, but it doesn't last long without food" ("Save Our"). Atwood goes on to reference the story of King Midas, who welcomes the power to turn all he touches into gold, until he starves to death ("Save Our").

At first glance, Positron Prison seems to honour the prison-farm model, since the resident-prisoners grow most of their own food: the many vegetables, grains, legumes, and fruit crops "are supposed to produce the fresh food, both for Positron Prison and for the town of Consilience. Not only the fresh foods but the frozen ones, and not only food but drink" (*The Heart* 65). Whereas food is scarce on the outside for Stan and Charmaine, the inside world of the Positron Project seems to offer abundance. However, the reality is that Positron remains dependent on external resources. Furthermore, its emphasis on high-production rates skews the project towards unethical practices (such as the breeding of headless chickens) and perpetuates an unsustainable future: "Some items are brought in from outside – quite a few items, in fact – but that state of affairs is viewed as temporary. In no time at all, the Project will be self-sustaining. Except for paper products, and plastics, and fuel, and sugar, and bananas, and …" (65; ellipsis in original). In other words, Positron foodways remain deeply ensconced in the neoliberal, late-capitalist system from which Stan and Charmaine supposedly sought refuge. In Positron, profit margins persist as the highest social value, with unreflective consumerism permeating all aspects of life.

Positron's neoliberal values are further underscored through the conflation of human lives with capital, as made clear by Atwood's second prison-related model for her novel. In an interview with Rachel Giese in *Chatelaine*, Atwood admits that real-life precursors for Positron include institutions with "incentive[s] to create more criminals," such as today's privatized prisons or Australia's history as a penal colony ("Legendary"). In the case of Australia, Atwood notes that female prisoners were eventually sent to the colony "to settle [the male prisoners] down.… But there simply weren't enough women … to meet the demand, so they lowered the bar, criminalized more behaviours and sentenced … more harshly to supply the demand" ("Legendary"). This dehumanizing commoditization of inmates is central to Atwood's conceptualization of the Positron Project, which posits itself as a solution to the economic collapse of 2008 by exacerbating social inequities and greed through the continued exploitation of human lives, rights, and labour. As one character in *The Heart Goes Last* notes,

> Even when prisons were privatized, even when the prisoners were rented out as unpaid labour to international business interests, the cost-benefit charts did not improve, because American slave workers couldn't outperform the slave workers in other countries. Competitiveness in the slave labour market was linked to the price of food, and Americans … weren't ready to starve their prisoners to death while working them to the bone.…
>
> Then it occurred to the planners of Positron … that if prisons were scaled out and handled rationally, they could be win-win viable economic units. So many jobs could be spawned by them … an ever-flowing cornucopia of jobs. And if every citizen were either a guard or a prisoner, the result would be full employment: half would be prisoners, the other half would be engaged in the business of tending the prisoners in some way or other. Or tending those who tended them. (39–40)

This utopian dream may be pitched as "full employment," but Positron deals in illusions promoted via marketing spin since the experiment depends upon an imprisoned slave-like economy through which the resident-prisoners give up their civil rights and liberties. Indeed,

Positron's false claim echoes Frederic Jameson's own observation in "The Politics of Utopia" that "capitalism cannot flourish under full employment; it requires a reserve army of the unemployed in order to function and to avoid inflation" ("The Politics").

In *The Heart Goes Last*, the prison model is marketed to allay consumers' fears that they have not permanently lost their middle-class status or purchasing power by appealing directly to their appetites and desires. The fact that part of Positron's sales pitch – "you can't eat your so-called individual liberties" (38) – and the explanation for people's eagerness to sign up for the Project – "People were starved for hope, ready to swallow anything uplifting" (41) – are both couched in the figurative language of food and ingestion suggest that this utopian project offers more of the same by replicating the outside world's neoliberal capitalism. Consumerism, advertising language and ideals, and socio-economic status remain all-encompassing. In *In Other Worlds*, Atwood notes, "Many utopias and dystopias emphasize food (delicious or awful)" (191), and in the case of Positron, the figurative dimensions of food signal early on that the value of Positron is highly questionable, inviting readers to look beyond the nicely packaged surface of familiarity and comfort and to be wary of what the characters consume, value, and believe.

In light of Atwood's real-life models, the twinned community that is Positron Prison and the gated town of Consilience provides a satiric critique of neoliberal capitalism as an imprisoning construct that has permeated human perceptions, systems, and experience. The inside and outside worlds are interconnected in profound ways, and food and food-related behaviours from both sides of the enclosure have much to communicate about socio-economic realities, human appetites, and lost freedoms.[2] In her analysis of food politics in women's writing, Sarah Sceats argues, "By looking right across [Atwood's] work it is possible to put together a picture of how food, eating and appetite in her fiction relate to 'how people order their societies,' on micro (individual, interpersonal) and macro (cultural) levels, not just in specific instances, but woven into an overall political analysis or vision" (94). Through this critical lens, Positron foodways, through their connection to the outside world, form a strategic part of Atwood's macro and micro satire, since prison food operates as both an implement and symbol of the neoliberal capitalist system, perpetuating its superficial pleasures, hierarchies, and abuses. Characters must move beyond the material comforts and abundance of this supposed utopia to see the exploitation and coercion that ultimately furnish their commissary tables and their own personal complicity within the system.

Literalizing the Metaphor: Imprisoned Thinking and the Positron Project

To understand Atwood's satiric depiction of a total institution through its prison food, I turn first to Frederic Jameson's postmodern theorizing of utopian fiction in *Archaeologies of the Future* and "The Politics of Utopia," and Michel Foucault's conceptualization of power in *Discipline and Punishment*. According to Jameson, utopian fiction is a kind of "socio-economic sub-genre" of science fiction (*Archaeologies* xiv), particularly since utopian imaginings are embedded within, and a response to, already existing systems of power. In "The Politics of Utopia," Jameson notes that utopia's "function lies not in helping us to imagine a better future but rather in demonstrating our utter incapacity to imagine such a future – our imprisonment in a non-utopian present without historicity or futurity – so as to reveal the ideological closure of the system in which we are somehow trapped and confined" ("The Politics"). One can readily turn to Thomas More's foundational text *Utopia* to see this ideological entanglement at work. In his book, More criticizes English noblemen who "live like drones off the labors of others" (35) and protests land enclosures as wealthy landowners "leave no ground to be tilled, enclose every bit of land for pasture, pull down houses, and destroy towns" (37), making tenant-farmers homeless and destitute. Paradoxically, when More imagines a solution to these inequities through the island of Utopia, where "citizens consider themselves to be cultivators, not owners, of what they hold" (59), he perpetuates exploitation, as made evident during the communal meals, since "slaves perform all tasks that demand heavy work and soil the hands" (71). If utopian thinking, or what Lyman Tower Sargent calls "social dreaming" (3), is about imagining an improved collective future, which ironically remains delimited by the current socio-economic system and its values, then it is important to note that Atwood literalizes this ideological imprisonment through her twinned depiction of the Positron Project as both an incarcerated town and a prison that are not so very different from the outside world from which Stan and Charmaine seek refuge.

As a total institution, Atwood's Positron Project is a satirical late-capitalist rendering of Foucault's model of modern incarceration with its "exhaustive disciplinary apparatus," which regulates "all aspects" of a prisoner's life and "takes possession of man as a whole," from his physical self to his consciousness (Foucault 235–6). For Foucault, punishment is not solely about inflicting bodily pain, but about subjecting "the heart, the thoughts, the will, the inclinations" of the prisoner to a larger politics of power relations (16), with food being one means of enforcement. According to sociological studies of present-day North American penitentiaries, prison food operates as a multifaceted form of punishment, especially in terms of the lost freedom of choice. Meals are typically low in nutrition, high in calories, prepared in questionable ways, and served at set times whether prisoners are hungry or not. In her article on "Penal Subjectivities," Lori Sexton notes that prison food is identified as a daily form of punishment that is both concrete and symbolic, with one female prisoner categorizing the low-quality, unappetizing meals as "dog food," a metaphor that placed her and her fellow inmates "lower on the food chain than other human beings" (122). Rebecca Godderis similarly argues in "Dining In: The Symbolic Power of Food in Prison" that a prisoner's sense of self and bodily autonomy are eroded through prison meals, especially since they often have no access to cultural dishes and have no say in how the food is prepared, which means they are unable "to make beneficial consumptive choices and thus, they could not be in full control of their own health" (258). Atwood's historical novel *Alias Grace* provides a ready example of prison food's purpose as a form of punishment. The opening pages include an excerpt from Kingston Penitentiary's *Punishment Book* of 1843 that lists "Bread and Water" (sometimes in addition to physical lashings) as a consequence of the prisoners' sense of entitlement, such as "Finding fault with rations," or for their non-compliant behaviour, such as "Staring about inattentive at breakfast table" (9). If, in accordance with the famous adage, "You are what you eat," then in prison, inmates have very little say not only in what they consume, but also in who they are. With respect to prison food's symbolic power, Godderis argues that it represents near-total control over prisoners' decisions and daily lives; citing Foucault, Godderis concludes that prison food is a striking example of how "power reaches into the very grain of individuals, touches their bodies and inserts itself into their actions and attitudes ... and everyday lives" (259).

While prison food is an indelible part of institutional control over the human subject, rarely is that control absolute. Indeed, the previous examples from Atwood's *Alias Grace* indicate that prisoners are punished for misbehaving during mealtime, such as voicing their distaste for the food in a kind of rebellion against institutional control. Godderis notes that "food-based resistance" is a key part of prisoners' narratives, since "prisoners use consumptive spaces to negotiate and contest the power inequalities resulting from the prison's highly regulated environment" (255). Prisoners' agency can vary in degree and kind, from the refusal to behave according to the rules during mealtime (260); to the intentional contamination of food, whether it be the guards' meals or those of fellow prisoners (261); to stealing food and using it as part of the "bootlegged food market" within the prison (263).[3] Ultimately, Godderis reveals that "prisoners access the symbolic power of food to structure, develop and maintain their individual identities – ones that are separate from the institutional designation of 'inmate' and the societal label of 'criminal'" (265).

This conceptual model of prison food not simply as a form of control but also as a means of resistance applies to Atwood's *The Heart Goes Last* in ways that underscore the distinct, near-insurmountable challenge of resisting a neoliberal system that drives consumerism and indulges the human subject's seemingly insatiable desires. In actual prisons, inmates do not want to eat the food but have little choice; in Atwood's Positron Project the inverse is true: the inmates desire the food and believe they have little choice. Ultimately, critical self-reflection and responsible actions are necessary for keeping appetites in check and for working towards a less exploitative present and future.

Through this combined framework of Jameson's notion of an imprisoned utopian imagination and Foucault's theorizing of the total institution that is a prison, I propose that within the Positron Project, foodways serve at least three key functions in enforcing neoliberal capitalism, and a fourth function in critiquing it. The first function is *replication*, in that Atwood's food imagery points to the inability of Positron to furnish a solution that does not break from the past. The second function is the power of *coercion* or *persuasion*, in that Positron's foodways uphold prisoners' consumer-driven attitudes and desires at the expense of their critical questioning of, or divergence from, imprisoning neoliberal values. And the third function is *objectification*, in that the conflation of humans with food perpetuates a system in which commodities are paramount to the greater social good. Finally, the fourth symbolic function of Atwood's prison food is to suggest the possibility of *resistance* via individual efforts to thwart, or at least deviate from, total institutional control and subjugation.

Food and Replication

Modelled nostalgically after American suburbia of the 1950s, an era of economic prosperity, the Positron Project's selling feature is the promise of happiness and material comfort in exchange for signing over one's civil rights and liberties. While Positron offers the appearance of security, its prisoners' well-being is, in fact, secondary to the financial interests of the top investors who manipulate the rules and use the system's ideological confines for their own benefit. In this way,

Positron remains firmly grounded in the current abuses of capitalism by the wealthiest 1 per cent. As a backward-looking model, the Positron Project offers nothing new, and Atwood accentuates this replication through a series of enclosed homes in which individuals struggle to safeguard their tenuous socio-economic status within a cut-throat neoliberal system. Whether it is Stan and Charmaine living in the small space of their car and facing threatening night-time attacks by thieves, the super wealthy who live in isolation on "tax-free sea platforms just outside the offshore limit" (9), or Stan's criminal brother Conor who moves from a "boarded-up bungalow" (19) to a guarded trailer park – "a fortress of sorts" (21) – with his gang, these confined citizens survive by any means necessary in the so-called outside world.

Given this recurring imagery of confinement both inside and outside Positron, it is not surprising that certain foods also repeat, with chicken and eggs being the most significant items. According to Jim Thomas, "prison diets reinforce a class-bound, leveling regimen by imposing a standard menu that … reflects what some have described as 'plebian fare'" (170). Just as real prisons serve the same meals in continual rotation to underscore prisoners' lack of choice and their subjugation (Thomas 169), Positron furnishes its commissary tables and Consilience's suburban kitchens through the mass production of its poultry and egg farms with little variation. Within the prison, chicken dumplings (63), chicken salad (138), chicken stew (121), and chicken wings (177) punctuate the prisoners' days. Outside, Consilience's resident-prisoners regularly greet their mornings with fresh eggs (124, 183, 253, 260) or snack on egg salad sandwiches at funerals (207). The uniformity of these cost-effective, mass-produced sources of protein signals the resident-prisoners' servitude, a classification made even more apparent by the fact that one of the only people to consume the more expensive meal of steak is Positron's top executive, Ed (224–5). Atwood's choice of chicken and eggs as staples of Positron is not surprising, since chicken has become a kind of twenty-first-century fare for the masses. As Samantha Noll argues in relation to Atwood's dystopian novel *Oryx and Crake*, in which chickens are genetically modified not to have a head (a disturbing innovation that also occurs in *The Heart Goes Last*), Atwood critiques today's poultry industry, in which large-breasted chickens are purposely bred to "provide humans with the majority of our protein needs," as an indictment of unethical practices that drive a capitalist agenda (275). Through the poultry industry of prison foodways, *The Heart Goes Last* exposes the ongoing subservience of its resident-prisoners contained within a total institution, especially since eggs and chicken also make appearances in Stan and

Charmaine's pre-Positron life. Indeed, one of the reasons Charmaine cannot wait to escape her outside life is to rid herself of the "rancid fat smell of the chicken-wings place next door" to the bar where she works (27). Charmaine may want to shed her chicken-bound, indebted identity, but Positron merely offers a continuation of the same foods and the same self, albeit with nicer packaging and lost freedoms. Just as Stan tends the chickens in Positron prison, letting them out "for a run twice a day, which is supposed to improve their morale," the resident-prisoners are given an illusory taste of freedom when they exchange places with their Alternates every month, moving between the jail and suburbia yet remaining fodder for the larger profit-driven enterprise (66).

With dietary staples repeating across the inside and outside worlds and the prison foods reflecting and upholding the values and social structures of the neoliberal capitalist system, Atwood not only uses food strategically for her social satire, but also appears to be having fun with her symbolism, prompting readers to ask that proverbial and confounding question: Which came first, the chicken or the egg? For now, I would like to focus on the egg as a potent if misleading symbol of new beginnings, which brings me to the second function of food within Positron: the power of persuasion.

Food and Persuasion

If real prisons deprive inmates of nourishment to inflict punishment, Positron exerts its authority through the inverse approach, supplying its resident-prisoners with both real and symbolic bounty to maintain their subservience to a neoliberal system. Apart from the chickens, eggs – both real and symbolic – appear regularly, as they have in Atwood's other dystopias, as potent signs of new-yet-imperfect beginnings.[4] Eggs are not only central to the industrial and unethical farm practices at Positron Prison, but they are also associated with the idyllic domestic morning scene of family, hope, routine, and middle-class comfort for which Charmaine longs: "She did love Stan.... A different kind of love. Trusting, sedate. It went with pet fish.... And with eggs for breakfast, poached, snuggled in their individual poachers. And with babies" (53). At one point, however, the egg becomes a model of the Positron Project itself: "First the town wall, like an outside shell; then, Consilience, like the soft white part of an egg. And inside Consilience, Positron Prison: the core, the heart, the meaning of it all" (189). If the prison lies at the heart of Positron's promise of new beginnings and its egg symbolism, then Atwood prompts her readers to reflect critically on the naive ways in which Stan and Charmaine understand and embrace this dream of security.

A key part of the recruitment campaign, food is the great temptation, as Positron plies would-be residents with reminders of a former life of affluence. The evening before signing up and giving away their freedom, Stan and Charmaine are provided with a night in the top hotel, the distraction of olives, a carafe of wine, and a restaurant meal voucher to tempt them into giving up their lives on the outside (32). These enticements cannot be underestimated since, on the outside, the "high-end places ... were drying up" because no one could afford to eat out in restaurants (8). In addition, the grounds of Positron seem near-paradisal, boasting "extensive greenhouses" and "several acres of apple trees, in addition to the outdoor market gardens" (65). In this enclosed community of abundance, it is telling that Jocelyn, one of Positron's top executives responsible for surveillance, majored in English literature and wrote her thesis on John Milton's *Paradise Lost* (110): she is well versed in narratives that speak to fundamental human desires and fallibilities. In Milton's rendering of the Christian myth, Eden is the original utopia, a place where all needs are fulfilled, but it also becomes Adam and Eve's lost home, a place forfeited because of temptation and to which humanity yearns to return. Positron seems to offer a tangible and quick-and-easy paradise regained to would-be resident-prisoners who come from the outside world of scarcity where "[p]eople are starving. Scavenging, pilfering, dumpster-diving" (33).

The presentation of Positron as a kind of food-rich paradise resonates with the pleasures and "wish-fulfillment" that Jameson highlights as having long been a part of utopian thinking: "Such wishes are even more obvious when we come to the various utopias where old peasant dreams of a land of plenty, of roasted chickens flying into the mouth, as well as more learned fantasies about paradise and the earthly garden, linger close to the surface" ("The Politics"). The flying chickens refer to the Land of Cockaigne from Middle English poetry, which Atwood describes elsewhere as a kind of edible world with rampant sex and gluttony, and "although a paradise of sorts, it was – officially at any rate – a fools' paradise" (*In Other Worlds* 68). In his analysis of food's metaphoric role in literature, Mervyn Nicholson similarly notes that in Christian and classical contexts, "paradisal visions depict the origin of human society in a setting of *human* harmony expressed as *natural* harmony – as abundant food, typically vegetarian.... The Fall is signalled by the start of a struggle for food; the sentence laid on Adam to toil by the sweat of his brow marks the constitution of food as *coercion*, not just the coercion *of* humans but coercion *by* humans – of earth, its creatures and subtextually of other humans" (199). In the context of Positron, its appearance of abundance distracts from its fallen state and the conformity and coercion that underlie its operations. As a former Milton scholar turned Positron executive, Jocelyn fully appreciates the power of paradisal narratives in that she knows all the "twists and turns" (110), including the temptations of food. Of course, equally telling is the fact that Stan has never read *Paradise Lost* and so is not as alive to its parable: that is, the consequences of appetites, the shared responsibilities that come with the freedom to choose, and the need to find a new garden, a new refuge. Indeed, *The Heart Goes Last* is filled with multiple references to lost homes, dreams, and frontiers that were supposed to bring harmony and abundance, but this myth of a promised land, as Jameson argues, is indelibly tied to a capitalist myth of progress and unending profits, since "capitalism also requires a frontier, and perpetual expansion, in order to sustain its inner dynamic" ("The Politics"). Stan and Charmaine are, therefore, likely to keep replicating the story of lost homes in an endless quest for new resources and abundance if they themselves fail to heed the warnings of the past and to adjust their consumer attitudes and desire-ridden behaviours by choosing to live and relate in responsible and sustainable ways.

In his research on utopian foodways, Robert Applebaum cautions that utopian thinkers often suffer from a blind spot when representing food as a resource of transcendence and pleasure, detached from the socio-economic and environmental conditions in which it is produced ("Concepts"). Atwood scholars have made similar claims with respect to *The Edible Woman* and the prose poem "Bread," noting that Atwood's depictions of consumerism and greed often foreground a "disconnect between food and conscious thought," between the meal on one's plate and the suffering of animals and other human beings (Murray 491). As Stuart Chipman summarizes with respect to "Bread," in which Atwood situates this staple within contrasting contexts of privilege and scarcity, "We deceive ourselves when we try to believe that satiating our self-serving appetites does not deprive others of life and well-being" (3). In *The Heart Goes Last*, food's similar implication within the total institution is clear: it plays a powerfully persuasive role by tempting resident-prisoners to follow their appetites and not their minds, and to wilfully ignore how their Positron lifestyle is sustained through the exploitation of resources, including humans in the form of slave labour or, as some resident-prisoners suspect, as "Protein-enriched livestock feed" (70). In this extreme social experiment, food is the great distraction through its alignment with wealth, pleasure, and socio-economic status. For example, when Stan and Charmaine first sign up as new recruits, the

PowerPoint sales pitch concludes with the phrase "A MEANINGFUL LIFE" beside an image of a golden egg in a nest, a symbol of material wealth and a promising future (42). For sceptical readers, this golden egg invites questions. Literally, nest eggs are real or artificial eggs placed in the nest to encourage hens in their laying. Positron's brand of egg symbolism also recalls the cautionary tale of the goose that laid the golden egg, a fable that ends badly for the goose when the owner, driven by short-sighted greed, kills the bird to find the source of the gold and ends up empty-handed. Despite these fabled warnings, Positron's resident-prisoners are mostly captivated by the gold and rarely hold space for prolonged contemplations of the injustices and exploitation of resources needed to perpetuate their enclosed world of consumer ease, which brings me to the third function of prison food: objectification.

Humans as Food

If an imprisoning ideology of endless profits and consumerism defines the Positron Project, then Atwood pushes her readers to contemplate where this total system of control inevitably leads, particularly through the conflation of humans, animals, and food. Theorizing the phrase "eat or be eaten" across various models of nature and human society, Nicholson argues that neoliberal capitalism and the market system have been conceptualized in ways similar to Charles Darwin's "paradigm of natural selection," with survival and competition as the driving principles (202). In this light, "Natural selection is … transformed … [in]to the appropriation of *others'* resources," and ultimately "those who can not [sic] obtain food" will "become the food for others" (202). Nicholson's argument resonates with Atwood's novel on several levels, as humans and chickens (and even eggs) become interchangeable in a convergence of Positron's major industries: poultry and egg farming, and sex-doll manufacturing.

In *The Heart Goes Last*, sexual desires are often communicated through images of food and acts of devouring, indicating how consumer ideology has infiltrated human relationships. Humans relate to one another in terms of capital, something Stan appreciates when he witnesses the sex-robot factory, which, like the chicken farm, is described as a "slaughterhouse" but without the blood (187), as body parts move down conveyor belts, ready for assembly. Male customers can order from a "menu" of options regarding women's appearance and expression, and these custom-designed companions take the place of the intricacies and responsibilities of real-life partnerships (192). Collapsing the categories of human and manufactured product facilitates the resident-prisoners' transformation from worker to commodity within a system bent on profiting from consumers' sexual appetites. Just as Positron designs a headless chicken to promote meat efficiency, it masters a high-end line of sex dolls by performing a brain-altering procedure on real women without their consent, so that they will imprint like ducklings onto whomever is in the room (204). When Charmaine realizes that Ed intends to perform this procedure on her, she recognizes that her autonomy and personhood are irrelevant: Ed "has no interest in who she is really. She's mostly just a body to him, and now he wants to turn her into only a body. She might as well not have any head at all" (274). In *The Heart Goes Last*, Atwood builds on the ethos of profit-driven production-within-confinement that is Positron's poultry industry of headless chickens and extends it to humans.[5] In this regard, Positron as a total institution has realized near-absolute control over the minds, bodies, and desires of its resident-prisoners, who are transformed into commodities and sold to the highest-paying consumer.[6]

Food as Resistance: Tiny Tims

When we reflect on the three functions of food touched on so far – replication, persuasion, and objectification – it is difficult to imagine escaping Positron's control as a total institution. Although food functions as part of Stan and Charmaine's enclosed neoliberal society, prisoners also have the capacity to use food as a means of resistance. In studying actual prisons, Godderis notes that "prisoners use consumptive spaces to negotiate and contest the power inequalities resulting from the prison's highly regulated environment" (255) and goes on to argue that "the 'prison food experience' [is] an opportunity to work towards a view of the prisoner as both agent *and* subject" and to identify acts of resistance (257). Godderis identifies several overt modes of defiance, such as "verbal altercations" in the dining area (260), "the contamination of food" by prisoners working in the kitchen (261), "violent clashes between prisoners and prison authorities" when congregated in the dining area (264), and "personally-defined eating rituals" (264). Food-related rebellions are certainly present in Atwood's novel, albeit primarily during the earlier phase of the Positron Project when actual convicts lived side-by-side with Positron's recruited resident-prisoners. For instance, Stan recalls when lunch hour used to be contentious and violent: "At that time there were still some bona fide criminals in the place. Drug dealers, gang enforcers, grifters and con artists, assorted thieves.… There were shovings in the cafeteria lineup, there were glarings, there were standoffs. Stan learned some ingenious combinations of words he would never have put together himself.... Scuffles broke out over muffins, plates of scrambled eggs were shoved into faces" (63). These altercations eventually cease when Stan notes that "the worst troublemakers vanished," with the ominous, unknown nature of that vanishing resulting in the remaining prisoners' overall compliance and improved conduct (65). While these violent acts of food-related resistance mostly disappear, Atwood still affords her characters space for questioning authority, disrupting imprisoning routines, and reassessing societal values through food's expressive possibilities.

According to Godderis, because of its "symbolic power," food is "a form of communication through which expressions of domination and resistance can be made. Consumptive habits allow institutional authorities and prisoners to develop and express an understanding of their situation and of themselves" (256). For the mostly compliant Stan, resistance often comes to him through imagined protests of his brother Conor (or Con, for short), an individual who always flouted the system to his advantage. Conor is a projected alternative, or voice of dissidence in Stan's head, whenever Stan questions his own compliance with Positron. For example, on the night before Stan and Charmaine enter the Positron Project, Conor prophetically warns Stan that it is not a trustworthy venture and that the couple will lose their freedom, since they will not be able to leave, "Except in a box, feet first" (35). Once inside, Stan repeatedly imagines how Conor would respond to life in Positron. When at the town meeting Stan learns to his horror about the proposal to breed headless chickens to "increase meat growth efficiencies" (79), he drinks his beer from the newly established Consilience brewery and imagines what Conor would say: *"You're joking. It's not beer, it's horse piss. What's it made out of, anyway?"* (80). With Con's voice in his head, Stan questions the authenticity of everything that is being fed to him both literally and figuratively, including the entire profit-getting system of the Positron Project:

> Hold on, thinks Stan. What's underneath all the horn-tooting? Some folks must be making a shitload of cash out of this thing. But who, but where? Since not that much of it is trickling down inside the Consilience wall. Everyone's got a place to live, true, but no one's richer than anyone else.
>
> So are they all being lied to, played for suckers? Duped into doing the work while others roll around in the cash? Conor always said Stan was too trusting, that he could never sniff out a bent motive, that given the choice he'd pay top dollar for a baggie full of baking soda and stuff it up his nose. Fuck, said Conor, he'd probably even get high on it. (81)

Conor clearly serves as an imagined alternative that enables Stan to scrutinize the world around him, including his own naive decisions and alignment with the system. For example, when Stan is reassigned to Positron's secret and highly lucrative sex-robot industry, he reassesses the chicken dishes in the cafeteria: "Sucking the fat off a wing, he reflects that he himself might have tended the *owner* of this wing when it had been covered with feathers and attached to a chicken" (177; emphasis added). The language is key here, indicating a world view through which living beings are understood in terms of capital, ownership, and usable parts. While enjoying his meal, Stan appreciates his own complicity with the system in which he is subjugated to others' wills just as he benefits from his control over the chickens.

Charmaine similarly experiences moments of critical insight into her compliance for the purpose of ensuring her ongoing comforts and relative freedom. During a lunchtime scene in the prison, Charmaine contemplates the sources of her food as she grapples with her job as executioner. Having never seen orchards in Positron, Charmaine eyes the plum crumble with suspicion and "can't help thinking it looks like curdled blood" (138), the simile here communicating the darkest aspects of Positron's lethal disposal of its resident-prisoners. Although Charmaine is having "qualms" about her role, ultimately she works to convince herself that she is just "having dessert. Plum crumble. The women at her table are making *mmm* sounds. Red crumbs cling to their lips" (139). Self-interest necessitates Charmaine's continued, wilful ignorance of the power structures that she both submits to and upholds to secure her own relative advantage.

Because prison food can offer a means of resistance, a significant dimension of this fourth function is food as knowledge. In his theorizing of utopia, Jameson notes that "our wildest imaginings are all collages of experience, constructs made up of bits and pieces of the here and now" (*Archaeologies* xiii), and that ultimately this genre works to "modify or correct the past" (xv). Jameson's description of utopian fiction as an intertextual form (2) resonates with Atwood's own approach to the genre. Her novel is rich with allusions to fairy tales, Milton, and her own earlier works, such as her dystopian fiction. This critical convention of the genre resonates with Atwood's food-as-resistance approach through food's symbolic and allusive possibilities, by signalling openings for change within what appears to be a totalizing institution. In addition to the numerous *Paradise Lost* allusions and the lessons that Christian parables relate, Atwood also includes subtle nods through food-related symbolism to other key intertexts, such as Charles Dickens's *A Christmas Carol*. In *The Heart Goes Last*, Atwood makes multiple allusions to Tiny Tim, a Dickens character who plays a transformational role in Ebenezer Scrooge's self-correction from miser to social benefactor. The first reference to Tiny Tim appears in the form of food during Charmaine's prison lunch: chicken salad served with Tiny Tim tomatoes grown on the Positron farms followed by the bloody-looking plum crumble for dessert (138).[7] Despite not being hungry, Charmaine forces herself to eat in order to conform to expectations of inmates' mealtime behaviours even as she inwardly questions the sources of the food and reflects critically on her own executioner's role in her "Medications Administration job" (139). Additional allusions to Tiny Tim appear later, but in a different form, when Stan escapes Positron through the secret password "tiptoe through the tulips" (194), taken from a novelty song from the 1920s repopularized in the 1960s by folk singer Tiny Tim. When Stan operates undercover as an Elvis-for-hire in Las Vegas, he knows it is time to deliver his precious cargo of smuggled-out data from Positron when he watches his brother, Conor, perform as part of the Green Man Group to the song "Tiptoe Through the Tulips" (267–8). Readers learn that Jocelyn, who is working secretly to undermine the Positron Project, is the one who chose the "annoying tune" as the secret password (177). Because she is a former literary scholar and figure of subterfuge, Jocelyn's chosen password and the repeated references to Tiny Tim merit reflection. With respect to Jocelyn's other calculated actions, Rano Ringo and Jasmine Sharma note, "Unlike her allotted function to ensure the success of the Project, she works towards its failure" (78). While Ringo and Sharma focus on Jocelyn as an agent who "subverts [the Positron Project's] phallic authority by maintaining her feminist presence within the system" (79), the allusions to Tiny Tim also highlight her critical intervention within the total institution of neoliberal capitalism. The Tiny Tim allusions signal that Stan's and Charmaine's journeys in and out of financial prosperity and life and death scenarios are not unlike the time travel of Dickens's *A Christmas Carol* when, in one night, the miserly Scrooge visits different eras of his life and realizes the potential impacts of his actions on others, especially Tiny Tim, in time to change his ways. Clear parallels become evident when readers further consider that Scrooge's initial response to a request for charitable donations "for the poor and destitute" is instead to pose the question, "Are there no prisons?" (16), and that Scrooge learns from his capitalistic greed after witnessing a speculative future determined by his past- and present-day choices. As with Scrooge's resolution to reform his behaviour upon witnessing the possible demise of Tiny Tim, in *The Heart Goes Last*, the many Tiny Tims – from tomatoes to the secret password – appear during moments of self-reflection when Charmaine and Stan question or even disrupt the individualistic, profit-driven system through their decisions to act responsibly and ethically.

In her essay "Scrooge: An Introduction," Atwood notes that Dickens's story is a "fairy tale or ghost tale" with "the traditional three-part structure of a fairy tale – three Spirits of Christmas, three ages of Scrooge (past, present, future) and it also has a fairy-tale ending, in which light triumphs over darkness, goodness and harmony reign, and an innocent life in peril – Tiny Tim's – is saved, not to mention the gnarly old soul of Scrooge" (119). *The Heart Goes Last* follows a similar fairy-tale structure by detailing Stan and Charmaine's three phases of socio-economic circumstances and by picturing their seemingly innocent middle-class life and marital romance restored by the conclusion, replete with a healthy child. However, the overlay of the prison motif further complicates the supposedly distinct past, present, and future of Stan and Charmaine's journey as Atwood brings these intertextual allusions to bear on her satirical critique of neoliberal capitalism. Indeed, the past seems to have replicated into the future with the same individualistic, consumer-focused attitudes and desires threatening to undermine a seemingly paradisal state, a conundrum that Atwood again communicates through food metaphors when Stan reflects on his renewed sex life with Charmaine, who has been supposedly programmed to fulfil his every desire: "Charmaine is toffee in his hands. She'll do it all, she'll say it all; she's everything he once longed for in the imaginary Jasmine, and more. True, the routine has become slightly predictable, but it would be surly to complain. Like complaining that the food's too delicious. What kind of complaint is that?" (302). Yet again, this supposedly utopian-like existence perpetuates the same ideological structures of Positron, including the conflation of humans with food.

Although Stan and Charmaine eventually escape the imprisoning environs of Positron, their so-called new life on the outside appears to be a return to the same enclosed neoliberal system. The couple takes up residence (again) in a suburban home in Vegas, a city associated with pleasure, money, and consumerism; Stan has resumed employment (again) in a sex-robot factory; and Charmaine confronts temptations (again) in her lingering sexual daydreams about Max. This time, however, Charmaine has supposedly been reprogramed to imprint sexually on her husband, and with the couple's garden, secure resources, baby girl, and intact marriage, this new enclosure appears nearly paradisal in fulfilling their every wish. So, is this truly an escape or just renewed compliance, and a repetition of the past?

Within *The Heart Goes Last,* characters' perceptions and choices are key to manoeuvring beyond their absolute conformity to the neoliberal system and repetition of previous mistakes. At the conclusion of the novel, the couple sits poised either to remain imprisoned or to make a conscious choice to safeguard each other and the greater good of their own private institution of marriage through ethical choices. On the couple's one-year anniversary of being "out," Jocelyn informs Charmaine that the brain procedure did not take place and that for the past year, she has resisted her own self-serving desires all on her own. The novel concludes with Jocelyn paraphrasing a line from John Milton, "The world is all before you, where to choose" (306), implying that Charmaine in her Eve-like role has the freedom to choose, to act in ways that will preserve the collective good of her marriage and the near-idyllic sanctuary of love and material security. The fact that their series of enclosed circumstances within neoliberal capitalism – first in their car, then in the Positron Project, and now in a Vegas suburb – have replicated from the past, to the present, to the future, gives the couple an advantage if they are willing to reflect carefully on the system that contains them, learn from the consequences of their actions, and not prioritize selfish appetites.

Atwood notes that in *A Christmas Carol,* Dickens's "covert intention – signalled by the work's one-time working title, 'The Sledgehammer' – was to strike a few more blows for the social justice he was so keen on by contrasting avarice and poverty, then proposing his usual antidote: an outflowing of private benevolence. For, as George Orwell has commented, though Dickens burned with anger at social injustices, he never went so far as to urge a whole-scale political revolution" ("Scrooge" 119). Dickens is an informative, intertextual allusion within Atwood's novel, and *The Heart Goes Last* similarly suggests that the all-pervasive capitalist system cannot be overthrown or escaped entirely. Instead, Atwood points to the possibility of learning lessons from past experiences and the possibility of benevolence and unselfishness, both of which provide the means to deviate within the master plot.

Conclusion

Ultimately, *The Heart Goes Last* concludes with the suggestion that there is always a degree of choice within confinement: Charmaine can risk paradise again through the pursuit of selfish desires, or she can embark with Stan on a new way of being in the world by curbing their appetites and acting responsibly, even within the systems and institutions that surround them. Throughout Atwood's ustopian parable, prison food plays a significant concrete and symbolic role in communicating the values of the neoliberal capitalist society, including ideological and systemic replication, reward for compliance, and objectification in the name of profit and use-value. This food also has the potential, however, to facilitate and communicate acts of resistance, by prompting consumers to reflect on the impacts of their actions and interconnectedness with other living beings. As much as supposedly utopian designers, such as the profiteers behind Positron, see food as an effective means of operationalizing and enforcing their vision, food ultimately remains grounded in material realities, open to other symbolic possibilities, and subject to individual consumers' scrutiny and choices, all of which serve as reminders of the limitations, responsibilities, and potential wrapped up in social dreaming and its satiric lessons for the future that are inescapably tied to the past and the present.

NOTES

1 For a related analysis of gendered modes of spatial confinement within Atwood's dystopian fiction, see Mabiana Camargo's chapter on the *MaddAddam* trilogy, in this volume.

2 In some respects, the twinned worlds of Consilience and the Positron Prison are examples of Augé's notion of "non-place" as described by Jessica McDonald in her essay in this volume, in that "individuals' identities become largely irrelevant as it is primarily their roles as passengers, consumers, or customers that define them" (179–80). In Atwood's *The Heart Goes Last*, the institutionalized mass identity of imprisoned consumer is so pervasive in every aspect of life, that it is nearly impossible to separate from it.

3 See McDonald's related discussion of urban foraging and the reimagining of one's environment through food as a form of personal agency within a systematized urban landscape (185–7).

4 For further discussion of Atwood's use of egg symbolism, see both Sceats's *Food, Consumption and the Body in Contemporary Women's Fiction*, and my article, "Ustopian Breakfasts: Margaret Atwood's *MaddAddam*."

5 In her research on broiler chickens through the fictional example of *Oryx and Crake*, Samantha Noll notes that Atwood's depiction of the "blob chicken" (genetically engineered to be headless) is not that different from today's industrially farmed chicken, "commonly called the 'designer chicken' … [which] is selectively bred to live in confinement and to produce more breast meat at the expense of the development of their internal organs" (274). Atwood carries this critique of the industry across her

dystopian novels as an example of how neoliberal capitalism permeates human society's unethical ways of relating to the world.

6 For related discussions of Atwood's representations of women as meat and as sources of sexually consumable parts, see Camargo's chapter in this volume.

7 Tiny Tim tomatoes were first propagated as a new variety in 1944 and were named after Dickens's character because the plant was "capable of being matured in a 5-inch pot for purposes of Christmas decorations" (New Hampshire 54).

WORKS CITED

Applebaum, Robert. "Concepts of Utopia, Concepts of Food." Utopian Appetites: The 21st Symposium of Australian Gastronomy, 3 Dec. 2016, Melbourne, Australia, unpublished conference paper.

Atwood, Margaret. *Alias Grace*. McClelland & Stewart, 1996.

– "Bread." *The Iowa Review*, vol. 12, no. 2/3, 1981, pp. 7–8. *JSTOR*, https://www.jstor.org/stable/20155632.

– *The Heart Goes Last*. McClelland & Stewart, 2015.

– *In Other Worlds: SF and the Human Imagination*, McClelland & Stewart, 2011.

– "The Legendary Margaret Atwood on Modern Love." Interview by Rachel Giese. *Chatelaine*, 15 Aug. 2015, https://chatelaine.com/living/books/margaret-atwood-modern-love-government-snooping-normal/.

– "Save Our Prison Farms Rally, Kingston, Ontario, June 6." *Margaret Atwood: Year of the Flood*, 7 June 2010, https://marg09.wordpress.com/2010/06/07/save-our-prison-farms-rally-kingston-ontario-june-6/.

– "Scrooge: An Introduction." 2009. *Burning Questions: Essays & Occasional Pieces, 2004–2021*, McClelland & Stewart, 2022, pp. 119–23.

Augé, Marc. *Non-Places: Introduction to an Anthropology of Supermodernity*. Translated by John Howe, Verso, 1995.

Boyd, Shelley. "Ustopian Breakfasts: Margaret Atwood's *MaddAddam*." *Utopian Studies*, vol. 26, no. 1, 2015, pp. 160–81.

Chipman, Stuart. "Margaret Atwood's *Bread*: A Deceptive Argument against Inhumane Indifference." *2009 Writing Awards*, Ruth & Ted Braun Awards for Writing Excellence, vol. 12, Saginaw Valley State U, pp. 2–3, https://svsu.edu/media/writingprogram/docs/writingprogrampdf/Chipman.pdf.

Dickens, Charles. *A Christmas Carol: The Original Manuscript*. Dover Publications, 1967.

Foucault, Michel. *Discipline and Punishment: The Birth of the Prison*. 1975. Translated by Alan Sheridan, 2nd Vintage ed., Random House, 1995.

Godderis, Rebecca. "Dining In: The Symbolic Power of Food in Prison." *The Howard Journal of Crime and Justice*, vol. 45, no. 3, 2006, pp. 255–67.

Jameson, Frederic. *Archaeologies of the Future: The Desire Called Utopia and Other Science Fictions*. Verso, 2007.

– "The Politics of Utopia." *The New Left Review*, vol. 25, Jan./Feb. 2004, https://newleftreview.org/issues/ii25/articles/fredric-jameson-the-politics-of-utopia.

McDonald, Jessica. "Small Acts of Urban Place-Making in Nalo Hopkinson's *Skin Folk*." *ReVisions: Speculating in Literature and Film in Canada*, edited by Wendy Roy, U of Toronto Press, 2025, pp. 179–201.

Montgomery, Marc. "Canada's Prison Farms Redux." *Radio Canada*, 29 June 2016, http://www.rcinet.ca/en/2016/06/29/canadas-prison-farms-redux/.

More, Thomas. *Utopia*. 1516. Broadview Press, 2010.

Murray, Sean. "Food for Critical Thought: Teaching the Science Fiction of Margaret Atwood." *Pedagogy*, vol. 14, no. 3, 2014, pp. 475–98.

New Hampshire Agricultural Experiment Station. "Agricultural Research in New Hampshire, 1944, Bulletin, no. 354." *NHAES Bulletin* 316, 1944.

Nicholson, Mervyn. "Eat – or Be Eaten: An Interdisciplinary Metaphor." *Mosaic*, vol. 24, no. 3–4, 1991, pp. 191–210. *JSTOR*, http://www.jstor.org/stable/24780473.

Noll, Samantha. "Broiler Chickens and a Critique of Epistemic Foundations of Animal Modification." *Journal of Agricultural Environmental Ethics*, vol. 26, 2013, pp. 273–80, https://doi.org/10.1007/s10806-011-9362-y.

Ringo, Rano, and Jasmine Sharma. "'Do Time Now, Buy Time for the Future': Phallic Deception and Techno-Sexual Agency in Margaret Atwood's *The Heart Goes Last*." *Messengers from the Stars: On Science Fiction and Fantasy*, no. 4, 2019, pp. 73–87.

Sargent, Lyman Tower. "The Three Faces of Utopianism Revisited." *Utopian Studies*, vol. 5, no. 1, 1994, pp. 1–37. *JSTOR*, http://www.jstor.org/stable/20719246.

Sceats, Sarah. *Food, Consumption and the Body in Contemporary Women's Fiction*. Cambridge UP, 2000.

Sexton, Lori. "Penal Subjectivities: Developing a Theoretical Framework for Penal Consciousness." *Punishment & Society*, vol. 17, no. 1, 2015, pp. 114–36.

Thomas, Jim. "Passing Time: The Ironies of Food in Prison Culture." *Food for Thought: Essays on Eating and Culture*, edited by Lawrence C. Rubin, McFarland & Company, 2008, pp. 166–79.

"Like the Voice of a Mad Angel": Hungry Ghosts in Kai Cheng Thom's *Fierce Femmes and Notorious Liars: A Dangerous Trans Girl's Confabulous Memoir*

KAI MCKENZIE

In Kai Cheng Thom's novel *Fierce Femmes and Notorious Liars: A Dangerous Trans Girl's Confabulous Memoir*, images of hungry ghosts create storied connections across space, generations, and time. Ghosts represent historical trauma and the ways in which those who are marginalized, excluded, erased, and disappeared continue to make themselves known. Thom's story extends speculative fiction's capacity to create "cognitive estrangement" as it draws on magic, horror, and the uncanny to unleash "forbidden desire" and reveal the mutuality of abjection (Booker 5, 8).[1] These sites of fracture also become sources of new possibilities as the surfaces of encounter shift and interpenetrate. Thom reveals the oppressive distortions of ciscentric society, which assigns and assumes gender and marginalizes and monstrifies those who do not cooperate with its institutionalized gender code. To do so, she uses the Chinese hungry ghost figure, drawn from stories about ancestors who, having acted badly out of greed during life, are left to haunt the living after death as starving figures with bloated bellies and tiny mouths. She also draws on the ritual power of the hungry ghost festival and the way it creates an atmosphere of change.[2] Her poetic novel is full of multifarious, culturally hybrid hungry ghosts, which represent the different ways in which ciscentric society haunts the trans girl at the centre of Thom's novel.

Using theories of abjection, affect, and the Gothic to analyse the Chinese hungry ghost and other monstrous figures, I argue that Thom uses these monstrosities to represent all aspects of internalized trauma, but also possibilities for healing. Thom's culturally situated themes of desire and haunting speak to affective and material forms of exclusion and abjection as projected onto gender-non-conforming embodiments and practices, as well as to possibilities for relational healing. In relation to Matthew Cormier's discussion in this volume of the character

Gerry's struggle to find balance and ground as non-binary in a frightening and changing world in Nancy Lee's *The Age*, Gwen Rose's appreciation for Indigenous resurgence in Cherie Dimaline's *The Marrow Thieves*, and Jessica McDonald's insights about the possibilities of transforming perspectives through simple acts of connection in Nalo Hopkinson's *Skin Folk*, I show that Thom's fantastical trans memoir demonstrates both internalized transphobia and the means to shift and transform perspectives. Like Gerry, Thom's protagonist struggles with shame and rage after internalizing the outer world's transphobic hatreds. Like the young characters in Dimaline's novel, she finds healing through community. And like the characters in *Skin Folk*, she discovers and facilitates small shifts in perspective through food preparation and other simple acts of caretaking which lead to large-scale and powerful transformative changes in the world.

In accord with affect theory, the gender-diverse characters in this novel respond to systemic exclusions and projections, with experiences of shame driving them towards new positions and new understandings. Affect theory provides a means of understanding the way feelings move through society, the way transphobic exclusions create an oppressive cultural atmosphere which generates trauma. According to Melissa Gregg and Gregory Seigworth, "Affect arises in the midst of *in-between-ness*: in the capacities to act and be acted upon.... At once intimate and impersonal, affect accumulates across both relatedness and interruptions in relatedness, becoming a palimpsest of force-encounters traversing the ebbs and swells of intensities that pass between 'bodies'" (1–2). Gregg and Seigworth's arguments suggest that the body's outer skin is no defence against the way society's transphobia invades, unsettles, and destroys a person from the inside. Transphobia is not simply a one-way transfer of abjection onto an object, but rather an experience of mutual tension. By projecting monstrosity onto the trans person's body, the surrounding cisworld becomes equally monstrous, because the projection is not really a distancing, but rather a drawing towards. This is the essential problem that Thom addresses: how to heal from this mutual horror, in which all are caught.

Transgender literary theory, building on queer theory, positions the rage resulting from the internalization of society's projections of monstrosity as a source of transformative power. In her essay "My Words to Victor Frankenstein above the Village of Chamounix: Performing Transgender Rage," Susan Stryker compares the rage of Frankenstein's creature to her own rage at being cast as monstrous. Stryker's arguments illuminate how resistant identities are born and position transgender ways of birthing and shaping sexed bodies as natural, and cisgender ways of assigning gender at birth as oppressive and disturbing.

Like Stryker, Thom uses queer gothic tropes in designing the spaces and affective atmospheres through which her protagonist moves, treating trauma experienced in the past as alive and present as hungry ghosts roaming the land and living in the bodies, psychic modes, and relationships of the characters. Eve Kosofsky Sedgwick argues in *Touching Feeling* that, "like a stigma, shame is itself a form of communication" that develops prior to an infant's ability to conceptualize their feelings (36). By moving both "toward painful individuation [and] toward uncontrollable relationality," shame lives in the spaces where selves develop (37). Julia Kristeva theorizes abjection as referring to "the jettisoned object [which] is radically excluded," approaching "the place where meaning collapses" (246). Similarly, Sara Ahmed argues that the "impossible" figure of the stranger conceals social differences and forms of displacement by revealing "processes of inclusion and exclusion, incorporation and expulsion, that constitute the boundaries of bodies and communities" (5, 7). Shame develops from broken relationships, from exclusion and abjection, yet the sites of exclusion are also sites of connection. The very act of rejecting others in a phobic response signals a specific kind of relationality because the need to reject indicates the need to define self in response to that which is rejected. Thus, sites of encounter with difference in Thom's novel can be read as sites of struggle that are productive of new forms of relationship and identity.

This edge of abjection upon which the protagonist travels explains Thom's use of queer gothic patterns. Laura Westengard points out that buried in the structure of gothic narrative "is an ongoing state of disruption that reflects insidious trauma" (6). This type of trauma is a persistent and devastating state resulting from constant micro-aggressions and an all-pervading hostile atmosphere. According to Westengard, the tradition of gothic writing involves the use of "atmospheric gloom," "the structure of embeddedness through stories within stories and frames of found manuscripts and letters," a "power-hungry sexually predatory older male" (8), as well as "[d]oubling and paranoia," "splitting, replicating, merging, fear, and desire," which make "indistinguishable the line between 'murderous or amorous'" (9, quoting Sedgwick). Although the genre traditionally involves a conservative return to the status quo after representing "difference and transgression" (9), its circuitous pathways involve "shape-shifting abilities of a form built on indeterminacy" (11). Gothic narrative, therefore, provides powerful generic space to explore the pressures placed on gender nonconforming people in a cisnormative, patriarchal society, the feelings those pressures evoke, and the difficult and dissociative aspects of identity that result. These pressures lead characters in Thom's novel towards new and hybrid possibilities.

The gothic narrative tradition centres on a female protagonist who is contained and cloistered and evokes fear of the monstrous feminine as the underside of this containment. The monstrosity in which trans women are cast has roots in the Euro-pagan and Christian history of the monstrous feminine in Western literature and culture. Barbara Creed explains that representations of feminine monstrosity, "terrifying creatures who were part-woman and part-animal" and who "haunt the myths of the ancient world" (180), express masculine-centred cultural fears and contain women within a patriarchal and repressive frame. The Sphinx, with "the face and breasts of a woman, a lion's body and the wings of a bird," the gorgons, "winged women with hair made of living snakes [who] could turn men to stone with their deadly stare," the lamia who "devoured children" and featured a "serpent's tail," and the "sea-dragon, the echidna, … half woman and half-serpent, [who] ruled over the earth's corrupt substances such as fetid water, slime and disease" (180), all haunted the imagination of cultures centred around men, laying the foundation for the transphobic cultural obsession with trans women today.

Creed demonstrates how the Catholic Church persecuted women, executing them as witches after gruesome torture sessions which demonstrated an obsession "with the nature of female sexuality and the kinds of sexual acts witches were said to perpetrate" (181). Witches were seen as chimaera, connected with animal nature, perceived to be sinful and lustful. Sexualized as either "lesbian, masculine, androgynous" (18), or hyperfeminized (15), in either case they were presented as a threat to traditional feminine domesticity and expressive of "current anxieties" including "epidemic contagion" (Creed 14, xv). Horror films of the late twentieth and early twenty-first century carry on this tradition, casting monstrous feminine characters as werewolves or vampires who "draw on the powers of the uncanny to terrify audiences," sometimes "disturb[ing] the boundaries that divide culture from nature and human from animal" (185). The monstrous feminine continues to haunt Western culture in representations of the "female vampire, cat woman, leech woman, ape woman, *femme fatale*, spider woman, mother alien, and female werewolf" in modern horror films (Creed 180). Vampires, in particular, express the fear of the returning dead in a way that is comparable to the Chinese hungry ghost tradition upon which Thom draws, and they connect with histories of feminine monsters who are perceived to suck the life force out of people (Creed 6).

Ghosts represent these haunted sites and the ways in which those who are marginalized, excluded, erased, and disappeared continue to make themselves known. As Avery Gordon points out in *Ghostly Matters*, haunting "registers the harm inflicted or the loss sustained by a social violence done in the past or in the present" (xvi). These sites of fracture also become sources of new possibilities as the surfaces of encounter shift and interpenetrate.

Cynthia Sugars and Gerry Turcotte recognize the unsettled and unhomely aspects of Canadian life. These include the "unresolved memory traces and occluded histories resulting from experiences of colonial oppression, diasporic migration, or national consolidation" (vii) and the way European settlers are haunted by "fear and desire" (viii). In their introduction to *Unsettled Remains: Canadian Literature and the Postcolonial Gothic*, Sugars and Turcotte argue that fear of Indigenous people who have been rendered ghostlike in settler imagination, through annihilation of their lands and livelihoods and from desire for a stable sense of home which eludes them, leaves settlers with "haunted minds rather than a haunted wilderness" (ix), while for Indigenous people, unhomeliness results from "historical crisis and dispossession" (x). Like Gordon, Sugars and Turcotte understand the "ambivalence, liminality, mimicry, boundary dissolution, and epistemological destabilization that characterize negotiations that occur in these locations" (viii). In this sense, Canadian spaces carry a history and aura of gothic uncanniness.

While of course there are enormous differences, some parallels are evident between the unhomed experiences of Indigenous Peoples in Canada and the ways in which trans characters in Thom's novel struggle with deprivation and dispossession of self, home, and security. In both situations, there is a sense of displacement that impacts and undermines relationships, as boundaries between self and other become fraught. Colonization involves theft of land and genocidal practices of destroying livelihoods, lifeways, food sources, and cultural integrity, while transphobia involves theft and erasure of gender-diverse cultural histories and practices of destroying lives and possibilities for survival; both share atmospheres of fear, stigmatization, and destruction of possibilities for living. They are also interconnected, as colonizers of what we call North America made a point of targeting and destroying gender-diverse Two-Spirit people and enforcing the normative European binary gender system on Indigenous Peoples.

Thom creates an expansive Canadian Gothic by creating a landscape haunted by both colonization and transphobia. The city of Gloom where the protagonist experiences a transphobic and stifling childhood is also dark, grey, and gloomy because white colonizers "won it in so corrupt a fashion" (7). This fusion of influences speaks to the intersectional experiences of the protagonist, who faces both racist and transphobic forms of violence and exclusion.

Through her creative use of the gothic mode, Thom blends the European monstrous feminine with Canadian literary histories of haunting and the Chinese hungry ghost tradition. Stories of Chinese hungry ghosts revolve around greedy ancestors who haunt the living after death. The starving, ghostly ancestors can never satisfy their hunger. In Thom's *Fierce Femmes and Notorious Liars,* haunted hunger is used to express the sense of lack that a young, diasporic Chinese-Canadian trans woman experiences through imposed shame and abjection. The family home of Thom's unnamed protagonist is the place where her shame, hunger, and desire for release from a stifling, transphobic, and racist environment is linked to her parents' hunger for success as new immigrants from China and the restrictions imposed on them (42). Their fears and needs prevent her from satisfying her own desires for fulfilment.

As an example of speculative fiction, a genre that works "to formulate challenges to the status quo and to imagine the possibility of alternatives" (Booker 5), Thom's coming-of-age novel bridges realism and fantasy to enter into the dangerous and difficult spaces of a young trans woman's psyche and to unlock healing powers. The protagonist moves from a more realistic space towards a more fantastic one, yet realism and fantasy overlap and interconnect in both her childhood landscape and the magical city to which she flees. Speculation allows Thom to access deeper truths about trauma and healing, to represent what her narrator calls "something kick-ass and intense with hot sex and gang violence and maybe zombies and lots of magic" (3), instead of the "11,378 transgender memoirs out there, which are just regurgitations of the same old story that makes us boring and dead and safe to read about" (3). Instead of trying to package trans lives so that they are acceptable to a cisgender world, Thom wants to delve into the intense psychological and sociological challenges that result from the ongoing transphobia and ever-present hostility in which trans people live. She plays with the idea of memoir, by calling her novel a "Confabulous Memoir." By working at genre boundaries between memoir and speculative fiction, she is able to get into the emotional places that become locked under conditions of trauma and find the keys that can release healing possibilities.

Told in first-person voice in a diary-like format, *Fierce Femmes* relates the story of a young transgender girl fleeing her oppressive parents for a magical yet devastatingly real community of trans women. The protagonist's parents project their own fears and failures onto her, their hungry unmet desires as new immigrants, as well as their transphobia. The protagonist's childhood home, a "crooked house in the heart of gloom," located in a Vancouver-like coastal city, is expressive of a blend of desire, hunger, and fear. In this landscape, the protagonist's body becomes a haunted site, filled with killer bees and a gentle ghost friend. When she travels to a fantastical place "West of the ocean and east of the wind, ... the City of Smoke and Lights" (20), she finds an emerging community of trans women haunted by the demonization of feminine power in Western culture and protected by the ghost of a murdered trans woman. The opposing ghost of a killer policeman represents oppressive authority, but also the mutuality of violence, as the protagonist and the cop join and meet in agonizing recognition. Finally, stories themselves are cast as ghosts. Mad and haunting tales emerge from the ground spontaneously like spirits. Hungry ghosts represent all aspects of oppression and containment for the trans girl, but also the means and resources for release.

The hungry house of the protagonist's childhood represents the thwarted hungers of her Chinese-Canadian immigrant parents, for inclusion, recognition, and wealth, "in a place called Gloom, where the sky is always grey and the rain is always falling" (7). The place is gloomy because it is haunted by European colonial conquest. In this place of colonial gloom, her childhood home is like a Chinese hungry ghost; it is "a crooked house whose walls curved and bulged in the middle and narrowed at the top and the bottom, like a starving person with a swollen belly" (7). With its bulging middle and narrow neck, it wants "to devour [her] and digest [her] whole" (21). She compares this house to "a giant spider web: the walls and floor trembled with every move you made, so that you could never be sure you were completely alone. And it stuck on you, grasped at you with its hungry windows and hungry doors, pulling you in so you couldn't leave, couldn't breathe, couldn't dream or achoo" (42). This hungry ghost house image connects the protagonist with the tradition of her ancestors.

The Chinese hungry ghost tradition has ancient roots. Mu-chou Poo discusses concepts of ghosts in ancient Chinese religion and points out that "the haunting dead, and their ghosts," those who died in a violent or unfortunate way, unlike those peacefully and ritually buried, "are the product of the unsettled conscience of the living" (183), but that ghosts could also be benevolent, sacred, and revered. Ghosts are entwined with beliefs about the need to respect and worship ancestors (184). In a visual study of the hungry ghost festival in Singapore,

Terence Heng explains that the rituals of the festival, which originated in China and spread through the diaspora, take place in the seventh month of the Lunar Calendar (usually August), and "involve a syncretic mix of animism, ancestor worship, Taoism and Buddhism" (148). Ancestors are believed to be released from purgatory to roam the earth and need "sustenance, entertainment and spending money" (148). The rituals involve providing offerings of food and burning incense and paper money for the ancestral spirits, who will give back in turn in the form of material blessings (156).

Hetty Lanier Keaton looks at the way Chinese-American women authors Maxine Hong Kingston, Amy Tan, and Lan Samantha Chang use hunger and food imagery connected with the Buddhist mythological figure of the hungry ghost to present problems of family breakdown, failures of communication, and unsatisfied longings. Keaton points out that in the works of these authors, unlike in the conventional hungry ghost tradition, there is no clear and satisfying resolution to the problems of family hunger, which remain perpetually unsatisfied (iii). Thom, in contrast, weaves a satisfying resolution to the problem of hunger in her novel by having her protagonist learn how to bake a magical and transformative healing cake. The resolution of her novel reads like a hungry ghost festival, in which the unsatisfied, desiring ghosts are fed and fulfilled, when the aura of the forgiveness cake spills out into the world and heals fractured relationships, trauma, and cultural wounds.

The thwarted hungers of the protagonist's parents are expressed as the hungry ghost of the swollen, unsatisfied house, which consumes the protagonist alive, carrying unresolved past trauma forward and generating new trauma in a complex mix of haunting desire. The protagonist's hunger for release from the oppressive house combines desire for release from transphobia, from the parents' heavy demands and expectations, and from the generalized racism of the landscape as the Chinese hungry ghost takes on new associations and connections in diaspora. These haunted margins are characterized by hybridity. A key aspect of their haunted nature is the way ghostly hungers mix, so that the protagonist's hunger to be fully enabled as a woman is interwoven with her hunger for connection and place in diaspora and for freedom from her parents' oppressive hungers. Haunting hunger is enhanced, made more uncanny and more horrific, by virtue of being impossible to purify as singular. Instead, its uncanny plurality makes locating causes more difficult.

In this haunted landscape, the protagonist herself becomes a ghost as her body and spirit internalize the trauma of her surroundings. Her parents' frustrated and unsatisfied hungers, leaving them "dead tired from their dead-end factory jobs" and eager to map their hopes onto the protagonist, keep her "trapped in the belly of the crooked house" (8). She feels pressured to be the filial and studious son and improve the family's standing in Canada (9). When they shout at her, spank and beat her as she fails school tests and uses her "mother's black stockings," pretending they are "a princess's long, black hair" (9), they mix their desires for full standing in Canada with their gendered expectations for their child. These pressures cast the protagonist into a haunted world, as she "slip[s] away into the darkness and run[s] off to the nearby playground ... overrun with weeds, the wooden jungle gym rotted and collapsed," with "leftover needles" underfoot and bats that "flutter overhead" (9). She hurls herself "toward the heavens" on "a rusty metal swing set": "The family of mangy three-legged coyotes that roamed our neighbourhood would yip and howl, and I would feel my whole body clenching up with hungry hope as I planned my Great Escape" (9–10). She learns how to pick locks and sneak around, haunting the world just as it haunts her. References to bats and coyotes help to create the haunted landscape through which the protagonist moves, while her efforts to propel herself into a connection with heaven and flight serve to emphasize the intense hunger that drives her and speak of spiritual possibilities.

Her body becomes a haunted site through the invasion of killer bees and the gentle ghost friend who supports and soothes her when she feels anxious. The bees teach her that sometimes you have to surrender to forces that are greater than you. Thom's narrator provides two alternative versions of the nature and outcome of this invasion, which represent the way society preys on the trans girl, beginning with the first and then correcting herself to provide the second as the true version. In the first version, "[f]at golden honeybees" begin to swarm (17) when the protagonist is six years old and playing in "neighbour Old Man Tom's garden," with its "jungled snarl of vines and spiky shrubs and sticky orange flowers that dripped a sweet-smelling clear liquid," pretending to be "a princess riding a unicorn into battle against the Shadow Army" (16). As "a furious cloud," the bees land on her hair and skin; her ability to manage her terror, pray, and beg forgiveness leads to a resolution as "[l]ittle by little, the bees and I made peace" (17). In the second version, this event happens "[o]n a cold winter evening, [when her] mother opened the door to the back porch of the crooked house so she could smoke a cigarette" (17). The bees "raced past her, ... a boiling cloud of rage and desire, searching for the sweetest, softest thing they could find" (17), entered the child's body through "every orifice, and … drank up all the nectar they could hold" (17). Once they drain her of life, some stay, "[a]addicted to [her] sweet blood" (18). These two versions of the manner and nature of the invasion of the bees, which end up haunting the protagonist's body and psyche, suggest possible qualities of relationship between the trans girl and the society at large.

The first version seems to represent the desired relationship, even as it signals the threats, fears, and shadows of a transphobic world. Fat and friendly honeybees come and check her out, and once she and they get to know each other, they make peace. What actually happens, according to the narrator protagonist in the second version, seems more in tune with the kinds of insidious trauma described by Westengard. Society, in the form of killer bees, drinks up all her sweetness, all her life-sustaining moisture. Some bees become addicted to her sweet blood and stay, in a representation of insidious trauma, that overwhelming and debilitating sense of being preyed on, of having society's projections of abjection within oneself. A person's skin provides no defence against this invasion. The external becomes internal. Even though the protagonist uses her "small, silver, reliable" pocketknife to try to get rid of these bees, "angry – alive – wriggling – under my skin," by "open[ing] up mouths in my skin / to try / and let them / out" (19),[3] they stay and haunt her every time she feels anxious or threatened. The bees specifically threaten her when she feels sexually in danger or challenged. Then they "swarm through [her] body, snarling and stinging" (58). These images of bees which feed on the protagonist mirror the way the protagonist describes her childhood home, which "ate you, that house. It kept you in it, but it didn't keep things out" (42). These images evoke transphobia, which generates insidious trauma that pins, traps, suffocates, and feeds on its victims.

The protagonist's Ghost Friend, in contrast, is supportive, rather than threatening. Ghost Friend echoes Poo's point that in ancient Chinese culture ghosts could be either dangerous or supportive and revered. This ancestral energy connected with ghosts suggests that Ghost Friend might represent historically lost threads of support for the trans girl. The protagonist first meets Ghost Friend while having "a picnic in a local cemetery" (23),[4] across the street from "this really amazing fried chicken place" run by "the Korean lady" who is the only person to recognize her womanhood. The protagonist reminds this restaurant proprietor of her granddaughter, because of her long hair (24). As she sits on a bench enjoying her lunch, she feels "a hand on [her] shoulder" (24). At first responding with fear, she comes to realize that she is "being contacted by a ghost.… And Ghost Friend wasn't at all threatening.… There was just something about the way they touched me – gentle, tentative, almost apologetic. Like a warm breeze, if breezes had fingers. And I realized Ghost Friend was shy" (24). After sharing these warm, friendly touches, they develop a special form of communication.

Ghost Friend is able to move through the protagonist's sexual inhibitions and bring her to orgasm, something that was always impeded in the past by what she describes as "the sensation of dark black bees buzzing and wriggling inside me, wherever I was touched" (25): "But Ghost Friend was so slow, so barely substantial, so responsive to my direction, that the bees and buzzing and wriggling did not come" (25). Ghost Friend soothes and comforts her whenever the bees warn her of danger, "brushing against [her] shoulders like flower petals" (26). Later, when the predatory physician she consults for gender-affirming medical care, whom she calls Dr. Crocodile, touches her, the killer bees swarm inside her. At the same time, "Ghostly fingers brush [her] neck" (58), indicating that, though opposed, the two ghost presences seem to play mutual roles, with the bees alerting her to sexual and predatorial danger while Ghost Friend helps to calm her.

The City of Smoke and Lights, to which the protagonist flees to escape her oppressive home, contains both goddess-like trans women and the spirits of murdered trans women. With its spaces devoted to pleasure, winding streets, and red lanterns, it is a realm symbolic of both violence toward trans women and longing for release from that violence. As the narrator says of this city, here "You can be the mango sweet golden skin woman swinging her hips to the bass at three in the morning or the androgynous skeleton running cold bone hands through the sweat of her hair" (20–1). These dreamed and desired possibilities place the trans girl between hope and fear, between life and death, between the sweet and golden images of satisfaction and the stone-cold fears of hunger and despair. Hunger represents both the desire of the trans girl for a sense of wholeness, connection, and community, and the way those desires are haunted by society's deathly fears of trans people, which she has internalized as fears of self. Hunger is that edge upon which she must travel and the reason she herself is portrayed as haunting even as she is haunted by the world.

In the city, haunting is connected to the powerful spirit of First Femme, the first trans woman to be murdered there, who protects the trans women who work as sex workers. The all-pervasive ghosts of murdered trans women make up the atmosphere and air of the city, which is "stained ash grey from the glamorous cigarette lips of hungry ghosts swimming through the fog" (20). These hungry ghosts are somehow connected with the air of transformative possibility which pervades the place, where "[y]ou can be anything you want: baller, biker, bad girl, punk rocker, faerie queen, goth, artist, stoner, vampire, dominant, submissive, witch, man, woman, medusa, monster, mother, poet, demon, lost boi, foxfire phantom gleaming out of the night, superhero, goddess, strong, beautiful, powerful, untouchable, whole" (20). This transformative power and multiplicity of possibilities mark the protagonist's journey, as she begins to affirm her womanhood through physical transformation and emotional connections with other trans women. The ancestral spirits of dead trans women provide the more supportive atmosphere through which the protagonist moves.

The hungry ghosts of murdered trans women who haunt the City of Smoke and Lights also form the supportive background for the spirit of the legendary First Femme, whose "bones still lie somewhere beneath the cobblestones" of the Street of Miracles, "along with her ossified heart, calling trans girls to her. Exhorting them to live their lives boldly, no matter the price" (38). Her murder marked the origin of the street "over seventy years ago," when she "was beaten to death by a would-be john in front of a dozen bystanders" (38). The spiritual power of First Femme and her accompanying multitude of hungry trans ghosts parallels the living power of the trans women, whose "magic, more than anything else, … sustains the everlasting festival that the Street of Miracles is so well-known for" (38). These "fiercest and most powerful femmes" generate the atmosphere of this Street, where "[t]ime is slow and memory fluid" (37), suggestive of a ritual space where past and present fuse and interpenetrate.

The community of goddess-like trans women in *Fierce Femmes* has a long European supernatural lineage. However, Thom works to dis-identify with that tradition,[5] reclaim transfeminine power, cast the men who prey on trans women as monstrous, and recognize that monstrosity embraces both those demonized and those who demonize. In her fusion of Chinese hungry ghost and Euro-pagan traditions, Thom creates a hybrid landscape on the Street of Miracles. "Red-gold lanterns float on invisible strings between the rooftops of restaurants, theatres, bars, sex shops, lounges, strip clubs, hookah dens," and "[c]louds of fragrant smoke waft through the air" (37–8), reminiscent of both the Chinese Lantern Festival, heralding return of light after winter,[6] and the Hungry Ghost Festival, with its wafting smoke from incense. But on this Street a "pantheon of goddesses" and assorted spirits and ghosts out of ancient Greek and European folklore live and work. This hybrid landscape of ghosts and traditions from Europe and Asia leads to a sense of openness and possibility. By combining features of Chinese festivals with imagery of European mythological history, Thom creates a fantastic space of cultural fusion.

Figures from each realm of tradition are no longer contained in that space, but are let loose upon the world, ready to mix, blend, and inspire new forms and new ideas. The women who form the protagonist's new community include Rapunzelle, who "blocks out the sun wherever she goes, an obsidian globe of a woman, always in boat-sized hot-pink leopard-print heels," with "[h]er weave … a forest of long gold braids" (38); Lucretia, "a white, blond princess with legs a mile long" (38); Valaria, "who is six feet tall with a shaved head" and "earrings made with a chain of spiked hoops," who "rarely speaks, but when she does, her voice rolls like quiet thunder" and who "looks like the Goddess of War"; Alzena the Witch, "who is all bones and enormous golden eyes and long, painted fingernails"; Esperanza, "who speaks only Spanish and always wears bright red lipstick"; and Marie-Eve, "whose face is covered in wrinkles" (39). These women are strong, powerful, and dangerous, new expressions of the European monstrous feminine, reclaiming their space and agency in the face of a world that continues to persecute them. Though clearly real in the frame of the novel, they also have ghostlike auras in connection with the many persecuted witches, goddesses, werewolves, and vampires of the European past.

In contrast, Dr. Crocodile represents the haunting presence of medical doctors who fetishize and prey on trans women and echoes the gothic inclusion of a predatory and sexually hungry older male. His office waiting room is full of ghostlike patients, including "a person who looks like a skeleton with skin tacked onto the bones as an afterthought [and] rattling breaths coming in and out of their mouth," "a bald person who must have once had gigantic blackbird wings, but most of the feathers have fallen out," and a vampire-like "old woman with ratty orange-striped fur and a tail" who "once had a mouth full of fangs" (54). Dr. Crocodile's presence is uncanny, "[h]is palm … hot and moist, like a swamp" with "a toothy grin" that never leaves his face and eyes that never blink (57). He fetishizes the protagonist's body by touching her "everywhere" (58) and offering free service in exchange for her participation in "[a] little program.… All in the interest of science, of course" (59). When he whispers his price into her ear, the implication is that he is sexually and medically abusing his clients and that medical practices controlling access to care for trans people are inherently abusive.[7]

Through multiple forms of hungry ghosts, Thom explores possibilities to link with ancestral powers and shift outcomes. First Femme magically absorbs a dead policeman's body during the trans women's war of vengeance against the men who abuse and murder them. The protagonist escapes from the heavy battle into a "small, high-walled courtyard" surrounding "an empty fountain with a huge shape in the middle," which is "so overrun with vines that [she] can't tell what it's supposed to be" (109). She is followed by a policeman dragging and beating Lucretia, and she ends up murdering him to save Lucretia. In the pained moment following this brutal and self-protective act, when the women are expecting the police to arrive and haul them off to jail, the fountain comes alive. The vines pull the cop into the well and the statue is revealed as "a stone statue of an enormous woman with a round belly and giant breasts. Her eyes are closed, a beatific expression on her face. She is wearing a sleeveless dress with a flowing train and plunging neckline that shows off her Adam's apple like a magnificent jewel, and her hair falls in ringlets to her waist" (116). As they watch in amazement, "[w]ater begins to run down her stone cheeks, in a trickle at first, then in rivulets, then steady streams. It gushes over the curves and valleys of her body, and into the well, which fills up impossibly quickly" (116). This image of the sacred spirit of First Femme coming alive to save them demonstrates the close relationship between ghosts, which carry the pain of past and present trauma, and mythical or legendary spirits, who create the foundation for strength and resilience.

The ghost of the dead policeman, who haunts the protagonist's nightmares, represents her agonizing recognition of and reconciliation with her own propensity for violence, in accord with the gothic tradition of fusion of the murderous and the amorous. He also demonstrates the mutuality of abjection, the way those casting others as abject become equally abject, and those cast as abject get drawn into the pain and violence of the situation. Instead of being an act of exclusion which keeps danger at bay, abjection is an act of mutual interpenetration, which is both violent and strangely intimate. The protagonist agonizes over her propensity for violence. When a man tries to take advantage of her during her bus ride to the City of Smoke and Lights, she nearly murders him with her martial arts frenzy and "animal fury" (28). When Lucretia teases her for not having breasts, she attacks Lucretia, "spinning her around and slamming her face into the stained cushions" (52), challenging anyone to disagree with her claim that she is just as much a woman as Lucretia.

After killing the policeman, she recognizes her propensity for violence: "*You like hurting people. That's why you killed that cop; it wasn't to save Lucretia, that's for sure. You're not the kind of girl who saves people. You're the kind who kills them*" (114). The vengeful action taken by the trans women as "Lipstick Lacerators" against the murderous men involves violence which almost destroys them. Even the protagonist's response to her first own cocoon-like apartment involves a desperate love that verges on violence. She loves it "with fierce, starving joy," saying, "I pummelled the futon with my feet and my fists like I wanted to kill it, like I wanted it to know how it hurt to love it so much" (43). The insidious trauma that has governed her life has left her unable to experience sex without the killer bees of predatorial transphobia roiling inside her (except with her gentle Ghost Friend) and unable to experience love without pain and violence.

The problem of her intimate relationship with violence, both as victim and as perpetrator, comes to a moment of confrontation and recognition when she meets, in a nightmare, the ghost of the policeman whom she has killed. In the gothic tradition of encounter with an intimate other who exposes the secrets of the self, she and the man meet in a moment charged with erotic attraction and mutuality. She feels followed by something that she cannot outrun, which appears as "Him. The cop. The monster. The zombie. Tyler. The cop I killed" (124). Initially, "[h]is body starts out rotting and horrible – full of pits and gaping holes, exposed organs the colour of raw, putrid meat," with a head that is "caved in" and "hangs at that unnatural angle" (124, 125). However, she notes, "[a]s he gets closer and closer, he starts to heal. The ragged edges of the holes smooth and close, his flesh reknits itself and blooms into living colour. His neck rights itself and his skull mends, covered by glinting golden hair. His eyes shine bright blue" (125). Instead of running and screaming, she feels paralyzed, even as the bees buzz through her dream body: "By the time he reaches me, his body is fresh and perfectly formed in the image of blond, muscled, porn-star masculinity. Like a fascist angel. His tattered uniform falls away and crumbles to dust, and then his underwear. His dick juts out from his abdomen, like a stabbing weapon. He looms naked in front of me, huge and menacing" (125). As a ghost returning, he represents her guilt, her culpability, as well as her fears.

Through their conversation, he names and reveals her deepest fear about herself, with a gentle lover's voice: "I know you.... Longing for the power to make other people afraid, because that's the only way you know to get rid of the fear in yourself. You hit people because you hate your body. You hate people like Lucretia, people you think are beautiful, because you don't love yourself" (126). This truthful information delivered by the ghost of the man who chased and nearly killed her friend Lucretia, and whom she has killed, paralyzes the protagonist in her dream. Then, he delivers her deepest fear up to her while invading her sexually: "'You were the real monster all along,' he says, and then he is kissing me, kissing, with his hot invader's tongue" (126). With the killer bees swarming and raging inside of her, the two become one, with "his razor-angled Asian body" in her "muscled, blond-haired arms" and "his longish black hair" in her "heavy-knuckled hands," while "his slender hips" grind against her "larger ones" (126). In this moment of terrifying fusion, she wakes up screaming and "full of a buzzing swarm of killer bees" because it is her "killer cop cop killer body that is stirring, blazing, devouring devouring devouring devouring swallowing him/her/me whole" (126). This nightmare encounter is the culmination of the invasion of the trans girl's body that began with the bees and represents ongoing insidious trauma generated by transphobic society, turning her body into a haunted site. Her fusion with the dead cop, horrific victim of the violent rage and self-protection resulting from her experience of victimhood, is the ultimate horror of transphobia, with the victim becoming monstrous, filled with rage and the desire for vengeance, because of the constant onslaught. Through the complete invasion of the trans woman's body and psyche, she loses herself and becomes instead one with this violent man. The encounter also demonstrates the mutuality of abjection. By abjecting her, the cop becomes monstrous. The two end up in a horrific, monstrous embrace.

This ultimate confrontation with the ghost that haunts her helps her to realize that the fear and violence she wants to externalize do in fact live within her. By murdering him, she has become that which she wishes to overcome and denounce. After this, she moves towards a more self-reflective encounter with self and other, through forgiveness, and learns how to bake a forgiveness cake that works magic and rearranges the world: "I release a spoonful of food colouring into the mixing bowl, and an explosion of red overtakes all. Crimson, carmine, scarlet, vermilion. There is blood on my hands, blood in my batter. Sweet wet blushes stain my forearms, my palms" (159).[8] The stain of violence and cruelty, which she recognizes to be part of herself, blends with "the scent of hot sugar" which "diffuses in a thick cloud" as "Ghost nails rake over [her] shoulders and back." As "the world spins and spins," she realizes that "there is nothing you can do but surrender" (159–60), just as she had to surrender to the bees, but this time she is surrendering to something empowering, rather than paralyzing. This transformative power of food, with its smells and tangible substance, reminding us of the Hungry Ghost festival with its offerings of food and incense filling the air night and day, goes out into the world and works change.

Ghosts represent sites of relationality which become charged with intensity around mutual or contrasting expectations, around the way the inner and outer influence each other, around the desire for affirmation and congruence, or separation and distinction. These tensions emerge as affective force fields which take on a haunting presence.

While internalized bees and fusion with the killer cop represent transphobia, Ghost Friend conveys an aura of ancestral support. The hybrid ghostly landscape of the City of Smoke and Lights communicates the hybrid cultural landscape through which the protagonist moves, which includes the haunting spirits of trans women who were killed, the empowering First Femme, and multiply shaped Euro-pagan beings as spirits of the past carrying traditions forward. In addition to this multiplicity of ghosts and spirits, stories themselves become ghosts in Thom's novel. Written stories, like that of Ghost Friend, have "no body and no voice" (26), yet they haunt us. They charge us with feelings. They connect us with memories and past experiences. Thom builds on this haunting quality of story by presenting stories as ghosts, which nevertheless have real impact.

Thom's protagonist demands real stories of trans girls and women. These are not the "very old archetype that trans girl stories get put into: this sort of tragic, plucky-little-orphan character who is just supposed to suffer through everything and wait, and if you're good and brave and patient (and white and rich) enough, then you get the big reward … which is that you get to be just like everybody else who is white and rich and boring" (2). Neither are they stories about the "poor little trans girl desperate for a ~~fairy godmother~~doctor to give her boobs and a vagina and a pretty face and wear nice dresses! Save the trans girls! Save the whales! Put them in a zoo!" (2). No, Thom's protagonist wants a real story, "The kind of story that doesn't wait for you to invite it to enter, but bursts through the doors of your rat-infested house like a glittering wind, hungry, hungry, to snatch up the carpet and scatter your papers and smash every single plate in the kitchen. That surges, howling, up the battered stairs to blast the stained sheets off your filthy bed and sweep your secrets out of the closet and send them shrieking outside, overjoyed to be finally set free" (1). These dangerous stories are "like the voice of a mad angel whispering of the revolution you are about to unleash" (1), driven by hunger for release, like the rising, insistent hunger of the trans girl for release from the oppressive conditions of her life. The play between the real and the ghostlike in Thom's novel, the way the ghostly becomes more real than normative TV stories, signals the aspirational and transformative power of story. Story is not bound to what is, but to what might be. Story has living power to break through stifling systemic structures of containment, like the tall tale in the City of Smoke and Lights: "As soon as a tall tale leaves your wicked mouth, it falls to the ground, moist and warm, wriggling with thick possibility. It sinks in deep, puts down roots. Splits the pavement as it rises, tall and spindly" (20). This power to crack through the facade of cisnormative life is what characterizes transgender stories such as Thom's. Stories are ghosts that haunt, renew, and inspire change.

This raging hungry story drives the protagonist to leave home and seek community with a magical group of friends in a mythical space, generating unstable genre boundaries between memoir and speculative fiction. First Femme, as a ghost of trauma, is also a spirit of hope and renewal, suggesting a mythic origin. The spirit of the dead cop is a reflection of self, in which the protagonist's own violence is mirrored, and the external enemy meshes with internal fears.

Ghosts in Thom's novel represent affective relational tensions, parental hunger in the form of the hungry house, transphobia that manifests as swarming bees and the spirit of the dead cop, and foundational trauma as the hungry ghosts of murdered trans women. Foundational support arrives as ancestral spirit power through the soft touches of Ghost Friend, the fierce and tender anchoring love of First Femme, the power of language to work change through stories, and the affective power to shift perspectives, which results from the transformational energy of the forgiveness cake. In each case, ghostly abilities to diffuse, transform, get past surface layers and into the core of problems generate opportunities to rework relationships and find new planes and platforms for healing. The blending of memoir and speculative fiction allows the trans protagonist, and Thom and Thom's readers vicariously, to open up their own lives, probe the dark and difficult, twisted and knotted spaces resulting from the transphobic pressures of the ciscentric world, and release new kinds of hope and resilience.

NOTES

1 Darko Suvin suggests in *Metamorphoses of Science Fiction* (1979) that science fiction creates cognitive estrangement: "*SF is, then, a literary genre whose necessary and sufficient conditions are the presence and interaction of estrangement and cognition, and whose main formal device is an imaginative framework alternative to the author's empirical environment*" (7–8). Booker also discusses Rosemary Jackson's ideas in *Fantasy: The Literature of Subversion* (1981) that link "the genre of fantasy both to political subversion and to the forbidden desire that psychoanalysis sees in the unconscious mind" (Booker 8). These include "The fantastic traces the unsaid and the unseen of culture: that which has been silenced, made invisible, covered over and made 'absent'" (Jackson 4).

2 Hun Yeow Lye points to the hungry ghost festival and associated rituals as a means of shaping cultural worlds (39).

3 Parts of Thom's narrative are presented in the form of poetry.
4 Lye recalls that during the ghost festival in Penang, Malaysia, a state with a large ethnic Chinese population, people were advised not to swim or go near cemeteries after dark, which suggests a connection between cemeteries and encounters with ancestral Chinese hungry ghosts (1).
5 José Esteban Muñoz defines "disidentification" as "a strategy that tries to transform a cultural logic from within, always laboring to enact permanent structural change while at the same time valuing the importance of local or everyday struggles of resistance" (11–12). Disidentificatory performances or moves involve using cultural features while shifting meanings and connections in ways that provide more space for those who are marginalized.
6 See J. Gordon Melton's "Lantern Festival (China)."
7 Nate Super discusses the ways in which the medical establishment has abused and misused transgender patients in a study of the interactions of transgender writers with ideas and pressures from sexological research and medical practice (40).
8 This image compares to the cake that Marian bakes at the conclusion of Margaret Atwood's *The Edible Woman*. Marian also uses the power of baking a cake that can be eaten and shared to reclaim her agency as a woman.

WORKS CITED

Ahmed, Sara. *Strange Encounters: Embodied Others in Post-Coloniality*. Routledge, 2000.

Atwood, Margaret. *The Edible Woman*. McClelland & Stewart, 1969.

Booker, Keith M., editor. *Critical Insights: Contemporary Speculative Fiction*. Salem Press, 2013.

Creed, Barbara. "*Ginger Snaps*: The Monstrous Feminine as *Femme Animale*." Priest, pp. 180–95.

Gordon, Avery. F. *Ghostly Matters: Haunting and the Sociological Imagination*. U of Minnesota P, 2008.

Gregg, Melissa, and Gregory J. Seigworth, editors. *The Affect Theory Reader*. Duke UP, 2010.

Heng, Terence. "Hungry Ghosts in Urban Spaces: A Visual Study of Aesthetic Markers and Material Anchoring." *Visual Communication*, vol. 13, no. 2, 2014, pp. 147–62.

Jackson, Rosemary. *Fantasy: The Literature of Subversion*. Methuen, 1981.

Keaton, Hetty Lanier. *Feeding Hungry Ghosts: Food, Family, and Desire in Stories by Contemporary Chinese American Women*. 2002. U of Tulsa, PhD Dissertation.

Kristeva, Julia. "'Approaching Abjection,' 1980." *The Routledge Critical and Cultural Theory Reader*, edited by Neil Badmington and Julia Thomas Routledge, 2008, pp. 245–66.

Lye, Hun Yeow. *Feeding Ghosts: A Study of the* Yukie Yankou *Rite*. 2003. U of Virginia, PhD Dissertation. *ProQuest*, https://doi.org/10.18130/V3S82Z.

Melton, J. Gordon. "Lantern Festival (China)." *Religious Celebrations: An Encyclopedia of Holidays, Festivals, Solemn Observances, and Spiritual Commemorations*, vol. 1, edited by J. Gordon Melton, ABC-CLIO, 2011, pp. 514–15.

Muñoz, José Esteban. *Disidentifications: Queers of Color and the Performance of Politics*. U of Minnesota P, 1999.

Poo, Mu-chou. "The Concept of Ghost in Ancient Chinese Religion." *Religion and Chinese Society. Volume 1: Ancient and Medieval China*, edited by John Lagerwey, Chinese UP, 2004, pp. 173–87.

Sedgwick, Eve Kosofsky. *Touching Feeling: Affect, Pedagogy, Performativity*. Duke UP, 2003.

Stryker, Susan. "My Words to Victor Frankenstein above the Village of Chamounix: Performing Transgender Rage." *GLQ*, vol. 1, no. 1, 1994, pp. 237–54.

Sugars, Cynthia, and Gerry Turcotte. "Introduction: Canadian Literature and the Postcolonial Gothic." *Unsettled Remains: Canadian Literature and the Postcolonial Gothic*, edited by Cynthia Sugars and Gerry Turcotte, Wilfrid Laurier UP, 2009, pp. vii–xxvi.

Super, Nate. *Cycles of Knowledge: Trans Life-Writing and the Sexological Bodymind*. May 2022. Ohio State U, Honours Research Thesis. *Knowledge Bank*, http://hdl.handle.net/1811/101450.

Suvin, Darko. *Metamorphoses of Science Fiction: On the Poetics and History of a Literary Genre*. Yale UP, 1979.

Thom, Kai Cheng. *Fierce Femmes and Notorious Liars: A Dangerous Trans Girl's Confabulous Memoir*. Metonymy Press, 2016.

Westengard, Laura. *Gothic Queer Culture: Marginalized Communities and the Ghosts of Insidious Trauma*. U of Nebraska P, 2019.

Interlude

Someone Is Dead

AMY LEBLANC

Item Description: a work of fiction (researchers cannot determine the facticity of the events described).

M

M lifts her shirt and tucks it under the band of her sports bra. She rips open the packaging of an alcohol wipe and uses it to disinfect a patch of skin a few inches to the left of her belly button. Circle left, circle right, circle left. She counts to thirty to make sure that the alcohol dries. She forgot to let it dry once and the needle carried the wet alcohol into her body. It stung and she vowed never to do this again, knowing that she would be back in the bathroom with a new needle and a new alcohol wipe in one month's time. She took the syringe from the fridge thirty minutes ago so she wouldn't have to feel freezing liquid as it entered her body. She pinches a bit of fat from her belly at the spot she's disinfected. She breathes in. She takes the syringe between her fingers and plunges it into her belly. Once the needle is nestled into her skin, she pushes the plunger, which always goes down slower than she'd like, and she feels the fluid as it seeps inside her. When she did her injection three months ago, Gus had stood on the other side of the bathroom door.

"How's it going?" he asked.

"It's in," M said. "It doesn't sting too bad this time."

The plunger is pushed almost as far down as it will go. When she pushes it that little bit more, the plunger clicks into place. When she removes her finger, the needle retracts fast enough that she barely feels anything as it leaves her skin. She breathes out. She's hardly heard the music she painstakingly selected beforehand. Now that Gus isn't there to fill the silence, she needs something to listen to. She was tempted to search "music for self-injections" in the YouTube search bar the way she might have done for music with which to exercise, study, write, have sex, sleep. A search would be fruitless, so she chose the first song that came up on shuffle.

"I'm done," M says, as though Gus is still there to listen. She puts a bandage over the injection site where a bead of blood is forming. She opens the door and almost expects to see Gus standing on the other side with a fresh cup of coffee in his hands. Instead, she enters an empty doorway. Negative space, she thinks. Nothingness.

Gus has been gone for three months. In the first weeks after his departure, M had not left the bathtub except to sleep and use the toilet. Her mother had come by once a day to bring sustenance and to try to convince her daughter to leave the tub. If her mother, Josephine, wasn't bringing her food, M wouldn't eat. M didn't want to go back to Gus's apartment to get her things. Her sister, Nora, had gone and collected what she needed: some clothes, her laptop, her phone charger, and a toothbrush. She wasn't going to use any of it. She was going to stay in the tub until she became part of it, and it would become a part of her. She was going to ignore everything that was happening outside, the fever, Gus, the increasing sense of panic and dread she felt radiating from her mother and sister. That could all happen outside and she would stay here beneath the warm water.

She had placed her hands on her belly beneath the water, which was more tepid than warm. It would be time to drain the tub and refill. She pushed slightly, a habit she'd developed when she still thought she was going to have a baby.

"Where'd you go, little bean?" she asked.

Nora

Olive stands in the kitchen doorway with her arms full of blankets in plastic wrap, canned goods, and bottled water. She has put on another pair of sweatpants and her cheeks are the colour of figs.

"Did you get candles?" she asks.

Nora had meant to buy candles at the store and had completely forgotten. They had been going to the grocery store every two weeks to minimize contact with the outside world. She had been at the store in the early days of the fever when a woman collapsed at the cash register and later died in hospital. Every time she left the house, she mentally prepared to see something similar.

"Shit," she says. "I'm sorry, love."

Olive turns around without a word and goes further into their house. Nora knows that when Olive is truly pissed off, she won't say anything at all. Sometimes, Nora wishes Olive would let her have it. Just as she is about to stand up and follow Olive to apologize again, the power goes out. Olive's phone beeps to let her know that it is no longer charging, and the lights flicker once, then stay out until the room is enveloped in heavy silence – the kind of silence that comes quickly when all background sounds disappear. The blackness outside creeps through their windows. They don't have Wi-Fi, or a battery-powered radio, and the cell towers must be down because data won't work, either.

Nora keeps one hand on the wall as she searches the house for the stubs of any remaining candles, but her eyes aren't adjusting. She knows that Olive used to light a candle each night before bed (back when they had time to worry about self-care), but she doesn't know where they are kept. The candles used to make their bedroom smell like candy or burning cinnamon. Once the candle was lit, Olive would ask Nora to read to her, like a child, until she fell asleep. When reports of the fever were first surfacing, they tried to study what was coming. Nora and Olive read novels, medical journals, historical accounts, but these did nothing to assuage their fears. They had dog-eared the page of a fairytale and underlined this phrase: *As she wrapped herself around his lungs and stomach, she whispered: You must take me everywhere. Leave no stone unturned, leave no mouth unkissed, leave no meal untainted.* They read poetry. Anne Sexton wrote "someone is dead, even the trees know it."

After a while they stopped reading.

M

When M was a child, she'd gone to an outdoor swimming pool with her mother on weekends during the summer. There was another girl, Agatha, who would be there with her own mother at the same time. Agatha and M weren't friends and they didn't plan their timing to go swimming together, but their mothers sat underneath the same striped umbrella while the girls swam circles and tried to avoid speaking to each other. M didn't have anything against Agatha – she just wanted to be alone, completely isolated under the water. M could hold her breath for two lengths of the pool and wanted to be able to do three lengths by the end of the summer. Agatha usually trailed behind, dog paddling because she wasn't as strong a swimmer. After an hour or so, they got out of the water, hair full of chlorine and whatever else had been deposited into the pool, and sat in front of their mothers' crossed legs to dry themselves in the sun. Agatha's mother had eyebrows like caterpillars, and she always smelled slightly like dust.

One weekend in August, M's mother had a cold, so they didn't go to the pool; when they arrived the next week, M didn't see Agatha or her mother or their red and blue striped beach towel that usually sat beside the snack shop. In fact, there were probably half as many people at the pool as usual. M wasn't sure if her mother was really friends with Agatha's mother, or if it was a relationship of convenience, like hers and Agatha's, but her mother asked around until she found out that Agatha was in the hospital. She'd stayed under the water too long – had swallowed masses of pool water, and she'd coughed it up and vomited over the side of the pool. A teenaged lifeguard had lifted Agatha from the pool by the armpits and had rubbed her back while she coughed up everything that was inside her. Once she was finished, all seemed to be well.

A few hours later, that last bit of water she'd swallowed was still in her lungs, which became inflamed until she couldn't breathe. Agatha collapsed next to the rope swing that hung from their poplar tree – her mother had seen her fall from the kitchen window. Dry drowning.

Agatha died in the hospital a few weeks later. M's mother cut an obituary from the paper to show her; the photo they had selected was a school photo with Agatha's head tilted the same way they'd posed M at her own school photos.

Nora

Nora digs in every drawer, sifting through old receipts, letters, and sympathy cards that they will never send. In the bedside table drawer, she finds a lighter and unscented pillar candles that are nearly burned down to nothing. She loads as many candles as she can into her cupped hands and props the lighter between her lips. As she leaves their room, she plans to tell Olive she is sorry for being difficult. She has barely opened her mouth when she sees Olive lying on the couch with a blanket wrapped around her shoulders.

"Olive?" A moment.

"I'm fine." Olive's voice is muffled through her elbow. The truth is that Olive feels an ache that goes deep into her spine like a small pair of scissors is working its way through her vertebrae one by one. She has never felt anything like this before and the visibility of her pain makes Nora panic.

"What if the power doesn't come back on?" Nora asks. "What if this is all part of the fever?" Sweat stains form beneath her underarms and seep through the fabric of her sweatshirt.

Olive rolls over and nestles deeper into the blankets.

"Mr. Almater next door probably tried to plug in too many things and blew something for the street. You know how forgetful he is. I'm sure everything is fine."

"You're right. I'm sure you're right," Nora says as she looks down at her feet.

They both know that she doesn't believe it.

Olive doesn't know if she believes herself. The darkness spreads so far beyond their bungalow and it is suffocating them minute by minute. Olive feels a slight constriction in her lungs and imagines they are full of cotton balls. And so, they wait.

M + Nora

The same week that the fever began, M and Gus had hosted their engagement party at her mother's house. M was eighteen, Gus was twenty-nine; they had been dating for two hundred and seven days, and M had missed her period.

Gustav Jackson – she told Nora he preferred to be called Gus or by his last name – was a painter. She texted her sister a link to his online portfolio. One of his paintings sold for $7,000 last month. Nora doesn't understand their relationship but is sure that M sees something in him. She hopes that whatever she sees will actually be there when she needs it to be. M invited Olive and Nora to Gus's most recent exhibition. He stood in the centre of an empty warehouse, naked, and slowly covered his body in bright red barbecue sauce. It was reviewed in the *Calgary Herald*, and an art critic called it "a splendiferous example of postmodern art." Nora prayed that there would be no barbecue sauce at their engagement party.

When Nora and Olive arrived at the party, it looked like they'd walked into a frat house. A banner of golden letters was stapled through the wall (*Mom will not be pleased*, thought Nora) that spelled out *SAME PENIS FOREVER!* with small bits of penis-shaped confetti on the floor. The confetti was stuck in M's hair. Nora couldn't see their mother anywhere; she was either in the kitchen, or she had decided to take herself away from the party and be elsewhere for the evening.

"You're late, Nora! I didn't think you were going to make it." M yelled right into her sister's ear. The music was loud and she smelled like she had already drunk quite a lot. "You know you're going to have to give me away at the wedding. I don't think Mom is even going to be there." She leaned over to kiss Olive on the cheek, and she put miniature red solo cups into their hands. Nora jiggled hers, and when the liquid didn't slosh over the sides of the cup, she understood that it was a Jell-O shot.

"Where *is* Mom, anyway?" Nora asked.

"Who knows? She's been against Gus and me being happy together since day one."

"Which was how many days ago?"

"Two hundred and seven days, to be exact." M downed another Jell-O shot.

"I'm going to go check her bedroom. Try not to be too tough on her, M. You're her baby and she loves you."

M was too busy throwing penis-shaped confetti at Olive to hear her sister. Nora looked at Olive to make sure she was okay with being left with M, and Olive gave a small nod and kissed her fingertips before touching Nora's face.

Nora pushed her way through boys who looked like high school quarterbacks, remembering that they probably were high school quarterbacks, until she could get to her mother's room. The door was closed, but a sliver of light shone through the space underneath.

"Mom? It's me. Can I come in?"

Nora opened the door a crack and found her mother sitting cross-legged on her queen-sized bed. The floral quilt was perfectly placed so that equal parts hung off all corners of the mattress.

"You're not going to join the festivities?" she asked her mother.

"I would rather eat penis confetti off the floor," was her response. So, she had seen the staples in her living room wall.

"It's not ideal, I'll grant you that," Nora said.

"Not ideal? You and I both know she's making the biggest mistake of her life." Josephine closed her eyes and pinched the bridge of her nose between her fingers. "She's only eighteen. How can she possibly know what she wants yet?"

Nora paused before saying, "It *is* possible that they really do love each other." Josephine pulled her knees into her chest and hugged them in tight but said nothing. "Do you want anything to eat? I can bring you something. A Jell-O shot perhaps?" Nora knew her mother would feel only marginally better if she ate something.

"I'm fine. But Nora, can you try to talk some sense into her? *Please.*"

"I'll try, but you know M. When she sets her mind to something, it's like trying to stop a bus on an icy road."

Nora left her in the room and closed the door behind her. The door clicked shut, and when she turned around, Gustav Jackson was standing outside the door.

"Nora, long time no see." He leaned in for a hug, which she accepted, but not without crinkling her nose. With her face pressed into him, she noticed how the sides of his neck smelled like meat.

"How's your mother doing?"

"Fine. She's fine."

The most disconcerting part of Gus's appearance was that he had floating irises. They hardly ever seem to settle in one place, and if they did, it was as though they saw straight through all people and all things. Nora felt like he was looking through her and into the back side of her skull. His eyes were blue and cold like ocean water.

"Listen," he said, "I know I'm asking a lot of your family, and I know that this was very sudden. But Emilie is my life now. I can't imagine doing anything without her. You understand that, right?" Nora nodded, but said nothing, because she didn't understand it. She and Olive had been together for four years – they hadn't jumped into an engagement. "I'm glad we're on the same page. I think I'll need your help getting Josephine on board." She tried, and failed, to keep her left eye from twitching when he used her mother's first name, as though they were friends, and not what they actually were: people who didn't know each other beyond interactions forced by M and who had no desire to know each other. "She's very protective of you both, isn't she?"

"It's just the three of us and it has been for a long time. It's hard to change gears." He nodded at her and his blue irises floated until they focused on the painting on the wall behind her head: a print of a painting by James Tissot called *The Dance of Death*; skeletons led a procession of people across the canvas, presumably to their deaths. Josephine always had peculiar taste in art. She'd bought a death mask of Napoleon Bonaparte at an auction a few years back.

"Anyway," he said stretching out the beginning vowel, "we ought to get back to the party and my bride-to-be. Wouldn't want her thinking we prefer each other's company over hers."

As he snaked past to go down the hallway, Nora felt his hand tracing a slight circle at the small of her back and she smelled the meaty-ness of him again. Her skin crawled where he touched her, and all she wanted to do was go home and shower for hours. As she entered the living room behind him, she locked eyes with Olive, who sent a reassuring smile. At that moment, Nora wanted to leave and go home and be only with her; instead, she rested her head on Olive's shoulder when she was close enough. She smelled like campfire.

"Jell-O shot?" Olive asked, holding one out in front of her.

"Please," she took it and tried to tip it back all in one go, but the Jell-O slowly slid down the side of the cup until it reached the back of her throat. It felt like swallowing sludge, so slow that she needed to swallow a few times to get it all down. She knew she'd pay for this drink the next day, but she couldn't get through this party without at least a little bit of alcohol.

"I think I may have just been hit on by Gus," Nora finally said – the part of her back that he'd touched tingled still, not in a pleasant way, but more like sunburn when the skin begins to peel. Olive's eyes widened slightly like she wasn't even a little bit surprised.

"He's probably the kind of guy that thinks he can turn me straight or something," Nora said. Olive glanced behind her shoulder and saw him watching. She pulled Nora in with a gentle hand around the back of her neck and kissed her. Her lips tasted like red Jell-O and tequila, and the feeling made something in the sides of both of their ribs tighten.

"There. Maybe he'll get the message this time."

Nora's phone buzzed in her back pocket. She didn't usually have her volume on because there was never anything urgent, but she'd put it on vibrate that night so that she would feel the alarm go off as a reminder to take her medication. The doctor had recommended taking her corticosteroids first thing in the morning, since they have a stimulating effect on most patients. For Nora, however, they were as good as sedatives. They sunk her energy so low that she could hardly move without aching or wanting to cry within a few hours of taking them. In the late evening, the lows coincided with sleep, so she didn't need to feel them as much. She took the pills out of a container in her purse, a "shopping and popping" pill carrier that Josephine had bought when Nora received her diagnosis. Both Nora and M took medication frequently – Nora took corticosteroids daily and M did self-injections of biologics once a month. Nora was born before the genetic testing craze and M was such a surprise that their mother didn't even think to try and alter her genetic makeup.

Nora slid the pill into her mouth, relegating it to the back of her tongue because it always tasted a little like copper. She downed it with a swig of water from the glass on the end table. She didn't think her doctor would advise washing her corticosteroids down with a Jell-O shot.

"Was that your glass?" Olive asked.

"Wasn't it yours? It was right by you, I just assumed you'd put it there."

Olive shook her head. "Well, that settles it, you're definitely going to get mono. You won't be able to kiss me for months and months and I'll have to find someone else to satisfy me."

With her hand on the small of Olive's back, she pulled her in and kissed her softly.

"There. Now you have mono with me. We'll be like two Victorian ladies afflicted with consumption and with nothing but each other for comfort."

"Fine by me," she said. In the corner of the room, M was gesticulating, probably explaining her hopes that Gus would make some kind of artistic centrepiece for their wedding. He, however, was looking straight at Nora with his floating eyes that didn't settle. He wasn't drinking Jell-O shots. Instead, he had a glass of what might have been scotch in a tumbler that looked like the ones Nora's father used to drink from. Nora knew the glasses were on the top shelf in the kitchen and the scotch was at the back of one of the cupboards. Apparently, Gus knew it too. He tilted his glass in her direction as though saying *cheers* from across the room and slowly nodded.

"God, what a creep," Nora said before she could stop herself.

"Do you want to get out of here?" Olive asked as she was jostled to the side by one of the teenage quarterbacks.

"Let's. We came, we saw, now let's say our goodbyes."

As they came to the corner, M stopped gesticulating and lit up.

"Everyone, this is my big sister, Nora, and her partner, Olive. Nora, this is Declan, Molly, Leah, Samuel, Caleb, Jeremy, and Noah. You've met Grace and Sophia." M pointed to each person as she said their name. Nora would never remember them all but tried to smile and at least pretend it was nice to meet them, even though she felt like they were generations younger than her – in experience if not in years. Grace and Sophia had been M's friends since childhood and would inevitably be her bridesmaids. They all stood in an uncomfortable semicircle and smiled at one another. "You and Declan would actually have a lot to talk about – he's a poet!" Declan's eyes looked like he'd been high for months on end and Nora gave him a smile that was more a tightening of the lips than anything. The only person who caught Nora's eye for any length of time was Jeremy. The only reason he caught her attention was because of his pallor. He looked white and dewy and sweaty, except for his cheeks. Two blemishes across his cheekbones that were a shocking shade of blue. *Make-up?* Thought Nora. *Or possibly some kind of condition?*

"We're going to be taking off. Thanks for having us and I hope you enjoy the rest of the party," Olive said while Nora looked at Jeremy and tried to discern what might be wrong with him. His eyes were unsettled like Gus's, but not because of floating irises. It almost seemed like his pupils might roll up and under his lids at any moment.

Nora's focus came back to the conversation. "Congratulations again to you both," she forced herself to look Gus in the eye and smile. "I think you'll be very happy together."

"Oh, Nora. That means the world to me, it really does – to know that we have your blessing," M lowered her voice and looked around to see if anyone other than Nora and Olive were listening. "There's one little thing I still need to tell you. Can you keep a secret?"

Nora nodded and M leaned in, smelling of Jell-O and tequila, and whispered *I think I might be pregnant*. It was no surprise to Nora, but she wanted to take her sister out of the room, lecture her about drinking while pregnant, or even only possibly pregnant, and then give her the biggest hug because she was desperately unprepared for everything that was about to come. Nora wanted to wrap herself around M like a protective shield and keep her from getting any older, or any more pregnant, or even any more drunk that night. But she couldn't. She leaned away as Gus took M by the elbow and guided her towards a conversation happening on the other side of the semicircle.

"Emilie, we need you to help settle something. We were looking at that ghastly painting Josephine has on the wall and wondering how one might come across a piece of art like that. Did she see the painting before she bought it? Or did a skeleton deposit it in the night and demand it be displayed?"

"I would have to assume the latter," she'd never heard M say "latter" before. "A skeleton crept into her bedchamber and after having his way with her, he left the painting as reminder of her mortality. That's why she's so damn miserable and mean all the time."

The crowd gathered around M began to laugh and hoot. Nora hadn't heard her be so cruel before, especially not about their mother, but she looked at Gus and he smiled as though she was a dog who had finally performed the right trick. If their mother was still sitting on her bed, she would have heard the whole conversation.

Nora took Olive's hand in hers and said, "Let's get home. I've had enough celebration for one night." She wondered if the baby would be born with a caul like M had been, or if it would be born screaming into bright hospital lights with a father whose eyes would never settle and a mother who was too young to know any better than to trust him.

In the days that followed the engagement party, there were twenty-two positive cases of Cerulean Fever in the city. Ten of them had come from the party. One week later, Gus got in his car to leave the city, an extra-large coffee with five sugars in the cupholder beside him. His destination was an arts commune he'd once visited when he was younger. He planned to call M to apologize for his cowardice once he got there. But he never arrived. The fever got him first.

Nora

Nora walks into the kitchen to make tea, places circular teabags in mugs, fills the kettle, and only remembers the power outage when the electric kettle won't turn on. It doesn't matter how many times the power goes out; she can't stop the impulse to reach for the light switch or the thermostat or the TV remote. When she comes back from the kitchen without tea, Olive is shivering on the couch with a second blanket draped over her shoulders. Nora hesitates before she reaches out and holds Olive's body against her own and tries to warm her. Nora feels that they have their own language of looks and movements – she runs a hand across Olive's forehead, much too hot, moving the hair from her eyes, hoping that their shared language of touch still means something. With her hand against Olive's forehead, she asks if Olive thinks she's contracted the fever. Olive responds by placing her own hand over Nora's, which is beginning to sweat from the heat of Olive's forehead. *Yes,* that movement says, *I think I caught it.* Nora brings herself to Olive's eye level and kisses her on her dry lips. Even though Olive says she hasn't smoked in ten years, her lips always taste like cigarettes.

"Did you know that there are massive spikes in birth rates nine months to the day after major power outages?" Nora asks, trying to lighten the darkness.

Olive nestles deeper into the blankets.

"So many accidental pregnancies," Olive says. "We couldn't get pregnant even if we were trying… Do you want to have a baby? When this is all over, I mean."

"Let's talk about it when it's all over," Nora says. When Nora calls 911, the dispatcher tells her that an ambulance won't be there for an hour.

Nora places the leftover candles around the bathroom and along the edge of the tub. She manages to find some of Olive's favourite lavender bubble bath in the cabinet under the sink. She fills the tub with water that might be just hot enough and empties half of the bubble bath into the water. The water heater usually retains enough heat for a lukewarm bath. Olive looks like she is asleep. Her lips are dry and almost blue. Nora picks her up and struggles under the weight of her. Even though she looks like she weighs nothing, it is as though exhaustion has made it impossible for her to stand up on her own. She somehow feels both solid and liquid, stiff and unyielding. Olive wakes to the scent of the bubble bath, offers a little smile, and tries to support some of her own body weight.

Nora helps her undress, layer by layer, and feels something shift in her stomach at the sight of her. Olive looks up unflinchingly, and Nora is reminded of why she picked Olive – she remembers when they first met, Olive with her with her fiery hair and a jean jacket covered in enamel pins. She was sitting at a café, alone, reading a book of Renaissance poetry. Nora waited until she was leaving to speak to her. The first time they kissed, it was in a change room at The Bay. Olive had asked her to come in to give an opinion on a new dress; they snuck into a room while the attendant was helping someone else. Once Olive was in the dress, orange and tucked against her ribs and hips, she climbed up on the bench, beckoned Nora closer, and then she leaned down and kissed her. When Nora later asked why she'd climbed on the bench, she'd said it was so that if the attendant came by, she would only see one pair of shoes beneath the door and they wouldn't be interrupted.

Nora helps Olive sink her body into the water, caressed by bubbles and shadows from the candles. Beneath the bubbles, the dark bruises on Olive's skin disappear and she seems so much lighter. She lifts an arm from the water, reaches out and wraps a soapy hand around Nora's, dragging it down into the water with hers. Nora will wash her hair and massage her scalp. She sits on the edge of the tub and holds her hand below the surface and waits.

M

M sits on the closed toilet seat and stares at the pregnancy test in its horrible pink box. She had bought it the day of the engagement party when her period was six days late. She had never actually taken a pregnancy test – she just had a feeling. But she found spots of blood in her underwear later that night and Gus left the next day. It is three months later and her period is late again.

She opens the box, slowly pulling the glued tabs away from the cardboard. Within the box is one pregnancy test wrapped in thin plastic with a surprisingly large set of instructions. She reads them front to back, twice, to make sure she's doing this correctly. She wonders how many women have sat on toilet seats next to bathtubs and read these same instructions; all of them hoping for something – all praying for different outcomes.

She removes the plastic cap from the test, stands up to lift the toilet seat lid, holding the absorbent part of the stick beneath her. She gets some urine on her hands, but she doesn't care. Once she's held the test under for ten seconds, she puts the cap back on and places the test on the counter, horizontally. She washes her hands and waits. She counts two hundred and seventy loud drips from the leaking faucet. Once five minutes have passed, she picks up the test, reads the screen, exhales.

If it's a girl, she thinks, *I'll name her Theodora. If it's a boy, I'll name him Joseph.*

M pulls the plug from the bathtub by its chain, takes her housecoat from where she'd dropped it on the tiled floor, and hangs it on a hook behind the door.

Apocalyptic World-Making: Comic Books, Enclosed Spaces, and Short Stories

Other Worlds within Other Worlds: Comics World-Building and Identity Formation in Emily St. John Mandel's *Station Eleven*

JASMINE REDFORD

Hybridic by nature and form, the comic book inherently embodies a juxtaposition of media, primarily visual art and the written word. Emily St. John Mandel's 2014 novel *Station Eleven* complicates the comic's relationship to other text(s) and art by including repeated reference to and description of a fictional comic within its pages. This relationship is further complicated through the naming of the various texts in the novel: while the comic as a whole is called *Dr. Eleven*, after its protagonist, one issue is titled *Station Eleven*. This cyclic intertextual naming links fictional author Miranda Carroll[1] to real-life author Emily St. John Mandel, but invites confusion about which text or place is referenced: *Station Eleven* the novel or *Station Eleven* the comic book or Station Eleven the fictional space station from which the issue takes its name? By acknowledging that world-building, the development of an imaginary world or universe complete with its own fictive history, is not simply a creative leisure activity that leads to speculative franchise opportunities, Mandel uses Carroll's comic as an apparatus for the characters, specifically Kirsten Raymonde and Tyler Leander, to create their new, lived realities. Mandel's novel posits that world-building through so-called disposable media and art forms, identified in the novel as comics, *Star Trek* episodes, and tabloid magazines, is not simply an exercise in nostalgia but instead serves as the cornerstone of contemporary and future personal and cultural identity.

Historically, comics – Carroll's fictive *Dr. Eleven* series included – offer a look into fantastic, sometimes melancholy pocket universes whose themes comment on contemporary issues and/or anticipate future problems in the world in which they were authored. According to Mark West in his essay on Shakespeare and salvagepunk in *Station Eleven*, by "imagining and depicting a fallen world, the comic is a cultural product that testifies to the pleasure found in imagining destruction" (16).

Mandel's *Station Eleven* places Carroll's *Dr. Eleven* at the centre of a new, post-pandemic, world in which beauty is still found, not despite, but because of, the wreckage left behind. The world of the *Dr. Eleven* comic – a future-facing narrative that paradoxically reminds its readers about the past – exists in a dreamlike wonderland where there are no established conventions, a parallel to the post-collapse anarchy and survivalism that Mandel's survivors experience.

Worlds within texts are first conceived and built by authors. The culture and ecosystems of Mandel's and Carroll's imaginary worlds lay the foundation for what will become reality within the novel. Theological scholar Mark Godin, who equates world-building with the practice of understanding fictive truths, explains the process: "The concept focuses critical attention on the cumulative effect of details which add depth and shape to the world of the text, and which work together to suggest a breadth of dimension to that world, allowing readers to find it 'believable' to the point of being able to situate their own imaginations within it" (55). This technique connects the fictive fantastical with realistic potentiality. Stories and the elements within them are objectively fictional and yet, to the reader's understanding, they are *possible*. As an example, technologies in various *Star Trek* episodes, such as tablet computers, flip communicators, and Bluetooth headsets, were seemingly not so much imagined as they were anticipated. This practice is observable in Mandel's loose prediction of the COVID-19 pandemic that temporarily shut down the international socio-economic world (the reverberations of which are still ongoing) in the novel's virulently more devastating "Georgia Flu" (17). In "Trauma and the Ethics of Literary Culture in the Time of Pandemic," Wendy Roy suggests that an author's world-building verisimilitude is inspirational to its audience, as the comics and other media of *Station Eleven* "have enduring significance in the post-apocalyptic world" (58). Indeed, Carroll's authorship informs and transforms her own reality within the novel; in the chapter in which she realizes that her marriage to her philandering husband, actor Arthur Leander, is ending, she autobiographically identifies with the lonely isolation of her character, Dr. Eleven. The narrator notes that "Station Eleven is all around them" (Mandel 107), an observation that both references the artwork in her office and the "untenable situation that the comic-book setting evokes" for her in that moment (Roy 58). For Carroll, the *Dr. Eleven* comic book is a proxy for her lived experiences; however, for the post-collapse carriers of the obscure comic, it is an old-world touchstone upon which to craft new-world realities.

Comic books are sometimes a deprecated art form, but the novel's pre-pandemic youth base, small as it is, matures into post-pandemic adults who reconstruct their world out of comics and popular culture. Pablo, Miranda Carroll's abusive artist boyfriend, is Mandel's stand-in for those who cannot appreciate or distinguish among graphic narratives: "He has no interest in comics. He doesn't understand the difference between serious graphic novels and Saturday-morning cartoons with wide-eyed tweetybirds and floppy-limbed cats" (87). In the post-apocalyptic world, what was once ephemeral mass culture, easily rejected by so-called serious artists like Pablo and Arthur, is demonstratively unique. This rarity may be a result of the material disposability of the medium in a world in which survival is prioritized, as much as for Carroll's decision to release her work in a minuscule print run. Scarce or not, comics are cultural objects, and their value as commodity texts is post-pandemically altered. In a new world of beauty built upon ruin, survivors prize the corporeal. Comics in general were formerly expendable – a disposable medium printed on cheap paper with high acid content, prone to disintegration, which Carroll avoids by using archival paper (42). However improbably, Carroll's comics, portable and material, still exist, and it is the textureless internet that becomes an inaccessible dream. Children born after the apocalyptic event "remembered the stories they'd been told about WiFi and the impossible-to-imagine Cloud, wondered if the Internet might still be out there somehow, invisible pinpricks of light suspended in the air around them" (38).[2] The unfathomable Cloud disintegrates, insofar as it is inaccessible to the survivors, but the physical comics, treasured by Tyler and Kirsten, and the world these texts offer upon which to reframe new cultures, remain.

The comic world of *Dr. Eleven*, with its titular protagonist, Dr. Eleven, coalesces with the post-pandemic world of Carroll, blurring the line between a fantasy created in the past and the reality in which Mandel's characters presently survive. The created world includes an (almost) nuclear family unit: Carroll's former husband, Arthur; his son by his second wife, Tyler; and a child actor Arthur takes under his wing, Kirsten. Significantly, both Tyler and Kirsten were given copies of the first two issues of *Dr. Eleven* by their father/father-figure. The main character of Caroll's imagined world, Dr. Eleven, is cherished and held close to the hearts of his bearers, while Carroll dies during the pandemic and is thus sacrificed and *anonymized* to secure the posthumous legitimacy and legacy of her efforts. Her comics become one of the sacred foundations for the unrestrained, misguided monotheocracy led by Tyler, who takes on the identity of a post-apocalyptic prophet, and at the same time the basis for Kirsten's secular comfort during her work as an actor in a travelling theatre company. Station Eleven is, all at once, a space station within a comic book series within a novel, and through the carriers of the *Station Eleven* comic – Tyler/the prophet and Kirsten – Carroll builds a new world in a world penned by Mandel. As Godin notes, "world-building is particularly apt for considering complex structures of thought which shape human purpose and belonging" (56). It is through the creative construction of Carroll, along with other inspirations such as *Star Trek*, Shakespearean plays, and the *New Testament*, that Kirsten and Tyler, children of the old and the new world, develop their personal realities through literary nostalgia. Post-pandemic identities and societal possibilities are directly formed from pre-pandemic literatures and art forms.

In science fiction, superhero comics, and other forms of speculative writing, characters often rewrite their own identities. Carroll's comics indulge in this genre convention, but in Mandel's post-pandemic reality, Kirsten and Tyler use the conventions of identity formation in the comics as grounding for the development of their own identities. In *Station Eleven* the novel, reassignment of identity becomes a bedrock in a post-collapse world where there are "No more avatars" of online communication (Mandel 32). Mandel's new communities, post-collapse, encompass the other-worldly made worldly, as alter ego transitions to ego proper. Many members of the Travelling Symphony, of which Kristen is a part, are known only by their chosen instrument(s) and chair numbers,[3] while the actors are frequently conflated, in name, with their Shakespearean identities. Carroll's fictions, born from her own experiences, undergo a rebirth in the new world as speculative world-building moves in and out of reality. Kirsten cannot remember her parents or her past and continues to reflect on what was. Tyler, who may have "had the misfortune of remembering everything" (304), abandons his name to embrace the role of prophet because, as he freely admits, "Sometimes names are an encumbrance" (300). The convention of renaming oneself, a common trope in speculative literature, is one of the first steps in the creation of new personal and cultural identity.

Dr. Eleven, so named by Carroll, embodies the intersections of the past in which he was authored and the dystopic future he is written into. As the eponymous character in the comic series, his experiences and feelings reflect the characters in *Station Eleven*. Like his melancholy and introspective creator, Dr. Eleven is chiefly a detached observer who monastically records his meditations and stoically "never whines" about his situation (83). He escapes the enslavement of Earth by the ambiguously identified "hostile civilization from a nearby galaxy" (83) and, later on, the flooding of his new home, Station Eleven. Apart from his loyal friend, Captain Lonagan – a loose phonetic translation of (a) lone again – Dr. Eleven survives by employing isolation as a defensive mechanism. Like the subjects of the quarantined airport in *Station Eleven*, or the perpetually misplaced characters of *Star Trek: Voyager*, another intertext of Mandel's novel, Dr. Eleven lives on a station meant for arrivals and departures but offering neither. The station is compared to a planet "the size of Earth's moon," but because its "artificial sky was damaged in the war, ... on Station Eleven's surface it is always sunset or twilight or night" (83). No one on Station Eleven can wake up from perpetual night and no one can go home to Earth; in this world, there is no transitional change of place, only acceptance of placement. Fittingly, Kirsten, who treasures the *Dr. Eleven* comics and has freedom of movement, migrates towards the airport/station, and the accompanying Museum of Civilization, effectively and metaphorically docking the space station and returning it home. Carroll's Station Eleven has all the technological advancements that the post-pandemic world of Mandel's *Station Eleven* lacks, although they, too, are damaged. Similar to the other characters in the *Dr. Eleven* fellowship, Dr. Eleven adopts an alter ego that becomes his primary identity: he has a quantitative name. If ten represents a maximum value – ten out of ten on a quiz, ten on a speaker dial, ten fingers – then eleven is one step beyond known possibility. Eleven, the comic's protagonist, comes to numerically represent the new millennium that Mandel's survivors exist within.[4]

Comics, both literature and art, are formative media that young readers often use to understand and construct their own reality. As an art form, one that Pieter Vermeulen argues in his essay on Mandel's novel "engages the social through the collisions, overlaps, and intersections of literary and social forms" (10), comics are customarily the outcome of a cooperative effort: writers, pencilers, inkers, colourists, and editors all take part in development. However, Carroll works on her *Station Eleven* comics as a personal project without fellowship, and as noted above, the character Dr. Eleven is similarly isolated. The carriers of *Station Eleven*, Kirsten and Tyler, interpret this estrangement in different ways. Kirsten values her community, the Travelling Symphony, and does not endow the *Station Eleven* comics with a religious reading or what Vermeulen argues is "object-oriented ontology" (9). Tyler/the prophet misreads *Station Eleven*, alongside the more influential *New Testament*, and uses the exploits of Carroll's lonely physicist in the formulation of a religion in which he is godlike. From the creation of his new religion, built upon his understandings of comic and biblical literatures, Tyler shapes a new, dangerous culture.

Considering the comics from a religious angle invites an evangelical reading of Carroll as biblical scribe. Working alone, Carroll fills the position of a monastic chronicler, like the observant Friar John Clyn, recording the events of the Black Death during the fourteenth century (Clyn and Dowling), who appeals to future readers: "so have I reduced these things to writing; and lest the writing should perish with the writer, and the work fail together with the workman, I leave parchment for continuing the work, if haply any man survive, and any of the race of Adam escape this pestilence and continue the work which I have commenced" (qtd. in Butler vii). Like Clyn, Carroll embodies a tradition of creation, observation, and writing as a vehicle for contemporary fears and future meditations – in her case, pre-pandemic and bound up in the hybridic form of the comic, which is itself a form of illuminated manuscript. Carroll and Clyn witness, record, and speculate on devastation and survival, and their efforts endure to move nomadically across time from ships to airports to space stations. This portrayal of movement is connotative of how disease and death is aided by technological advancements in travel. The Black Death is transported on ships, the Georgia Flu by airplane, and the foregone conclusion is that "diseases [are] mobilized by global trade networks" (West 10). Carroll's comic is produced before the flu explodes "like a neutron bomb over the surface of the earth" (Mandel 37), killing her and nearly everyone else on Earth. However, the worlds of the comic and the novel exhibit significant parallels, including isolation, displacement, fear of capture by bad actors with ill intentions such as Carroll's denizens of the Undersea and Tyler's "doomsday cult" (83, 62), and the longing for home or an approximation of what-once-was. This longing becomes foundational in identity and culture creation, as Tyler combines his impressions of the comic and *The New Testament*, which were both introduced to him when he was a young and impressionable age.

Mandel places Tyler's ownership of graphic literature within a Christian context; thus, the comics are imbued with a degree of world-building divinity. The authorship of the *Station Eleven* comics, like the authorship of many parts of the Bible, is initially unknown or disputed by the citizens of the post-pandemic world. Anonymous authorships usher both comic and *New Testament* into the traditional field of apocrypha, where both messages absorb into one unit of doom. For Tyler, *Station Eleven* exists figuratively and literally within the Bible. In a retrospective passage, Mandel reveals that Tyler's last conversation with his father, in an allusion to passing into heaven by "going up onstage" (325), involves the boy excitedly proselytizing about the world of *Station Eleven*. In that world, Dr. Eleven's enemies from the Undersea chase you and pull you under, "but they're not really bad. They just want to go home" (325). He later references this scene to Kirsten when he has her held at gunpoint as he and Kirsten enact "A face-off between Dr.

Eleven and an adversary from the Undersea" (302). Tyler intertwines his interpretation of the Bible with Carroll's comic mythology, setting him on the path of the prophet where he can perform his own world-building by shaping his post-pandemic reality, with past literature thus connected to present troubles.

In Mandel's *Station Eleven*, intertextuality is continually used to blend literary culture with the lived reality of the novel's characters. Mandel offers allusion to other past plagues metatextually, using William Shakespeare, a plague survivor, as the vehicle. The narrative begins with the Shakespearean stage play *King Lear* in which actor Arthur, a tragic Lear figure, dies of a heart attack, while in the next section of the book the Travelling Symphony performs *A Midsummer Night's Dream*. Time collapses and Kirsten recites the "Lines of a play written in 1594, the year London's theatres reopened after two seasons of plague" (57). Another character, Dieter, acknowledges that "Shakespeare had lived in a plague-ridden society with no electricity and so did the Travelling Symphony," but the clarinet player, Sidney, otherwise known as the Clarinet, responds that "In Shakespeare's time the wonders of technology were still ahead, not behind them, and far less had been lost" (288). As Shakespeare's scripts are carried on to live another day, so too are Carroll's comic books in this newly created world, levelling the contemporary distinction between high and popular culture. As West notes, the relevance of all of these works exists in "art's mimetic function, [and the] comfort and stimulation audiences receive from seeing representations of their own experience" (8). While the plays continue to travel through the Symphony's performances, the comics travel with their carriers. They become objects of cultural exchange and transmit their messages in this new society, knowingly or unknowingly, through both Tyler and Kirsten.

Tyler/the prophet and Kirsten, foils and happenstance siblings, represent different readerships. Both characters are children of the old world and reach their respective maturities in a post-pandemic society. Both have Arthur – a nod to Arthurian mythology intermingling with Shakespearean mores – as their father figure. Both, like Arthur, have trouble with, or refuse to engage in, monogamous relationships. Like his father, Tyler collects wives, and Kirsten abandons old-world pair bonding, but not at the expense of her communal ties. Significantly, after Tyler's death, Kirsten discovers that he has been carrying a scrap of Carroll's *Station Eleven* in his copy of the New Testament, "the first page of *Station Eleven* she'd ever seen that hadn't come from her copies of the books" (Mandel 304). This revelation in Revelations is epochal and, understanding both its serendipity and significance, Kirsten places the torn page of the comic back into Tyler's lifeless hand after he is shot (304), uniting reader and media.

In the early days of Mandel's fictive pandemic, when Tyler is still a child quarantined with other survivors at the Severn City Airport, a connection between his love for the comics and religion is tentatively forged: "Tyler spent his days curled in an armchair in the Skymiles Lounge, reading his comic books over and over again. [His mother, Elizabeth,] sat near him with her eyes closed, lips moving constantly, rapidly, in some repeated prayer" (245). Later, readers are told, "He kept to himself mostly, reading his comic books or Elizabeth's copy of the New Testament" (252). Tyler carries this obsession with women, apocryphal Christian theology, and Carroll's comics together into adulthood. While Tyler grants *Station Eleven* sacredness with little care given to the hard copy, Kirsten does the reverse; receiving the comics from Arthur was "the clearest memory she retained from before the collapse" (41). These texts, protected in a ziplock bag, travel everywhere with her in the faded Spider-Man backpack that carries her important treasures alongside other resources like bottles of water (66). Tyler, identified alongside his mother early on as "unsettling" (258), continues to mistreat and obsess over the texts in his care and, like Carroll's inhabitants of the Undersea, is willing to engage in violent acts to secure his ideological ascendancy.

If the comic operates as a cornerstone of world-building in Mandel's post-apocalyptic universe, then the physical neglect or care afforded to it by its carriers is significant. Kirsten does not bestow divinity upon the *Station Eleven* comics but recognizes that her affection for them – and for the unpractical paperweight and the magazine articles about Arthur that she also carries – reflects her desire to collect and better understand pieces of the past: "'You're like an archaeologist,' [her friend] Charlie said, when Kirsten showed off her findings" (41). For Kirsten, art is not meant for worship, but for an understanding of the past and the human condition. Kirsten's concluding sacrifice of a comic to the Museum of Civilization that Arthur's friend, Clark Thompson, has started in a repurposed airport illustrates her desire that a relic should be kept safe and serve a human interest. As the narrator notes after Kirsten gives Clark one of her two issues of *Dr. Eleven*, he "could see that it pained her to part with it, but the Symphony was passing into unknown territory and she wanted to ensure that at least one of the comics would be safe in case of trouble on the road" (331). Kirsten's sacrifice is done for the greater good and is comparable to other donations of prized originals or copy-texts (art, prints, or manuscripts) that are gifted from a private collection to a museum or gallery.

Both characters build a personal ideology and pedagogy, respectively, on collection culture.

Tyler's ownership of the comic is also used to enrich his post-pandemic attitudes and teachings, and the reveal of his copy draws him figuratively closer to Kirsten, even as he is about to kill her. Without the end-of-novel disclosure that Tyler was also gifted the *Dr. Eleven* comics by Arthur, nobody, least of all the hapless reader, knows for certain whether or not Tyler is the prophet, although Clark does make a connection between the two close to the end of the book (280). While Tyler and Kirsten share a mutual fondness for the comics, they have conflicting philosophical approaches to Carroll's *Dr. Eleven* comic series. These become evident during their final, fatal encounter, as they re-enact Arthur's gift and Carroll's words like actors at a table read. When confronted with Tyler's knowledge of the world of *Station Eleven*'s Undersea, Kirsten offers a liturgical performance of the play script they have shared: "'We long only to go home,' Kirsten said. This was from the first issue, *Station Eleven*.... The prophet's expression was unreadable. Did he recognize the text?" (302). Tyler does not engage in the offered sacrament. His refusal or inability to acknowledge his connection to another person and to participate in a reading of *Station Eleven* with that person suggests hypocrisy – and perhaps that is Mandel's intended effect – but, for Tyler, *Station Eleven* is a hidden text. It is sacrosanct to him alone and reminiscent of an era in which only a select few were qualified to preach a sacred text. Kirsten offers him a fellowship in script, but Tyler challenges her right to share those words and that divinity. There are many ways to engage with a beloved text. Martin Paul Eve notes in his essay on Mandel's novel that Tyler and Kirsten, effectively siblings at war, exist on opposite ends of the readership spectrum in a novel featuring "acts of interpretation and reading as among its central concerns" (3), and that opposition "invites us, at its surface level, to read symptomatically by offering depictions of characters reading and misreading objects" (6). Eve's analysis of *Station Eleven* focuses on the metadata of ruined objects within the novel to comment on interpretive and political readings of Mandel's dystopia, which supports my reading of the novel's antiquated materials as makers of myth, culture, and meaning, as evidenced through Tyler and Kirsten's opposing interpretations of the comics.

Station Eleven observes the distinction made between superior and inferior art culture but concludes that both are capable of forming and reforming lived reality. The high art of the new world – the Travelling Symphony and their Shakespearean stage plays – is headlined by the low art of the old world, in a quotation from *Star Trek: Voyager* stencilled on the lead caravan: "*Because survival is insufficient*" (58). This "additional line of text" (58) is an intertextual thematic touchstone that invokes a cornucopia of elements of humanity within inhumanity, reaching out from a moment within televised science fiction and including collective memory, diaspora, and art. *Star Trek: Voyager* is a unique entry in the *Star Trek* mythos, as the crew members of the Voyager are not explorers, like the characters of their sister series, but instead misplaced travellers trying to find their way back home, as are the characters of Mandel's novel and Carroll's comics. It is significant that Mandel's characters are inspired to create their new reality from the world-building efforts of so-called low art franchises such as *Star Trek* and *Dr. Eleven*. However, this connection does not go unchallenged as Dieter, a member of the symphony, states, "that quote on the lead caravan would be way more profound if we hadn't lifted it from *Star Trek*," to which Kirsten responds, "it remains my favourite line of text in the world" (119). In Mandel's novel, the seed of profundity in art, required as more than a supplement for survival, finds provenance in artefacts that are often not considered art.

The efforts of Tyler, Kirsten, and Clark demonstrate that it is the collectors of media who preserve and influence history. Disposable media that have been assigned more value as they age, such as *Star Trek* merchandise or comic books that are kept in good condition, eventually find their way into the hands of personal collectors or museums. Similarly, Clark's Museum of Civilization at the Severn City Airport begins with an artefact that initially seems to have little cultural significance. When the quarantine survivors break into the airport's Mexican restaurant and some question whether this is theft, a survivor named Max jokingly says, "I'll cover it on my Amex"; he then leaves his credit card "next to the cash register, where it remained untouched for the next ninety-seven days" (243). At the end of those ninety-seven days, Clark retrieves the card and places it in his museum in what was once an airport lounge (254). Cultural objects and abstractions – comic books, *Star Trek* episodes, abandoned credit cards – become foundational stepping stones for (re)building in a new world. In "Postapocalyptic Curating: Cultural Crises and the Permanence of Art in Emily St. John Mandel's *Station Eleven*," Carmen Méndez-García notes that the museum's goal is to "pass down a sense of shared culture with its collection of donated, useless remnants of technology … and assorted objects found in abandoned baggage" (111). The characters clearly exhibit "a deep nostalgia for the role objects occupied while there was still electricity" (114), but this post-pandemic curation is an impulse "doomed to failure: a museum that celebrates objects that *were* markers of a civilization, but which are now unusable, just beautiful, empty signifiers" that idolize the past while disregarding the future (121). I disagree that the fervent admiration of broken or otherwise useless relics is problematic; instead, I consider the curation of these objects, as performed by Mandel's characters, a humanistic impulse. Evan Williams's definition of "salvagepunk" – "the post-apocalyptic vision of a broken and dead world, strewn with both the dream residues and real junk of the world that was, and shot through with the hard work of salvaging, repurposing, détourning, and scrapping" is particularly useful in interpreting this fictional world ravaged by the Georgia Flu (19–20). Shakespeare, the Bible, and the *Station Eleven* comic are all, in one way or another, revered, despite the objections of various characters. Those who continue the outdated practice of valuing one form of cultural expression over another do not survive to the end of Mandel's novel, for "What has come to an end is the globalized world" (West 7). The divide between high and low art has collapsed, thus imbuing artefacts such as comics and credit cards with culture-creating, abiogenetic power.

Myths fade or can be altered to fit new sociocultural needs, but they do not die, and as *Station Eleven* demonstrates, neither do comic book heroes/protagonists. Miranda Carroll – whose surname evokes another speculative overworld/underworld split, Lewis Carroll and *Alice in Wonderland* – creates Dr. Eleven, star of his own graphic narrative volumes, the first two entitled *Station Eleven* and *The Pursuit*. As a character, Dr. Eleven continues to exist in a post-pandemic world that concerns itself less with reconstruction and more with inauguration. The bearers of the *Station Eleven* comics are understandably mortal, but Dr. Eleven is the same age as he was the day Carroll set him to paper. He arguably exists *above* mortality. As West argues, "The comic … depicts two destroyed worlds – the Earth itself and the space station proxy for it, the former destroyed by violence, the latter by floods" (17). That Dr. Eleven has survived at all and is able to elegize his attempts to "*forget the sweetness of life on Earth*" (Mandel 42) suggests a degree of superheroic immortality in an ironically dispensable medium. However, the novel appreciates and prizes this disposability. Matter, organic or otherwise, is beautiful because it is timely, not timeless: the wearing down of vinyl each time a record is played; how a loved one is committed to memory the last time they say goodbye; when Clark watches an airplane fly for the last time (247). The comic book was (and arguably still is) a literature of limited life, but Dr. Eleven, unable to return home, remains, at first with Kirsten and Tyler and then, later, in the Museum of Civilization – an artefact of the past world infused with a new immortality as Mandel's survivors use it to imagine new futures.

Relevant to the reimagining of personal and cultural creation via the immortality of comic book characters is the timeless nature of the medium. Comic books, especially but not exclusively American franchises, never seem to end, and as Mandel's novel takes its name from Carroll's work, *Station Eleven* also never ends. The nature of publication infinity is proportional to the medium's economic profitability. Carroll's *Dr. Eleven* stands apart: she brings the series to temporal closure, although it cannot be said for certain whether she would have penned a sequel, as she was one of the many casualties of the Georgia Flu. How does the value of a work change when the author, or principal actor in its creation, is inaccessible? Regarding this conundrum, West observes that the "Survivors attempt, as Kirsten does here, to read the traces of [the departed's] stories" in a "landscape [populated] with their absence" (5). It is this inaccessibility that enables a work to be (potentially) misinterpreted. The prophet's men kidnap the Clarinet, but the paper she leaves behind is misread as a suicide note when it was actually "the first line of [an] opening monologue [of a play], which she'd envisioned as a letter" (Mandel 289). Mortality and the completion, or incompletion, of art and text manifest again in the minor character Frank, who aims to finish authoring the project he was hired for before he commits suicide. A post-apocalyptic narrative is invariably gothic when all stories become ghost stories, and archaeologists like Kirsten, tattooed with graphic representations of death in a depopulated world, end up "dragging souls across the landscape like cans on a string" (297).[5]

The absence of use for an object or of life for a person seemingly cements their legacy. Miranda is the only character in Mandel's *Station Eleven* to have her death from the Georgia Flu expressly recounted. Perhaps she is a prophet herself and her fate cannot come as a surprise as, according to West, "throughout her life, Miranda is imagining destruction" (17). Until her death, she continues undauntedly to engage in the creation of her *Dr. Eleven* comic series, running on passion-project energy and having the books "printed at her own expense" (Mandel 213). Carroll herself is sacrificed to secure *Dr. Eleven*'s legitimacy, thus continuing the macabre tradition of a mortality/art disconnect. Additionally, her comic legacy secures her own irrelevancy through the combination of her rejection of community – very few surviving characters knew she was engaged in the creation of *Dr. Eleven* – and her choice of authorial obscurity: "There is no biographical information in either issue, initials in place of the author's name. 'By M. C.'" (42). Appropriately, her death combined with her anonymity imbues the work she leaves behind with immortality, as art becomes more valuable when the creator is dead; the value of art from the past, arguably, is that it is foundational for new culture creation.[6]

In *Station Eleven*, there is no possibility that the so-called death effect will have any capitalistic agency in its post-collapse world, but the *Dr. Eleven* comics left in existence are infused with an alternate worth by Tyler and Kirsten. Art begins to acquire a different type of investment potential, existing not just as cultural object but as culture and world builder. Carroll herself eschews the mercenary considerations of the art market through her refusal to produce for the masses (Mandel 42). Kirsten curiously observes that "In the inside cover of the first issue, someone has written 'Copy 2 of 10' in pencil. In the second issue, the notation is 'Copy 3 of 10.' Is it possible that only ten copies of each of these books exist in the world?" (42). It is almost inconceivable that a traditionally mass-produced medium would be constricted to such a small print run. By her own design, *Station Eleven* and *The Pursuit* are not appreciated in Carroll's lifetime, particularly not by her ex-spouse, Arthur, who at his earliest opportunity re-gifts them to Tyler and Kirsten. But the comic series, once out of Carroll's hands, transitions from undervalued and obscure artefact to seminal text of a new age.[7]

Fittingly, the bearers of Carroll's *Station Eleven* narratives obtain the texts from Arthur when they are young, and this endowment evokes a religious narrative in which the father passes down an influential, sacred text that furnishes the ideologies of a new world or a world made new. An outgrowth of political satire and newspaper "funnies," comic books, historically, were a medium created for the children of the early twentieth century, and despite their recent legitimization within academic and literary circles, they are still connected to a juvenile readership. Uncoincidentally, Carroll's *Dr. Eleven* comics are most intimately affiliated with the only characters originally presented as children. The suggestion is that children have mastered the art of ardent and obsessive affection towards objects: Tyler excitedly recounts the entire plot of the comic *Station Eleven* to Arthur over the phone (324–5), while Kirsten thanks Arthur happily by declaring that she loved the comic books he gave her (328). Whatever Carroll's purpose may have been for her compositions, Mandel manifestly indicates that the *Station Eleven* comics initially resonated more with children than they did with adults. Arthur himself leans creatively upon the predominately adult medium of movies and, more recently, Shakespearean theatre. Kirsten bridges the gap between the categorical mature artistry of theatre and the historical juvenile artistry of comics. She is the cultural offspring of Arthur Leander and Miranda Carroll, a child of their collective influence and more than a simple foil to Tyler Leander. The final confrontation between Kirsten and Tyler, performed over the script Carroll pens and their father hands down to them, reads as melodramatically as any science-fiction epic or comic narrative in which the hero discovers that the villain is, in actuality, a close relation.[8] The communion over the contents of a so-called disposable comic between Kirsten and Tyler, upon whose lines of text each participant has granted a measure of personal identity, accords their shared nostalgia further significance by moving the comic from the sphere of personal treasure to that of shared cultural artefact.

Station Eleven – comic and book – offer complementary readings about the world-building, culture-growing essentiality of artistry, including literature, music, celebrity culture, and the comic book series from which the novel takes its name. Miranda Carroll's apocryphal mythopoesis informs Mandel's collapsed world, but Carroll was created by Mandel. There is an irony implicit in world-building, insofar as it is often the disadvantaged and the young who create new worlds and thus formulate new values for later generations to build upon. Similarly, comic books that are not appreciated in their own time become the seed of a central narrative for Tyler and Kirsten, liminal characters born in the old world who mature in the new one. The lack of interaction between communities in Mandel's *Station Eleven* encourages the growth of mythicality in missing or ruined abstractions; in these isolated societies, the significance granted to old-world ephemera multiplies. Mandel's post-pandemic survivors prize legacy and, like Dr. Eleven – a fictional character in a fictional comic in a fictional storyline – also prize the agency inherent in choosing a personal alter. Carroll's incorporation of life into art informs Mandel's *mise en abyme* narrative. Like a play within a play, the series is a passion project within a book – speculative fiction within more speculative fiction – and Miranda's need to express herself through graphic fiction becomes worthy of entry into the Museum of Civilization. Here, the hybrid form of the comic makes its locale an apt choice for the name of the book, but there is a conflation of art, text, and form. Mandel intertextually collapses universes – text within text, myth within myth, world within world – to create the Station Eleven space station, which exists within the comic *Station Eleven*, which also exists within the novel *Station Eleven*. These iterations are at once an active literary kaleidoscope and a static comic book panel, trapped in time like the never-ending dinner party at Arthur and Miranda's Hollywood home that, recreated in the comic, brings "tears [to Clark's] eyes because all at once he recognizes the dinner party, he was *there*" (332). The fictional comic is also, to an extent, a text of non-fiction – a comic drafted from personal history that

Kirsten and Tyler use as a basis for their own personal histories. Fiction thus bleeds into reality or vice versa, until the two are entwined. Arguably, Miranda Carroll has the honour of scripting her own hereafter. Kirsten Raymonde, by novel's end the only living inheritor of this legacy, becomes a mortal intersection of apocalyptic chronology, art, and survivalism, insufficient as it may be. Her Shakespearean career gazes upon the past and her space comics look to the future, each alike in dignity and in glorious dilapidation, as pre-collapse fictional world-building in Carroll's comic series assists the post-collapse survivors in (re)building their reality.

NOTES

1 Characters within texts are generally referred to by their first or full names. However, despite her status as a fictional person, I refer to Mandel's character Miranda Carroll by her surname when I am speaking of her as an author.
2 In a similarly futile thought exercise about the inaccessibility of the online world during a powerless pandemic, the character M in Amy LeBlanc's "Someone Is Dead," in this volume, recalls a time where she would once use YouTube for background music, but now such a "search would be fruitless" (248).
3 Within band/orchestra culture, chair order generally identifies the competency of the player, but other factors come into play when ordering the chairs. First chair trumpet, for instance, will often get the harder parts and the solos (and a higher rate of pay), and second and third chair trumpets typically support the first chair in harmony and sound.
4 In *Station Eleven*, the theme of constant revitalization is realized in the dog Luli, the only named character to effectively travel through multiple universes: first as Miranda's pet in the pre-pandemic world, then as Dr. Eleven's dog in the *Station Eleven* comics, and then again as the pet of Tyler – and later Kirsten – in the post-collapse world.
5 Members of the Travelling Symphony tattoo on their bodies the number of times they have killed another person in self-defence. Each death is recorded individually and is represented by the weapon that was used; Kirsten, for example, has two knives tattooed upon her wrist (Mandel 295–6). Similar visual iconography, the representation of an experience or ideology through a symbol, is often used in graphic literatures and comic books.
6 This effect is often, and unkindly, called the "death effect," which is "traditionally conceived of as the price bump an artist gets after her death" (Sussman).

7 William Shakespeare, ever-present in *Station Eleven*, noted in "Sonnet 81" that the pen-holder will disappear, but the script will remain for future generations: "Which eyes not yet created shall o'er-read, / And tongues to be your being shall rehearse" (lines 10–11).
8 See, for example, *Star Wars: The Empire Strikes Back*.

WORKS CITED

Butler, Richard. "Introduction." *The Annals of Ireland*, by John Clyn and Thady Dowling, Irish Archaeological Society, 1849, pp. i–xxxvii.
Carroll, Lewis. *Alice in Wonderland*. 1865. Pearson Education, 2008.
Clyn, John, and Thady Dowling. *The Annals of Ireland*. Irish Archaeological Society, 1849.
Eve, Martin Paul. "Reading Very Well for Our Age: Hyperobject Metadata and Global Warming in Emily St. John Mandel's *Station Eleven*." *Open Library of Humanities*, vol. 4, no. 1, 2018, https://doi.org/10.16995/olh.155.
Godin, Mark. "Make-Belief Translation: Fictive Truths and World-Building from *The Lord of the Rings* to Theological Institutions." *Literature and Theology*, vol. 35, no. 1, 2021, pp. 55–78, https://doi.org/10.1093/litthe/fraa037.
LeBlanc, Amy. "Someone Is Dead." *ReVisions: Speculating in Literature and Film in Canada*, edited by Wendy Roy, U of Toronto P, 2025, pp. 247–59.
Mandel, Emily St. John. *Station Eleven*. 2014. Harper Perennial, 2017.
Méndez-García, Carmen M. "Postapocalyptic Curating: Cultural Crises and the Permanence of Art in Emily St. John Mandel's *Station Eleven*." *Studies in the Literary Imagination*, vol. 50, no. 1, 2017, pp. 111–30, https://doi.org/10.1353/sli.2017.0000.
Roy, Wendy. "Trauma and the Ethics of Literary Culture in the Time of Pandemic: Emily St. John Mandel's *Station Eleven* and Saleema Nawaz's *Songs for the End of the World*." *Studies in Canadian Literature*, vol. 47, no. 1, 2022, pp. 50–72, https://doi.org/10.7202/1095236ar.
Shakespeare, William. "Sonnet 81." *The Complete Works of Shakespeare*, edited by Bevington David, 4th ed., Longman, 1997, p. 1680.
Star Trek: Voyager. Paramount Network Television, 1995–2001.
Star Wars: The Empire Strikes Back. Directed by Irvin Kershner, Lucasfilm, 2004.
Sussman, Anna Louie. "The 'Death Effect' on Artists' Prices Actually Occurs When They're Alive." *Artsy*, 2 Jan. 2018, http://www.artsy.net/article/artsy-editorial-death-effect-artists-prices-occurs-alive.
Vermeulen, Pieter. "Beauty That Must Die: *Station Eleven*, Climate Change Fiction, and the Life of Form." *Studies in the Novel*, vol. 50, no. 1, 2018, pp. 9–25, https://doi.org/10.1353/sdn.2018.0001.

West, Mark. "Apocalypse without Revelation?: Shakespeare, Salvagepunk and *Station Eleven.*" *Open Library of Humanities*, vol. 4, no. 1, 2018, https://doi .org/10.16995/olh.235.

Williams, Evan Calder. *Combined and Uneven Apocalypse: Luciferian Marxism.* Zero Books, 2011.

Gender Oppression through Enclosed Spaces in Margaret Atwood's *MaddAddam* Trilogy

MABIANA CAMARGO

In the *MaddAddam* trilogy, Margaret Atwood investigates the geography of patriarchal social systems through an exploration of a fictional dystopian and post-apocalyptic society. In the trilogy's central narrative, neoliberal techno-capitalist practices plunge the world into a decaying state, before its total devastation by a manufactured pandemic that eradicates almost all of humanity. The first and second novels of the trilogy, *Oryx and Crake* (2003) and *The Year of the Flood* (2009), depict a post-apocalyptic present with a few survivors and a dystopian past characterized by a classed society based on corporate power. The trilogy's last novel, *MaddAddam* (2013), is settled in a post-apocalyptic present and provides glimpses of a new posthuman future with the presence of human and non-human survivors, including a bioengineered, posthuman species.

The *MaddAddam* trilogy is a complex work of speculative fiction, a category that according to Atwood has two main features: it poses "what if" questions and is governed by real-world laws that validate the plausibility of the fictional setting. In explaining how she came to write the first novel in the trilogy, Atwood asserts that she spent a long time "considering dystopic 'what if' scenarios" ("*Oryx and Crake* Introduction" 365). Because the trilogy revolves around imagined futures that are transformed and compromised by technological advances and corporate power, the novels raise innumerable "what if" questions regarding the uncertainties of such forces in reinventing life on the planet. Atwood also asserts that her novels depict things that humans have "already invented or started to invent" (365). Her trilogy has at its core, then, the most signifying features of speculative fiction: to question – or speculate on – matters pertinent to an author's time and society, while not defying the rules of reality.

As a speculative trilogy, *MaddAddam* explores how technology and climate crises might impact humanity's future while questioning our present social, political, and economic organizations and systems. Atwood's novels encourage discussions of gender relations in a capitalist society through female characters whose lack of spatial possibilities exemplifies their subjugation. In this chapter, I focus primarily on the dystopian past timeline of Atwood's trilogy as depicted in *Oryx and Crake* and *The Year of the Flood*, and I analyze how Atwood's female characters Oryx, Toby, and Ren are confined to enclosed spaces and have limited mobility. These characters live in a social zone of exclusion built upon ideas about their bodies that are aligned with and concretized by the materiality of physical spaces. Each location exemplifies the asymmetrical power relations between men and women, with the women usually under male control and/or suffering gendered abuse. Through the female characters' movement in space, ideas about women's bodies, sexuality, and behaviour are reinforced, determining their social roles and identities.

Space is not a passive venue of human relations but a complex, relational, and autonomous dimension. In his 1974 study *The Production of Space*, French theorist Henri Lefebvre claims that space is socially produced by our modern mode of production, and for this reason becomes not only "a means of production" but also "a means of control, and hence of domination, of power" (26). For Lefebvre, space plays a crucial role in the division of labour and the ordering of life itself. Expanding on Lefebvre's arguments, feminist geographer Doreen Massey discusses the "positionality" (1) of individuals in the social sphere; she sees space and place as imbricated in social relations, particularly those that shape class and gender. Massey argues that the spatial is "constructed out of the multiplicity of social relations across all spatial scales" (4), relating to both globalized economic activities and more local places such as the workplace and the household. She proposes the term "space-time" (5) to indicate the dynamism of the spatial, which derives from the interconnection of social relations that happen simultaneously. Linda McDowell, who is also concerned with how gender relations are spatially produced, attests that "social practices, including the wide range of social interactions at a variety of sites and places – at work, for example, at home, in the pub or the gym – and ways of thinking about and representing place/gender are interconnected and mutually constituted" (7). For McDowell, how people interact with one another is part of a culture grounded in history but also space. As these discussions suggest, space plays a significant role in shaping individuals' identities and human societal organization.

Spatial exclusion is thus a social product whose dynamics must be examined and challenged.

The oppressions that the *MaddAddam* trilogy's Oryx, Toby, and Ren experience result from unequal spatial opportunities tied to and shaped by gender in a neoliberal capitalist world. Through expected behaviours performed by the individual, gender produces the reality of the sexed body. In her 1990 study *Gender Trouble: Feminism and the Subversion of Identity*, Judith Butler proposes that sex is socially understood through gender, which is not only the effect of cultural meanings about biological sex but also the "very apparatus of production whereby the sexes themselves are established" (11). For Butler, repetitive acts and actions constitute gender, a socially produced corporeal marker that creates a sexed body. Similar to Butler, feminist geographer Jennifer Fluri highlights how the body is one of the main products of social relations. She argues that "the body is a surface upon which various forms of social, cultural, and political meaning are inscribed" (26), and for this reason, the body communicates various meanings. Based on these notions of gender performance and the body, I discuss how gender is established through spaces allotted to the characters in Atwood's *MaddAddam* novels, and how their bodies themselves become spaces of contention.

Pleeblands and Compounds: The *MaddAddam* Trilogy's Dystopian Spatiality

A macro view of the geography of the novels' dystopian society can help in understanding the specific locations and systemized spatial oppressions of Atwood's female characters. In the past timeline of the trilogy, Oryx, Toby, and Ren belong to a world in which life is completely out of balance, with "plagues," "famines," "floods," "droughts," and "wars" (*Oryx and Crake* 253–4). Environmental crises and social dysfunctions shape the world's decaying state, leading to its collapse. Two main spaces define *MaddAddam*'s dystopian past: the enclosed suburban areas called "compounds" and the open cities or "pleeblands." The former are projects and products of the ruling corporations, dedicated to "the top people" (*Oryx and Crake* 26), including the wealthy, scientists, and their families. The latter are the urban spaces destined for the working and unemployed poor. Whereas the compounds provide their inhabitants with a high-quality, comfortable, and secure infrastructure for housing, work, and leisure, in the pleeblands people live with limited resources, pollution, and violence.

The division between the cities and the compounds represents how a classist society places bodies through the division of labour.

For Lefebvre, social space embodies social interactions, particularly regarding the biological differences between people ("*social relations of reproduction*") and the hierarchical division of labour ("*relations of production,*" 32). Because all individuals are assigned a specific location through their entanglement in socio-economic interactions, space enables a political economy. In the *MaddAddam* trilogy's pre-pandemic world, techno-capitalism and the division of labour reinvent its society's spatial relations by redesigning the extreme edges of the borders that separate individuals through social relations of both reproduction and production.

New technological inventions are part of the imagined society of the trilogy and help to shape it in different ways. These include species that are genetically modified, such as pigs that have had their DNA altered in order to host human-tissue organs (*Oryx and Crake* 22) and engineered posthumans informally called Crakers.[1] Crakers are supposedly better versions of humans: they are vegetarians and have no conception of racial or other differences or hierarchies (*Oryx and Crake* 305). Initially, until they are released into a post-apocalyptic world, they are also confined to an enclosed space, a research dome with a ceiling that seems like a blue sky but is in fact "a clever projection device that simulated dawn, sunlight, evening, night" (302). The once-imprisoned Crakers become significant agents of societal transformation after their release, particularly when they create bonds with ordinary humans.

In the *MaddAddam* novels' imagined past, corporate interests and actions alter life by objectifying and modifying everything. This voracious techno-capitalism also anticipates many of the catastrophes of the novels' current world, including the pandemic that wipes out almost the entire human race. Asymmetrical power relations among people and speciesism are foregrounded by limitations to social space. In Atwood's unequal system, women from less privileged backgrounds are the most affected by sexist violence, as seen in the spatial mobility (or lack of it) of Oryx, Toby, and Ren.

Intersections of Gender, Class, and Race in Oryx's Confined Spaces

Despite being a title character in *Oryx and Crake*, Oryx plays a secondary role, appearing only through recollections of the dystopian past by the main character, Jimmy, a survivor of the pandemic who renames himself Snowman.[2] Oryx is a woman from an impoverished Asian community whose life has been marked by human trafficking and sexual exploitation. During her childhood years, she is purchased from her family and forced to be a street flower vendor and an actor in child-pornography films; as a teenager, she is apparently confined to a garage by a sexual predator; as an adult, she works as a paid companion for the powerful scientist Glenn, also known as Crake, in a corporation compound. There, Oryx becomes part of a love triangle with Crake and his friend Jimmy, leading to her death. She spends her entire life serving men and being a victim of them, and her spatial oppression intersects with gender, race, and class.

Oryx's identity is never fully revealed, as her original name is not provided in the narrative; it is implied that even she does not remember it. While working for Crake as an adult, she receives the nickname Oryx Beisa; like the names adopted by Glenn, Jimmy, and others in their circle, the name refers to an extinct or near-extinct animal.[3] Oryx's precise place of birth is unknown. She comes from a village "with trees all around and fields nearby, or possibly rice paddies ... where everyone was poor and there were many children" (*Oryx and Crake* 115). This description suggests a country that faces poverty because of colonialization in a globalized world. Although Atwood does not allow readers to map Oryx's exact origins, through her character the author points to colonialism as one of the primary spatial factors that sparks her oppression.

Oryx is consistently both physically and metaphorically enclosed. Her image first appears in *Oryx and Crake* on a website called HottTotts when she is about eight years old, watched by teenagers Jimmy and Glenn. In the video, Oryx and other girls perform oral sex on an adult man while looking "frightened" (90). The video illustrates how Oryx is physically exploited but also metaphorically imprisoned in the computer frame, and thus doubly subjected to male gaze and control. As a child, she is objectified and commodified, exemplifying how "media representation complements and promotes the image of women [and children] as 'body,' a sexual commodity supposedly always available for the consumption of men" (Irshad and Banerji 588). In the virtual frame, Oryx's infant body becomes a venue for men's desires, normalizing violence against female bodies of all ages.

Both Jimmy and Glenn are struck by the little girl's image and are complicit in the child abuse they witness. While young Jimmy describes her as "three-dimensional from the start" (90), Glenn snaps stills of her face, selects one in which she looks into the camera, and hands Jimmy a printed copy. Years later, Glenn/Crake uses Oryx's picture as a gateway for the virtual game *Extinctathon*, a clandestine meeting room for bioterrorist activists (215). Again, Oryx is enclosed metaphorically in the virtual frame, becoming an object and product for men in the group to observe and consume. Her objectification on screen can be compared to the objectification of Offred discussed in MacKenzie Read's "Vision and Re-Visioning in *The Handmaid's Tale* and Two Adaptations," a chapter in this collection. Read argues that in Atwood's acclaimed 1985 novel, the oppressive and pervasive masculine "gaze" helps to constrain female characters. This constraint parallels Oryx's subjugation through acts of observation in which she is taken only as an object to be consumed.

As Oryx later recounts in her story to Jimmy, her spatial oppression begins after she is sold by her family to "Uncle En" and transported with other children in the back of a car with locked doors (125). Smuggled into a different country, they encounter the unknown space of a big city, described as "chaos, filled with people and cars and noise and bad smells and a language that was hard to understand" (127). In the urban centre, Oryx becomes SuSu (129); she sleeps in a "small room" with "a barred window" (127) that is crowded with other children, and during the day she is forced to work illegally selling flowers to white tourists. To do this work, "She was given a dress that was too big for her, and in it she looked like an angelic doll" (130). Fluri argues that a dress "operates as a way of marking corporeal identities, which [are] malleable and often manipulated for various social, cultural, economic, and political purposes" (41). In Atwood's novel, the dress not only creates a performative femininity to define the child but also produces a stereotypical image of Oryx as a "doll" (*Oryx and Crake* 130), innocent and adorable, but also an object that can attract potential clients on the city's streets.

Oryx/SuSu's role as an urban flower seller is socially accepted because she now belongs to "the city of men," as Leslie Kern defines the urban space in *Feminist City*. For Kern, "the city has been set up to support and facilitate the traditional gender roles of men and with men's experiences as the 'norm,' with little regard for how the city throws up roadblocks for women and ignores their day-to-day experience of city life" (6). Cities disregard women's experience through different dynamisms and at different levels. In Oryx's case, a little girl being exploited goes unremarked, even though "the police knew all about it" (*Oryx and Crake* 129). Her exploitation in the urban space also relates to how her body is categorized through race. According to Fluri, "race and gender are spatially organized bodily markers. This means that race and gender are visible both on the body and by way of different geographies" (31). Relating to Fluri's claim, the city embraces Oryx's oppression because she is both a girl and an illegal alien.

Oryx's oppression on the urban streets is intensified when she is exposed to male predators, many of them Western white tourists. She is told by Uncle En to accept offers to accompany men to hotel rooms. During these ventures, inside a confined space, Oryx is asked to "take off her dress" (*Oryx and Crake* 131). When both she and the man are naked, Uncle En arrives to rescue her, but primarily to blackmail the man into giving him money so he will not be reported to the police. Atwood's presentation of male violence and domination over female child bodies is a critique of child sexual exploitation as a capitalist social disease. Further, this exploitation is clearly related to colonial power, as Oryx is a victim of the misery of her home country and becomes both a sexual commodity and part of a cheap labour force. Recalling Massey's ideas about how different and simultaneous interrelations and interactions happen "at all spatial scales" (264), Oryx's spatial positioning in the urban sphere suggests that she is located between the global and the local through colonial relations. The fact that Oryx is used and abused on the streets of a different country relates to how her Asian home country (a colonized space) sustains another richer country (a colonizing space), and how both spaces are interrelated in a complex dynamism of economic and political relations.

After Uncle En apparently dies, other men take Oryx from the street and force her to perform in pornographic movies with other children (*Oryx and Crake* 136, 140). These probably are the films Jimmy and Glenn watch on the website HottTotts and through which her body is sexualized in the virtual world. Later, she is apparently discovered in another enclosed space: a garage in San Francisco. As adult Jimmy learns through a news item on television, Oryx, or a girl who looks very much like her, was purchased by a North American man who found her on the web. Not only her, but "a wave of adolescent girls found locked in garages" share their stories: some of them would say that "[t]hey'd been rowed across the Pacific Ocean on rubber rafts, they'd been smuggled in container ships, hidden in mounds of soy products" (254). After Jimmy meets Oryx in the compound where they both work for Crake, he questions her about this experience; while patronizing her, he tries to force her to confirm that she was the girl in the news item (315–16). Other than saying that the garage "was more like an apartment" (316), Oryx avoids telling Jimmy details, including about her abductors. The sex-slave scandal in Atwood's pre-pandemic society is additional evidence of how exploitation of marginalized girls and women is related to colonized and confined spaces.

Oryx ends her life in the North American corporate compound as Crake's "devoted employee" (310). She is, in fact, his mistress, but she also performs other duties, including helping the Crakers learn about the world around them (309). Oryx is even more confined while working as the Crakers' mentor; she enters the dome that artificially imitates a paradisiac natural spot to teach them simple ideas related to botany and zoology, so that they can understand the environment and learn how to survive. Oryx and the new posthuman species are both hemmed in and controlled in this space.

The first time the adult Jimmy sees Oryx in the compound is through a window into the dome: "Like the Crakers she had no clothes on, and like the Crakers she was beautiful," Jimmy thinks (308). Again, she is an object to be observed inside a frame. Her virtual image collected from minicams again strikes adult Jimmy: "She turned into the camera and there it was again, that look, that stare, the stare that went right into him and saw him as he truly was" (308). Because Oryx and the Crakers are erotic and scientific objects, they can only mimic "normal" human relations. They become the "the signified – not the signifier," as Read defines the observed subject in *The Handmaid's Tale* (365). Thus, within the compound, Oryx is both physically and metaphorically imprisoned.

At the same time, her mobility is not completely constrained, as she becomes a saleswoman responsible for selling Crake's creation, the supposed aphrodisiac BlyssPluss. He defines Oryx as "an expert businesswoman" who "had useful contacts in the pleeblands" through her previous role as a sex worker (313). In this new role, Oryx serves as a bridge between the compounds and the pleeblands, but also as an unwitting vector for the global pandemic since, unknown to her, Crake has deliberately inserted a highly contagious virus into BlyssPluss. Because the cities have qualities such as "anonymity, energy, spontaneity, unpredictability, and yes, even danger" (Kern 12), Oryx's mobility in the city spaces reinforces stereotypes surrounding her as a woman. Jane Rendell claims that "femininity is connected with chaotic and disorderly space" (107); this idea, when associated with Oryx's spatial practice as a businesswoman whose actions are as dangerous and dirty as the cities themselves, suggests that she personifies chaotic femininity because she brings chaos to the landscapes she enters.

Further, Oryx's relationship with Crake and love affair with Jimmy evolve into a tragedy. At the end of *Oryx and Crake*, she is murdered by Crake in the enclosed space of the entrance to the compound, provoking Jimmy to kill him (329). Her death exemplifies confinement and consumerism, as she has become a product owned by Crake, who uses brutal violence to end her life.[4]

Oryx's body is repeatedly subjected to masculine control, and she learns to play different roles to survive a hostile and cruel world. Her social roles are the frame that holds her identity, while spatial limitations determine the course of her life. Oryx is part of a world that values capital controlled by masculine power. For this reason, throughout her life, she is marginalized, commodified, enslaved, and locked in, forced to be obedient and submissive. The absence of Oryx's real name and place of birth in the narrative emphasizes her oppression. She is alienated from her subjectivity as she cannot assert who she is and where she comes from. However, this alienation allows her identity to be fluid and adaptable in an oppressive world, which is also one of the facets of her resilience.

Toby's Mobility and Enclosure in the Pleeblands

The Year of The Flood focuses on the lives of two survivors of the pandemic, Toby and Ren, and provides more details about the trilogy's initial dystopian, corporate-ruled world, particularly the urban spatiality of the pleeblands. This second novel depicts the challenges the women face in the dystopian past; during the pandemic, when they are both in isolation; and in the post-apocalyptic world, which is almost devoid of life.[5]

In the past of the *MaddAddam* trilogy, Toby, similarly to Oryx, has her body commodified and her spatiality limited because she is a working-class woman. Throughout her life, Toby is metaphorically and physically imprisoned, and she is always susceptible to male violence. She is physically confined in rooms and buildings and metaphorically enclosed in costumes and garments, and she also undergoes body modifications to survive economically and to protect herself.

The Year of the Flood starts with Toby living post-apocalypse, isolated in a building that once was the AnooYoo Spa where she previously worked as a manager. She has access to the roof in this building, where she goes to watch the quasi-empty landscape around her (3), and to the enclosed garden in the grounds (15). During her days locked in the spa, she fights to maintain her life, always on alert. The narrator says, "She's prepared. The doors are locked, the windows barred. But even such barriers are no guarantee: every hollow space invites invasion" (5). Her need for safety imprisons her, although, in her confinement, she shows how powerful and resilient she is.

Toby's isolation at the spa before and after the pandemic is a consequence of the economic and gendered oppression she experiences in a techno-capitalist, patriarchal world. At the time she is a teenager, the corporations begin intensifying their presence in society, including establishing a security agency called CorpSeCorps. Toby's family is affected in different ways by the intense corporate activities. First, her mother becomes the victim of a corporate scam to profit through a human-created disease spread through health supplements (25–6).[6] After her mother's funeral, Toby's father, in despair at the loss of his wife and the bankruptcy of his family, takes his own life (27). Afraid that the corporations will inquire about her father's death and family's debts and perhaps imprison her, Toby decides to change her identity and flee to the pleeblands.

In the chaotic urban space, Toby is confined both physically and metaphorically. She first lives in a tiny room in a building with illegal immigrants, in an area called the Sewage Lagoon "because a lot of shit ended up in it" (30). Her life exemplifies physical enclosure due to poverty. She is also metaphorically imprisoned and susceptible to masculine violence in the first job she finds in the pleeblands. Working as "furzooter," Toby advertises businesses by wearing an animal suit and hanging a sign around her neck; she is imprisoned in the furry costume, which is "hot and humid" with a limited "range of vision." While performing her job, she is frequently attacked by "fetishists who knocked her over … and rubbed their pelvises against her fur" (31). Although she does not classify these attacks as sexual violence, because her skin cannot be touched, she finds it "creepy" (31), and she is, in fact, sexually assaulted.[7] Further, struggling to survive in the "city of men" (Kern 6), Toby uses her body as an asset for her survival: she sells her hair and her ova on the black market (*Year of the Flood* 31, 32). Her health is eventually compromised, making it impossible for her to "donate any more eggs, or – incidentally – have any children herself" (32): Toby loses her reproductive capacity as a result of her position as a marginalized body living in extreme poverty.

Her oppression in the pleeblands is maximized when she works in a fast-food chain called SecretBurgers. As he has previously done with other female employees, the manager, Blanco, obliges Toby to engage in sexual activity, at the cost of her job and life. Scholar Dunja M. Mohr claims that for Blanco, "woman *is* the sexualised, abused, enslaved, raped, and tortured body, a replaceable object, to be literally consumed as meat" (294). Atwood's use of the metaphor of meat or "SecretBurgers" to represent women's bodies, as pointed out by Mohr, satirizes the idea of consumerism that trespasses on female bodies in patriarchal cultures. The metaphor indicates the real danger they are exposed to, since violence, slaughter, and consumption are part of the semantic field that constitutes the meanings of "meat."[8]

Toby is able to end the objectification and violence she experiences at SecretBurgers when a friend who has joined the eco-group God's Gardeners initiates a rescue operation in the guise of a fight near the restaurant (*Year of the Flood* 41–2). In the company of these "bizarre people" with a "wacky religion" (44), as they are first described, Toby lives on the rooftop of an old factory building, a place called the "Garden" (42). From her perspective, the Garden is "so beautiful, with plants and flowers" and "vivid butterflies" and "bees" (43), although in an "unlikely and somehow disturbing location" (44). The Garden is an attempt to reanimate life in a decaying world in which human actions and climate crises are destroying nature. Through their religion, the Gardeners condemn consumerism and technology and aspire to a more communal and eco-friendly way of living: they plant their own organic food, manufacture their own medicines, and eat a vegetarian diet, and every member plays a productive role in the community.

As a Gardener, Toby has more freedom and a better quality of life; however, she is still in a confined space, and her body is gendered through the Gardeners' organizational hierarchy. The eco-religious group claims that everyone is "equal on the spiritual level" (45) but that they must be divided in the material world. The leaders are called Adams and Eves and are assigned numbers according to their areas of expertise or degrees of power. As a Gardener, Toby wears "dark, sack-like garments" and long hair, as this is believed to be God's "aesthetic preference" (46). The dress of Gardener women embodies a patriarchal perspective about women's bodies – they are a venue for men's lust and therefore must be hidden – and is performative in that it assigns cultural acts to specifically gendered bodies.

Eventually, Toby becomes an "Eve" (181) after the death of senior Gardener Pilar, who has been her guide and role model. Although Toby has a calmer and better life with the Gardeners, she is not completely safe with them. A male Gardener tries to sexually assault her (103), and every time she leaves the Garden to wander the pleeblands, "she'd cover herself well and wear a nose cone and a wide sunhat" (97) so as not to be seen and recognized by Blanco. On the streets, she is metaphorically imprisoned by the garments she wears to hide herself.

After Toby's abuser attacks the Garden in order to get at her, the Gardeners' leader sends Toby to hide in the AnooYoo Spa. In her journey to this space, she is again metaphorically and physically imprisoned as she is hidden under a furzoot costume (258) and has to sleep in a "former hydraulic-lift pit" (259) and later in an old "bank vault" (261). To further ensure her safety, Toby submits to cosmetic procedures. She changes her fingerprints and her skin and hair to a darker colour, is given a lower voice, and starts using green contact lenses (261). With a new look, Toby embraces a new persona, becoming Tobiatha, "Less angla, more latina. More alto" (262). Her disguise encapsulates the city's violence concerning her body. Kern argues that women always "experience the city through a set of barriers – physical, social, economic, and symbolic – that shape their daily lives in ways that are deeply (although not only) gendered" (5). Applying Kern's claim to Toby's spatial practice, she can never be free in the urban space due to her social class and the fact that she is a woman. Although she disguises herself to become unnoticed, her invisibility is only possible in the enclosed space of the spa, not on the city streets.

The AnooYoo Spa reinforces patriarchal notions of femininity that are performative through its ideologies and design and through the bodies that belong to this space. For Butler, gender "performativity is not a singular act, but a repetition and a ritual, which achieves its effects through its naturalization in the context of a body, understood, in part, as a culturally sustained temporal duration" (*Gender Trouble* xv). Gender is an effect of the performance of cultural acts that design and constrain the body over time. In the dystopian world of *The Year of the Flood*, most of the spa's employees are women, and most of its clients are wealthy women looking for cosmetic treatments that will help in their performance of femininity.

In the spa, beauty is a commodity. Toby reads from the staff instructional booklet, "We're not selling only beauty.... We're selling hope" (264); the spa thus posits beauty as an ideal that relates to social worth. In *The Beauty Myth* (1990), Naomi Wolf claims that beauty is a myth that operates through a political economy that hinders women's freedom while safeguarding male dominance. According to Wolf, the myth "is not about women at all. It is about men's institutions and institutional power" (13). Wolf suggests that ideologies about women's beauty "undermine women's advancement" (20) in a culture that fears and despises women when they claim power. In Atwood's novels, AnooYoo reinforces the beauty myth as part of a patriarchal society that values women's appearance above all.

Feeling weak and hallucinating while surviving post-pandemic, Toby occasionally "hears voices – ... the voices of women, the women who used to work here, the anxious women who used to come, for rest and rejuvenation" (*Year of the Flood* 5). Her memory confirms that AnooYoo's female clients were "anxious" if they could not comply with societal standards of beauty and youth. Further, the dominant presence of the colour pink in AnooYoo's design reinforces a performative femininity. At the spa, Toby recalls, there were "pink sheets and pink pillows, and pink blankets too" (96); "everything was pink" (297). The spa materializes femininity by reproducing the social and cultural codes of a patriarchal society.

As the spa manager, Toby acts rebelliously and clandestinely to help women fugitives of the corporations hide from persecution (266). At the same time, she stockpiles food, preparing herself for a future apocalyptic event, a precaution she has learned previously from the Gardeners (265). While in the spa, an ex-Gardener visits Toby and invites her to "play" the virtual game *Extinctathon,* which is how the eco-resistance group MaddAddam communicates. To enter the cyber gateway, Toby takes on code names of extinct animals, first Dodo and then Inaccessible Rail (269). Through the virtual game, she learns about the destruction and break-up of the Garden and gets ready to face the pandemic or "Waterless Flood" (20), in the Gardeners' words. Although the virtual frame allows Toby to be an activist, she is also metaphorically imprisoned by the computer screen; she depends on the information and orders her colleagues pass along to her. When the pandemic hits, she locks herself in the spa; her choice to remain in a confined space saves her from contracting the fatal illness.

Almost as much as Oryx, Toby is oppressed because of the exclusionary values of the patriarchal society to which she belongs. She loses her family because of harmful capitalist practices. She is left in extreme poverty in the pleeblands, where she learns about the dangers of the "cities of men." Ironically, she also learns the value of her young female body, and, like Oryx, she trades it in order to survive. Toby is metaphorically imprisoned in own her skin, and like Oryx, she is obliged to perform roles that are dictated by the intersection of her gender and class.

As seen in Toby's story, gender oppression has severe and traumatic consequences. The abuses she experiences affect her in different ways: she will not be able to bear children, and she shuts down many of her feelings, becoming what Gardener children call a "Dry Witch" (62). However, with the Gardeners, Toby finds healing as well as safety. Later, when she encounters other human survivors post-apocalypse, she becomes an important community member, acting as a leader, a caregiver, and a storyteller and teacher for the Crakers, as Oryx was before her. Toby's resilience in surviving a masculine world and a pandemic shapes her into a strong female character in Atwood's third novel, *MaddAddam.*

Ren's Survival through Sexual Quarantine

Ren, whose birth name is Brenda (*Year of the Flood* 302), is another survivor of the pandemic whose body is objectified and whose life is at risk in a masculine-controlled world. Younger than Toby, she has lived in both the compounds and the pleeblands. Because her father is a scientist, Ren first inhabits a compound, but later she spends part of her childhood in the city as a God's Gardener. When Ren is a teenager, she returns to the compound, where she becomes one of the young women who is sexualized and objectified by Jimmy as described in *Oryx and Crake*.[9] Some years later, Ren ends up by herself in the pleeblands, where she works at a nightclub for men. Ren is vulnerable to abuse and endures different kinds of oppression; she is able to find a modicum of freedom only when she meets other survivors post-apocalypse. However, in Atwood's trilogy, Ren is the female character with the most power, not only because she inhabits two worlds but also as evident in the novel's narrative structure: she is the only protagonist who is allowed to narrate her own story.

In *The Year of the Flood*, Ren narrates her life after the pandemic while isolated in a building that once was the nightclub Scales and Tails, where she worked as a trapeze dancer and a sex worker. Locked in a quarantine room called the "Sticky Zone," Ren describes it as a "fortress" (281): "I can't see out the window, it's glass brick. I can't get out the door, it's locked on the outside" (6). Female employees of Scales are confined to the Sticky Zone if clients have potentially infected them. Because Ren was assaulted by a client who "got carried away and bit [her], right through the green sequins" (6) of her Biofilm Bodyglove, she is in isolation until her test results are released. Ren's imprisonment at Scales is a result of the sexual abuse she suffers, and, ironically, is the reason she survives the pandemic brought about by BlyssPluss, a product she has seen consumed at the club (202).[10]

Ren ends up in the confined space of Scales as a consequence of being a marginalized woman in the pleeblands. When she is a child, her mother leaves her scientist husband in one of the compounds to live with her new lover, a God's Gardener. Ren lives with them in an old factory near the Garden, a place she describes as "a big room, with some cubicles curtained off" (63). Despite the simplicity of their new surroundings, Ren and her mother find a certain comfort and security. As Gardeners, "everyone, including children, had to contribute to the life of the community" (69), and so Ren not only studies but also works as an apprentice at tasks such as botanicals and cooking (61). When Ren's mother becomes disenchanted with her lover and returns to the scientific compound, Ren is forced to accompany her. Ren struggles with readapting to compound living because her view of life is now affected by the Gardeners' eco-friendly principles and ideologies. After Ren's mother tells her that she cannot afford her college fees, Ren decides to return to the pleeblands (293–4). Once again in this open space, she first gets a job at the AnooYoo Spa, where she works under Toby, whom she has known in the Garden. Having the privilege of only "working with women" (295), Ren initially feels safe. However, when her mother, now living with another man, comes to the spa as a customer and ignores her daughter's existence, Ren decides she wants to be "someone else entirely" (301) and takes a job she has been offered at Scales and Tails. While her life at Scales is a consequence of her quest for autonomy and freedom, it also indicates her limited options as a young woman in a sexist world.

Scales and Tails materializes the misogynist practices of the *MaddAddam* trilogy's dystopian society. At the club, women are hypersexualized, and their bodies are commodified through their roles as erotic dancers and sex workers: each is "a valuable asset" (7), an object of consumption by the club's male clients who want "epidermis and fantasy" (307). The club's clientele does not see women as whole human beings with thoughts, feelings, wishes, and imperfections. Women have little agency and mobility in this space compared to the men who circulate in it. Here, sexual discourses about female bodies are constructed and manifested. As Butler argues, "the regulatory norms of 'sex' work in a performative fashion to constitute the materiality of bodies and, more specifically, to materialize the body's sex, to materialize sexual difference in the service of the consolidation of the heterosexual imperative" (*Bodies that Matter* 2). Scales materializes sex by offering women as products to be consumed by men. Focusing on the pleasures of a male audience, the club also reinforces heteronormative behaviour in which traditional gender roles and sexualities are maintained. Further, the club's name and the pictures at its entrance (74) suggest a hybridism of women with animals. Scales promulgates the idea that women need to be animalistic and wild. The club's name and social practices create and reinstate idea(l)s of femininity that are performative and that in effect dehumanize women.

At the same time, women like Ren who work in the club can find some autonomy and financial security. Ren is proud of being a trapeze dancer, since it is a skill that allows her to make a decent living. As the manager tells her, she is not "a disposable" but a "talent" (282). She knows she has a place in a hostile society, and her confidence is part of her empowerment and resilience. The women workers at Scales have some prestige because they serve the most important men in the dystopian society. In Ren's words, "we were known as the cleanest dirty girls in town" (7). Atwood's use of an oxymoron, "the cleanest dirty girls," ironizes patriarchal meanings surrounding female bodies: they need to be "dirty" in sexual terms and "clean" in relation to their health in order for the club to maintain its status as an ideal place of consumerism for men. At the same time, as Ren's injuries indicate, the club can be a dangerous place for female employees.

In the novel's present, while locked in the Sticky Zone at Scales, Ren recollects events from the past and describes what happened during the pandemic outbreak. She recalls talking to her friend Amanda by phone (56) and watching TV news about the beginning of the epidemic (279).[11] Through the cameras available to her, she also sees a fight in Scales with three former convicts, called Painballers, in which customers and club employees are killed.[12] The men want to get at her, but her manager refuses to give them the door code and is killed. From this day on, Ren is locked in a room in an empty club. She watches the news about the worldwide epidemic, riots, and killings, and then sees no more news (283). She later claims that she is "very lucky" because her lockdown "kept [her] safe" (6), sheltering her from both the predatory men and the pandemic.

In her past life as a Gardener, Ren has been told that writing is dangerous and forbidden because written words can denounce one to an enemy. Believing that in the post-apocalyptic world it is "safe" to do so, she repeatedly writes her name on a wall with a make-up pencil, "*Renrenren*, like a song" (6), so that she will not forget who she is while being trapped. Ren is alive, Ren is Ren, and her writing is a defiant act that exemplifies a transition to a new world and identity. She does not want to be Brenda, a child in a compound, but instead Ren, a past Gardener, dancer, and survivor. She is only released from the quarantine room, and her survival ensured, when Amanda arrives and helps her to decipher the code that unlocks the door.

Like Oryx and Toby, Ren's life is marked by quasi-imprisonment in confined spaces. Ren experiences spatiality through circulation in both the compound and the pleeblands; however, she is never allowed to choose freely where she wants to be, and she is marginalized in both spaces. In *The Year of the Flood*, Ren becomes a sex worker mainly to survive but also to forget the pain of a broken relationship with her mother and her abandonment in the pleeblands. Like Oryx and Toby, Ren learns that her body is her most valuable asset, and she exchanges it to make a living. Despite becoming autonomous in certain ways while at the club, Ren is always subjected to men's gaze and control.

In *The Year of the Flood*, Ren has more narrative control than either Toby or Oryx because she is allowed to tell her own story. Ren is not a leader, as Toby becomes, but she is a resilient female character who shows her strength as a young woman in a decaying male-controlled world. Her resilience can be seen in her courage to become Ren and forget Brenda; her capacity to endure a solitary life; and her loyalty to Amanda, whom she helps and protects.

Posthumanity and Sisterhood in the Post-Apocalyptic World

In Atwood's trilogy, gender differences and women's oppression continue to exist after the pandemic. At the end of *The Year of the Flood*, after Ren is released from the Sticky Zone by Amanda, both women almost immediately return to being sexual commodities: they are kidnapped and sexually assaulted by Painballers who also survived the pandemic. Ren is able to escape and goes to the Spa to meet Toby, and together they flee through the near-empty landscape to save Amanda from men who think of her as "a sex toy [one] can eat" (417): both a sexual object and a literal "piece of meat" they can consume if times get desperate.

Toby, Ren, and Amanda are able to regain a certain amount of freedom when they join other survivors, including ex-Gardeners and Crakers. However, the three women still suffer gender oppression in different ways. In this new community in an urban park, gender roles reflect previous social organization, with men going on missions and most women staying home (*MaddAddam* 342). Amanda and Ren are both sexually assaulted by Craker men, whose way of mating, despite lacking emotions and desires, reflects the sexist perspective of their creator, Glenn/Crake. In an occasion defined by Toby as a "major cultural misunderstanding" (13), the Craker men act towards Amanda and Ren as they would towards Craker women. Both women become pregnant, as does a third survivor who engages in consensual sex with the Craker men. At the same time, Toby fights feelings of sadness and jealousy because she cannot have a child of her own (91, 274).

In *MaddAddam*, even though the pandemic has completely devasted human culture, the new social organization bases itself on humanity's past. Although the human survivors in *MaddAddam* strive towards more egalitarian relationships, some of the ideologies from the past dystopian society are still present in their behaviours and those of the Crakers. The living humans and Crakers epitomize human history – fractured, inconsistent, full of contradictions and multiple meanings. Even post-apocalypse, women are in a subjugated position and are vulnerable to male dominance. The new world presented in the last novel of the trilogy, despite pointing to a better posthuman future, is not an ideal one for women as it is still filled with patriarchal ideologies and performances.

The *MaddAddam* trilogy does not project a completely hopeless view of the future of human behaviours and relations, however. Atwood's post-apocalyptic world exhibits a feminist impulse through the alliance and sisterhood of the women. In *The Year of the Flood,* the narrative focuses on the female characters, who are heroines for each other and themselves. As Mohr argues, "Atwood foregrounds with Ren/Amanda and Toby … a strong feminist thread of resilience" (293). The sorority created by these women is essential to reestablishing a new world, as presented in the final novel, *MaddAddam.*

Reconsidering Contemporary Societal Organization through Speculative Fiction

Atwood's speculative trilogy enables a deep examination of the specifics of our current space-time, which Massey identifies as a continuum of practices and realities throughout history (4). When dystopian social organization and apocalyptic events interrupt the space-time that regulates the fictional society, they provoke an examination of real oppressive institutions that constrict human life: the neoliberal techno-capitalist state, patriarchy, and colonialism.

The *MaddAddam* novels uncover a complex spatiality that provides a radical critique of modern societies and their modes of production. According to Lefebvre, space "embrace[s] a multitude of intersections" (33) that relate to the social; at the same time, it becomes the product of the social. Further, space is linked to "productive forces, including technology and knowledge," the "social division of labour," and "the superstructures of society" (85). The geography of the early part of Atwood's trilogy is marked by division between the cities and the compounds, which are complementary opposites in which one side profits from the other. The techno-capitalism of the dystopian society transforms every segment of life and is represented in the urban architecture: most individuals are condemned to marginalization and poverty as a result of exploitation of one group over another.

In Atwood's *Oryx and Crake* and its sequels, the position of the characters in space results from the construction of corporeal meanings through their society's political, social, and economic ideologies. Oryx, Toby, and Ren are unequally treated because of bodily markers derived from class relations, but also those of race and gender, all of which are spatially produced. Their social positions are enforced through what McDowell identifies as everyday interactions shaped by institutional and structural power (11). They are physically confined and must play roles connected to their sexuality. Thus through these three characters, Atwood exposes how a patriarchal society objectifies women and imprisons them in their own bodies.

In her 2012 essay "Future Shock: Rewriting the Apocalypse in Contemporary Women's Fiction," Susan Watkins claims that apocalyptic fiction can dismantle dominant narratives, including patriarchal ones, "by rethinking the relationship between technology, science, gender, and empire" (120). Atwood's trilogy proposes a revision of these narratives and relationships while challenging the material boundaries of space and the binarism of gender. The *MaddAddam* novels denounce the exclusionary geography created by capitalism aligned with patriarchy. Taken separately or as a group, the novels thus can be read as speculative critiques or re-visions of contemporary geopolitical-societal organization.

NOTES

1 In Atwood's trilogy, the young scientist Glenn, a.k.a. Crake, whose adopted name is part of the title of *Oryx and Crake*, creates both the Crakers and the future pandemic.

2 *Oryx and Crake* is narrated in third person, but from the perspective of Jimmy/Snowman.

3 The men's adopted names refer to two birds, the red-necked crake and the thick-knee or "Thickney" (81, 299). However, after the disaster, Jimmy tells the Crakers he is the mythical Abominable Snowman (7, 348).

4 Oryx's deadly commodification inside the corporate compound resonates with that in Atwood's *The Heart Goes Last* (2015), in which characters live in a prison-compound town. In "The Possibilities of Prison Food in Margaret Atwood's *The Heart Goes Last*," published in this collection, Shelley Boyd claims that the town is "an imprisoning construct" that permeates people's minds and lives (206).

5 The sections of *The Year of the Flood* focused on Toby are narrated in third person, although from her perspective, while Ren is given a first-person voice.

6 As Boyd argues, food carries neoliberal power and control over bodies. In *The Year of the Flood*, this power is exemplified by the deadly health supplements.

7 The sexual assault Toby suffers while a furzooter alludes to zoophilia. Piers Beirne (2006) calls forced sexual acts between humans and non-humans "*interspecies sexual assault*" because of its similarity to "the sexual assault of women, children and infants" (326). For Beirne, just like sexual violence on humans, interspecies sexual assault is a consequence of a "malicious masculinity" (328) that sees animals, as well as women, as commodities (329).

8 Some time after Toby frees herself from Blanco, he sees her on the street and yells, "You're meat!" (*Year of the Flood* 255), alluding to his desire

to continue to abuse her or perhaps kill her. Carol J. Adams claims that animals are the absent referent in the meaning of the word "meat"; similarly, when women are conceived as meat, they are "treated as inert objects, with no attention paid to their feelings or needs" (65).

9 Ren/Brenda first meets Jimmy when they are in high school. When he learns she was previously a Gardener, he calls her "a little enviroserf," something he thinks is "[s]exy" (*Year of the Flood* 217). Jimmy thus objectifies and sexualizes Ren, as his words mean that what makes her attractive is the fact that she is supposedly an ex-slave.

10 At Scales, Ren encounters the scientist Glenn/Crake, whom she met in high school, as well as Oryx.

11 Amanda is another female character whose marginalization has a strong spatial character. She comes from a family of farmers in Texas who lost everything due to drought and ended up living in a refugee camp (*Year of the Flood* 84). With no other options, both mother and daughter trade their bodies to get shelter and fulfil their basic needs.

12 Painballers are condemned criminals who engage in a televised, deadly fight-to-the-finish (*Year of the Flood* 98).

WORKS CITED

Adams, Carol J. *The Sexual Politics of Meat: A Feminist-Vegetarian Critical Theory.* 1990. Continuum, 2000.

Atwood, Margaret. *The Heart Goes Last.* 2015. Emblem, 2016.

– *MaddAddam.* 2013. Vintage Canada, 2014.

– *Oryx and Crake.* 2003. Vintage Canada, 2009.

– "*Oryx and Crake* Introduction (2018)." *Burning Questions: Essays & Occasional Pieces, 2004–2021.* McClelland & Stewart, 2022, pp. 363–7.

– *The Year of the Flood.* 2009. Vintage Canada, 2010.

Beirne, Piers. "Rethinking Bestiality: Towards a Concept of Interspecies Sexual Assault." 1997. *Green Criminology*, edited by Nigel South and Piers Beirne, Ashgate, 2006, pp. 117–40.

Boyd, Shelley. "The Possibilities of Prison Food in Margaret Atwood's *The Heart Goes Last.*" *ReVisions: Speculating in Literature and Film in Canada*, edited by Wendy Roy, U of Toronto P, 2025, pp. 203–23.

Butler, Judith. *Bodies that Matter: On the Discursive Limits of "Sex."* Routledge, 1993.

– *Gender Trouble: Feminism and the Subversion of Identity.* 1990. Routledge, 1999. E-book edition, Taylor & Francis e-Library, 2002.

Fluri, Jennifer. "The Body, Performance, and Space." *Feminist Spaces: Gender and Geography in a Global Context*, edited by Ann M. Oberhauser, Jennifer L. Fluri, Risa Whitson, and Sharlene Mollett. Routledge, 2018, pp. 25–46.

Irshad, Shaista, and Niroj Banerji. "Gender as a Social Construct in Margaret Atwood's *Oryx and Crake*." *Academic Research International*, vol. 2, no. 2, 2012, pp. 585–94. *SAVAP International*, http://www.savap.org.pk/journals/ARInt./Vol.2%282%29/2012%282.2-65%29.pdf.

Kern, Leslie. *Feminist City: Claiming Space in a Man-made World*, 2019. Verso, 2020.

Lefebvre, Henri. *The Production of Space*. 1974. Translated by Donald Nicholson-Smith, Blackwell Publishing, 1991.

Massey, Doreen. *Space, Place and Gender*. U of Minnesota P, 1994.

McDowell, Linda. *Gender, Identity and Place: Understanding Feminist Geographies*. U of Minnesota P, 1999.

Mohr, Dunja, M. "Eco-Dystopia and Biotechnology: Margaret Atwood, *Oryx and Crake* (2003), *The Year of The Flood* (2009), and *MaddAddam* (2013)." *Dystopia, Science Fiction, Post-Apocalypse*, edited by Eckart Voigts and Alessandra Boller, Wissenschaftlicher Verlag Trier, 2015, pp. 283–301.

Read, MacKenzie. "Vision and Re-Visioning in *The Handmaid's Tale* and Two Adaptations." *ReVisions: Speculating in Literature and Film in Canada*, edited by Wendy Roy, U of Toronto P, 2025, pp. 363–82.

Rendell, Jane. "Introduction: 'Gender, Space.'" *Gender Space Architecture: An Interdisciplinary Introduction*, edited by Jane Rendell, Barbara Penner, and Iain Borden, Routledge, 2000, pp. 101–11. E-book edition, Taylor & Francis e-Library, 2003.

Watkins, Susan. "Future Shock: Rewriting the Apocalypse in Contemporary Women's Fiction." *LIT: Literature Interpretation Theory*, vol. 23, no. 2, 2012, pp. 119–37. *Taylor & Francis Online*, https://doi.org/10.1080/10436928.2012.676490.

Wolf, Naomi. *The Beauty Myth*. 1990. Vintage Canada, 1997.

"Show Me You're Still Human": Uncertainty and Humanity in Apocalyptic Short Stories by Canadian Women Writers

WENDY ROY

Despite the origins of speculative fiction in magazine stories, much of the recent critical focus on apocalyptic writing by Canadian women has been on novels. These include Margaret Atwood's *MaddAddam* trilogy (2003, 2009, and 2013) and, more recently, books such as Emily St. John Mandel's *Station Eleven* (2014), Larissa Lai's *The Tiger Flu* (2018), Cherie Dimaline's *The Marrow Thieves* (2017) and *Hunting by Stars* (2021), Saleema Nawaz's *Songs for the End of the World* (2020), and Catherine Bush's *Blaze Island* (2020). There is also, however, a substantial though much less studied body of short-form apocalyptic fiction in Canada, published much earlier than these novels. In the twenty years between 1964 and 1985, four well-known Canadian women writers used short stories to explore fears about nuclear war and climate change, focusing in particular on human and gendered communication during times of crisis. Margaret Laurence's 1964 "A Queen in Thebes" makes pointed commentary about language, power, and gender during a nuclear apocalypse, while Atwood's haunting 1975 "When It Happens" presents a woman's imaginings about her fate in a potential war-related disaster. P.K. Page's 1979 "Unless the Eye Catch Fire ..." portrays climate catastrophe as causing *othering* and scapegoating at the same time as it brings about posthuman communication, while Carol Shields's 1985 "Words" suggests that humans need to continue to speak to one another during an environmental crisis, even if that communication might bring about their own deaths. These short stories use a compact, spare, and sometimes poetic genre to represent gender as a factor in survival, but also to explore the idea that fear of the *other* and even of annihilation might be mitigated by maintaining essential human connectedness. The power of the stories comes from their narrative uncertainty: what is going on is always in question, providing a heightened sense of disquiet and anxiety. The four texts suggest that uncertainty is a key characteristic not only of persuasive short stories, but also of successful apocalyptic and post-apocalyptic fiction.

In her study of early women's speculative fiction in Canada, Marcelle Kosman points to its origins in short stories published in pulp magazines. She examines how these early works of speculation have fallen out of literary conversation, including stories such as A.E. (Alice Elizabeth) Burton's "The Discovery of Nil" (1939), which presents an apocalyptic vision of Earth from the perspective of interplanetary explorers. Kosman argues that the obliteration from "cultural memory" of both such stories and the magazines in which they were published resulted from "the midcentury nationalist imperative," which focused on and brought about "high cultural production and, eventually, canon formation" (27, 28).[1] While after the mid-twentieth century, speculative short stories by women writers were no longer published in pulp magazines, such speculation did not die out altogether; instead, it resurfaced in stories by canonical Canadian writers published in literary magazines or collections. All four authors in this study have won Governor General's Awards for their writings and are Companions of the Order of Canada. All are best known for their novels or, in the case of Page, her poetry. However, while Atwood has received worldwide acclaim for her apocalyptic and dystopian novels, forays into such fiction by the other three writers are anomalies.

Gerald Lynch and Angela Robbeson acknowledge in their introduction to *Dominant Impressions: Essays on the Canadian Short Story* that while genre categories are malleable and indefinite, "family resemblance[s]" among short stories include "brevity, concision, [and] unity of impression and effect" (2). Included on Lynch and Robbeson's list of well-known short-story writers in Canada are three of the four on whom I focus – Laurence, Atwood, and Shields – while the work of Page, an award-winning late-modernist poet, fits their assessment of the short story as perhaps "closer to poetry than to the traditional novel" (2). While Lynch and Robbeson criticize how commentators have focused on "the exquisitely crafted modern story" with its "concision, indirection, and unhappy endings" (1), this indirection – indeed, uncertainty – is a key focus of this essay. I argue that uncertainty over historical events, the meaning and significance of words, and what it means to be human provides narrative power in the stories' considerations of gender and humanity.

The contention that the short story can be a political genre because of its uncertainty is not new. In *Dreams of Speech and Violence*, a study of short fiction in Canada and New Zealand, W.H. New suggests that writers in Canada have "sought ways of structuring stories so that they might break free from received conventions of speech and form, hence break formally free from the shaping social conventions that were lodged in their inherited language" (239). He calls this restructuring "part of a twinned process of affirming and masking reality" (239) and points in particular to the use of techniques of ambiguity such as irony and paradox, "which ask for double-hearing" (242). Ultimately, New contends that the "narrative indirectness" of these stories "is a form of orderly violence against received order (whether imperial, European, Protestant, or male)" (240).[2] If one accepts this argument (and New presents detailed evidence from short stories in Canada to forward it), then protests against cultural and political marginalization, including as a result of gender divisions and colonization, can be seen as a characteristic of many Canadian short stories. This may be one reason four writers who are best known as either novelists or poets chose the short story to write about apocalyptic events, and especially about women during imagined times of crisis.

The power of uncertainty is evident in contemporary fiction in general, and apocalyptic and dystopian fiction in particular. Mette Leonard Høeg argues in the introduction to *Literary Theories of Uncertainty* that undecidability is often used either "to disrupt the seeming naturalness of a narrative" or to "render the uncertainty of reality and human perception" (1). While Høeg focuses on canonical mid-twentieth-century literature, her claims about disruption and perception can be applied more specifically to works of speculative and especially apocalyptic and dystopian fiction. Jason Bartles suggests that such fiction can challenge the status quo, in part through its emphasis on what Høeg calls the "uncertainty" of human experience. In his essay on narratives by Ursula Le Guin, Angélica Gorodischer, and N.K. Jemisin, Bartles argues that the "ambiguity at the center" of these authors' "open-ended … imaginaries" serves to "challenge dogma, pessimism, and complacency" (107). The same kind of implicit challenge, I argue, is evident in the ambiguity inherent in the stories by Laurence, Atwood, Page, and Shields under consideration in this essay.

These four stories frame uncertainty in the context of apocalyptic events (and by this I mean world-changing catastrophes, in popular rather than religious terms) and what happens both during and afterward.[3] In her 2020 study *Contemporary Women's Post-Apocalyptic Fiction*, Susan Watkins outlines key characteristics of post-apocalyptic fiction: first, "the world before the disaster is in living or cultural memory"; second, there is a "clear attribution of blame for the apocalyptic disaster" on such things as "human carelessness for the environment" and "capitalist exploitation of natural resources"; and third, the text focuses on "taking the chance to rebuild in a different way" (9–10). Building on Frank Kermode's argument that "the apocalyptic mode ... indicates the specific concerns of people living in particular places and spaces" (Watkins 4–5), Watkins contends that apocalyptic works by women writers are "related to their specific subject positions in the contemporary moment" (2) as they explore "the ways in which patriarchy and neocolonialism are intrinsically implicated in the disasters they envision" (1). She argues further that these writers "transform and rewrite the traditions of the apocalyptic genre" in order to focus on "its intrinsically gendered aspects" (2),[4] including the relationship "between structural inequalities generated by patriarchy, misogyny and racism and issues such as climate change, global capitalism and techno-science" (10). Watkins concludes that as a political tool, "the post-apocalyptic genre can be used not merely to warn, look back and mourn, but also to generate new ideas and possibilities for humanity" (11). Springboarding from this discussion, I argue that as examples of post-apocalyptic fiction, stories by Laurence, Atwood, Page, and Shields explore concerns of the mid- to late twentieth century to examine patriarchal and exclusionary social structures and their connections to war and climate change, and either implicitly or explicitly to suggest avenues for change.

War and Gender: Stories by Laurence and Atwood

"A Queen in Thebes" is one of Margaret Laurence's lesser-known stories. It appeared in the summer 1964 issue of *Tamarack Review*[5] and stands in counterpoint to her other works published at around the same time: two books set in Africa (the story collection *The Tomorrow-Tamer* and the travel memoir *The Prophet's Camel Bell*, 1963) and the first of the much more well-known Manawaka books (*The Stone Angel*, 1964).[6] Unlike the collection, memoir, and novel, which reflect her experiences and those of people around her in Africa and Canada, "A Queen in Thebes" speculates on the future; it is what Laurence called "a fantasy look at a post-nuclear world, and an extremely bleak look" – "a kind of horror story" (qtd. in Xiques 334, 333). Laurence's story stems from what Watkins would term an author's position as a subject "in the contemporary moment" (2). It can be considered among the tradition of nuclear disaster stories that proliferated after the Second World War, including American Ray Bradbury's "There Will Come Soft Rains" (1950), British-Australian Nevil Shute's *On the Beach* (1957), Canadian Hugh Hood's "After the Sirens" (1960), and Phyllis Gotlieb's *Sunburst* (1964).[7] Laurence's story was written shortly after the Cuban missile crisis of 1962. While Bradbury's story portrays a world without humans,

Shute's novel the end of the world for the last survivors, and Gotlieb's the fate of a few affected monstrously by radiation, Laurence's story, like Hood's, explores the post-apocalyptic lives of ordinary survivors – in Laurence's case, an unnamed young woman and her child. "A Queen in Thebes" outlines a bleak struggle for existence that concludes in the re-establishment of harshly patriarchal social structures through family hierarchies and religious practices.

Uncertainty is fundamental to Laurence's narrative. "A Queen in Thebes" begins with a pervading sense of fear and ambiguity regarding a potential war. The third-person narrator notes that "Everyone had feared war for so long that it seemed it might never happen after all" (337) and that the protagonist has taken her baby, Rex, to the family's isolated cabin not because of the possibility of conflict but simply to get him into cooler mountain air for the summer. The woman sees the flash and "poisonous toadstool" of a nuclear explosion in the distant city to which her husband has returned (336). While she never learns exactly what happened or how it came about, "she knew the thing had come which everyone had feared" (336). She waits for her husband to return for them in their car, but he never does. When she walks to a nearby gas station, she finds it empty of people, with not even a working telephone. Uncertainty is evident in how her thoughts are described: "She wondered dully" if the people who ran the garage had found a safer place, "or if they had only run into other deaths, other polluted places, other cities shattered and lying like hulked shadows of the earth" (337). Evoking Bradbury's story, and through it the real examples of nuclear shadows in Hiroshima, the protagonist imagines "the human shadows which she had long ago heard were etched on stone" after a nuclear blast (338).

By the first snowfall, she knows that she and her child are "condemned to life" (338). She wonders how long the food supplies will last (337), and in the months and years that follow, she works relentlessly on their survival: fishing, hauling wood, snaring rabbits and birds. She and her son are "always cold and usually hungry," and she becomes obsessed with keeping the fire burning (338). Her repeated trips to find other survivors are futile: part of the horror of her experience is that she is never sure what has happened to her husband and to others, or if indeed anyone else is left alive. She thinks of what has occurred simply as "the Change" (340), an enormous and horrific alteration in the direction of her life.

One of the key themes of Laurence's story is the nature of humanity as related to speech, self-identity, and religious practice. The woman looks forward to the time when her son can speak, because what she misses most is "the sound of human voices" (339). But once Rex can talk, they communicate only "briefly, abruptly" about practical tasks (340). The boy learns from her and soon becomes a better hunter, but now she begins to experience fear, "not of the many things that there were to fear outside, but of something inside the dwelling, something unknown" (341). While the source of this fear is ambiguous, the implication is that without contact with other people, the mother and child may not be able to maintain their humanity, including the ability to speak about things other than immediate survival and to relate to one another in humanistic ways. Laurence herself wrote that the story highlights the "struggle towards humanity.... But it also suggests that survival as human beings is virtually impossible in total isolation, without other people, without human society" (qtd. in Xiques 334).

The drive towards religious explanation for life events is explored near the end of the story, with the narrative concluding that it can be a negative rather than positive aspect of human relations. The woman has long since stopped praying, but Rex becomes interested in her religious explanation that "All life comes from God" (343). When the fire goes out due to the mother's carelessness, the now-teenaged Rex berates her, repeatedly calling her "stupid" (341). He travels to a lightning strike outside their area to bring back fire for their hearth, now no longer in their dilapidated cabin but in a cave, the implication being that their move into the cave is a regression in their status as humans. When he returns with a smouldering brand, Rex demands that his mother get on her knees to pray to the god of fire (343). Eventually, he determines that the real god is not fire but the sun, and he prepares an offering to it, telling her, "But you are not to touch this stone and this fire and this meat.... That is for me to do" (345). Their new religious practice has not helped them to maintain their humanity, but it has led to the institution (or reinstitution) of a patriarchal exercise of power.

The concept of self-image plays a part in this new example of gendered oppression. An object from the woman's previous life has kept her feeling human: a hand-mirror, which she keeps hidden (346). When her son, referred to for the first time as "the man," catches her looking at herself in it, he destroys the mirror and hits her "again and again and again" (346), yelling, "You are unclean!" The only image of her that he allows is his own. While not of her volition, a violent, patriarchal, and oppressive relationship has somehow risen from the ashes of their lost world.

The irony of the titular reference to Thebes, the setting of Sophocles's *Oedipus Rex*, becomes evident only in the story's last lines. While scraping hides with a bone – metal tools are reserved for the man – the woman realizes that she must start cooking dinner, since "He did not like to be kept waiting" (347). She no longer remembers her own name, but she does remember fragments of a song, in some way "connected with the name she had once held" (347). The song is "Lavender's Blue," including the line "When you are king … I shall be queen" (347). Her son is the king – Rex – and she is the ironic queen – Jocasta. While he has not killed her husband, Rex has usurped his place, as the last chilling lines of the story confirm: "Then, inside the cave, one of the children began crying, and she went to give comfort" (347). The lack of connection to a larger social world has resulted in male domination in social, sexual, and reproductive terms.[8]

While Laurence's story is a cautionary tale about the dissolution of human relations and the reinstatement of oppressive gender norms after a nuclear war, Atwood's 1975 "When It Happens" reflects on gender relations during an unspecified forthcoming disaster from the perspective of a fifty-one-year-old rural woman known only as Mrs. Burridge. In breaks between writing items on a shopping list, Mrs. Burridge considers the resources she may have to help her survive an apocalyptic event. The uncertainty of "When It Happens" is evident in the title: something is happening or is about to happen, but what is "it" and "when" will it happen? The menace and anxiety surrounding the potential for unspecified war or conflict is emphasized through both the focus on the domestic and the shifts in verb tense, from present to future and back again.

Like Laurence's story, "When It Happens" is a product of uncertain times. Fears of nuclear and other types of war were still current in the mid-1970s, with India detonating a nuclear bomb in 1974 and the Vietnam war ending in spring 1975, only a few months before Atwood's story was published. "When It Happens" first appeared in September 1975 in *Chatelaine* and was republished two years later in Atwood's first story collection, *Dancing Girls* (1977).[9] The story anticipates her 1981 novel *Bodily Harm,* which features a protagonist in a struggle for survival. It also predates by ten years Atwood's most well-known foray into the dystopian and apocalyptic genre, *The Handmaid's Tale* (1985), followed by the more obscure short stories "Freeforall" (1986, republished in 2023) and "Hardball" (1992).[10]

"When It Happens" initially hones in on the domestic through a description of Mrs. Burridge's production of green tomato pickles. The opening section touches on the mundane lives of women such as Mrs. Burridge, identified only by their married names, at the same time as it points to the ways in which such women have traditionally helped their families survive difficult times by growing big gardens and preserving the produce. As the third-person narrator notes, during these implied uncertain times, others "were having to learn all over again" how to preserve foods (126). But while once it made Mrs. Burridge "feel safe to have all that food in the cellar ... [i]t doesn't make her feel safe any more. Instead she thinks that if she has to leave suddenly she won't be able to take any of the jars with her, they'd be too heavy to carry" (127). The homemaking skills that once provided security have now become a liability. The narrative thus alternates in an unsettling way between the ordinary of the domestic and the extraordinary of crisis and change.

Why Mrs. Burridge feels threatened is never made clear, and the sense of combined indeterminacy and menace increases as the story progresses. Four to five times each day, readers are told, she "goes to the back door, opens it, and stands," looking for "something burning, smoke coming up from the horizon" (126), but she sees nothing. As the narrator notes, taking on Mrs. Burridge's thoughts, everyone, including her husband, seems powerless and hesitant: "They are all waiting, just as Mrs. Burridge is, for whatever is to happen" (128); "Everyone knows something is going to happen, you can tell by reading the newspapers and watching the television, but nobody is sure what it will be" (129).[11] The sense of uncertainty is highlighted through phrases such as "whatever is to happen" and "nobody is sure," and indeed the story implies that the threat may be simply in Mrs. Burridge's imagination.[12]

Since the domestic act of preserving food for survival seems fruitless under such circumstances, Mrs. Burridge wants to ask her husband to teach her to use one of their guns, a traditionally masculine implement. However, she cannot explain that she needs to know because, she thinks of Mr. Burridge, "*Maybe you'll be dead. Maybe you'll go off somewhere when it happens, maybe there will be a war*" (128). The story's language of uncertainty is evident in the repeated use of the word "*maybe*," in a series of italicized sentences that include the three indefinite words of the story's title.

The remainder of the narrative takes place as Mrs. Burridge writes a grocery list, at the same time looking around the kitchen at what she will have to leave behind, as she imagines details of the future disaster.[13] First, she imagines, the world will quiet; planes will stop flying overhead, and the noise from the highway will disappear. Television and radio will turn to soothing music and then be censored (130). Again using language of uncertainty, the narrator notes that "Mrs. Burridge is not positive about what will happen next; that is, she knows what will happen but she is not positive about the order" (130). She expects, though, that oil and gas deliveries will stop and telephones will be disconnected. There will be no explanation, "because of course they – she does not know who 'they' are, but she has always believed in their existence – they do not want people to panic" (130). Young men will "begin to appear on the back road" (131). She will hide the shotgun and shells behind the barn – "She has already picked out the spot" (131) – and she "will feel things are getting serious on the day the electricity goes off and does not come back on" (132). As these details are presented, the narrator repeatedly enters into not just Mrs. Burridge's musings about what might occur, but also her regrets about the results within her home, such as thawing and rotting vegetables when the freezer no longer works (132).

During this part of the narration, the story's verb tense shifts repeatedly from future to present, as though what Mrs. Burridge has imagined is not in the future but is currently happening: "One morning she goes to the back door and looks out and there are the columns of smoke, right where she's been expecting to see them" (132). She thinks about her children, from whom she has not heard in weeks, because now there is no mail delivery. Her husband goes to investigate "a little trouble down the road," and "she knows he will not come back" (133). She gathers food that is light enough to carry, unearths the shotgun, and opens the gates so the livestock can go free. She thinks of the future of her preserves, "shattered on the floor in a sticky puddle that looks like blood," and she considers burning down the house herself, before someone else can do it (134). Instead, she walks north, carrying her parka, food, and gun. At this point the narrative returns to the list, with Mrs. Burridge writing supplies needed in the present moment, with the impending disaster still in the future: "*Oatmeal*," "*Shortening*" (134). The story then reverts to describing the crisis as though it is happening in the present: at nightfall, Mrs. Burridge stumbles upon two men near a fire. One comes towards her, "His teeth bare," thinking "she will be easy, an old woman" (135). He then "says something, but she cannot imagine what it is, she does not know how people dressed like that would talk" (135).

The narrator makes it clear that these events are still in Mrs. Burridge's imagination, but an imagination so vivid that it is as though it is happening. She knows that the men want her gun and that she must kill them before they kill her, although "she does not want the loud noise or the burst of red that will follow" (135). These are pictures she has conjured, perhaps through a paranoia that does not reflect reality, but "She has no pictures beyond this point. You never know how you will act in a thing like that until it actually happens" (135). In the last lines of the story, Mrs. Burridge writes one more item on her list ("*Cheese*"), then gets up to look out the door, anticipating once more that she will see the smoke of the forthcoming destruction.

An incredible sense of menace is produced in Atwood's story through the juxtaposition of the domestic mundane – preserving vegetables and writing a shopping list – with an imagined crisis or conflict. At the same time, like Laurence's, the story also explores a woman's power, or lack of it, during such an event. Mrs. Burridge has worked all her life on the farm, and she knows how to keep her family fed during difficult times. But she cannot use a gun, and she imagines that when she is left alone during a time of conflict, men will think women like her easy prey.

Global Warming and the Human/Posthuman: Stories by Page and Shields

In contrast to the stories by Laurence and Atwood, Page's "Unless the Eye Catch Fire …" and Shields's "Words" are non-realist works that employ uncertainty to explore the potential and need for human connectedness during climate disaster, rather than specifically gendered violence as a result of war. Both were written at a time when human responsibility to the environment was entering public consciousness in a meaningful way. Rachel Carson's *Silent Spring*, about the effects of pesticides on living creatures, had been published in 1962; in the late 1970s global temperatures had begun to increase to a noticeable and measurable extent; and in 1987 an international treaty was signed to ban chlorofluorocarbons for their role in ozone depletion. Writers of fiction had begun to speculate about climate disaster as early as the 1960s, including J.G. Ballard's *The Drowned World* (1962) and *The Burning World* (1964, a.k.a. *The Drought*), and stories based on human-caused climate change began to be published in the late 1970s and early 1980s. They include Kim Stanley Robinson's 1981 short story "Venice Drowned," which explores the effects of rising sea levels on coastal cities such as Venice.

Page's story was first published two years earlier, in 1979, and Shields's a few years later, in 1985. Both feature uncertainty: the cause of the environmental disaster is never truly known in Page's story, and it is imaginatively presented as the result of human speech in Shields's story. Because neither story states explicitly that humans are causing climate warming because of their excessive use of hydrocarbons, the messages about what could happen to the earth and to human relationships during a time of crisis are perhaps easier for readers to "hear."

Page did not write much fiction; other than her pseudonymously published novel *The Sun and the Moon* (1944) and fewer than twenty short stories, collected in *A Kind of Fiction* (2001), she is known primarily as a member of the Montreal group of poets and a modernist poet who continued to write until close to the end of her life. Some of her poems address sight or inner vision,[14] while others tackle human responsibility to the planet, including "Planet Earth," which the United Nations chose in 2001 to be read simultaneously in New York, the Antarctic, and the South Pacific to celebrate the International Year of Dialogue Among Civilizations. "Unless the Eye Catch Fire ..." first appeared in *The Malahat Review* in April 1979.[15] The story focuses on the earth's disintegration because of an unspecified climate catastrophe, with the othering of those who have extraordinary new vision (and are held responsible for the earth's warming) eventually replaced by a sense of togetherness. As part of its indeterminacy, "Unless the Eye Catch Fire ..." employs a striking collapse of binary oppositions that forces readers see how connected humans are to what seems separate from us.

Not surprisingly given Page's writing and publication history, the prose of her story is highly metaphoric, like an extended prose poem (perhaps one reason the story was republished in two collections of poetry). Structured as a journal, written over several years by an unnamed first-person narrator,[16] the story documents one woman's experience of the gradual but unexplained heating of the earth's surface. The earth has become what she calls, using a domestic metaphor, "a self-cleaning oven" (56): it is purging itself of humans and indeed all other life on the planet.[17] However, shortly before this disaster is identified, Page's narrator discovers a new and deeper way of seeing. The world "shakes" and fills with intense colours, and she and a few other visionaries perceive vivid connections between its parts: *there* becomes *here*, *without* becomes *within*, *darkness* becomes *light*, and she is "flooded out, dissolved in that immensity where subject and object are one" (38–41). For these few, the perceived oppositions in the world no longer exist.

Several possible ways of interpreting Page's story are inherent in the title and epigraph. The title suggests something omitted and indeterminate and then trails off in an ellipsis, leading to questions: how can an eye catch fire, and what will occur if that does or does not happen? The epigraph, which appears in the story as republished in *Evening Dance of the Grey Flies* and Page's collected works, but not in the original in *The Malahat Review*, helps to explain the title: "*Unless the eye catch fire, / The God will not be seen....*" The quotation is from Theodore Roszak's 1972 *Where the Wasteland Ends*, a complex book about both the visionary eye and the devastating effects of industrialization on the planet; the lines appear in Roszak's book as part of an uncredited poetic epigraph to a chapter about Blake, Wordsworth, and Goethe.[18] Through the epigraph and title, one possible interpretation of the focus of Page's story – the negative effects of humans on the planet – is complemented by another – the concept of visionary and potentially posthuman imagination.[19]

This latter idea is evident not only in what happens to the narrator and others like her, but also in the extraordinarily metaphoric language used to describe their experiences. In the opening pages of the story, repeated and intermingled metaphors related to colour, light, water, fire, music, and technology all lead to a sense of indeterminacy and yet clarity about what is happening. As an example, the narrator says,

> Random leaves on the cherry twirled like gold spinners. The garden was high-keyed, vivid, locked in aspic.
>
> Without warning, and as if I were looking down the tube of a kaleidoscope, the merest shake occurred – moiréed the garden – rectified itself. Or, more precisely, as if a range-finder through which I had been sighting, found of itself a more accurate focus. Sharpened, in fact, to an excoriating exactness.
>
> And then the colours changed. Shifted to a higher octave – a *bright spectrum*. Each colour with its own *light*, its own *shape*....
>
> I don't know how to describe the intensity and speed of focus of this gratuitous zoom lens through which I stared, or the swift and dizzying adjustments within me. (38–9)

The multiple, piled-on metaphors both aid in an understanding of the phenomenon the story is describing and, at the same time, preclude complete, literal comprehension. The uncertainty evoked by the words "I don't know" is emphasized later through words such as "[p]erhaps" and "I can't help wondering" (43, 44), as well as repeated questioning and the statement that "[t]rue accounts" of the phenomenon are "inarticulate, diffuse, unlikely – impossible" (43).

One inexplicable and impossible phenomenon – the shake that leads some people to see the world brilliantly and perceive it as part of themselves rather than separate – is quickly followed by another – the unexplained heating of the earth. Again, this occurrence is described in the story through a language of uncertainty, with the narrator referring to rumours, multiple explanations, and inconsistencies in measurement and reporting (44–5). There is never a clear explanation for what is happening, although theories such as "bacteria from outer space; a thinning of the earth's atmosphere; a build-up of carbon-dioxide in the air; some axial irregularity; a change in the earth's core" (47) are all proposed. In this section of the story, the potential for humans to have caused this disaster is explored, and the results are enumerated: thawing northern ice (46–7), rising ocean waters (55), drastically increasing air temperatures (55), extinction of birds, and leafless trees (54–5). The narrator concludes that humans may indeed be at fault: "mankind at large – improvident, greedy mankind – whose polluted, strike-ridden [sic] world is endangered now by the fabled flames of hell" (47). Her language of hell and damnation evokes the traditional, religious meaning of apocalypse, as a time of judgement of the wicked.

Threats to the planet's ecology lead to social and cultural transformation and eventually collapse: as in Atwood's story, transportation systems, mail, newspaper, telephones, schools, and electricity all come to an end (51); the world becomes quiet, and the only communication medium is the radio, which plays mostly emergency announcements (52, 59). While the connection is never made explicit, the two uncertain events or processes then come together, paving the way for an additional reading of the story as an exploration of othering resulting in scapegoating. The few people with extraordinary vision are singled out and blamed for the heating of the earth (46). The narrator is glad she has not told people that she is one of them, but when she denies her ability, she says, "I felt faithless … as if I had not borne witness to my God" (43). As this passage suggests, what has happened to her is transformative. Comparing herself and other so-called "shakers" to a flock of quails she has seen rise all at once, she says that they "share one brain – no, I think it is one heart – between us" (49), and that when she looks at the world around her, she understands that she is "part of this vibrating luminescence" (50). Farouk Mitha argues in "Catching Fire: Allegories of Alchemical Transformation in the Art of P. K. Page" that the story presents "a vision of mystical transformation," focusing on "processes of transmutation by fire" (118). While I would not call the experience described alchemical, it is certainly a transformation through visions of light, colour, and oneness.

As these transformative experiences multiply, the earth also changes into a burning and uninhabitable place. As Mitha puts it, "Page creates a dramatic tension between two simultaneous types of transformation, between that of a lyrical individual and that of an apocalyptic world" (123).This change eventually brings about unity: there are no longer "desperate gangs of angry citizens," since "[w]e seem at last to understand that we are all in this together" (Page, "Unless" 51). While the narrator has been *othered*, put into a separate and dangerous category, her experience of "seeing" has also broken down oppositions: the outer world becomes inner; inanimate becomes animate; self becomes other; and, as she euthanizes her dog, death becomes life as the two consciousnesses merge into one. Again, this process is described in a highly metaphoric way, with the narrator questioning, "But how to describe what is beyond description?" (58).

The enigmatic ending of Page's story enforces the collapse of oppositions through its representation of the journal writer's solitary but connected world; through a switch in pronouns, from "I" to "we"; and through the use of water as a metaphorical avenue of transformation from life to death. As she waits in her house for her own death, the narrator notes that she feels "part of that whirling incandescent matter – what I might once have called inorganic matter!" She then says,

> We are together now, united, indissoluble. Bonded....
> We share one heart.
> We are one with the starry heavens and our bodies are stars.
> Inner and outer are the same. A continuum. The water in the locks is level. We move to a higher water. A high sea.
> A ship could pass through. (60)[20]

The end of the world is represented as a place of beauty and cohesion, as humans shed their sense of difference and become one with each other, with the stars, and finally with water, allowing the ship of human existence to pass through. The story raises the question of whether some people, in facing the end of humanity, might in fact be able to go beyond the confines of the human, especially the anthropocentric belief that people are at the centre of the universe. Instead, Page's story suggests, the consciousness of humans as only one small part of the world, and as intimately interconnected with all other parts, both animate and inanimate, might allow for an existence outside of and beyond that of normal human life.[21]

While Page's story imagines a posthuman future, Shields's "Words" is about the necessity for people to continue to communicate through human speech, even if that means the end of humanity. Shields is best known for her novels, especially the Governor General's Award–winning *The Stone Diaries* (1993), but she was also a poet, a dramatist, and a writer of short stories. While most of her work is formally realist, several stories published in 2000 are based on speculative propositions; these include "Weather," which imagines that a strike of meteorologists means a world without weather, and "Windows," in which a window tax results in people blocking off their windows to live literally and metaphorically in the dark. "Words" was first published fifteen years earlier, in Shields's 1985 story collection *Various Miracles*. As the title suggests, the story focuses on parts of speech, through the imaginative premise that the human voice is causing the planet to warm to unsustainable levels. Two of the delegates to the first International Conference in Rome, Ian and Isobel – whose names both start with "I" and thus evoke the first-person singular of the reader – fall in love, in part because of Isobel's beautiful voice (67).[22] As they court, she "place[s] long, ribbony Spanish phrases into Ian's mouth," and he speaks the same words in English: "table, chair, glass, cold, hot, money, street, people, mouth" (68). While some of these words are related to objects and concepts of everyday life, the last two relate to humans and the part of their bodies needed for speech and sustenance as well as love.

While there is initial uncertainty about the cause of the warming, ten years later, the third-person narrator tells us, "no one really doubted that it was the extravagance and proliferation of language that had caused the temperature of the earth's crust to rise, and in places … to crack open and form long ragged lakes of fire" (68). The link between the imaginary world described in "Words" and the real potential for global warming because of climate change is clear, although never explicitly stated, allowing for an objective perspective that could potentially lead to more nuanced understanding. With countries "still reluctant to take regulatory action," and with Isobel at home with the children, Ian jumps to his feet at the most recent International Conference to claim that, as with the current experience of global warming, "We are living in a fool's dream, … and the time has come for us to wake" (69). He notes that "Voluntary restraints were no longer adequate to preserve the little earth, which was the only home we know" (69). He lists problematic human activities – use of percussive or emotional words, multilingualism, call and response, and metaphor, all of which are essential for communication on a global human level – and he concludes by stating that "by refusing to make linguistic sacrifices, the human race had willed its own destruction" (70). Carried away by the prolonged applause, Ian announces that he will take "a vow of complete silence for the sake of the planet that had fathered him" (70). This statement immediately suggests an implicit critique of his actions, as he calls upon not mother earth but instead father planet to authorize his decision.

As the narrator notes, Ian regrets his promise almost immediately, but "hubris kept him from recanting" (70). In contrast to his silence, once he returns home, an angry and hurt Isobel talks even more and at a louder volume, "anything to furnish the emptiness of the house with words" (71). Her voice, once "as rare and fine as a border of gold leaf" (67), becomes "loud and shrewish": "She rambled on and on, bitter and blaming, sometimes incoherent, sometimes obscene" (71). More pointedly, Isobel taunts her husband by implying that speech is a fundamental characteristic of humanity: "'Show me you're still human,' she would say. 'Give me just one word'" (71). The uncertainty about whether one can be human without verbal communication is evident in how Ian's family responds to him: his children "poked at him, at his face and chest and arms, as though he were inert" (70–1), and eventually Isobel starts treating him as an inanimate object, "crossing in front of him as though he were a stuffed chair" (71). Like Laurence's character, she forgets his name and then his existence, "for how could anything be said to exist … if it didn't also exist in the shape of a word" (71).[23]

Years later, Ian follows Isobel on a clandestine visit to "an ancient, dilapidated building … where children had once gone to learn to read and write" (72). In the fire and smoke of what is never explicitly named but is clearly an abandoned school, he hears a contrasting "waterfall of voices." A dozen people are talking about poetry, among them his wife, and the sound of "her old gilt-edged contralto … made him draw in his breath so sharply that something hard, like a cinder or a particle of gravel, formed in his throat" (72). The next day, he finally speaks, "a sound that was only half-human," but which Isobel interprets as her own name.

The story ends with Isobel calling the children inside, closing the windows and doors "against the unbearable heat," and then beginning as she and Ian had when they were courting, with "table, chair, bed, cool, else, other, sleep, face, mouth, breath, tongue" (73). Listed again are objects of everyday life, but also words that suggest both *otherness* and parts of the human body needed for spoken language. Shields's story circles back to Laurence's in its claim that humans need speech, and must name one another and their relationships, in order to be fully human, even if it brings their own destruction. Here, however, the parallel with current environmental warnings becomes untethered, because Shields does not seem to be saying that action against climate change is futile. Instead, her story is a commentary on the importance – indeed, the essentialness – of humans talking to one another about crises in the world, in order to try to solve them. This communication starts within families but must also radiate out to the larger world.

Conclusion: Apocalyptic Uncertainty

All four of these brief but powerful Canadian portrayals of crisis times raise challenging and controversial questions related to their contemporary moment. Is it inevitable that patriarchal social structures will be reinstated after the collapse of a society? Are women always helpless during war? Do humans have to reach their end before they see themselves as one with other human and non-human beings, and with the natural world? Are spoken words necessary to humanity, and if so, what does that say about languages such as American Sign Language? These questions are never fully answered in the narratives, with the texts' open-endedness and uncertainty adding to their narrative force. The more pessimistic stories by Laurence and Atwood, which focus on gendered power pre- and post-apocalypse, are followed by the more optimistic (if stories in which human life ends or comes close to ending can be called optimistic), imaginative, and broader human explorations by Page and Shields. These stories paradoxically suggest that people need to be open to communication through both speech and non-verbal means, even as those human and posthuman communications accompany or bring about the end of human times.

The central uncertainty of these short stories indicates that indeterminacy is a key component not only of successful short fiction, but also of speculative fiction. As Watkins argues about other examples of the post-apocalyptic genre, such stories do not just look back to the past nostalgically or to the future with trepidation; they also generate "new ideas and possibilities" – and, I would add, new questions – for humanity (11). As New concludes in his study of short fiction, for readers to follow authors into "alternative narrative options" and thus "alternative social choices" "requires each reader to embrace uncertainty awhile, to listen for the stories that indirection and interruption tell, and to accept the broken, open – and to that degree 'violent' – forms of narrative as legitimate processes of reclaiming a valid history and constructing a valid speech" (244–5). The alternatives suggested in the stories by Laurence, Atwood, Page, and Shields are based on uncertainty and in some cases violence. These narratives both interrupt conventional understandings of gendered conflict and of what it means to be human, and suggest or imply alternatives to the apocalyptic situations and relationships they imagine.

NOTES

1 The main focus of Kosman's dissertation is how early Canadian women writers of SF used "fantastical and scientific tropes" to support the ideology of white supremacism at the core of their texts' "feminist and nationalist politics" (27).

2 New also posits that "authorial uncertainty" about whether a message is heard is "the very subject of literature" (244).

3 In *Rewriting Apocalypse in Canadian Literature*, Marlene Goldman reminds readers that the word "apocalypse" literally means "revelation," and that in St. John's Book of Revelation in the Christian Bible, the word refers to "the destruction and judgement of the old, earthly world and the creation of a new, heavenly paradise" for a small group of the "elect" or chosen people (16). Goldman argues that rather than focusing on the annihilation of the existing realm and a joyful future for the elect, contemporary Canadian authors of apocalyptic fiction concentrate on "the traumatic experience of those barred from paradise," especially the "victimized non-elect": "women, children, minorities, and nature itself" (5, 16). She suggests, further, that contemporary apocalyptic fiction functions as "crisis literature" that reflects political and social forces (17).

4 Watkins notes a "minimising of gender and sexuality" in typical apocalyptic fiction that she does not see replicated in works by many women authors, including Atwood (7).

5 *Tamarack Review* was a Canadian literary magazine published between 1956 and 1982. "A Queen in Thebes" was not republished in a collection of Laurence's stories, but was considered in 1981 for a science-fiction module planned for an Ontario correspondence course (Xiques 333) and was reprinted in Donez Xiques's 2005 book *Margaret Laurence: The Making of a Writer*.

6 As well as the story collection and the memoir, Laurence's seven-year sojourn in Africa resulted in two studies of African literature, published in 1954 and 1969, and the novel *This Side Jordan* (1960). Her five books set in the fictional Manitoba town of Manawaka (1963–74) include the linked story collection *A Bird in the House* (1970) and the novel *The Fire-Dwellers* (1969), which explores, among many other topics, a woman's fears of nuclear war.

7 See Allan Weiss's "The Canadian Apocalypse" for a listing of additional Canadian works of fiction that reflect on both nuclear war and environmental collapse. Matthew Cormier's chapter in this volume analyzes apocalyptic thinking in two recent novels set during the Cold War, Nicolas Dickner's *Apocalypse for Beginners* (2009) and Nancy Lee's *The Age* (2014).

8 In her dissertation on twentieth-century Canadian post-apocalyptic speculative fiction, Ariel Petra Kroon argues that "by the end of the story, the woman is truly reduced to the status of object: she has forgotten her own name, is barred from participation in her son's new religion, subject to his verbal, emotional, and sexual abuse, and responsible for taking care of their children" (107).

9 The Canadian women's magazine *Chatelaine*, launched in 1928 and still in print, originally included fiction in its roster. During the time that

Atwood's story was published, editor Doris Anderson used the magazine to raise concerns about gender relations.

10 Several decades later, Atwood's status as a post-apocalyptic and dystopian writer was secured by the publication of the *MaddAddam* trilogy (*Oryx and Crake* 2003, *The Year of the Flood* 2009, and *MaddAddam* 2013), followed by "Torching the Dusties" (2014), *The Heart Goes Last* (2015), *The Testaments* (2019), and "Impatient Griselda" (2020). Atwood, who began her writing career as a poet, calls these novels and stories *speculative fiction* rather than *science fiction*. Such fiction, she argues, does not include "things that could not possibly happen" but instead focuses on "things that really could happen but just hadn't completely happened when the authors wrote the books" (*In Other Worlds* 6).

11 When the story appeared in *Chatelaine*, it was preceded by a subhead: "Everybody who read the papers or saw television knew that something was going to happen. But nobody, except Mrs. Burridge, knew quite what. As she made up her shopping list, she also made her plans." The subhead underplays the uncertainty of the narrative by suggesting that Mrs. Burridge knows what is happening, when, as the story makes clear, she does not. "When It Happens" was also accompanied in *Chatelaine* by a page-and-a-third illustration of a middle-aged woman standing at a screen door and looking out.

12 Albert Rau notes in his essay on Atwood's short stories that "there are several hints in the story that she is imagining things" (23).

13 It is noteworthy that most of the story takes place in one room, the kitchen of a farmhouse. The closest Mrs. Burridge gets to the outdoors is when she goes to the kitchen door to look for signs of war, and in her vivid imaginings of the future. Mabiana Camargo analyzes the political implications of the confinement of women to enclosed spaces in her chapter on the *MaddAddam* trilogy, in this volume.

14 See, for example, "The Stenographers," "Photos of a Salt Mine," and "Stories of Snow."

15 *The Malahat Review* is a Canadian literary journal established in 1967 and still published. Page's story was republished in *Evening Dance of the Grey Flies* (a poetry collection, 1981), *The Hidden Room: Collected Poems*, vol. 1 (1997), and *A Kind of Fiction* (2001). It was adapted into a one-woman play by Joy Coghill in 1994, "arranged by Coghill as a duet for actor and flutist (Robert Cram)" ("1990–1999"). "Unless the Eye Catch Fire ..." was the inspiration for a 1999 reading by Page accompanied by a concert of original music by Gavin Bryars, both of which were recorded for the fifty-minute film adaptation of the story by Anna Tchernakova, broadcast on CBC television in 2000 as *Last Summer* ("*Unless The Eye Catch Fire...* (2000, Canada))."

16 The narrator identifies herself as a woman and is given the nickname "Babe" by a friend but otherwise is not named. As the story progresses, the labelling and dating of her journal entries becomes more uncertain and provisional, with the last entry labelled simply "The End."

17 References are to the story as published in the 1981 collection *Evening Dance of the Grey Flies.*

18 The poem is often attributed in online sources to William Blake, but does not appear in his collected works. Victoria Jones speculates that it has been identified as a poem by Blake because it appears as an epigraph at the beginning of a section about his work in Roszak's book ("Catching Fire"). However, Roszak does not include a source for the epigraph, suggesting that he himself is the author of the poem.

19 As David Hickey argues in his thesis on light in Canadian literature, Page's story "seeks to make plain the precarious place of the planet and its peoples within the broader universe" (231).

20 Minor revisions from original publication to reprinting include altering the last sentence, from "A ship can pass through" (1979: 86) to "A ship could pass through" (1981: 60). I argue that this change to a verb of possibility leads to increased indeterminacy.

21 While there is some debate about the meaning of the term "posthuman," I use it to denote existing in a state beyond what is generally considered human, especially in terms of understandings and capabilities. In this sense, it is different from Donna Haraway's 1985 concept of the cyborg, a hybridized transhuman resulting from technoscience (475–6), and from Alena Cicholewski's related representation of the posthuman in YA fiction, in her chapter in this volume.

22 Ian is apparently from Canada, although his nationality is never stated explicitly, while Isobel is from Spain or a Spanish-speaking country.

23 Students in a class at the University of Saskatchewan who studied this story pointed out that the characters could have used sign language to engage in human communication without sound. Since Shields wrote about sign language as an articulate mode of exchange in the conclusion to her first published novel, *Small Ceremonies*, it appears as though she was exaggerating in this story to emphasize verbal communication as necessary for humanity.

WORKS CITED

"1990–1999." *Joy Unsorted: The Life and Work of Joy Coghill*, https://www.joycoghill.com/copy-of-1990-2010.

Atwood, Margaret. *Bodily Harm.* McClelland & Stewart, 1981.

– "Freeforall." *The Toronto Star*, 20 Sept. 1986, pp. J1, J4. Reprinted in *Old Babes in the Woods*, McClelland & Stewart, 2023, pp. 127–36.

– *The Handmaid's Tale*. McClelland & Stewart, 1985.
– "Hardball." *Good Bones*, Coach House Press, 1992, pp. 93–6.
– *The Heart Goes Last*, McClelland & Stewart, 2015.
– "Impatient Griselda." The Decameron Project, *The New York Times Magazine*, 7 July 2020, pp. 1-14, https://www.nytimes.com/interactive/2020/07/07/magazine/margaret-atwood-short-story.html. Reprinted in *Old Babes in the Woods*, McClelland & Stewart, 2023, pp. 95–101.
– *In Other Worlds: SF and the Human Imagination*. McClelland & Stewart, 2011.
– *MaddAddam*. 2013. Vintage Canada, 2014.
– *Oryx and Crake*. 2003. Vintage Canada, 2009.
– *The Testaments*. McClelland & Stewart, 2019.
– "Torching the Dusties." *Stone Mattress*, McClelland & Stewart, 2014, pp. 241–86.
– "When it Happens." *Chatelaine*, Sept. 1975, pp. 50–1, 93–9. Republished in *Dancing Girls and Other Stories*, McClelland & Stewart, 1977, pp. 124–35.
– *The Year of the Flood*. 2009. Vintage Canada, 2010.
Ballard, J.G. *The Burning World*. Berkley Books, 1964.
– *The Drowned World*. Berkley Books, 1962.
Bartles, Jason A. "Navigating Uncertainty: The Ambiguous Utopias of Le Guin, Gorodischer, and Jemisin." *Utopian Studies*, vol. 33, no. 1, 2022, pp. 107–26.
Bradbury, Ray. "There Will Come Soft Rains." 1950. *Science Fact/Fiction*, edited by Edmund J. Farrell et al., Scott, Foresman, and Co., 1974, pp. 289–94.
Burton, A.E. (Alice Elizabeth). "The Discovery of Nil." *Fantasy: A Magazine of Thrilling Science Fiction*, vol. 1, no. 2, 1939, pp. 93–9.
Bush, Catherine. *Blaze Island*. Goose Lane, 2020.
Dimaline, Cherie. *Hunting by Stars*. Penguin, 2021.
– *The Marrow Thieves*. Dancing Cat Books, 2017.
Goldman, Marlene. *Rewriting Apocalypse in Canadian Fiction*. McGill-Queen's UP, 2005.
Gotlieb, Phyllis. *Sunburst*. Gold Medal Books, 1964.
Haraway, Donna. "A Cyborg Manifesto." 1985. *The Feminism and Visual Culture Reader*, edited by Amelia Jones, Routledge, 2003, pp. 475–96.
Hickey, David. *After Dark: Reading Canadian Literature in a Light-Polluted Age*. 2013. U of Western Ontario, PhD Dissertation. *Western Libraries*, https://ir.lib.uwo.ca/etd/1805/.
Høeg, Mette Leonard. Introduction. *Literary Theories of Uncertainty*, edited by Mette Leonard Høeg, Routledge, 2022.
Hood, Hugh. "After the Sirens." 1960. *Flying a Red Kite: The Collected Stories*, Porcupine's Quill, 1987, pp. 137–47.
Jones, Victoria Emily. "Catching Fire." *Art and Theology: Revitalizing the Christian Imagination*, 3 June 2022, https://artandtheology.org/2022/06/03/catching-fire/.

Kosman, Marcelle. *The Super Unknown: Canadian Women's Science Fiction, Fantasy, and the Circulation of White Feminist Politics, 1896–1941*. 2020. U of Alberta, PhD Dissertation. *Education and Research Archive*, https://doi.org/10.7939/r3-zzca-cy34.

Kroon, Ariel Petra. *Moving Beyond Survival in Twentieth-Century Canadian Post-Apocalyptic Science Fiction 1948–1989*. 2021. U of Alberta, PhD Dissertation. *Education and Research Archive*, https://doi.org/10.7939/r3-m30f-v186.

Lai, Larissa. *The Tiger Flu*. Arsenal Pulp Press, 2018.

Laurence, Margaret. *A Bird in the House*. McClelland & Stewart, 1970.

– *The Diviners*. McClelland & Stewart, 1974.

– *The Prophet's Camel Bell*. McClelland & Stewart, 1963.

– "A Queen in Thebes." *The Tamarack Review*, summer 1964, pp. 25–37. Reprinted in *Margaret Laurence: The Making of a Writer*, by Donez Xiques, Dundurn Press, 2005, pp. 333–47.

– *The Stone Angel*. McClelland & Stewart, 1964.

– *This Side Jordan*. McClelland & Stewart, 1960.

– *The Tomorrow Tamer*. McClelland & Stewart, 1963.

Lynch, Gerald, and Angela Robbeson. "Introduction." *Dominant Impressions: Essays on the Canadian Short Story*. U of Ottawa P, 1999, pp. 1–8.

Mandel, Emily St. John. *Station Eleven*. Harper Perennial, 2014.

Mitha, Farouk. "Catching Fire: Allegories of Alchemical Transformation in the Art of P. K. Page." *Journal of Canadian Studies*, vol. 38, no. 1, 2004, pp. 118–28.

Nawaz, Saleema. *Songs for the End of the World*. McClelland and Stewart, 2020.

New, W.H. *Dreams of Speech and Violence: The Art of the Short Story in Canada and New Zealand*. U of Toronto P, 1987.

Page, P.K. "Photos of a Salt Mine," "Stories of Snow," and "The Stenographers." *The Hidden Room: Collected Poems*, vol. 1, Porcupine's Quill, 1997, pp. 48–9, 53–4, 102–3.

– "Planet Earth." *The Hidden Room: Collected Poems*, vol. 2, Porcupine's Quill, 1997, pp. 203–4.

– (pseudonym Judith Cape). *The Sun and the Moon*. 1944. Reprinted in *The Sun and the Moon and Other Fictions*, Anansi Press, 1973, pp. 1–137.

– "Unless the Eye Catch Fire ..." *The Mahahat Review* no. 50, 1979, pp. 65–86. Reprinted in *Evening Dance of the Grey Flies*, Oxford UP, 1981, pp. 38–60; *The Hidden Room: Collected Poems*, Porcupine's Quill, 1997, vol. 1 pp. 187–207; *A Kind of Fiction*, Porcupine's Quill, 1997, pp. 159–84.

Rau, Albert. "'Until It Actually Happens': Margaret Atwood Speculates About the Future of the World." *Inklings*, vol. 31, 2014, pp. 15–28.

Robinson, Kim Stanley. "Venice Drowned." 1981. *Clarkesworld Science Fiction and Fantasy Magazine*, no. 131, 2017, https://clarkesworldmagazine.com/robinson_08_17_reprint/.

Roszak, Theodore. *Where the Wasteland Ends: Politics and Transcendence in Postindustrial Society*. Doubleday & Company, 1972.
Shields, Carol. *Small Ceremonies*. McGraw-Hill Ryerson, 1976.
– *The Stone Diaries*. Random House Canada, 1993.
– "Weather" and "Windows." *Dressing Up for the Carnival*, Viking, 2000, pp. 24–31, 96–106.
– "Words." *Various Miracles*. Random House Canada, 1985, pp. 67–73.
Shute, Nevil. *On the Beach*. Heinemann, 1957.
Sophocles. *Oedipus Rex*. Translated by George Theodoridis, *Poetry in Translation*, 2005, https://www.poetryintranslation.com/PITBR/Greek/Oedipus.php.
"*Unless The Eye Catch Fire*... (2000, Canada)." *Gavin Bryars – Works*, https://web.archive.org/web/20210219173520/https://gavinbryars.com/work_film/unless-the-eye-catch-fire-2000-canada/#.
Watkins, Susan. *Contemporary Women's Post-Apocalyptic Fiction*. Palgrave Macmillan, 2020.
Weiss, Allan. "The Canadian Apocalypse." *Worlds of Wonder: Readings in Canadian Science Fiction and Fantasy Literature*, edited by Jean-François Leroux and Camille R. La Bossière, U of Ottawa P, 2004, pp. 35–45.

Interlude

Children of the Affect

CYNTHEA MASSON

Breathe in. Breathe out.

So easy to instruct. So difficult to remember when the stones begin to fall. The first pebble causes only a temporary sting. *One breath in. One breath out.* The first rock diverts attention. *One breath in.* The plan to remain calm is thwarted. The first boulder leaves a permanent dent. *One gasp in.* The body can be pelted – whether by literal or figurative stones – only to the point of near collapse. Then, if viable, the mind must make a choice: die or surrender. She had surrendered under the guise of faith. *Take me in, Brother.* Now, a devoted Sister of the Affect, she stepped onto the portal platform awaiting transport initiation.

Jasper, she whispered. The word caught in her throat. *Jas-per,* she emphasized its two syllables, its paired breaths: *Whisper. Jasper.* Yes, the appointed name would work – sly, lethal. She stood confident in purpose, a stalwart convert to the cause. *Breathe in. Breathe out.*

Jasper paused outside the entrance for slated encounter 3 of 8. Though they had veered into Scenario C enactment territory, encounters 1 and 2 had been otherwise uneventful. During the first – inside the shop with window decals reminiscent of glyphs – an elderly male, appearing to originate from Encampment 5 or environs, merely nodded as Jasper spoke. She wondered if Maxwell had initiated the wrong location sequence or implanted an inaccurate language processor. Jasper reassessed, purchased a small box of red sweets – tapping a card against a device – and left. Outside, under a tree harbouring only a few remnants of leaves, she opened the box and placed one of its contents into her mouth: sweetness and spiciness together. Intoxicating. Its texture reminded Jasper of the delicacies Maxwell had provided recruits during a holiday lesson. Easter? No. Halloween. *Trick or treat.*

But Halloween had occurred weeks earlier here in Encampment 10, assuming Maxwell had correctly programmed the location sequence. The original schedule for the Final Affect would have placed Jasper into her designated encampment amidst New Year's festivities. But early landers had reported glimpses of success, so the Ecclesiast had ordered Stage 2 encounters to begin ahead of schedule. If only Maxwell had reassigned her to Stage 3! Then she'd be enjoying the treat-laden holidays of Christmas and Hanukkah. Instead, this box of sweets would have to suffice. She finished all but two before entering the building for encounter 2 of 8.

Here too, she'd had meagre success. A woman, whose diction and sentence structure read as inaccurate against the encoded grammar, never stopped speaking. Jasper learned of five great children. No. Grandchildren. Great-grandchildren. She learned of their ages and assessments, their sports, their awards, their enumerable skills. Met with this woman, Jasper had no time to practise her enunciations – no finessed *F*s or silken *S*s or perfect *P*s.

Fine, thank you. My name is Jasper. Is your business successful?

Jasper would never know. During this encounter, she was the one to nod in response.

Outside again, she ate another box of sweets – these ones also multicoloured but comprising nuts and chocolate. Interesting, she decided. But she preferred those of the first box.

Cinnamon.

ı|||ı|ı

During her first recruitment lesson for Children of the Affect, Jasper had expected a delay before the inevitable question.

"Are you willing to die?"

Fellow recruits, one after the next, responded: *Yes, yes, yes.*

Jasper paused, staring directly into the Ecclesiast's cloud-dampened eyes.

"I'm already dead," she answered.

All twenty fellow recruits – some shocked, some appalled, some jealous – shot piercing glances. Perhaps she would be transferred to one of the other fifteen sections. Or perhaps she would be ousted from the program. Dishonourable discharge: lack of respect equates to lack of faith.

"All the better," said the Ecclesiast, nodding, contented.

The living will die. The dead will be reborn. The faithful will inherit the realm, they recited at evening song. *And we, Children of the Affect, will inherit the earth.*

That night, after shadow elegies and tea service, the Ecclesiast offered each recruit a sanctioned glyph. Jasper hesitated only briefly before accepting the golden spoon, upon which rested a disc of yellow parchment embossed with indigo ink. The glyph depicted a single character – "8" – whose meaning, like its effect, depended on perspective. Unsure how to proceed, she watched the others. All but one stirred the glyph into their tea and then set the spoon onto the table. One recruit broke with routine. She rose, glided up the nave, extracted the glyph from the spoon with her tongue, and set the spoon upon the plinth of the Abstraction of the Divine Octet.

Undiluted, renegade: Octavia.

The location of encounter 3 of 8 harboured no sweets. Numerous and varied items stood within easy reach no matter which direction she turned. She recognized a few from Affect Centre lessons: playing cards, measuring tapes, flashing lights. No. *Flashlights.* One word. She then recalled that inhabitants of Encampments 8 and 18 called this item a *torch.* But given its *flashing* potential, Jasper preferred *flashlight.* Those housing a red flashing light among their features brought Jasper immeasurable satisfaction.

Emergency. Imminent danger. Assistance required.

She pulled one from a bin and pushed at its buttons to determine its flashing potential.

"It needs batteries," said a man who stood a few feet from her.

"Yes," said Jasper. "Batteries. Power."

"Let's see," he said, gesturing for the flashlight.

Examining it briefly, he turned and walked down the aisle. Jasper followed. They stopped at a revolving pillar displaying an abundance of battery choices.

"You'll need three of these."

He handed her the flashlight and a package containing four batteries.

She turned directly toward him and enunciated meticulously, "What is the purpose of the fourth battery?"

He laughed, then shrugged. "What's your pleasure?"

Jasper doubted this inhabitant would understand her pleasures.

"Do you want them or not?" he asked.

"Yes, please."

Yesss. Pleassse.

He pointed to the front counter and walked away.

"Could you please show me this flashlight's functions?" Jasper enunciated to the clerk.

"You need to pay first."

"Yes, of course. I will pay first."

She surrendered the flashlight and batteries, waited, then tapped her card against the device. *Remain calm*, she imagined Maxwell instructing. Standing only the counter's breadth from the clerk, Jasper exhaled slowly and soundlessly as she waited. *Breathe in. Breathe out.*

Soon enough, Jasper understood the code – which of the flashlight's buttons resulted in which features. Outside the shop, she stood in the shadow of a large, seemingly out of place evergreen tree, pressed the required buttons, and watched the flashing red light for a full minute. Thereafter, staring up at the sign above the shop for encounter 4 of 8, Jasper smiled at the result of her splendidly inconsistent vision. Even without a glyph, she could make the letters dance.

ı|||ı|ı

To Jasper, for the first year at the Affect Centre, Octavia's presence – Octavia herself – remained baffling. Other Children of the Affect revealed having lived predictable circumstances prior to recruitment – disheartening histories that trickled out over the months as piecemeal narratives whose plot points unnervingly paralleled Jasper's own. *Loss. Injury. Abandonment. Betrayal.* In the Graphic Era, such stories would have made nutrient-rich fodder for staged dramas. If only Jasper and the other recruits had existed during those foundational years. Surely, they would have taken alternative routes rather than follow roads carved by their neglectful ancestors. Now, before any such dramatic performances, Children of the Affect must restore the Bygone World to its idyllic glory – a task turned duty for the previously disenchanted.

But Octavia defied logic. The occasional story she shared over a glass or two of sapphire cordial was pleasant if not deliberately uplifting. *Wealth. Beauty. Acceptance. Love.* Less generous recruits eventually shunned her company in sardonic dismay. Only Jasper longed for more. Only Jasper understood that Octavia was painting a future rather than redrawing a past.

ı|||ı|ı

The pungent air in the shop of encounter 4 of 8 stopped Jasper cold. Her entire body shuddered – a tremor shot from head to feet before she regained composure. Barely able to breathe in, she neglected years of training in her attempt to breathe out. Moments later she wondered whether she was breathing air at all or merely inhaling aromatic fumes.

"May I help you?" asked a clerk.

"I … I thought this shop sold tea."

"No. Spices."

Floor to ceiling, jar after jar, box after box, bin after bin – spices.

"So, do you need any spices?"

Jasper contemplated the drop and roll. *Fire! Exit the building!*

The clerk gestured to his right. "Cardamom? Cayenne? Celery salt?" He paused before adding, "We're at the Cs."

She moved closer to the display and scanned the options. She gasped, then coughed.

"Cinnamon!"

"Medical grade is on sale," he said, pointing to a lower shelf.

ı|||ıı|ı

Jasper had not done well enough on the placement exam to warrant medical training at the Affect Centre. But she had attained permission to gain basic knowledge of exchange by watching the Level 8 recruits. Generally, Level 8s worked in pairs: doctor and patient. Repeatedly, her eyes landed on Octavia, whose stethoscope rested against the chest of her partner, their breathing paired. *Octavia* – her name an homage to the Divine Octet. What would Octavia hear through her stethoscope if it were placed against Jasper's chest? If only. *Big breath in. Big breath out.*

ı|||ıı|ı

For encounters 5 and 6 of 8, her thoughts disruptively mired in grief, Jasper managed to utter only one discernible sentence to the first inhabitant she stumbled upon in each location.

Excuse me, could you please tell me the time?

"Three twenty," said encounter 5.

"Three forty-five," said encounter 6.

The inhabitants' answers, though irrelevant to her mission's primary purpose, had an unforeseen effect on Jasper. She could sense time fleeting. Years at the Affect Centre, years of comradeship bound by a single goal, time spent distracted both from former regrets and recent despair, culminated in one mission on one day. No recruit would be sent on a second mission, at which point the risk of negative consequences quadrupled. Even the Ecclesiast knew to draw a line. Month after month, Jasper had prepared mentally and physically. But now the time ticked away one encounter after the next, hours of her existence evaporating with no tangible results beyond sweets and spices and flashing lights. No longer viable as an Affect Centre recruit, she would return to civilian life once recovered. What would her interactions matter? What would she matter?

Emergency. Imminent danger. Assistance required.

ı|||ı|ı

"What is your hope?" Jasper asked Octavia.

They lay on the dock under a quilted silk blanket watching swaths of light dance across the luminescent sky. Octavia responded immediately, as if her answer had been oft rehearsed.

"For our work to be valued by future generations who walk the paths we cleared."

Hearing that single sentence, Jasper unwrapped the first layer of Octavia's enigma. Before recruitment, Octavia had been shunned by those she had striven to help. Whether friends or strangers, whether assured in their assertions or frozen by their fears, the youth Octavia had fought to bolster, the peers she had sought to embrace, had pushed her out of their hastily chalk-drawn circles. *You are no longer needed. So, you are no longer welcome.*

ı|||ı|ı

Only the lack of a better option kept Jasper moving forward through this foreign realm.

"What time is it?" she asked, neglecting nuanced wording and enunciation.

She stood at the midpoint – both temporally and spatially – of encounter 7. At least four people heard the question. Three walked away. One remained and replied.

"I left my phone at home," said the woman.

This woman wore a purple hat. She did not know the answer, yet she had responded. Affect Centre lesson scenarios had not included such intriguing outcomes.

"On purpose?" Jasper asked.

"To break the routine."

ı|||ı|ı

Jasper spent a full thirty minutes progressing toward the location marker for her final encounter. She now stood at its threshold, hand against the door.

"What happened to your face?" a boy asked.

He sat on a wooden ledge that encased withering plants. Unlike her own, the boy's face was flawless. In the dazzling light of the evening sun, he stared at her: two dark spheres recessed amidst currently sun-drenched umber skin. Partially blinded by the light, partially by circumstance, Jasper could not readily distinguish his irises from his pupils.

Pupil. Both student and part of the eye.

As she watched his eyes and contemplated her response, the child waited, still and seemingly patient.

Patient. Both medical enactment role and required personality trait.

Patient pupils.

"An accident," she finally replied.

The boy nodded.

"So, you have a story," he said.

She stepped away from the unopened door and moved closer to the boy.

"A story?"

"Past tragedies make current stories," he said.

Such wisdom could have comprised a Central Precept at the Affect Centre.

"What is your age?"

"Eight," he said.

Eight of eight – a coincidence.

"What is your name?"

"Jerome."

"And what is your story, Jerome?"

ı|||ı|ı|ı

The cruellest level of betrayal begins in stealth – so quiet that it advances unnoticed. Early excuses from those whom you most cherish seem reasonable. Time is chiselled into novel configurations, but its dissonances are muted. Years of daily contact dwindle to once per week, but all will eventually be well. Sharing a meal amidst myriad commitments is hard won, but the exchange is all-the-more valued given the sacrifice. Then, abruptly, moss-obscured, the boulder of truth careens downward, felling all that it meets. A friend who has only a few hours for you spends an entire week, shortly thereafter, with a mutual friend – jovial vacation photos circulate. Another friend claims the need for a two-month silent retreat immediately after the three months you've spent rebuilding her home. Another misinterprets a complex situation – no consultation permitted – and shuns you eternally.

You jump off a cliff – metaphorical or otherwise. Your goal is to land in calm waters, but you fall short, impaling yourself. The world looks different through your one remaining eye.

"Transformation!" proclaimed Jerome.

They had been sharing stories for precisely thirty-three minutes. With each tale, Jasper had provided only highlights, neglecting specifics of a world Jerome could not comprehend. Yet after each, he responded initially with a single word or phrase – a beyond-his-years insightful summation – and then with a story of his own. The stories he proffered echoed hers – harsh lessons gleaned from a brief but heartbreaking existence.

His parents had died three years ago.

From his memories of their lives and in his dealings with their loss, Jerome had learned to interpret complex signs etched by people with both something to tell and something to hide. Thus, despite his immature age, he had honed a skill: interpreting and translating the hieroglyphic dances that wove their way through the anecdotes he gleaned from passersby.

Glyphs, thought Jasper, tasting the sour irony.

Early in their conversation, Jasper had learned that Jerome's grandmother would emerge at the workday's end from the yet unopened door, behind which lay the precise location for encounter 8 of 8: a failure of duty from Jasper's perspective, a vow to be kept from Jerome's. Tired but obligated, Jerome's grandmother had promised to take him to speak with Santa Claus.

Jerome told Jasper what he planned to request of Santa: a baby sister. As he expounded on his fantasy, she silenced the revelation of a plain and simple truth.

At the Affect Centre, while waiting for Octavia in the green corridor, Jasper had observed a Santa Claus training scenario. She had watched the recruits through the window, listening thanks to an open door. The red and white uniforms – the hats in particular – had caught her eye.

"Breathe in," the section Commander said. "Then three breaths out – *ho, ho, ho*. Short, staccato, forceful!" He paused. "Ready! Breathe in. Hold it. Breathe out."

"Ho, ho, ho," said the recruits.

"Power up! Christmas will be critical to Stage 3 success!"

"Ho! Ho! Ho!"

"Good! Again! Breath in! Hold it! Breathe out!"

"Ho! Ho! Ho!"

All the red and white uniformed recruits had loudly *ho-ho-hoed* at once, and Jasper retreated, into the alcove next to the fountain. Jealousy twinged, as if the *ho, ho, hoes* themselves were mocking her. She had already been reassigned to Stage 2: late November. Not Halloween, not Christmas, not even Thanksgiving, since her placement was in Encampment 10, a region whose holiday of food-enhanced gratitude occurred before Halloween.

"You will deposit seeds here, here, and here," Maxwell had demonstrated repeatedly in the weeks leading up to the mission. "Encampment 10, Region 23, District 35 is yours to sow."

Canada. Saskatchewan. Saskatoon.

Since Maxwell first assigned her location, Jasper had worked on her pronunciation multiple times a day. *Sas-katch-e-wun. Sas-ka-toon,* she had enunciated in the alcove of the green hallway next to the fountain awaiting Octavia: *Sassss-katchewan.*

"I've been good." said Jerome. "So, Santa will be good to me."

Silence.

"Did you hear me?"

Jasper returned to the moment.

"Yes, of course."

"Do you believe me?" Jerome asked.

He had perceived her lack of focus.

"Yes, I believe you. You have been good."

"For the entire year!"

"For the entire year," Jasper repeated.

Jerome clapped and laughed.

Hearing his laughter, her confidence faltered – his mirth more potent than spices.

The first unsanctioned glyph she had absorbed depicted the foot of a bird. One finger first pressed firmly against the embossed page, then moved from fingertip to tongue, and Jasper understood Octavia's entire story. Her mind took flight. She circled round and round and round, her wings spread like those of the hawks in childhood folklore – soaring above the mountains for an eternity and then spiralling downward for hours until she landed at Octavia's feet. *I understand,* she told her. *I understand now. Who could resist such delight?* But her words were lost against the shrill cry of the hawk, and Octavia turned away. Perhaps she had never tried a bird's foot, never learned to speak the language of raptors. Perhaps all Octavia's glyphs portrayed foliage – flowers and trees, grasses and grains whispering to one another in the breeze, lush and languid like Octavia herself. Jasper knew only of her beloved's final glyph, the golden leaf that had shattered her brain.

"Listen, Jerome," she said. "Perhaps–"

"What?"

"Perhaps visiting Santa is not the best way to make your request."

"He's one way!"

"Perhaps offer a prayer to your god."

"God doesn't bring Christmas presents," Jerome said.

Admittedly, Jasper knew little of the individual faiths or deities of these people – only in so much as they were false. Only in so much as the Divine Octet would rightfully reclaim the earth once Children of the Affect had chastised its current inhabitants for their blasphemy.

But here, outside encounter 8 of 8, in Encampment 10, Region 23, District 35, Jasper empathized with Jerome and debated with herself. Surely, he had crossed her path only by chance, not destiny. Surely, he was not meant to be part of her mission. Surely, even if infected alongside other blasphemous inhabitants, Jerome would survive, convert, worship Her Splendour, the Divine Octet. With time, he would age. And certainly, as he aged, he would find his bygone beliefs trite. He would recall both Santa and God only as long outgrown myths.

"If you–" she started, then stopped.

Jerome tilted his head. His curious eyes gleamed. The gloss of his hair caught the light.

"If you were to … contract a … sickness, what would you do?"

"What, like a cold?"

"A cold. Or another virus."

"I'd go another day. Santa's at the mall until Christmas."

"Of course. But if you became sick enough to need a doctor–"

"Do *you* need a doctor?" Jerome asked.

"No. I'm merely curious. If *you* were sick, do you have a doctor to help you?"

"Sure."

"Do you like this doctor?"

Jerome shrugged. "She lets me play with her stethoscope."

"Stethoscope."

"You know," Jerome said, pounding on his chest, "to listen."

ı|||ı|ı

"The inhabitants deserve no mercy," Maxwell had emphasized during the inhalation ceremony. "They kill themselves while eviscerating others. *Terrorists. Blasphemers!* Their only redeeming attribute is their willingness to die for their faith. What are you, Children of the Affect, sacrificing of yourself beyond a miniscule risk of death? *Nothing! Nothing!* Because you are valiant. May your mind, heart, and spirit stand strong as their strength diminishes!"

"What is our timeline?" Jasper asked after an attendant removed her mask.

"Rest assured," said Maxwell, "you'll remain asymptomatic until your return."

"No–"

"Oh! The inhabitants! The virus requires at least a week to replicate."

"No. No. The departure time – what time are we to be at the portal?"

"Ah!" he surveyed the room of recruits and then glanced at the clock above the door. "One hour for incubation, one for encounter review, then an attendant will escort you – all of the recently inspired – to the platform."

He manoeuvred the inhalation equipment to ease Jasper's movement.

"Reap the glory!" he said. "Reap the glory!"

ı|||ı|ı

Jerome was the child she had envisioned, the one she would have had with Octavia. If only.

"Come with me!" he pleaded, reaching for her hand.

"I would like to, but I cannot."

"Why?"

"I have to go home."

She extracted her encounter 3 purchase from her jacket pocket and set the buttons to engage the flashing red light.

"Merry Christmas," she said, handing the flashlight to Jerome.

"Thanks. What do you want?"

"Nothing, I–"

"I mean from Santa. I'll ask him for you! What do you want?"

Three seconds passed.

"A world without glyphs."

ı|||ı|ı

Jasper coughed. She sat in the hospital wing of the Affect Centre awaiting inoculation.

"The symptoms will dissipate within a few days," the attendant assured her. "No more troublesome than a common cold."

"For us," said Jasper.

"Of course, of course. For us, a cold. For them … well, a variation on a theme."

"A lethal variation."

The attendant smiled. Discarding the empty vial, he stood and saluted her. His hand moved so swiftly to the side of his mouth and out that Jasper saw only a blur of official respect.

"May you reap the glory of each breath!"

ı|||ı|ı

Jasper faced the attendant outside the Ecclesiast's office.

"Submission tray, please."

"Reason?"

"A suggestion."

"To what end?"

"To enhance the glyphs."

"You know as well as I," replied the attendant, "the dosage of sanctioned glyphs–"

"Not the dosage. The sensation."

The attendant replied via sceptical expression.

Jasper removed the box from her pocket and tipped its contents into her hand.

"Try one."

Head tilted to the right, the attendant now appeared both sceptical and curious.

"A flavoured sweet from the Bygone World," Jasper explained, coaxing in gesture.

He accepted one, sniffed at it, then cautiously bit off a fragment. His eyes widened. He transferred the remainder into his mouth. Chewing, no longer sceptical, he nodded.

"What is the name of this flavour?"

"Cinnamon."

Jasper retrieved a small bottle from another pocket and placed it on the submission tray.

"Cinnamon oil," she announced by way of explanation. "I submit to the Ecclesiast that glyphs should taste of cinnamon."

ı|||ııı

En route to the chapel, Jasper repocketed the box but kept the one remaining sweet clenched in her hand. At the Abstraction of the Divine Octet, she placed the sweet between two sanctioned glyphs, crushing the mixture against the plinth before placing it into her mouth.

She chewed. She waited. Nothing.

She noticed only the burning sensation left on her tongue by the sweet.

Jasper remained uncertain whether the spice, its aroma, or its taste had prompted clarity. Either way, she strove to break the Affect Centre's routine just long enough for the recruits to take a decisive step off the well-trodden path.

ı|||ııı

And our breath will spread across the lands, its spirit hover over the waters.

The weak will drop to the ground, as stones falling from a crumbling mountain.

The strong will trample, one upon other, deep in the trenches of a paradise lost.

And we, Children of the Affect, will inherit the earth.

ı|||ııı

Breathe in.

Gender and Indigeneity: Apocalyptic and Dystopian Film and Television

What If the Natives Were Immune? Dismembering Colonial Masculinity in Jeff Barnaby's *Blood Quantum*

JUNE SCUDELER

Mi'kmaw director Jeff Barnaby's 2019 zombie film *Blood Quantum* consumes colonial values about Indigeneity and highlights his own community's infection by colonizer rhetorics. Set in the same fictional Red Crow reserve as Barnaby's 2013 feature debut *Rhymes for Young Ghouls*, *Blood Quantum* uses the zombie apocalypse to dismember colonial impositions of blood quantum and masculinity. Writing about *Rhymes for Young Ghouls*, settler scholar Kristina Baudemann argues, "Colonialism *is* horror, and the colonized turn into zombies in a dehumanizing system" (159). In an anti-colonial twist in *Blood Quantum*, non-Indigenous people fall prey to the zombie virus to which Indigenous Peoples are immune. Although non-Indigenous viewers can enjoy the gore, *Blood Quantum* is really addressed to Indigenous audiences. As nêhiyaw actor Michael Greyeyes asserts, "We're survivors. We totally get it.... Who would be the best survivor in an actual apocalypse? Us.... We actually lived through the apocalypse: the colonial settler state is another kind of apocalypse for us. And we're here" (qtd. in Wong; first ellipsis in original).[1]

After the zombie virus is unleashed in *Blood Quantum*, the Red Crow members retreat and defend their territory. Barnaby uses the fortified reserve to show the importance of reciprocity and responsibility as the inhabitants debate whether to allow non-Indigenous people onto their land, maintaining that rez sheriff Traylor (played by Greyeyes) and his son Lysol (played by Kiowa Gordon, Hualapai) are a hindrance to Indigenous values of reciprocity because of toxic masculinity, particularly in Lysol's case. Barnaby shows what happens when the world is out of balance through male anger. *Blood Quantum*'s ending, however, upends reconciliation because several Indigenous people survive the destruction of Red Crow's fortified reserve: Traylor's ex-wife, Joss

(Elle-Máijá Tailfeathers, Sami/Kainai), who is a nurse, and their son Joseph (Forrest Goodluck, Navajo/Hidatsa/Mandan/Tsimshian), along with Joseph's newborn daughter. Barnaby explains in an interview with Jordan Crucchiola in *Vulture* that "there's no functional family unit in the film, but toward the end you get a sense that there's going to be a female presence – wise, steady – and there's going to be a young presence in the father, and you get the impression to a certain degree that they're going to be not necessarily okay, but better off" ("Jeff Barnaby"). *Blood Quantum* calls for a different kind of family based on caring and empathy among a strong woman, her empathetic son, and her granddaughter.

Barnaby shows a world that is devastated because it is out of balance and thus lacks complementarity. Settler scholar Leah Sneider defines complementarity as encapsulating "concepts of responsibility and relationship in the maintenance of social or communal balance," including "the overarching ideology behind actions or performances reflecting responsible, reciprocal, and respectful relationships" (63). Barnaby's film revolves around the relational differences between Joseph, who still has his mother, and his half-brother Lysol, who grew up in the foster care system. In the zombie apocalypse, building relations is the only way to survive. Survival means rejecting colonial notions of masculinity and embracing more Indigenous-centred notions of protecting community and solidarity. Barnaby emphasizes, "If you're talking about colonialism, I don't see how you do that without talking about the patriarchy or inherent misogyny within the system" ("Jeff Barnaby"). Discussing the film's critique of patriarchy and misogyny, Tailfeathers stresses that "It's Indigenous women who hold up our communities.… I think that's very true for a lot of communities, where it's the women who are putting in a lot of the work to hold us together and to keep our cultures and language strong" (qtd. in Yamato). In Barnaby's film, Joss is not only a nurse who is ready to fight for her community but also a truth-teller, unafraid to confront Joseph about his lack of responsibility towards his impending fatherhood. The mother and son's survival symbolizes a way forward out of colonially imposed ideas of Indigeneity and masculinity.[2]

Using conventions of horror films, speculative literature, and documentaries, *Blood Quantum* examines whether Indigenous people can survive colonization and the Canadian state's genocidal apparatus. Barnaby focuses on the larger forces outside the reserve; in an interview in *Canadian Dimension*, he compares such forces to a kind of zombie pandemic: "It's not even a fabled metaphor. It's pretty obvious what I'm driving at: colonialism and capitalism are pandemics. If you look at the way colonialism has consumed everything, how could you not compare it and late-stage capitalism to a cannibal that devours everything in its sight mindlessly?" ("Decolonizing"). This devouring can be termed *necropower*, what Cameroonian scholar Achille Mbembe positions as "the capacity to define who matters and who does not, who is disposable and who is not" (27), since the prefix "necro-" reminds us of corpses, the walking dead of colonization. As Renae Watchman (Diné) and settler scholar Michael Truscello argue, Barnaby inverts "the conventional racialized Other of the zombie narrative, to situate white settlers as the voracious *necropower*" (464). His film then adds a gendered lens to deepen the understanding of this concept. In *Blood Quantum*, Lysol is consumed by the necropower of the foster care system, the trauma of which leads to toxic masculinity and the destruction of his community. He is both damaged by whiteness and colonization and damaging to his own community.

Barnaby hints in *Blood Quantum* that environmental degradation is the cause of the zombie virus. It is highly significant that one of the film's three animated sequences occurs near the beginning of the film and focuses on what happens to motherhood during an environmental crisis.[3] This scene suggests that settler colonialism's insistence on seeing land as simply a place from which to extract resources has dire consequences for all living beings. The setting is a red-soaked landscape with burning fires, but in the middle of this hellscape is a pregnant woman perched on a rock. A green essence flows from her to a pond with a foetus in it, segueing into the filmic 1981 Red Crow reserve and the opening credits. In interviews, Barnaby focuses on the environmental impact of his film: "I would describe *Blood Quantum* as more of an environmental apocalypse film than I would a zombie film," with the planet "trying to shake off the fleas that are humanity to better its survival" (qtd. in Simonpillai). Environmental toxicity leaches into the community, especially into the male characters, affecting how they treat each other. Environmental degradation leads to personal ruin and to toxic masculinity; disrespecting the earth means loss of respect for self and for community.

In *Blood Quantum*, white settlers lose control over their bodies but still mindlessly try to infect Indigenous Peoples with colonialism. Barnaby's films show that Canada's relationship with Indigenous Peoples is one "steeped in colonial violence, governmental surveillance, racist hatred, and jealousy of Indigenous rights and sovereignties as perceived entitlements" (Baudemann 153), symbolized by the white zombies who unsuccessfully try to consume Indigenous people. Indigenous bodies, like the land, are perceived to be for the use of settlers.

Blood Quantum starts with a staple for the Mi'kmaw community, dead salmon, coming back to life. We later learn that the salmon and other traditional wild food have been infected with the virus through environmental destruction that devastates the Red Crow residents' use of traditional food. Moon, played by Gary Farmer (Cayuga), explains in the film that "the reason this virus has destroyed all the world is that the Earth is trying to revert to its old ways. It is trying to heal itself from the damage done to it due to the exploitative methods of the humans in the name of development." Part of the debate within the film is what the old ways mean. Six months after the outbreak, the members of the Red Crow community have made their land into a fortified compound to keep infected people out. Although Traylor is initially opposed to allowing white people onto the reserve, he and Joseph eventually do so. They become better community members and better fathers because of the zombie apocalypse, while Lysol is a colonially made monster who cannot grasp the helping hand his half-brother offers him. Instead, Lysol engineers the colonization of the community, leaving Joss, Joseph, and his newborn daughter to continue Indigenous life in the face of a colonial zombie apocalypse.

There is a long tradition of equating Indigenous Peoples with the monstrous. Barnaby turns this idea on its head, however, by presenting settlers as monstrous flesh-eating zombies. As Carol Warrior (Alutiiq [Sugpiaq]/Dena'ina Athabascan/A'aniiih) explains, "Native Americans have historically been represented by EuroAmerican authors as fearsome because their very Indigeneity and humanity threatens the legitimacy of colonial conquest.... Native Americans have been depicted as monstrous not because of what we do, but because of *where* and *what* we are: we are connected to place – that is, we have stood 'in the way of progress,' as defined by the west" (22). Seeing Indigenous Peoples as monstrous is an excuse for taking Indigenous lands, with people figured as inhuman and thus not deserving of land of their own or even of life. For settlers, Black scholar Robin R. Means Coleman argues, Indigenous Peoples and cultures are "so excessive that [they] could not be adequately contained or completely destroyed, forever rising up to haunt White domains and bodies" (149). Coleman is referring to the Indian Burial Ground trope in movies like *Pet Sematary* (1989) and *The Amityville Horror* (1979) that thwart white bourgeois property values, because, as settler scholar Colin Dickey argues, "deep in the idea of home ownership – the Holy Grail of American middle-class life – is the idea that we don't, in fact, own the land we've just bought" (Dickey). Barnaby extends this critique of bourgeois achievement, implying not only that white people cannot own properties because they are on unceded Indigenous lands, but also that they are unable to own their bodies when they turn into zombies. These events reverse the ways that Indigenous bodies are controlled by colonial governments, are forcibly removed from their lands, and have their children taken away, even as Indigenous Peoples resist these policies.[4] While the origin of the zombie virus in *Blood Quantum* is not fully explained, access to land is key as the Indigenous survivors debate who should be let into the secure compound.

Other films and books have covered similar territory as *Blood Quantum*. Horror film and literature – exemplified by *Get Out*, Black director Jordan Peele's 2017 evisceration of anti-Black racism and white liberalism – provides a fertile ground for social commentary on race relations. The young adult novels of Cherie Dimaline (Métis), *The Marrow Thieves* (2017) and *Hunting by Stars* (2021), create a dystopic future in which the Canadian government sets up schools to extract the marrow from still-dreaming Indigenous Peoples for non-Indigenous people who are going mad because they can no longer dream. Cree-Métis director Danis Goulet's 2021 film *Night Raiders* features a dystopic Canada in 2043 that takes children away from their caregivers to be placed in an assimilationist school called the Academy, a reference to Residential Schools. Similarly, Guatemalan director Jayro Bustamante's 2019 film *La Llorona* uses the haunted house genre to expose the Guatemalan military dictatorship's massacres of Indigenous Mayan peoples in the early 1980s.[5] Bustamante says that he decided to use horror after he "conducted a market analysis in Guatemala to understand what types of movie audiences [are] consuming in the country, and I learned that 90% of them are watching superhero blockbusters and horror movies. Based on that I started researching how to tell this story in the horror genre and I landed on La Llorona" (qtd. in Aguilar). *La Llorona* was nominated for multiple awards, suggesting that, as settler film journalist Alexandra Heller-Nicholas reminds us in her online review of the film, "horror can be turned into something with almost indescribably enormous ideological potency."

Zombie films are an ideal way of attacking topics like racism and colonization because of their popularity. Settler scholar Jeffrey Sconce argues that "zombie movies are often meant to be read as political statements.… They are more about the present moment than future predictions." As in revisionist Westerns that make "Indians" the heroes, Sconce states, in zombie films, "Wealth, power, imperialism, military force – all are useless in perpetuating tyranny and injustice over the rotting dispossessed.… It is now or soon will be their world and we are only living it … until the moment when we cross over and join them"

(97). Zombies are a shuffling (or sometimes fast-moving) metaphor that brings our worst fears to life. For this reason, George Romero's 1968 classic *Night of the Living Dead* struck a chord with Black viewers. Shot in the same year as Dr. Martin Luther King and Robert Kennedy's assassinations, the film features a Black man (Duane Jones) as the lead who survives a night in a farmhouse only to be shot by white police and locals. *Night*'s mixture of being a "prestige or social problem film" and an exploitation film with "a proud, smart, resourceful African American as its protagonist and star" (Coleman 146) ensured lineups for the film.

Of course, while a zombie apocalypse is probably not going to happen (we hope), *Blood Quantum* employs zombies as a visceral (and viscera-eating) metaphor for genocide that targets Indigenous viewers. Indigenous people in Barnaby's film do not become zombies but must survive a zombie apocalypse not of their making. Settler scholar Darryl Jones argues more specifically that zombies are "an expression of personal disempowerment and apocalyptic terror" (57), which is what makes them so terrifying. In *Blood Quantum*, white people have lost their agency but have still ideologically infected some of the film's characters. Indigenous people cannot become zombies in *Blood Quantum* but, as settler scholar Bruce F. Kawin contends, zombies "become the condition of the world, the backdrop against which the moral and immoral actions of the living characters are judged" (121). Barnaby uses the zombie genre to expose the effects of colonization particularly on Indigenous men but also to show that imbalance in gender roles is disastrous for Indigenous communities such as Red Crow. Non-Indigenous viewers are reminded that colonization is at the root of the apocalypse, including environmental degradation and toxic masculinity; these two strands cannot be untangled in *Blood Quantum*.[6]

The title of Barnaby's film has specific legal ramifications for Indigenous Peoples. Although blood quantum, the amount of so-called "Indigenous blood" in a person's ancestry, is a term more applicable to the United States, Canada's Indian Act, which does not include Métis or Inuit peoples, decides who qualifies as an "Indian." Blood quantum contradicts Indigenous conceptions of Indigeneity by focusing on blood and genetics rather than community acceptance. Although the Canadian government seems to be more benign than the US government, the second-generation cut-off means that First Nations children can lose their status depending on their parents' status.[7] The intended outcome of blood quantum is the extermination of Indigenous Peoples, which is made visceral in the film. Joseph and his girlfriend, Charlie, worry about whether their baby will be immune to the zombie virus, while Traylor is unable to stop an infected white mother from eating her child by a Mi'kmaw father.

In *Blood Quantum*, which was mostly shot in Barnaby's reserve of Listuguj, Quebec, Barnaby evokes a real-life colonial invasion motivated by Western capitalism as the basis for the film. On a global level, Barnaby argues, "We've all just fucking had it with late-stage capitalism. You're starting to see permutations of these ideas manifest themselves in all these dystopian apocalypse films" (qtd. in Bramesco). The film was inspired by the genocidal onslaught on his reserve by the Quebec Provincial Police on 11 and 20 June 1981 to enforce government restrictions on Mi'kmaw salmon-fishing rights. Barnaby was a small child when the raids happened, but they left a profound impression:

> In 1981, before I got put into the [foster care] system, I still lived in Listuguj with my mother and watched from our dumpy basement apartment as 800 plus Quebec Provincial Police and Department of Fisheries officers flooded the reserve, blocking off the only 3 entrance points.... They had come to kick the shit out of some fishermen for not listening after being told when, where, and how much to fish. During the raid, I was sitting on the back of a pick up truck when one of the S.Q. agents smashed me in the face with the barrel of his rifle while running down my uncle. I was four years old and it's the first thing I can remember in my life: someone I've never met busting my mouth for what I represented. ("*Blood Quantum* Press Kit")

Barnaby's memories of colonial violence help us understand Lysol's anger. Barnaby notes that his earlier scripts were angrier, but "For me the big change that happened was I became a dad. All of a sudden the most horrifying thing to me wasn't the dead coming back to life. It was whether or not I was going to be a good dad.... I grew up in foster care, but I knew my father, and he was just a terrible human being.... So the movie became a story about the intergenerational shittiness of being a father that isn't up to the task" ("Jeff Barnaby"). In *Blood Quantum*, however, Joseph and his more inclusive masculinity and paternal responsibility become the enduring model.

Barnaby's film uses images from renowned Abenaki filmmaker Alanis Obomsawin's 1984 documentary *Incident at Restigouche* that show the brutality of the QPP assault on Listuguj.[8] As Barnaby says, "That shaped my perception in a couple ways: first by showing me that film could be used as a safe form of social protest.... You hear Native people talking about learning self-perception through Hollywood depictions, but I was growing up watching real Mi'kmaq men and women onscreen, because of Alanis' film.... Around this time, I was also watching a lot of horror films, and my brother had brought home a Beta copy of *Night of the Living Dead*" (qtd. in Bramesco; first ellipsis in original). While Obomsawin's film is a documentary and Barnaby's is a zombie film, both directors use these very different genres as a lens for social justice. Barnaby recreates key scenes in Obomsawin's film; for example, an elder in *Incident* says in Mi'kmaw about his axe, "I draw a line [on the ground] for them not to come any further," which is echoed in *Blood Quantum* by rez sheriff Traylor's father, Gisigu. Barnaby also recreates the iconic photo and scene reproduced in Obomsawin's *Kanehsatake: 270 Years of Resistance*, a documentary account of the 1990 Mohawk resistance to the proposed development of a golf course on a cemetery in Kanehsatake. The photo, taken by Shaney Komulainen for Canadian Press, is of an Indigenous warrior staring into the eyes of a Canadian army private; in the film, Lysol stares menacingly and with some curiosity into the eyes of a zombie soldier.[9]

Echoing *Incident at Resigouche*'s depiction of Mi'kmaq asserting their fishing rights, *Blood Quantum* begins with a striking image of Gisigu fishing off the Red Crow Reserve in 1981. He gathers his fish, taking them to a gutting table on the shore near his small cabin. Barnaby fuels our anticipation for something horrific to happen, with close-ups of the fish being gutted and thrown into a bucket. Gisigu works methodically, until one of the eviscerated fish starts flopping on the table. Startled, Gisigu steps away as the fish flops onto the ground. The camera pulls back to reveal a wrecked boat to the left of the cabin, a tableau that gestures to the ongoing suppression of Indigenous fishing rights and polluted rivers and oceans. This aspect of the film evokes the history of environmental disasters on First Nations, such as the Northern Pulp paper mill at A'se'k (Boat Harbour, Nova Scotia) pumping toxic waste into Pictou Landing First Nations' lake for thirty-five years. Advocacy by Elders and community members resulted in the closing of the mill (Meloney). In Barnaby's film, eating wild fish and game can lead to being infected as a zombie, an indictment of the lack of care of the environment.

Blood Quantum shows that the world is out of balance environmentally but also in terms of gender. Settler scholar Sam McKegney notes that while stereotypes of Indigenous men as bloodthirsty warriors "offer relief from often-untenable social conditions as well as a sense of masculine agency that colonization has rendered difficult for many Indigenous men to attain in other ways," they are "problematic" because they present men who "seek power through dominance and violence" (259–60). *Blood Quantum* emphasizes the effects of toxic masculinity on the

Red Crow Reserve through Lysol's grasping towards power and violence and his lack of community solidarity, which leads to the destruction of the community's fortifications. He cannot entirely be blamed for his actions; he grew up in the foster care system which alienated him from his family and community. However, even if he had grown up on the reserve, the film implies, the lack of a good father and the violent death of his mother means that he might have gone down the same path. Barnaby shows the emotional distance between the father and son as they talk to each other sitting in their respective cars, which face in opposite directions. Lysol angrily drinks a beer, offended that Traylor refuses his offer of one, yelling "sperm donor" as Traylor drives off.

Joseph tells his mother that Lysol "doesn't have anyone. Traylor fucking abandoned him." The use of his father's name rather than "dad" reflects the strained relationship he, too, has with his father. Lysol jealously refers to Joseph as the "good son," even as Joseph is both in awe of Lysol and afraid of him, drawn to and repulsed by Lysol's anger. Joseph tries to best Lysol in the toxic masculinity competition, getting drunk and shitting on a white woman's car as she drives under him while he is perched on the bridge between the town and the reserve. With Traylor and Lysol on the side of a damaged masculinity, and Joss and Charlie, whom he clearly loves, on the side of a constructive future, Joseph is pulled in two directions, but finally chooses to side with his mother and partner.

Although Barnaby focuses on masculinity in *Blood Quantum*, Joss is also central to the film. Tailfeathers said she carried a community of "beautiful Indigenous women" in her role ("*Blood Quantum* TIFF Premiere"), and while Joss holds the community of survivors together she is not portrayed only as a "lifegiver," a stereotype of Indigenous women solely as mothers. Joss does not mince words when she picks up Joseph from jail at the beginning of the film, telling him, "I know your heart's in the right place but your head's up your ass." When Joseph expresses his ambivalence about being a father because of the example Traylor has set, Joss reminds Joseph, "if you're more focused on being a brother to Lysol than being a father, and if the question ever came up if you're ready, the way you're prioritizing your life right now is your answer." Joseph does not seem like anybody's idea of father material, but as with Traylor, the zombie apocalypse turns him into a supportive father, partner, and community member. A scene in the compound between Charlie and Joseph shows his shift away from his brother. The couple lies on their bed behind a makeshift blanket curtain discussing Lysol. While Joseph sympathizes with his brother's anger and places it firmly within the context of family breakdown and the genocidal child welfare system, he also says, "I gave him a pass in so much fucking nonsense.... It has to stop sometime. You can't just be an asshole." However, even as Joseph begins to distance himself from Lysol, viewers understand that Traylor bears responsibility for not being there for Lysol, potentially because of his problems with addiction; however, they also understand that Traylor was dealing with his own trauma, and that such trauma moves through generations.[10] We are never sure why Traylor is a less-than-ideal father, but we can hypothesize that colonial ideas of masculinity have influenced Traylor, demonstrated by his cowboy attire that echoes that of a sheriff in Western movies. Although he sports braids, he wears jeans and a denim jacket, with a big belt buckle and a bandana slung around his neck. Traylor has internalized stereotypes of what it means to be a man that damage relationships with his sons and his ex-wife. He sleepwalks through life, not sure how to be a better man.

In a strange way, the zombie apocalypse is the best thing that happens to Traylor as it makes him a protector of his community and forces him to question his priorities, including his love for his sons and Joss. As Greyeyes notes, "It takes the end of the world for him to be a better person" ("*Blood Quantum* TIFF Premiere"). Traylor shares a tender moment with Joss as she stitches up a zombie bite on his back; the camera lingers on Traylor's body, showing the multitude of bites he has received as a result of safeguarding his community. When the compound is overrun with zombies, he and a few of the community members race to evacuate people, particularly those in the makeshift nursing station.

In the end, Traylor sacrifices himself to save Joss, Charlie, and Joseph, telling them in Mi'kmaw, "I want you to tell my grandchild big stories about me." It is tough to watch Traylor being ripped apart and eaten by zombies because viewers have seen him grow as a character and embrace a more caring version of himself. However, he knows that sacrificing himself potentially saves the grandchild whom he never gets to meet. Greyeyes emphasizes that "This film is really an examination of fathers: good, bad and ugly" (qtd. in Yamato). While Traylor is in the latter category for much of the film, his father, Gisigu, consistently provides a role model for his son and grandson. After the gutted fish come to life, Traylor makes his dad a deputy because he is trustworthy and holds Mi'kmaw ways of knowing. Towards the end of the film, Gisigu appears in one of the three animated sequences, heroically fighting a horde of zombies with a machete as Joseph looks on from the boat. Viewers do not know if he survives – Barnaby stresses that the sequence is deliberately ambiguous – but in this scene Joseph's grandfather also proves to be a warrior for his community and family.

In contrast, Lysol's character arc is a condemnation of Canadian and provincial governments' forced removal of Indigenous children from their families and communities. According to the Canadian government's 2016 census, "52.2% of children in foster care are Indigenous, but account for only 7.7% of the child population" ("Reducing"). Clearly, the child welfare system is not working for Indigenous children, a system that Barnaby knows intimately. His character, Lysol, has been warped by the foster care system, becoming a young man hell bent on revenge who wants to drag his younger brother into his spiral of anger. The audience can both understand and condemn Lysol's destructive behaviour.

Forrest Goodluck, who plays Joseph, states that Lysol does not know how to reconcile his feelings: "The only way he knows how is through violence, what he grew up with." As Barnaby explains, "Lysol's mother died quite violently, or at least she met an early demise, and he's carrying this darkness around in him that manifests itself in misogyny. I felt like at some point this guy is going to turn into a barbarian and just start asserting dominance. There's a commentary on male toxicity there, but I wanted to present it in a way that didn't nice wash it" ("Jeff Barnaby"). Lysol's viciousness seems to be a result of the lack of positive female presence in his life and the fact he was abandoned by his dad and grew up in the foster care system. Barnaby muses that "way back when we first started testing the film, the question that popped up the most is why is Lysol so angry. I was like, *Really? You don't grasp why he's so angry within the context of the film, or as a broad overview of society*?" ("Jeff Barnaby"). As Joseph explains to Charlie, he went to foster care "an Allan and came back a Lysol," his nickname an apt metaphor for the toxically dehumanizing effects of the child welfare system.

Lysol, like his grandfather and the pregnant woman, features in an animated sequence, albeit of a darker nature. He is on top of a volcano menacingly holding a spear, a nod to his position on a path of vengeance. He stares intently and furiously at the viewer. As he breathes hard, the landscape turns to fire. This darkness is even extended to Joseph, who both adores Lysol and has a hard time accepting his anger. Near the beginning of the film, Lysol and Joseph are in a jail cell, unaware that the apocalypse is beginning. After Joseph informs Lysol that he got arrested only because he knows that their dad "wouldn't come to get you but he'd come get us," Lysol responds, "Any stupid shit you do your people are going to hang on me." In this scene, Lysol describes his family as "your people" clearly demonstrating that he feels like an abandoned outsider.

Lysol comes to an ignominious end. In a literal condemnation of toxic masculinity, his penis is chewed off by Lilith,[11] one of the white refugees at a compound party who reanimates into a zombie. In revenge for letting white people such as her into the secure area, Lysol uses the zombified Lilith to attack the compound, obliterating the fragile community. After confessing his act of genocide against his own community, he is stabbed by Joseph, and his grandfather fires a gun to attract zombies to eat him. Thus, in a strange way, Lysol also sacrifices himself, albeit unwillingly, as the zombies are slowed down as they feast on him, enabling Joss, Charlie, and Joseph to escape. In contrast, Joseph survives the zombie apocalypse because he learns to be gentle and supportive of Charlie and his larger community. He fulfils Lysol's earlier advice: "You don't have to be a trash dad. That shit's optional."

Settler scholar Sean Carleton argues in a preface to an interview with Barnaby that "Reconciliation is not dead in Barnaby's fictional world," because "survival requires Indigenous and non-Indigenous peoples to work together to defeat the undead, transforming themselves and their relations in the process" ("Decolonizing"). Signalling the importance of working with white people to survive the zombie apocalypse, Joseph states, "There is no us and them. There's only us." And while Traylor notes that "The bigger problem than the dead, walking-around townies is the live breathing ones" who are "coming across in almost the same numbers," he also argues that "we've got to do right by survivors."

The members of the Red Crow reserve debate whether to allow non-Indigenous peoples onto their territory. Barnaby acknowledges that "If you're going to talk about the character Lysol in the film being this postcolonial Indian that doesn't really grasp the concept of keeping the borders open or keeping an open heart or an open mind, which is traditionally what Native people have done when they welcome the survivors, I think you couldn't not address it. Because it's an issue within Native communities" ("Jeff Barnaby"). A line by Joss undercuts the notion of "reconciliation"; she tells Lysol that he is not wrong when he does not want to allow white people there, and he is not proven wrong as the compound is ultimately destroyed by white people who have become zombies. *Blood Quantum* thus put the possibility of reconciliation between members of the Red Crow reserve and settlers into question. Doing right by survivors costs Traylor his life even as he becomes a potential source of "big stories" for his grandchild. Barnaby pulls the rug from underneath settler viewers by having Joss, Joseph, and his daughter as the only human survivors at the end of the film, leaving the settler zombies behind.

Blood Quantum ends with Fawn Wood's (Cree/Salish) lovely lullaby "Mommy's Little Guy," a song of love to Joseph's daughter but also to Joseph himself, the son who embraces his gentleness. The three survivors leave behind not only toxic masculinity, but also the government-imposed confines of the rez, reclaiming the area outside as Indigenous lands. Echoing the ending of *Incident at Restigouche,* in which a young boy and his father fish together on a river, Joss, Joseph, and his unnamed daughter assert a new kind of community at the conclusion of *Blood Quantum*. But it is a fragile hope as the zombies of colonization still roam free, ready to consume Indigeneity.

NOTES

1 Grace Dillon (Anishinaabe) coined the term "Indigenous futurism" to highlight the importance of showing Indigenous Peoples thriving in the future with their ways of knowing intact. She explains, "It is almost commonplace to think that the Native Apocalypse, if contemplated seriously, has already taken place" (8), including the "Battle of Little Big Horn and Custer's demise (1876)" and the "Oka uprisings of the 1990s at Kahnesetake" (8–9). Cherokee scholar Daniel Heath Justice expands the concept: "For populations that faced eighty-percent mortality and higher due to European-inflicted disease, displacement, enslavement, starvation, military action, and internment … the 'end of days' isn't just the stuff of doomsday religionists or science fiction, but of historical memory and lived experience.… And that makes those of us living today the post-apocalypse survivors of world-shaking catastrophes" (167–8). The discovery of unmarked graves at former Residential Schools is just one horrifying example of Canada's genocidal policies.

2 For analyses of other Indigenous conceptions of post-apocalyptic societies, see the chapters in this volume by Gage Karahkwí:io Diabo on Waubgeshig Rice's *Moon* novels and by Gwen Rose on Cherie Dimaline's *The Marrow Thieves* and its sequel. These novels also address questions of masculinity, or what it means to be a man in an Indigenous community post-apocalypse.

3 *Rhymes for Young Ghouls* also contained animated sequences. Barnaby explains, "I find integrating those sequences lets you know that you're in a film, which I think is important when you're a Native storyteller to always let your audience know that you are indeed looking at a fictitious representation of Native people and not a documentary" ("Interview" by Stephen Saito).

4 In a recent example of many such resistances, in October 2021, chiefs, matriarchs, family members, and Gitanmaax councillors blocked social workers from taking a child from a Gitxsan community (Monkman).

5 Winnie Lee explains that "La Llorona is a well-known and pervasive legend who serves as a cautionary tale for multiple generations in Latinx households, often invoked to scare kids and stop them from misbehaving.… In some versions, she's an indigenous woman who's so enraged by her husband's infidelity that she vengefully murders their children in a nearby river, then drowns herself in grief and remorse" (Lee).

6 Environmental degradation and toxic masculinity are also disastrous for Indigenous women and Two-Spirit/Indigiqueer people. Unfortunately, there are no explicitly queer characters in *Blood Quantum*, although Kawennáhere Devery Jacobs (Mohawk), who played Alia in *Rhymes for Young Ghouls* and who identifies as queer, plays a part in *Blood Quantum* as James. Both Charlie and James can be seen as masculine names, with Jacobs playing an androgynous character in leather and combat boots.

7 The Native Women's Association of Canada has a primer that explains how second-generation cut-off works ("Indian Status in Canada").

8 *Incident at Restigouche* can be viewed at https://www.nfb.ca/film/incident_at_restigouche/.

9 The photo by Komulainen and the corresponding still from Barnaby's film can be found on the internet.

10 Other characters offer Traylor beer as if he is expected to want one, but he refuses as he realizes how alcohol use has alienated him from his family.

11 Regarding Lilith, "A medieval Jewish text called the Alphabet of Ben Sira describes her as Adam's first wife who disobeyed him and God and asserted her equality to Adam, giving a legendary origin to her demonic behavior.… The contemporary feminist movement found an inspiration in this image of Lilith as the uncontrollable woman and decisively changed the image of Lilith from demon to powerful woman" (Lesses).

WORKS CITED

Aguilar, Carlos. "Crying for Justice: Jayro Bustamante on *La Llorona*." *Rogertebert.com*, 5 Aug. 2020, https://www.rogerebert.com/interviews/crying-for-justice-jayro-bustamante-on-la-llorona.

Barnaby, Jeff, writer and director. *Blood Quantum*. Prospector Films, 2019.

– "Decolonizing the Zombie Apocalypse: An Interview with Jeff Barnaby about His New Film *Blood Quantum*." Interview by Sean Carleton. *Canadian Dimension*, 26 Apr. 2020, https://canadiandimension.com/articles/view/decolonizing-the-zombie-apocalypse-an-interview-with-jeff-barnaby-about-his-new-film-blood-quantum.

– "Interview: Jeff Barnaby on Developing Survival Skills for a Zombie Plague in *Blood Quantum*." Interview by Stephen Saito. *The Moveable Feast*, 7 May 2020, https://moveablefest.com/jeff-barnaby-blood-quantum/.

– "Jeff Barnaby Made an Apocalypse Movie to Watch the System Fall. Then a Pandemic Hit." Interview by Jordan Crucchiola. *Vulture*, 6 May 2020, https://www.vulture.com/2020/05/jeff-barnaby-is-worried-white-people-wont-get-blood-quantum.html.

Baudemann, Kristina. "Indigenous Futurist Film: Speculation and Resistance in Jeff Barnaby's *Rhymes for Young Ghouls* and *File Under Miscellaneous*." *Canadian Science Fiction, Fantasy, and Horror: Bridging the Solitudes*, edited by Amy J. Ransom and Dominick Grace, Palgrave Macmillan, 2019, pp. 151–65.

"*Blood Quantum* Press Kit – Production Audiovisuelle Canadienne." *RDVCanada.ca*, 22 Aug. 2019, https://rdvcanada.ca/wp-content/uploads/gravity_forms/7-b153bacda73dd76449b4941ad8241bc4/2019/08/Blood-Quantum-Prelim-press-kit.pdf.

"*Blood Quantum* TIFF Premiere: Cast & Crew on the Powerful Story at the Heart of This New Zombie Movie." *YouTube*, uploaded by HeyUGuys, 8 Sept. 2019, https://www.youtube.com/watch?v=CpyHJC4ORKM.

Bramesco, Charles. "'I'm Indigenizing Zombies:' Behind Gory First Nation Horror *Blood Quantum*." *The Guardian*, 28 Apr. 2020, https://www.theguardian.com/film/2020/apr/28/blood-quantum-horror-film.

Bustamante, Jayro, writer and director. *La Llorona*. Les Films du Volcan, 2019.

Coleman, Robin R. Means. *Horror Noire: Blacks in American Horror Films from the 1890s to Present*. Routledge, 2011.

Dickey, Colin. "The Suburban Horror of the Indian Burial Ground." *The New Republic*, 19 Oct. 2016, https://newrepublic.com/article/137856/suburban-horror-indian-burial-ground.

Dillon, Grace. "Imagining Indigenous Futurisms." Introduction to *Walking the Clouds: An Anthology of Indigenous Science Fiction*. U of Arizona P, 2012, pp. 1–12.

Dimaline, Cherie. *Hunting by Stars*. Penguin, 2021.

– *The Marrow Thieves*. Dancing Cat Books, 2017.

Goulet, Danis, writer and director. *Night Raiders*. Elevation Pictures, 2021.

Heller-Nicholas, Alexandra. "*La Llorona*." *Alliance of Women Film Journalists*, 8 Aug. 2020, https://awfj.org/blog/2020/08/08/la-llorona-miff-2020-review-by-alexandra-heller-nicholas/.

"Indian Status in Canada." *Native Women's Association of Canada*, https://www.nwac.ca/assets-knowledge-centre/Indian-Status-in-Canada-FINAL.pdf.

Jones, Darryl. *Sleeping with the Lights On: The Unsettling Story of Horror*. Oxford UP, 2018.

Justice, Daniel Heath. *Why Indigenous Literatures Matter.* Wilfrid Laurier UP, 2018.

Kawin, Bruce F. *Horror and the Horror Film.* Anthem, 2012.

Lee, Winnie. "How Mexico's Most Sorrowful Spirit Became a Cultural Phenomenon." *Atlas Obscura,* 30 Oct. 2019, https://www.atlasobscura.com/articles/the-weeping-woman-in-mexico.

Lesses, Rebecca. "Lilith." *Shalvi/Hyman Encyclopedia of Jewish Women,* 31 Dec. 1999, https://jwa.org/encyclopedia/article/lilith.

Mbembe, Achille. "Necropolitics." *Public Culture.* Translated by Libby Meintjes, vol. 15, no. 1, 2003, pp. 11–40.

McKegney, Sam. "Warriors, Healers, Lovers, and Leaders: Colonial Impositions on Indigenous Male Roles and Responsibilities." *Canadian Perspectives on Men and Masculinities: An Interdisciplinary Reader,* edited by Jason A. Laker, Oxford UP, 2011, pp. 241–68.

Meloney, Nic. "'It Looked Like Paradise:' Mi'kmaw Elders Reflect on How Paper Mill Pollution Changed Their Community." *CBC Indigenous,* 31 Jan. 2020, https://www.cbc.ca/news/indigenous/pictou-landing-first-nation-northern-pulp-1.5447179.

Monkman, Leonard. "Gitanmaax Members Stop Child from Being Taken from Community by Social Workers." *CBC,* 10 Dec. 2021, www.cbc.ca/news/indigenous/gitanmaax-child-welfare-workers-blocked-1.6217014.

Obomsawin, Alanis, writer and director. *Incident at Restigouche.* National Film Board, 1984.

– *Kanehsatake: 270 Years of Resistance.* National Film Board, 1993.

Peele, Jordan, writer and director. *Get Out.* Universal Pictures, 2017.

"Reducing the Number of Indigenous Children in Care." *Government of Canada; Indigenous Services Canada,* 7 June 2021, https://www.sac-isc.gc.ca/eng/1541187352297/1541187392851.

Romero, George, director. *Night of the Living Dead.* Image Ten, 1968.

Sconce, Jeffrey. "Dead Metaphors/Undead Allegories." *Screening the Undead: Vampires and Zombies in Film and Television,* edited by Leon Hunt, Sharon Lockyer, and Milly Williamson, I.B. Tauris, 2014, pp. 96–111.

Simonpillai, Radheyan. "TIFF 2019: Indigenous Artists Are Using Horror to Unpack Colonial Trauma." *Now,* 4 Sept. 2019, https://nowtoronto.com/movies/news-features/indigenous-horror-blood-quantum-tiff-2019.

Sneider, Leah. "Complementary Relationships: A Review of Indigenous Gender Studies." *Indigenous Men and Masculinities: Legacies, Identities, Regeneration,* edited by Robert Alexander Innes and Kim Anderson, U of Manitoba P, 2015, pp. 62–79.

Truscello, Michael, and Renae Watchman. "*Blood Quantum* and Fourth Cinema: Post- and Paracolonial Zombies." *Quarterly Review of Film and Video,* vol. 40, no. 4, 2022, pp. 462–83, https://doi.org/10.1080/10509208.2022.2026273.

Warrior, Carol Edelman. *Baring the Windigo's Teeth: Fearsome Figures in Native American Narratives.* 2015. U of Washington, PhD dissertation. *University Libraries*, https://digital.lib.washington.edu:443/researchworks/handle/1773/33820.

Wong, Jessica. "*Blood Quantum*'s Indigenous Actors Totally Get the Zombie Apocalypse." *CBC Entertainment*, 10 Sept. 2019, https://www.cbc.ca/news/entertainment/tiff2019-bloodquantum-1.5273257.

Yamato, Jen. "How Indigenous Zombie Horror Film *Blood Quantum* Became Prescient in the Pandemic." *Los Angeles Times*, 8 May 2020, https://www.latimes.com/entertainment-arts/movies/story/2020-05-08/blood-quantum-indigenous-horror-zombie-pandemic-jeff-barnaby.

Vision and Re-Visioning in *The Handmaid's Tale* and Two Adaptations

MACKENZIE READ

The notion that what has happened can happen again is evident both within Margaret Atwood's *The Handmaid's Tale* and in how the book has been revisited through multiple adaptations since its publication. Artistic choices in the 1990 film and 2017–25 television adaptations of Atwood's 1985 novel either perpetuate or dismantle the book's key concepts of surveillance and oppression. To film a representation of the novel's highly monitored society, as some critics argue, extends Gilead's interrogative surveillance practices to the viewer. While a valid concern, vision and re-visioning in the filmed adaptations connect the act of looking with power relations, suggesting that it is not the medium that is problematic but *how* it is used. Adrienne Rich's feminist idea of "re-vision" is useful in studying how the novel, film, and television series handle what Laura Mulvey calls "the gaze" – looking and being looked at – since those acts serve as the entry point through which audiences either conspire with Offred against Gilead or endorse its surveillance of her.

The Handmaid's Tale has been adapted into films, stage productions, ballet, radio plays, audiobooks, television series, and a graphic novel. These adaptations not only have transformed the narrative into different media but also collectively demonstrate the adaptability of Atwood's story. Critic Linda Hutcheon amusingly notes, "Given the adaptational impulse and genius that Atwood so clearly demonstrates, it is either entirely appropriate or nicely ironic that her own works have been adapted so often" ("Adapting" 252). Hutcheon believes that Atwood's works are revisited again and again because of her "uncanny ability to have her finger on the pulse of the *Zeitgeist*" (252). Although cultures change and attitudes shift, what concerned Atwood in the twentieth century persists into the twenty-first: issues of gender(s) equality, misogyny, reproductive rights, personal autonomy, extremist views, and political issues impacting marginalized groups.

Besides their contemporary relevance, adaptations of *The Handmaid's Tale* are worth investigating because they revisit and reimagine Atwood's story. These adaptations do what Hutcheon calls a "double process of interpreting and then creating something new" (*Theory* 20). The result is not a replica of the inspiration text, but a fully formed work that Hutcheon argues functions according to Darwin's biological theory of evolution: "Adaptation, like evolution, is a transgenerational phenomenon" (32). As such, adaptations are what Sarah Cardwell describes as "points on a continuum, as part of the extended development of a singular, infinite meta-text: a valuable story or myth that is constantly growing and developing, being retold, reinterpreted and reassessed" (25). In this way, adaptations add to the "meta-text" rather than replace or live secondarily to their predecessors. Adaptation is, in Hutcheon's words, "repetition, but repetition without replication" (*Theory* 7). In their multiplicity, adaptations can threaten hegemonic institutions because they celebrate and live in heterogeneity.

A creator's impulse to adapt is to bring a new vision to the story, and this impulse can be political. Although not specifically referring to adaptations, Rich's notion of "re-visioning" is a feminist process of engaging with existing texts with a new outlook to understand and, in turn, resist patriarchy's construction of women: "Re-vision – the act of looking back, of seeing with fresh eyes, of entering an old text from a new critical direction – is for women more than a chapter in cultural history: it is an act of survival. Until we can understand the assumptions in which we are drenched we cannot know ourselves. And this drive to self-knowledge, for women, is more than a search for identity: it is part of our refusal of the self-destructiveness of male-dominated society" (35). To reclaim identity by reconsidering the constructions of women in a patriarchal culture demonstrates the power of deliberately looking anew. Ultimately, it affords the opportunity to understand the dominant language in order to engage with it subversively or reject it entirely. In doing so, women can rescue their identities from the limiting parameters established by patriarchal societal structures. This potential for rescue is applicable to Atwood's Offred, who is quite literally forced to take on a new name and identity in the theocratic Republic of Gilead, but also to others who suffer under patriarchal norms.

A textual "re-visioning" occurs in the cinematic adaptations of *The Handmaid's Tale*. Adaptations not only bring fresh eyes to the work but also present the narrative in a way that requires different contexts and engagement from audiences. One of the great challenges for filmed adaptations of the novel is their association with what Mulvey calls "the male gaze." Using the term "objectification," Mulvey employs psychoanalytic theories to argue that a woman on screen can be viewed "as erotic object for the characters within the screen story, and as erotic object for the spectator within the auditorium, with a shifting tension between the looks on either side of the screen" (19). Referring to the ideas of art critic John Berger, Mulvey makes the point that women on screen are often vessels of meaning but rarely the makers of it. Moreover, as objects of the male gaze, women are acutely aware of being looked at and thus commit the complicated act of seeing themselves through the gaze of men.[1] This analysis is important to the conversation about "the gaze" in *The Handmaid's Tale* because Offred (along with all women in Gilead) is hyper-aware of how men look at her and how she must present herself to satisfy them and, ultimately, stay alive. While at times this dynamic is to her advantage, she is often the signified – not the signifier. Offred's vulnerability reminds readers that under a totalitarian state, looking the part is a matter of life or death.

While there are countless examples in the novel of Offred knowing she is being watched, her relationship with the Commander highlights the varying degrees of threat packed into looking and being looked at. This dynamic is present in their first encounter. As Offred walks down a dark hall to her room, she sees the Commander near her door. His back is to her, and Offred tries to retreat without being noticed. The Commander, however, sees her and approaches her without a word. Offred's panic signals fear at the uncertainty of his actions. She narrates, "I stop, he pauses, I can't see his face, he's looking at me, what does he want? But then he moves forward again, steps to the side to avoid touching me, inclines his head, is gone" (61). Since she relies on looking to gain information that could prepare her for a potential threat, this encounter is particularly unnerving. She reflects, "Something has been shown to me, but what is it? Like the flag of an unknown country, seen for an instant above a curve of a hill. It could mean attack, it could mean parley, it could mean the edge of something, a territory" (61). The ambiguity in their first encounter demonstrates Offred's reliance on seeing a face to gather valuable information and respond appropriately. This dance is a complicated one, but nevertheless an important one, as it ensures her continued survival.

Once the Commander invites Offred to illicit meetings in his private study, their growing intimacy complicates the gaze for both of them. For instance, Offred admits that the Commander is "of interest to [her], he occupies space, he is more than a shadow" (204). She also notes that he no longer sees her as "a usable body.... To him [she] is not merely empty" (204). Their mutual recognition of each other's humanity means that they cannot detach and objectify as they once did. Yet, their power imbalance keeps Offred from gazing at him the way he does her. When she receives a contraband *Vogue* magazine from the Commander as a gift, for example, she draws parallels between his looking at her and the objectification of fashion models (196). In another section, Offred grows self-conscious as the Commander watches her rub lotion onto her hands. His gaze makes her feel "shy of him" because "he was actually looking at [her], and [she] didn't like it" (200). Offred's objectification demonstrates what Mulvey calls a woman's *"to-be-looked-at-ness"* (19). She is keenly aware of the Commander's scrutiny and the potential danger associated with it.

Though Offred certainly lacks the agency that the Commander possesses, the meetings allow her to see and read material that is no longer permitted in Gilead. In this way, Offred is not just another object in the space she occupies. The Commander permits Offred to read books and magazines and play the board game Scrabble. Like a hungry animal, she describes these short bursts of time as trying to consume as much as possible "before the next long starvation" (231). She compares her reading to "the gluttony of the famished; [or] if it were sex it would be a swift furtive stand-up in an alley somewhere" (231). As she has her own private visual feast, she points out that the Commander's gaze is a "curiously sexual act, and [she feels] undressed while he does it" (231). Noting that her "reading … seems a kind of performance" (232), Offred always has the Commander in mind as she tries to escape into the imaginary worlds in her reading material. His mental commandeering – as even his title suggests – reminds her that it is because of his enjoyment in watching her read that she is able to do it at all. Not only does the Commander exude control over her through his gaze, but also she no longer has the luxury of being the quiet observer. She knows that in a highly monitored state such as Gilead, it is always safer to be an observer than observed. His watching is therefore as invasive as it is sexual since her objectification also means being vulnerable to his scrutiny.

This notion of performance becomes even more pertinent to the Commander and Offred's relationship when he takes her to Jezebel's, a place in which the high-ranking men of Gilead ironically indulge in all the sins they condemn publicly. To allow her to play the part of mistress, the Commander gives Offred a hyper-feminine disguise. Instead of her regular uniform of a winged cap and full-length red gown, she must wear a revealing dress, accessories, and make-up. In this sexy disguise, Offred uses her discerning perspective to reveal the complexities of masculinity and male identity. Specifically, Offred recognizes that her purpose is to mirror back to the Commander his power and confirm it to his colleagues. She narrates,

> It occurs to me he is showing off. He is showing me off, to them, and they understand that, they are decorous enough, they keep their hands to themselves, but they review my breasts, my legs, as if there's no reason why they shouldn't. But also he is showing off to me. He is demonstrating, to me, his mastery of the world. He's breaking the rules, under their noses, thumbing his nose at them, getting away with it. Perhaps he's reached that state of intoxication which power is said to inspire, the state in which you believe you are indispensable and can therefore do anything, absolutely anything you feel like, anything at all. Twice, when he thinks no one is looking, he winks at me. (296–7)

The Commander's motivation in bringing her there is to bolster his ego, but in doing so he reveals his dependency on her objectification to validate his image of himself. The fact that he winks at Offred when he believes no one is watching proves that he, too, is aware of the ways he must project and assert his power. In return, Offred's compliance gives her access to information she would not otherwise have. She understands how powerful and rare it is to look, especially unencumbered by her winged cap. In fact, this freedom allows her to spot her best friend, Moira, while at Jezebel's. Using her intense gaze, Offred wills Moira to see her from across the room: "Surely she must turn, I'm willing so hard, she must look at me, before one of the men comes over to her, before she disappears.... Moira swivels her head around again, checking perhaps for prospects.... This time her eyes snag on me. She sees me. She knows enough not to react" (301). Offred's fear of Moira disappearing at the arrival of a man is both literal and symbolic, especially given the fact that Moira's lesbianism is displaced by the straight sex she is forced to endure as one of Jezebel's workers. As objects and sexual playthings, both Moira and Offred are overlooked as threats to the status quo. Yet, it is because they are overlooked that Moira and Offred are able to connect and share illicit information with each other. This subversive activity goes unsuspected because, to the male patrons, these women are entertainment and serve as reflections of their own egos and nothing more.[2]

For Handmaids, the gaze functions entirely differently. As part of their uniform, the Handmaids' bonnets act similarly to horse blinders in that they limit the full view of the spaces they occupy. Offred describes this difficulty and the measures that Handmaids must take in order to see their surroundings: "Given our wings, our blinkers, it's hard to look up, hard to get the full view, of the sky, of anything. But we can do it, a little at a time, a quick move of the head, up and down, to the side and back. We have learned to see the world in gasps" (38). It is not by coincidence that following this passage, Offred and her shopping partner, Ofglen, first encounter the "Wall." Hung from it are men considered so-called "war criminals" by Gilead. In reality, their only crimes are holding professions now banned by the Republic. Around their necks are signs that give the reason for their execution. Offred remarks that most of the hanged men are scientists or doctors, with one specifically wearing around his neck a "drawing of a human fetus" (41), a symbol of the abortion services he provided "in the time before" (41). This menacing scene is intended to be witnessed by them to encourage submission and threaten disobedience. Moreover, Gilead's regressive annihilation of science, medicine, and literacy (all of which work to demystify the unknown) proves just how dangerous it is to see and possess knowledge.

Still, Offred and her fellow Handmaids are clever in finding creative ways to observe. A pivotal moment for Offred comes again when she is out with Ofglen. Unable to see and read her expressions, Offred is uncertain of her partner's allegiance to Gilead's mission. It is not until they stop in front of a shop window and lock eyes in their reflection that Offred learns of Ofglen's involvement in an underground resistance organization. At first, the intimacy of looking at one another makes Offred feel as if she is "seeing somebody naked, for the first time" (210). It is an image that echoes the nakedness she feels under the Commander's discerning watch. Offred thus registers that "there is risk, suddenly, in the air between [them], where there was none before. Even this meeting of eyes holds danger. Though there's nobody near" (210). That danger is realized minutes later when a man is violently and swiftly plucked from the street and put into a black van by the police force known as the Eyes. Though Ofglen instructs Offred to "pretend not to see" (212), Offred admits that she "can't help seeing" (212). It is a moment that demonstrates the full risk of looking in a highly monitored state. Ofglen's command to avert their eyes is an act of self-preservation and protection for the Mayday resistance organization. Yet Offred's inability to look away is also an act of self-preservation because she is aware that to survive, she must be alert to her dangerous environment.

The complexity of seeing and being seen is at its richest during the monthly Ceremonies. As she endures a practice that objectifies her entirely by using her only as a vessel for making children, Offred uses vision and her objectifying of the Commander to maintain her own agency. For instance, as she prepares to be raped by the Commander, Offred wonders what it must be like "to be a man, watched by women" (109). While the "man" takes on a more general identity, she is clearly referring to the Commander as well: "To have them watching him all the time. To have them wondering, What's he going to do next? To have them flinch when he moves.... To have them sizing him up. To have them thinking, He can't do it, he won't do, he'll have to do, this last as if he were a garment, out of style or shoddy, which must nevertheless be put on because there's nothing else available" (109). Despite the threat that men present to women, it is the women who act, not the man in Offred's narration. This reversal of the male gaze is intensified by the sexual innuendo of a man being "put on" out of necessity. While Offred also suggests that a man puts on a woman "like a sock over a foot" (109), the sexual politics become further complicated with her description of the Commander's phallus as having an eye and seeking vision through penetration:

> [H]is tentacle, his delicate, stalked slug's eye, which extrudes, expands, winces, and shrivels back into himself when touched wrongly, grows big again, bulging a little at the tip, traveling forward as if along a leaf, into them, avid for vision. To achieve vision in this way, this journey into a darkness that is composed of women, a woman, who can see in darkness while he himself strains blindly forward.
>
> She watches him from within. We're all watching him. (109)

The phallic eye conjures associations with the surveillance and oppression that are central to Gilead. After all, the police task force in Gilead is called the Eyes. Yet Atwood extends the eye metaphor to the entire patriarchal social structure because, as Jeanne Reesman argues, "light is the province of the male Establishment, while darkness is associated with women. The male/light/vision images, expressed in images of light conquering darkness and of 'seeing' people instead of addressing them, are harsh and oppressive" (308). Against the Commander's domination, Reesman suggests, Offred's puns and detailed description of his member challenge his phallic power with her words (310). If this is true, Offred's last lines confront the Commander's sexual power directly with the force of her intellect and her indomitable personhood: "But watch out, Commander, I tell him in my head. I've got my eye on you" (109). Though unable to speak such words, Offred's defiant thought puts the Commander in a position of vulnerability despite her own oppression. As a result, Offred proves that vision and its connection to power are more nuanced and malleable than her oppressors would like to believe.

Collectively, these examples of looking and being looked at demonstrate how complex and politically charged it is to be on either side of the gaze. In a totalitarian state such as Gilead, it is an especially complicated issue. As such, it is easy to see why Atwood's story takes great pains to explore these intricacies of looking. Her narrative presents examples in which the gaze traps its subjects, and it also illustrates how looking plays an integral role in defying oppressors. Without Offred's elaborate descriptions of being watched and covertly watching others, the horrors of Gilead would not resonate as they do. Perhaps most importantly, Offred's reversal of the gaze gives her agency in a world that actively suppresses her autonomy. It is imperative, then, that adapters of the novel also engage meaningfully with the gaze when creating their own adaptations. In fact, without this key theme considered, film adapters, in particular, run the risk of reobjectifying Offred with their cameras.

Some critics have argued that *The Handmaid's Tale* should not be filmed at all given the novel's intense criticism of patriarchal surveillance. This criticism is particularly directed at Victor Schlöndorff's 1990 adaptation of Atwood's novel. In Pamela Cooper's "Sexual Surveillance and Medical Authority in Two Versions of *The Handmaid's Tale*," she argues that the film's camera lens mirrors the ways that Gilead controls and objectifies its women: "To film *The Handmaid's Tale* is to duplicate the threatening strategies of visual surveillance that persecute the women depicted in the narrative. It is to force the audience's complicity by identifying the inherent voyeurism of movie-watching with the invasive examining of the disenfranchised by the dictatorial [*sic*] which the novel portrays. The very act of filming *The Handmaid's Tale* automatically shifts the issue of surveillance-enforced misogyny to a metafictional or metacinematic level" (57). Cooper is correct in pointing out that the film's camera shots replicate surveillance practices, since they are often static and positioned at a distance from Offred, or Kate, as she is identified in the film (played by Natasha Richardson). Since her point of view is rarely explored through the camera work and there is very little voice-over to reveal her interiority, the audience is forced to be an invisible "other" in the scene rather than Kate's conspiratorial mate. The result, Cooper argues, is that these shots "implicitly [endorse] the terms of that contract, so vehemently questioned in the novel, between totalitarianism and the gaze" (57). Indeed, viewers are always watching but never really identifying with Kate. Vision, therefore, is not treated with the complexity that is depicted in the novel; rather, it is flattened in its perpetuation of the male gaze. This problem in Schlöndorff's adaptation undermines the narrative's most valuable asset: Offred's point of view. Without this intimate connection to her frame of mind, the film seems to side with the oppressors rather than its heroine.

It is worth studying Schlöndorff's film, however, to examine the ways the male gaze reinforces the very powers that Atwood's novel tries to destabilize. This dichotomy is most prevalent in the Ceremony scene. In the novel, Offred establishes an intimacy with readers in her detailed descriptions of the furniture and decor of the room where the Ceremony is taking place. She admits that if her eyes were open she would see everything that she is describing, including the Commander's open eyes (117). However, cautious of experiencing this trauma in her body, she keeps her eyes closed and adopts a non-identity. She narrates, "One detaches oneself. One describes" (117). In Schlöndorff's adaptation, the Ceremony is filmed in such a way that the audience spends more time with the Commander than with Kate. In fact, the scene begins with the camera following the Commander as he approaches the bed. It then briefly cuts to Kate's writhing body as she fights against Serena Joy's tight grasp. In the darkened room, Kate's red-veiled face is obscured, making it difficult for the audience to connect with her suffering. Although she gasps and cries out, it is unconvincing and distracting to the scene. The camera then pans up to Serena Joy's uncomfortable expression before cutting back to the Commander. The only instance when the camera adopts Kate's point of view comes when the Commander has just finished his duty and is briefly bent over her. This complicity is short-lived, however, since the camera tilts up with the Commander as he rises, looks down at Kate, and leaves the room. In his analysis of this scene, Jeroen Gerrits points out that "the artifice of [Kate's] suffering (conveyed through Natasha Richardson's 'mechanic' [*sic*] acting and the obviously dubbed gasps) is no doubt to achieve a Brechtian distantiation effect. All the same, if the novel suggests that Offred and the Commander (and his wife) stick to the playbook, with Offred offering her body while keeping control over her mind, … Schlöndorff ends up offering up a rape fantasy to a male gaze" (218). Indeed, Atwood's Offred detaches from her trauma to preserve her mind – it is her only defence against the Commander and, by extension, Gilead. Schlöndorff's Kate, on the other hand, does not detach like Offred during this scene. Her sobs illustrate how violated she feels in this process, both physically and mentally. Of course, what happens to her during the Ceremony is traumatic; however, Kate's sobs paint her as more helpless than Offred, whose steely composure denies her oppressors' total control. Since Kate has no power over her autonomy apart from her private thoughts, it is disappointing that Schlöndorff visualizes her suffering without offering her any interiority to subvert the horrors she experiences.

While Schlöndorff's filmmaking is culpable in its reinforcement of patriarchal relations, the same problem infiltrates the mise-en-scène and tone. Light in the bedroom during the Ceremony, for example, is absent apart from two lit candles. In both the novel and the television series, however, the bedroom lights are on because, as Offred points out, "What's going on in this room ... is not exciting. It has nothing to do with passion or love or romance or any of those other notions we used to titillate ourselves with" (116–17). Since light in the novel is associated with male domination and surveillance, and darkness, by contrast, is the domain of the feminine, it is disappointing that Schlöndorff opts for a darkened bedroom for the Ceremony. After all, this is not a space where Kate nor Serena Joy revel in their femininity. Even more troubling is that without Kate's internal dialogue, viewers have very little opportunity to ally with her against the Commander and Gilead more generally. Ultimately, Schlöndorff's lack of consideration for these important aspects in the novel does nothing to challenge the ideologies that are so intensely examined and criticized in the novel.

Scenes between Kate and her fellow Handmaids are no better at amending the film's overarching problems. Where Atwood's Handmaids are justifiably suspicious of their surroundings, Schlöndorff's are far less timid and cautious. Even their costumes are more liberated, since his Handmaids do not wear the winged bonnets that limit visibility. As a result, they are depicted more casually talking with others and observing their surroundings. Kate herself is shown in scenes looking visibly horrified and angry without the self-consciousness or fear of being caught by an Eye or an informant. In this adaptation, there is little need for whispering or covert behaviour. As a result, the film undermines its own attempts to portray the horrors of Gilead. Consider the film's equivalent scene of Offred discovering Ofglen's affiliation with the resistance group. In the novel, Offred and Ofglen are wary of each other, since neither is sure of the other's loyalty to Gilead. This uncertainty is due, in part, to their inability to see each other's faces while walking side-by-side in uniform. It is not until their eyes meet in the reflection of the shop window that Ofglen reveals to Offred a secret network working against Gilead. When a pedestrian is violently abducted by the Eyes a moment later, it becomes clear just how risky and brave it is for these two women to conspire together. In Schlöndorff's adaptation, Ofglen confesses this sensitive information to Offred in a crowd of Handmaids and Wives at a party celebrating the birth of a new baby. As camera shots depict women merrily drinking and laughing, a live band plays soft jazz music. Indeed, the set design matches this joyous tone with what looks like a typical garden party. As Ofglen tells Offred that she is not alone and that "there are many of us," she makes no effort to lower her voice or act covertly. In response, Offred furrows her brow and looks obviously shocked by the news. Ofglen, more militant than afraid, instructs Offred to "watch [her] Commander. Study him." As she speaks, Aunts supervising the Handmaids walk by them. Yet, Ofglen makes no attempt to lower her voice or adjust her body language to protect their conversation. The opportunity for viewers to experience the tension of such transgressive behaviour is thus lost. This scene clearly lacks the ambiguity and risk that plagues Atwood's characters throughout the novel. For Ofglen to speak so plainly and freely to Offred is to disregard the gruesome circumstances of these women and the surveillance that keeps them from outright retaliating.

Schlöndorff's creative liberties not only impact the quality of the film, but also entirely miss the point of Atwood's dystopian work. As such, Gerrits determines that the film is not just an artistic failure but a political one too: "Schlöndorff's specific way of creatively responding to the challenges the novel poses … has ethical and political ramifications, and in Schlöndorff's case, these work to reinforce patriarchal structures" (218). While Kate does eventually kill the Commander in what seems more of a provoked attack than a calculated one, the narrative throughout the film has largely enforced a patriarchal position and, in fact, wins out with the film's final scene. Instead of Atwood's deliberately ambiguous ending for Offred, Schlöndorff's Kate is depicted safely hiding in a camper trailer in the mountains. She explains in the only voiceover in the film that she is waiting for the arrival of Nick, the Commander's former driver-turned-rebel fighter and her secret lover. Her round belly reveals that she is pregnant with his child. She narrates, "So, I wait. I wait for my baby to be born into a different world." Her dreamy stare into the distance suggests a regained hopefulness about her future. It evokes similar tableaus of women waiting at home while their soldier husbands are away at battle. Sadly, this ending misses the point of Atwood's novel entirely. Instead of a cautionary tale about the dangers of extremist political and patriarchal institutions, the film, as Peter Dickinson suggests, "reinscribes a patriarchal-heterosexual ideology based on the hegemony of reproductive sexuality – something that the novel seems to challenge at every turn" (17). By no means do these criticisms of Schlöndorff's film argue that his adaptation must remain faithful to Atwood's plot. Rather, they suggest that his adaptation weakens his own efforts to create a feminist dystopian film.

If Schlöndorff's film stands as an example of how *not* to film *The Handmaid's Tale,* the Hulu television series (also called *The Handmaid's Tale*) illustrates how the camera can be used to enhance the novel's themes and bond viewers with Offred. This chapter's exploration of the series will focus on only the first season, but it is worth noting that the series has since expanded *The Handmaid's Tale* universe in subsequent seasons. Television, after all, is an art form that is not bound to a feature-length time limit, as is the case for movies. For the sake of examining the gaze in the series, however, I focus on the first season, since it most closely aligns with Atwood's novel and the film adaptation's plot. In addition, examining certain camera shots in the television series serves to illustrate their superiority over their counterpart shots in Schlöndorff's film. Ultimately, the Hulu adaptation speaks to the legacy of *The Handmaid's Tale* and its continued relevance to modern audiences.

In the twenty-seven years between Schlöndorff's film and the Hulu series debut of *The Handmaid's Tale*, much has changed in film-making, technology, and storytelling. Media platforms like Netflix and Hulu have established themselves as places for films and series to exist outside of theatres and cable television. Advancements in technology also have made film-making more affordable and accessible. Moreover, television has expanded from the conventional episodic form into a more multifaceted and cinematic mode, attracting star-studded casts, larger budgets, and freer creative licenses. In his book *Complex TV*, Jason Mittel argues that the rise of this kind of television "employs a range of serial techniques, with the underlying assumption that a series is a cumulative narrative that builds over time, rather than resetting back to a steady-state equilibrium at the end of every episode" (18). With more flexibility and time to develop narrative, complex television adaptations have the same advantage as novels in their world-building. Episodes act as chapter equivalents in their story development and can dedicate time to details and alternate storylines without compromising the main plot. In the case of *The Handmaid's Tale*, the television series broadens its scope and includes other intertwining character storylines to show even more points of view than the novel or film offer. While Offred is still the central focus, the series' awareness of the audience, camera, and visible information on screen demonstrates how adaptations can not only successfully re-vision an original work, but also contribute new artistic elements that develop the story in profound ways.

In his video essay on the impacts of extreme close-ups and shallow depth-of-field filming in *The Handmaid's Tale* series, Evan Puschak thoughtfully explores how these techniques enhance the themes of oppression, surveillance, and uncertainty found in the novel. He argues that by keeping Offred's face tightly framed throughout the series, the film-makers help viewers develop an intimacy with her as she experiences her life under these oppressive conditions:

> The story of *The Handmaid's Tale* is really the story of the transition between America and Gilead told through the experience of Offred. To dial us into that horror, Reed [Morano] and [Colin] Watkinson [the film-makers] focus on the face. It is hard to remember a show that relied so much on one extreme close-up but Elisabeth Moss [who plays Offred] is definitely up to the task. With a camera near inches from her nose, the filmmakers combine a wide 28 mm Zeiss lens used only for these shots with a shallow depth-of-field to create an intense intimacy. With her bonnet on, it is almost as if we are under a blanket with the character. (Puschak)

Through its proximity, this camera technique shifts the audience from voyeurs to confidants. Viewers can see, in every muscle spasm in Offred's face and flicker of her eyes, the tension that she tries to suppress in order to maintain her safety. Although extremely subtle, these facial movements are powerful in connecting the audience to Offred's inner turmoil. David Roche argues more generally that "the series' poetics ... construct the face as a synecdoche of the subject, the mirror of the soul, a potential site of resistance to the order metonymized by the costume, and a topography our gazes explore" (131). In that sense, Offred's tightly framed face is vital to the progression of the series' narrative. Although Offred may not be able to speak up against her oppressors, close-ups offer a visual entry point into her interiority. Understanding what is beneath the surface of Offred's body language propels the tension and anticipation for what is to come. The series thus achieves the kind of intimacy between Offred and viewers that is so integral to Atwood's narrative.

Thanks to these film effects, the Hulu adaptation also aligns more closely with Atwood's novel in its depiction of the Ceremony. The scene begins with a tight camera shot of Offred's face. Her stare is blank and unfocused, as if she is a corpse. In slow motion, viewers watch her head move mechanically up and down on the bed. In the background, choir music can be heard with a voiceover by the Commander reciting biblical verses. The camera then cuts to Offred's perspective with a shot of her clothed body on the bed with her knees spread. Between them, the Commander's blurred torso is thrusting into her. A quick succession of cuts shows various items with a shallow depth-of-field. These shots force the audience to observe Offred's buttons, the Commander's watch, his tie, and Serena Joy's ring. There are also extreme close-ups of the Commander's furrowed brow and Serena Joy's equally vacant expression. In narrowing the visual information to these small details, the film-makers essentially mirror the novel's approach to the Ceremony. Recall that Atwood's Offred describes the room in order to compartmentalize the assault that is happening to her. She fixates on the details of the furniture in the room, including the colonial-style bed with a canopy that resembles a "sail of a ship" (115). In this scene, Offred is detached, and she describes (117). The film-makers of the television adaptation manage to depict a similar Offred with extreme close-ups of her blank face and hyper-focused shots of objects. The difference, however, is that viewers are seeing these details as Offred does. They are small but fixed in the blurry trauma occurring in and around Offred. Certainly, this scene is an impressive translation from text to film. It is one of many examples that demonstrate film's capacity to be nuanced and in tune with the inner thoughts of a character despite its reliance on visual storytelling.

The soft-focus aesthetic of the Ceremony scene is not the only instance in the series. In fact, shallow depth-of-field shots saturate most scenes in the first season. Despite its visual beauty, this type of filming is symbolic of the oppression that exists in Gilead. Reading, for example, is prohibited for most women, and consequently information available to Offred is restricted. The camera mimics this state because, as Puschak points out, "it literally narrows the visual information in focus" (Puschak). Just as Offred's perspective is limited, viewers are also confined to what little is sharply focused on onscreen. Although they remain spectators of Offred, viewers are thus aligned with her (and others who are oppressed) in their shared limited view of the world. In this way, the television series complicates the gaze using cinematic effects and camera shots that better serve the narrative than the omniscient and traditional placement of the camera in the 1990 film.

Soft-focused shots are particularly effective when Offred is engaging in risky behaviour. For example, when she discovers that Ofglen is not as she seems, the blurry world around them increases the tension between them, since the potential for danger is always present but not always clearly visible. As in the novel, Ofglen makes her first real attempt at revealing her motivations to Offred in the first episode after stopping in front of a shop window. Though Ofglen had already made subtle but detectable comments to Offred leading up to this moment, it is her ghostly reflection in the window that gives Offred and viewers a sense of the person she was before the rise of Gilead. To Offred, she says, "This used to be an ice cream place. They had the most amazing salted caramel. It was better than sex. Like, good sex" ("Offred"). As she speaks the last two lines, her eyes intensely focus on Offred in the window's reflection. That it is her reflection confessing this truth rather than Ofglen herself contributes to the ambiguous fear in the scene. Of course, the tension is already palpable since the women are risking their lives communicating in this way; however, also evident is Offred's (and the viewers') wariness of Ofglen's intentions. While the fuzzy outline of her translucent face is a visual metaphor for the person she once was, the same image lacks the stability of a direct gaze. Not being able to look Ofglen in the eyes makes it more difficult for Offred to discern her intentions. The camera echoes this problem in the next three cuts. First, the camera cuts to Offred's real face as she scrutinizes Ofglen's reflection. Since viewers already have access to Offred's internal thoughts and feelings, the shot of her face reinforces the stable link between viewers and Offred. Here, she says, "I always thought you were such a true believer." The camera then cuts back to Ofglen's reflection as she responds, "So were you. So frickin' pious." A quick cut back to Offred's real face once again reinforces the tension between their gazes. The camera cuts back again to Ofglen's face as she says, "They do that really well. Make us distrust each other." This response underlines the relentless uncertainty that colours the interactions between characters and the spectatorship of viewers. In fact, once the camera shows both the physical Offred and Ofglen, Offred bows her head and warns Ofglen that the Eyes are nearby. The ambiguity of Ofglen is now replaced with the very real threat of the task force responsible for surveilling its citizens.

At the end of the scene, Ofglen walks Offred to her home, where they speak between the bars of the tall gate that defines the Waterford property. As Offred is about to turn, Ofglen moves in closer and whispers, "There is an Eye in your house." The heavy black bars of the gate interrupting their faces suggest that both women are caged or in a kind of prison despite the soft, dappled sunlight in the background. This visual reinforces the oppression and paranoia that keeps these women from speaking and acting freely, even in a supposedly beautiful place. Still, the fact that their final exchange is face-to-face provides some stability in this tense moment. Offred looking into Ofglen's eyes works similarly to how viewers access Offred's face to discern her motivations. This intimacy is integral to their trusting one another, especially now that the tension has shifted to the question of the spy in the Waterford household. Ultimately, this scene demonstrates that storytelling can extend beyond dialogue. Together, camera techniques and mise-en-scène can be just as effective in supporting the plot and themes of the narrative.

With Offred at the narrative's centre, the television series also takes great pains to film from her perspective. Indeed, for cinematographer Colin Watkinson, the most important element in planning the shots for the series was to keep the point of view of the camera in line with Offred's. In an interview, he explained that "The title itself,

The Handmaid's Tale, meant that it was a point of view show, and that [the creators] would have to concentrate heavily on where the camera had to be to tell the story" (Wells-Lassagne 241). He also explains that in his conversations with director Reed Morano, he learned that they used lighting, symmetry, and aerial shots to help create the oppression that Offred feels. The first scene of the series, for example, is an aerial shot of a wintery forest. Beneath the stark branches, the small figures of June (soon to be renamed Offred) and her daughter are running to escape from military agents looking for them. The giant trees, by comparison, loom over them menacingly. It is a powerful visual that echoes their terror and powerlessness against Gilead. Of these shots, Watkinson said, "Looking down on this character, [the viewer knows] that she [is] trapped in this world.... So the overhead shot is not her perspective, but it's her perspective of her perspective" (Wells-Lassagne 241). His explanation points out that the camera does not necessarily have to be from Offred's perspective in a literal sense in order to keep the film's point of view as her own. In fact, as already discussed in the examination of her face, Offred is regularly the object of the viewer's gaze throughout the series, but the series' consideration of her viewpoint – even when it is not technically what she can see – keeps the camera from objectifying her in the same way that Kate is in the 1990 film. Whereas Schlöndorff's film seems to reinforce patriarchal surveillance, the series' camera shots are designed to create intimacy between viewers and Offred/June as well as evoke the terror of her situation in Gilead.

One striking difference between the novel and its filmed adaptations is Offred's rebellion. In Atwood's tale, Offred is often passive and compliant in her role as a Handmaid. When reflecting on the protests that were occurring in the United States before Gilead's takeover, she says, "I didn't go on any of the marches. Luke [her husband] said it would be futile and I had to think about them, my family, him and her" (226). Later as a Handmaid, Offred sometimes lacks the grit needed to actively rebel against Gilead. In one instance, Ofglen asks Offred to spy on the Commander to gain valuable information for the resistance group. Instead of agreeing to help, however, Offred refuses out of fear of being caught. To herself, she narrates, "I scarcely take the trouble to sound regretful, so lazy have I become" (338). Of course, Offred's fear and compliancy are understandable given the risk to her life. But in her inertia, she traps the readers just as she is trapped in Gilead. In novel format, this immobility is acceptable because its impact on the reader is similar to how Gilead confines Offred. In a visual format, however, the need for action to propel the narrative is imperative. Consequently, both the film and the television series make their protagonists bolder in their agencies.

While the 1990 film uses no voiceover until its concluding scene, in the television series voiceover is used repeatedly to illustrate the discrepancy between Offred's submissive exterior and her rebellious interior. Early in the series, this discontinuity between Offred's physical expressions and her feelings builds a conspiratorial rapport between Offred and viewers. When Offred introduces Nick in the series, for example, she explains that he is the Commander's driver and that he lives over the garage. Due to his "low status," she critically remarks, "he hasn't even been issued a woman" ("Offred"). Meanwhile, the camera shows Offred, eyes averted and head down in her winged cap and red uniform. She appears shy and humble. The camera then cuts to Nick who asks if she is going shopping. Her voiceover sarcastically responds, "No, Nick. I'm going to knock back a few at the Oyster House Bar. You wanna come along?" ("Offred"). It is one of the rare instances of humour in the series, one that demonstrates the significant clash of Offred/June's identities. To his face, she quietly responds with a "yes" before making her way down the driveway. In relation to the gaze, these differences connect the audience with Offred rather than objectifying her, since viewers are the only ones who are privy to her interiority – her true self.

By contrast, audiences must rely on and interpret Kate's physical cues alone for the majority of the 1990 film. It is only in the last scene when Kate is isolated in her hideout that Schlöndorff is forced to use voiceover, since there is no one for Kate to speak to. In this scene, however, voiceover is not used to reveal the complexity of her character. Rather, it is used to reinscribe the status quo and provide a conventional Hollywood ending. To achieve this happy ending without the audience having access to Kate's interiority for most of the film, Schlöndorff overcompensates by having Kate slash the Commander's throat before escaping with the help of Nick. It is a bold move and one that gives Kate some power back. Still, Gerrits criticizes the film's climax, noting that "Kate's assault appears less a determinate act by a resistance fighter than a provoked response of woman in need of a patriarch's protection but desperate enough to take revenge when he avoids responsibility for having put her life at risk" (219). The structure of the last act of the film may be more action-packed, but it fails to give Kate the self-empowerment and agency that June possesses in the television series. There is some irony in the fact that June ultimately has more subversive defiance than Kate, a murderer by the end of the film. However, the conspiratorial nature of the series' voiceover bonds June and the audience together in an act of disobedience that inevitably changes how viewers see her and relate to her.

While I have argued that the television adaptation of *The Handmaid's Tale* is more successful in its handling of the text's challenges than the film adaptation, together these adaptations attempt to re-envision Atwood's narrative through a new perspective and situate it in the political and creative contexts of their times. As Hutcheon points out, adaptations create "a kind of dialogue between the society in which the works, both the adapted text and adaptation, are produced and that in which they are received, and both are in dialogue with the works themselves" (*Theory* 149). It is perhaps because of these connections that *The Handmaid's Tale* remains so pertinent today. Certainly, these works extend the life of the story and expand upon its patchwork quilt of meanings. The television series especially utilizes the tools of its media to honour the themes in Atwood's novel while cultivating new ways of understanding Offred and her experiences. In particular, the film-makers' considerations about camera placement and cinematic effects in the series demonstrate the feminist possibilities of filming while avoiding the perpetuation of the male gaze. Unlike in Schlöndorff's film, the television series' approach to re-visioning Atwood's story dares to use the camera as a co-conspirator with Offred rather than the eye that fixes her in her place. This shift of the gaze comes, in part, from the television creators' understanding of the society in which this series was produced. As women's reproductive rights become increasingly tenuous and political extremism grows in North America, the threat of a patriarchal theocracy does not seem so farfetched. Yet, as adaptations prove, there is the opportunity to re-vision our future and refuse, as Rich says, "the self-destructiveness of male-dominated society" (35). This re-visioning is applicable to *The Handmaid's Tale* and it will certainly be relevant as the contemporary world navigates these challenging political times.

NOTES

1 Critics such as D.N. Rodowick and Gaylyn Studlar have challenged aspects of Mulvey's argument by pointing out that her "deterministic, polarized model leads to a crucial 'blind spot' in her theory of visual pleasure" (Studlar 213). Specifically, Mulvey avoids confronting the complexities of gender in relation to subject-object choices since "the place of maleness is discussed as both the subject and the object of the gaze (though only in a restricted fashion) and femaleness is discussed only as an object structuring the male look according to its active (voyeuristic) and passive (fetishistic)

forms" (Rodowick 11–12). *The Handmaid's Tale* demonstrates the difficulties with Mulvey's limited model, since Offred is both the gaze's object and a voyeur herself – sometimes simultaneously.

2 Mabiana Camargo's examination of the ways space shapes the subjectivity, identity, and safety of women in her chapter "Gender Oppression through Enclosed Spaces in Margaret Atwood's *MaddAddam* Trilogy" is relevant here. In particular, Camargo's discussion of the commodification of bodies through the character of Ren, a sex worker who dances at the Scales and Tails nightclub, demonstrates that "looking the part" circumscribes women as objects for male consumption while subversively affording women the ability to take in information to which they would otherwise have little access. Ren literally chameleons herself, wearing costumes made of shiny scales for the pleasure of men; in exchange, she is given access to society's most powerful figures. Furthermore, she can watch the news on television, converse with other women, and ultimately survive a pandemic outbreak (296). Like Offred, Ren suffers from the rampant misogyny in her society, but within the constraints of space and the circumscription of femininity, both women are freer than others to look and obtain information otherwise denied to them. This arrangement is critical to their survival.

WORKS CITED

Atwood, Margaret. *The Handmaid's Tale*. 1985. Seal Books, 1998.

Camargo, Mabiana. "Gender Oppression through Enclosed Spaces in Margaret Atwood's *MaddAddam* Trilogy." *ReVisions: Speculating in Literature and Film in Canada*, edited by Wendy Roy, U of Toronto Press, 2025, pp. 281–301.

Cardwell, Sarah. *Adaptation Revisited: Television and the Classic Novel*. Manchester UP, 2002.

Cooper, Pamela. "Sexual Surveillance and Medical Authority in Two Versions of *The Handmaid's Tale*." *The Journal of Popular Culture*, vol. 28, no. 4, 1995, pp. 49–66.

Dickinson, Peter. "Introduction: Reading Movies." *Essays on Canadian Writing*, no. 76, 2002, pp. 1–45.

Gerrits, Jeroen. "From Episodic Novel to Serial TV: *The Handmaid's Tale*, Adaptation and Politics." *Open Philosophy*, vol. 5, no. 1, 2022, pp. 209–30.

Hutcheon, Linda. "Adapting (to) Atwood." Wells-Lassagne and McMahon, pp. 251–61.

– *A Theory of Adaptation*. Routledge, 2006.

Miller, Bruce, creator. *The Handmaid's Tale*. Hulu Originals, 2017.

Mittel, Jason. *Complex TV: The Poetics of Contemporary Television Storytelling*. New York UP, 2015.

Mulvey, Laura. *Visual Pleasure and Narrative Cinema*. Indiana UP, 1989.

"Offred." *The Handmaid's Tale*. Season 1, episode 1, Hulu Originals, 27 Apr. 2017.

Puschak, Evan. "One Reason *The Handmaid's Tale* Won Emmys Best Drama." *YouTube*, uploaded by Nerdwriter1, 31 Aug. 2017, https://www.youtube.com/watch?v=cY4aCnfrqss.

Reesman, Jeanne. "Dark Knowledge in *The Handmaid's Tale*." *The CEA Critic*, vol. 53, no. 3, 1991, pp. 302–18, https://doi.org/10.1353/cea.2018.0040.

Rich, Adrienne. *On Lies, Secrets, and Silence: Selected Prose 1966–1978*. W.W. Norton & Company, 1979.

Roche, David. "Shallow Focus Composition and the Poetics of Blur in *The Handmaid's Tale* (Hulu 2017-)." Wells-Lassagne and McMahon, pp. 127–41.

Rodowick, D.N. *The Difficulty of Difference*. Routledge, 1991.

Schlöndorff, Volker, director. *The Handmaid's Tale*. Cinecom Entertainment Group, 1990.

Studlar, Gaylyn. "Masochism and the Perverse Pleasures of the Cinema." *Feminism & Film*, edited by E. Ann Kaplan, Oxford UP, 2000, pp. 203–25.

Wells-Lassagne, Shannon. "Filming *The Handmaid's Tale*." Wells-Lassagne and McMahon, pp. 239–49.

Wells-Lassagne, Shannon, and Fiona McMahon, editors. *Adapting Margaret Atwood:* The Handmaid's Tale *and Beyond*. Palgrave MacMillan, 2021.

"I'm Not Your Personal Manic Pixie Assassin": Reading *Killjoys*' Tough Woman through an *Alien* Lens

HEATHER SNELL

A romping Canadian space opera that wears its parodic orientation on its sleeve, Michelle Lovretta's 2015–19 television series *Killjoys* hilariously sends up sexist science-fiction tropes of the past. Among these tropes are those involving "tough" women, toughness being, of course, a malleable characteristic since what defines it varies over time. Part of what the show implicitly explores is how tough women have been represented in North American entertainment media since the release of Ridley Scott's *Alien*, whose central heroine inspired Lovretta's creation of killjoy Dutch, a.k.a. Yala Yardeen (performed by Hannah John-Kamen). Within the fictional world of the series, killjoys are not, as their name might suggest, feminists, but rather, bounty hunters. The show focuses on a trio of killjoys consisting of the central action heroine, Dutch, and the two brothers with whom she teams up: Johnny Jaqobis (Aaron Ashmore) and D'avin Jaqobis (Luke Macfarlane). As with *Alien*'s Lieutenant Ellen Ripley (Sigourney Weaver), Dutch battles a faceless, unnamed Company that variously symbolizes colonialist, imperialist, capitalist, and racist political forces. Beyond the obvious connections between Dutch and Ripley and the dystopias in which their heroism is set, *Killjoys* fans familiar with the entire *Alien* franchise are likely to catch more subtle references. These references offer rich sites of analysis because they register shifts in how tough women have been portrayed in North American entertainment media over the course of the four decades that separate *Killjoys* from *Alien*.

Many of the tough action heroines that have emerged throughout this period are, at least in part, indebted to the *Alien* films, the first of which, released in 1979, introduced a new model of white feminine toughness and resilience to American audiences.[1] Cool-headed and determined to survive, Ripley and her cat are the sole survivors of an extraterrestrial attack. With the exception of the final scene, in which she is depicted in skimpy underwear, she is the embodiment of a toughness free of the sexy girlishness that increasingly came to define the action heroines of the 1990s and 2000s. Ripley helped to pave the way for these later action heroines, including *The Terminator*'s Sarah Connor (Linda Hamilton) in 1984, who becomes, borrowing Yvonne Tasker's terminology, "muscular" over the course of the film's sequels; Sarah Michelle Gellar in *Buffy the Vampire Slayer*, created by Joss Whedon in 1997; Michelle Rodriguez in her various "tough woman" roles beginning in 2000, notably in *Girlfight* (2000) and the *Fast & Furious* series (2001–23); and Zoe Saldana in the 2011 film *Colombiana.* As these examples suggest, action heroines of colour have become more common in entertainment media; at the same time, as discussed later in this chapter, they tend to be included in a way that politically neutralizes any critique of systemic racism.

Killjoys pays parodic homage not just to Ripley but also to many of the iconic action heroines who have graced the screens of movie theatres since her debut. Registering a popular move towards irony and pastiche, *Killjoys'* Dutch is shamelessly brash and witty, sometimes seeming to channel Buffy more than the quietly resilient Ripley. Yet she also recalls Pam Grier's performance of toughness in Jack Hill's 1974 blaxploitation film *Foxy Brown,* in that in *Killjoys,* John-Kamen's Nigerian heritage is accentuated in the character she plays through lighting and hair styling. Rodriguez's performances of toughness are likewise echoed in Dutch's speech style and ability to physically fend off attackers. While Dutch is a fully fleshed-out character with her own fears, anxieties, and desires, she performs multiple versions of toughness, oftentimes with a large dose of irony. When interpreted within the context of major shifts in feminist discourse, she can be described as post-feminist in her simultaneous sexual objectification and subjectivization. In its representation of the central heroine, and in its sexual suggestiveness, *Killjoys* flirts frequently with "porno chic," a mode Rosalind Gill associates with a post-feminist sensibility (151). Following Jason Morgan, however, the series also flirts with "perversion chic" in its predilection for the queer underclass. One of the most remarkable departures from *Alien,* one of *Killjoys'* most pointed references, is Dutch's reliance on queer community. Whereas the price of Ripley's toughness is isolation, Dutch is rewarded with the love and support of characters who are in some way misaligned with the status quo. Whether or not *Killjoys'* celebration of queer community defines its Canadianness is a matter of debate, but it does mark a significant shift from the characterization of the action heroine as hopelessly masculine and, therefore, unrecuperable as a feminine figure.

In what follows, I briefly rehearse the feminist debates sparked by the *Alien* franchise before turning to *Killjoys* as exemplary of a pop-culture text that pays homage to and mocks its precursors and, in so doing, advances a critique of the sexist tropes that have tended to shape representations of tough women. While there is nothing purely oppositional about the series – it inevitably celebrates much of what it seems to want to critique, and in arguably post-feminist fashion – through analysis of its relationship with *Alien*, I argue that it draws attention to the continued contestability of the action heroine in an era that heralds new post-feminist sensibilities.[2]

The *Alien* Debates

To date, *Killjoys* has received little critical attention despite its parodic engagement with representations of tough women in American pop culture. In contrast, the *Alien* franchise has sparked the publication of at least fifteen scholarly essays and book chapters as well as a monograph. The films that make up the series describe human encounters with a hostile xenomorph whose appearance has sparked numerous debates about monstrous femininity and the politics of gendered representation. Not surprisingly, many critics side with or against Laura Mulvey's conception of the male gaze in attempts to grapple with the films.[3] In his analysis of the franchise, Stephen Scobie remarks that "From the start ... the most salient line of approach to the *Alien* films has been to explore the questions they raise about feminism and about the presentation of feminism in contemporary culture" (81). Pamela Church Gibson likewise argues that the "academic study of the Alien saga is indicative of the divisions and fissures within the discipline of film theory" (40). The first film marked the end of a decade of psychoanalytic theoretical fervour, and feminist attention to the body found a rich home in the series' attention to corporeal horror and unsettling images of embodiment. These images are made even more unsettling through their apparent upendings of gender norms (41).

Whether or not the films' representations of gender count as feminist has divided scholars. Even so, Ripley has become an icon of feminine toughness. She embodies strength without the typical trappings of femininity: her uniform resembles that of the other crew members on the spaceship Nostromo, the only differentiating mark being the "Lt. Ripley" badge on the left breast. Unlike the tight-fitting uniforms of *Star Trek: The Original Series* (1966–9), and the even tighter uniforms that would come to characterize *Star Trek: The Next Generation* (1987–94), Ripley's uniform is baggy and unflattering but proves ideal for battling the horrific alien xenomorph that births itself out of the chief engineer's chest after the crew answers a distress call emanating from the planet LV–426. The only departure from this style of representation occurs in the final scene of the film, when Ripley strips down to her underwear in preparation for a long hibernation, only to discover that the xenomorph has somehow managed to sneak on board her escape pod. This scene has generated considerable debate among the film's critics and framed many interpretations of its three sequels. The core argument across analyses by Barbara Creed, Ros Jennings, and Sherrie A. Inness is that it is anti-feminist in its compensatory function: the scene provides a spectacle of normative femininity in the wake of what one could describe as a transgressive display of heroism as Ripley succeeds where her crew members, plunged one by one into the depths of despair and hysteria, fail. The xenomorph itself is crucial to this reading, for it symbolizes what Creed calls an object of "the archaic mother," a "fetishized phallus" that castrates and must be repressed in accordance with the patriarchal logic of the film: "Compared to the horrific sight of the alien as fetish object of the monstrous archaic mother, Ripley's body is pleasurable and reassuring to look at" (23). Jennings amplifies this negative reading of the scene by comparing it to pornography, arguing that the alien's design, the cinematography, and Ripley's performance sexualize what should be a moment of terror (161). Inness remarks that the scene's sexualization of Ripley "does a great deal to limit the threat to gender norms posed by her tough persona" (107). Even though these three critics take different theoretical approaches to *Alien*, they agree that the final scene is, if not destructive of the film's feminist potential, troubling in its superfluity.

Less psychoanalytically informed critical engagements highlight the importance of moving away from rigid binary oppositions and the value of genres such as action, science fiction (SF), crime, and horror as venues where dominant gender norms can be exposed and subsequently critiqued. In her analysis of the *Dirty Harriet* films and *Blue Steel*, Cora Kaplan points out that "Some analysts even suggest that it is in these hybrid genres where mass market film comes closest to producing a progressive film text on gender, for it is when fantastic narratives exaggerate and make strange the ordinary everyday misery of sexual difference that its bizarre contours are most closely rendered" (54). Tasker coined the term "musculinity" in her influential 1993 book *Spectacular Bodies: Gender, Genre, and the Action Cinema* as a means of dissociating strength and muscularity from men. Referencing muscular action heroines such as *Blue Steel*'s Megan Turner (Jamie

Lee Curtis) and *Terminator*'s Sarah Connor (Hamilton), she argues that the seemingly contradictory combination of qualities traditionally associated with men and women in the same figure reinforces and challenges dominant gender norms. Elizabeth Hills similarly refuses the dismissal of "phallicized" action heroines in some feminist media criticism, insisting, as with Kaplan and Tasker, that they invite us to question essentialist views of sexual difference (38–9). In rejecting a dominant psychoanalytic schema in which women are positioned negatively as either figurative males or mere objects of the male gaze, she finds room in *Alien* for a less pessimistic reading of the film's action heroine. Drawing on Gilles Deleuze and Rosi Braidotti, she makes a case for Ripley as a "new active-heroine machine," which, by means of creative reassembly of typically gendered traits, functions within "the productive middle space between binaries" (46). Even though the *Alien* films were directed by different men and (with the exception of Weaver) featured different actors, they are remarkably consistent in their refusal to establish clear lines between heroes and villains and, correlatively, between male and female characters. It is within this grey area that the Ripley of all four films can be read, not necessarily as a feminist heroine, but as one who invites a rethinking of dominant gender norms.[4]

In *Tough Girls: Women Warriors and Wonder Women in Popular Culture*, Inness argues that "In a culture where women are often considered the 'natural' victims of men, tough women rewrite the script" (8). In so doing, they unsettle the logic that some traits properly belong to men and others to women (21). Jeffrey Brown notes that contradictory depictions of the action heroine as active subject and fetishized object signal a "double bind" (7). At the same time, he echoes Kaplan, Tasker, Hills, and Inness in his insistence that they blur the difference between "what we consider masculine and feminine, of desirable beauty and threatening sexuality, of subjectivity and objectivity, of powerful and powerless" (10), thereby providing rich opportunities for problematizing the reduction of the action heroine to mere fetish. He argues that action heroines are "contestable figures" (18). It is, at least in part, this contestability that makes heroines such as Ripley so easily dismissed as sexist. The blurring of boundaries can make the designation of a cultural text as feminist frustratingly difficult. In keeping with their status as action heroines, the plethora of tough and often muscular women who have featured in popular entertainment media since the 1970s similarly troubles boundaries and, by extension, the essentialism on which dismissals of action heroines as phallicized depend.

Enter *Killjoys*

Killjoys makes fun of and reproduces muscular-women precursors, creating a space for rethinking the action heroine in the twenty-first century. The sheer number of heroines in the series indicates an interest in examining the figure. In addition to Dutch, the series features several minor characters whose power resides in their knowledge, quick thinking, and, in some cases, prosthetic enhancement. Such enhancement sometimes appears to compromise the series, making it appear retrosexist, a quality that aligns it with post-feminism: both overturn sexist tropes while leaving intact the structures that activate them. In her examination of racialized dolls, Sarah Banet-Weiser points out that post-feminist gender identity is, for this reason, a "slippery category" (202). Retrosexism adds the element of nostalgia by involving imagery "where sexism operates freely within the frame of a period style" (Williamson). *Killjoys* could, perhaps rather ungenerously, be interpreted as "having it both ways," reproducing sexisms of the past while also pretending to subvert them. Gill points out that this strategy is common in post-feminist media culture (159). The willingness of the series to reproduce, however ironically, exploitative sexist tropes such as nuns with guns and women with machine guns for arms makes it vulnerable to charges of retrosexism.[5] The show's multiplication of minor, prosthetically enhanced female characters is hardly a clear and visible sign of a critical orientation, especially when one considers the politics of irony. The problem is that reading the show as parody requires familiarity with a vast intertext. As Linda Hutcheon points out, irony relies on insider knowledge and interpretive savvy (36). Where the show might be read as most feminist is in its casting of John-Kamen, but even this could be interpreted as exploitative. Banet-Weiser explains that "representations of race and gender work as a kind of cultural capital, in terms of which it increases the political and social clout of a network to be able to claim that it is 'diverse'" (203).

In his examination of the young-adult climate fiction of Monica Hughes in this volume, William Thompson points to the concurrent trend to spotlight whiteness in the literary industry, arguing that "white, adolescent girls have dominated the young adult dystopia and climate change novel, which thus far has framed the young adult response to political tyranny and environmental devastation in terms of white, able-bodied adolescent girldom" (148). Although Banet-Weiser and Thompson make these statements in the context of children's television and literature respectively, they apply to *Killjoys*, especially when one considers the show's interest in climate catastrophe and the tyrannical oppression of young people. In privileging an empowered Black girlish femininity, *Killjoys* certainly deviates from the trend Thompson identifies, and one could argue that the series' casting of bionic artist Viktoria Modesta alongside other actors with actual body modifications is a welcome change in an entertainment industry that has historically excluded people with disabilities. Yet these kinds of gestures also raise questions about the extent to which creators are willing to dismantle systemic racism and ableism in the industry.

In his discussion of racial diversification in action films featuring female leads, Jeffrey Brown points out that modern Hollywood strategically privileges mixed-race actors precisely as a means of avoiding substantive attempts to dismantle systemic racism in the industry: "By featuring actresses of mixed racial identities as heroines, the action genre is able to both utilize ethnic stereotypes about women and to sidestep other racial issues, such as discrimination or miscegenation" (80). Incorporating sexy action heroines in teams made up of men is likewise standard Hollywood practice. "Placing female characters on male-dominated teams, or partnering them with a male colleague," Brown asserts, "is a common strategy for including women but also tempering any threat they may pose to the ideal of manly heroism" (54–5). *Killjoys* reproduces this sexy-woman-on-an-all-male-team strategy, with Dutch leading the two men who help to make up their bounty-hunting trio. The show even goes so far as to develop a romantic subplot between Dutch and D'Avin, their very names signalling the inevitability of their coupling.

Killjoys' excessive multiplication of popular types and blurring of the hero/villain boundary nevertheless articulates a willingness on the part of the series and its performers to think beyond rigid binary oppositions. It establishes a queer orientation, moreover, in its inclusion of LGBTQ2S+ characters and embrace of misfits who dare to imagine a future that departs radically from a profoundly dystopian present structured by a brutal, heteronormative, and heavily racialized interplanetary capitalist system. The main conflict in *Killjoys* is deeply rooted in a form of advanced capitalism that recalls some of the most dystopian moments in American history. Plantation slavery in one place keeps wages down in another, and there are no social safety nets. Not surprisingly, riots and skirmishes with police are common. Although Black people and people of colour exist among the nine aristocratic families ("the Nine") that control the Company, poverty is racialized, with those of the darkest hue barely subsisting at the bottom of the social hierarchy. The show encourages viewers to root for the underclass and, with the exception of Delle Sayah Kendry (Mayko Nguyen) – a prominent member of the Nine – and Aneela, Dutch's antagonist and double also played by John-Kamen, situates its most interesting characters in the working-class district of Old Town on the moon of Westerley. As if to ward off charges of establishing a rigid political binary opposition, even the long-standing struggle between working-class people on Westerley and the Company – a dialectic that forms the backdrop for the action – is challenged early in the first season as *Killjoys* begins to unravel its complicated tapestry of power relations. The multiple settings, enabled by the action occurring in a fictional planetary system dubbed "the Quad," in turn help to animate the show's critical subtext. As the killjoys move from gritty urban environs to forests, deserts, and derelict labs, there are plenty of opportunities to parody tired generic tropes.

The series' parodic orientation most signals its Canadianness, if this label can be reasonably attached to any cultural text. While interpreting entertainment media within a national frame risks homogenization, Jason Morgan defends his application of the Canadian label by arguing that one way of avoiding homogenization is to read the nation as quintessentially queer. He draws on Eve Kosofsky Sedgwick to interpret "queer" as a word that "denotes both inclusiveness and transgression" (216). A queer reading of the nation is one that deftly sidesteps binary thinking and the attendant privileging of one term in the binary, in this case men and heteronormativity. Queer, moreover, need not be restricted to sex, gender, and sexuality; rather, "it is an *inclusive* category," well positioned to offer insight into any number of cultural, political, and social phenomena (Morgan 217). When applied to the nation, "queer theorizing speaks to the fundamental contradictions (the innate 'queerness') in the formation of any community" (217). To a large extent, the nation finds sameness where there is only difference; rather than embracing this difference, however, advocates of nationalism downplay it, reinforcing dominant norms and values in the process. To read the nation as queer is to expose and subsequently refuse this homogenizing operation.

In its celebration of misfits and its scathing critique of an interplanetary capitalist system that treats people like machines from which labour can be extracted, *Killjoys* is proudly queer. Announcing itself as such, it places the Royale bar, owned by the flamboyant, gender-queer Pree (Thom Allison), at the centre of the action. Pree presides over the primary watering hole for the series' characters when the going gets tough and they need to take refuge among others who share their experience of oppression at the hands of the Company. In episode 8 of the first season, entitled "Come the Rain," he makes this explicit by inviting everyone into the Royale during an acid-rain storm, where "safe haven" and "cold beer" are generously on offer. He gradually becomes the community builder capable of holding the killjoys together when they form "Team Awesome Force." The leadership role he adopts makes sense when his backstory is revealed: he is a former warlord whose home world embraced same-sex relations. The reversal of expectations around Pree – who ever heard of an openly gay warlord and an openly gay world of warlords? – provides the stuff of comedy and invites viewers to side with communities where queerness is accepted as normal. Community itself is defined as queer, since it is the oppressed workers on Westerley who meet at the Royale who most embody it. Any semblance of community elsewhere is exactly that, a semblance and not the real thing, for real community requires a transcendence of transactional relationships. Equality remains an impossible-to-reach ideal within the community over which Pree presides, and conflict is frequent, but it is utopian in contrast with the brutal regime of the Company. Unlike the zombified dancers of Utopia – a black-market node and never-ending electronic dance party suspended in interplanetary space – the patrons of the Royale socialize with one another. The central killjoy characters, Dutch, Johnny, and D'Avin, refuse to work with the Company, preferring instead to align themselves with the Reclamation Apprehension Coalition (R.A.C.), which they perceive to be at odds with the Company. Unfortunately, this organization is revealed to be a subsidiary of the Company. Not easily deterred from their mission to save their interplanetary system from a hostile extraterrestrial force that threatens the entire Quad, the killjoys and Team Awesome Force transform the R.A.C. into a capitalist-busting, queer organization.

Morgan suggests that mainstream English-Canadian film tends to be queer, and that this queerness is often manifest in a privileging of marginality in form and content; these elements are "used to tell stories that are strikingly different from most of those told by Hollywood" (211). Although *Killjoys* is a TV series that departs from the auteur films often cited as evidence for a Canadian film industry that spotlights the margins, it embodies what some commentators have dubbed *perversion chic*. Moving beyond the reductive definitions of perversion chic offered by casual observers of anglophone Canada's "dark movies, movies that are counter-Hollywood and anti-television" (Robert Lantos, qtd. in Morgan 211), Morgan makes a case for perversion chic as a queer subgenre. Films that might be collected under this umbrella, he argues, "invoke a *queer nationalism* that emphasizes the subversion of dominant models of belonging by positioning intersection and difference as the foundations of community" (212). *Killjoys* could be included among cultural texts in Canada that invoke a queer nationalism not simply because of its inclusion of LGBTQ2S+ characters but in its reimagining of the nation as queer. The closest thing to a nation, the moon of Westerley, is home to rich, diverse cultural communities despite its initial development as a hub of labour extraction for the Company. Pree demonstrates the laxity of norms in spaces such as Westerley's bar by donning elaborate, gender-bending outfits and engaging in flamboyant performances. While Pree could be interpreted merely as an attempt to capitalize on the trendiness of "queer chic" on the part of the show's producers, his previous life as a warlord in a community where queer love is the norm helps to distance him from the stereotype of the "queen."[6]

The big bad villain of the series – the Lady (Alannah Bale) – likewise plays with performances of identity, but in stark contrast to Pree's stylish dictatorship and management of the Royale, her costumes are literally Westerlyns. Rather than helping to build a collective committed to social justice, she plans on eliminating Westerlyns to make way for her clones. By multiplying herself, she mocks the community Westerlyns hold dear with an extreme form of narcissistic hyper-individualism. *Killjoys'* critical engagement with tired American sexist tropes takes place in this context, inviting a rethinking of the place of Canadian TV in a perversely chic entertainment universe. As a series that crosses the Canada-US border in its production – it was produced by the Canada-based Temple Street Productions in association with Space and the US-based Syfy – *Killjoys* also represents a kinship of sorts with US entertainment media, from which, and against which, so much entertainment in Canada positions itself.

Killjoys and the *Alien* Franchise: A Dialogue

Killjoys' implicit dialogue with the *Alien* franchise flirts with this transnational entanglement, particularly in relation to representations of tough women in popular culture. The first reference to the *Alien* films is a subtle yet revealing one. Near the end of episode 8 of season 1, entitled "Come the Rain," Johnny quips, "In the past ten days, I've been attacked by face-hugging biotech, stabbed by my brother, had major surgery, helped perform major surgery, been beaten, bullied and burned. I am done … fixing things." Crucially for a reading of this scene against *Alien*, two of the traumas Johnny describes involve penetration, which tends (inaccurately, many would argue) to be associated with passivity. Given the ubiquity of critical commentary about the xenomorph's mode of reproduction in the *Alien* movies – the films' facehuggers attach themselves to human hosts and insert long "fingers" down their throats – Johnny's susceptibility to penetration is significant. Part of what makes the *Alien* xenomorph so threatening is her embodiment of disparate gendered qualities: the initial discovery of her eggs occurs shortly after the Nostromo crew makes their way down a long, dark tunnel reminiscent of a vagina, but she reproduces through proxies in the form of facehuggers resembling hands yet suggestive of penises. The subjection of male characters to such beings is subversive of the sex/gender binary, because facehuggers transform men into passive receptacles. In so doing, they challenge long-standing associations of masculinity with activity. Much of the feminist purchase of *Alien* lies in this creative handling of the xenomorph's reproduction.

Even though the biotech to which Johnny subjects himself in episode 7 enters the back of his neck rather than his mouth, his status as receptacle warrants the *Alien* reference. On a symbolic level, the biotech device, similarly equipped with a long, penetrative appendage, is reminiscent of the facehugger's finger-like appearance, which, as Ximena Gallardo C. and Jason Smith suggest, evokes fellatio (37). Envisioned as a hand holding Johnny down from behind, the biotech can be interpreted as a symbolic rape that connects in troubling ways with the recent post-coital assault of Dutch by Johnny's brother, D'avin, and his subsequent stabbing of Johnny (the main plot events of the preceding episode). Far from manifesting bad character, D'Avin's assault of Dutch – with whom he has recently coupled up – is motivated by a chip that had been implanted in his head during his former life as a soldier and which is controlled by a sinister doctor. This first reference to the *Alien* franchise in *Killjoys*, therefore, occurs in the context of D'avin, Dutch, and Johnny learning how to work as a team again, a resolution that requires trust. The scene featuring Johnny complaining about the violence to which he has been subjected is intercut with a not-quite-consensual attempt at reconciliation between Dutch and D'Avin (Johnny has manipulated them into inhabiting the same spaceship, the only way out of which is to talk about the traumatic event that ruptured their relationship). That D'avin's assault of Dutch could qualify as a sexual one makes Johnny's face-hugging biotech quip even more noteworthy: Dutch and Johnny have been violated by D'avin's betrayal, but Dutch's sexual relationship with D'avin makes his assault seem even more invasive. While, technically, D'Avin does not rape Dutch, the timing of his assault makes it feel like rape. Johnny's quip about face-hugging biotech not only occurs in the episode in which Dutch struggles to trust D'Avin again, but it also expresses the challenges of forgiveness. That D'Avin has been bio-hacked further signals the ongoing struggle all three characters undergo in a world where technology threatens to take away agency. At the same time, *Killjoys* is careful to show that Dutch's violation is more troubling than Johnny's in its reflection of sexist violence in North America. The only thing that saves D'Avin as a heroic character is the element of mind control. While male characters blur gendered lines as frequently as female ones, conveying the message that gender is less important than other traits in determining character, the world of *Killjoys* is still a sexist one. If it was not, the queer performances of Pree and Johnny's almost boastful enumeration of his subjection to various forms of violence could not be seen as comically anomalous within the series' diegesis.

Killjoys' overall queerness, furthermore, means that there is much less anxiety about the prospect of men being impregnated than there is in the *Alien* movies. Unlike in *Alien*, in which facehuggers conjure up stereotypical male fears about female power, Johnny's tentacular experience prompts instead fears and anxieties around the lack of privacy and the ever-present threat of being hacked in an era of social media, enhanced artificial intelligence, and virtual, often pseudo, community. The Lady amplifies technology's threat to agency and privacy when she bio-hacks Westerlyns, effectively brainwashing them to prepare the moon for her clone-hatchlings; tellingly, she does this by catapulting them into simulated realities ostensibly designed to make them feel as though they have reached utopia.

The second reference to the *Alien* franchise is much less subtle yet far more revealing about the gap between Ripley and Dutch. In episode 2 of season 5, entitled "Blame It on the Rain," Dutch echoes Ripley's assault on the xenomorph's eggs in *Aliens* and *Alien Resurrection* by turning a flamethrower on the Lady's hatchlings. While she does not do so with quite the same vengeful fervour as Ripley in *Aliens*, the assault is similarly personal: Dutch has awakened from the cognitive prison in which the Lady has incarcerated her and in which she can only express the soft, feminine qualities ascribed to the stereotypical 1950s housewife. Not without a sense of humour, the Lady forces all three killjoys into virtual lives they would never choose for themselves, marrying Dutch to Johnny (who is like a brother to her), transforming the anti-establishment and countercultural Pree into a Company police officer, and isolating team-player D'avin as an independent killjoy. These designated positions achieve the Lady's aim in forcing queer characters to lead the straight lives they work so hard to avoid. In a bid to develop a subplot, Dutch is shown to be enjoying straight life in this brief episode, suggesting that her love for Johnny in the series' main plot is anything but brotherly. Her brief foray into what amounts to a false and (she protests) undesired heteronormative utopia drives her passionate destruction of the Lady's hatchlings. With all the wit one would expect from Buffy the Vampire Slayer and with homage to Ripley, just before destroying them, Dutch quips, "Come to mommy you slimey asswipes."

Dutch's channelling of Buffy is one marker of the distance between *Killjoys* and the *Alien* franchise even as her inner self-conflict mirrors Ripley's in the fourth *Alien* film; whereas many twenty-first-century vehicles for action heroines revel in witty repartee and comebacks, the *Alien* films are (with the exception of the fourth) quite serious. The distance between the two cultural texts no doubt registers shifts in feminist discourse: as action heroines become the focus of feminist debate, it becomes increasingly unacceptable to reproduce them without irony. This is especially true in the case of so-called phallicized action heroines, who are often accused of being merely figurative males rather than feminist figures. Dutch's tempering of Ripley's rage with humour can in this context be interpreted as a refusal to take the *Alien* films and, by extension, their entanglement in outdated gender politics, too seriously. Yet another and more important mark of departure from *Alien*, though, is Dutch's attachment to queer community. Unlike Ripley, Dutch is comforted by the queer love that surrounds her and which contrasts the hyper-capitalist individualism represented by the Lady. The other mother in *Killjoys* – the Lady – dredges up fears about losing oneself in a digital world of copies and simulated realities rooted in heteronormativity. In *Killjoys*, brainwashing is tantamount to straightwashing.

Later, in episode 7 of season 3, Dutch discovers that she has been birthed from the Green in the same way Ripley is birthed from the alien: the mother's material becomes the substance of the self. In *Killjoys*, the Green is a mysterious alien plasma that functions as an interplanetary computer network, an archive of personal and cultural memory, and the essence of life. Dutch's antithesis, Aneela, pulls Dutch out of a pool of Green through a laborious process of extraction from her spine. She frames this act within a fractured version of Rapunzel, who uses her own body to escape the tower in which she is incarcerated: "the girl saved up her magic and hid it from the man." The man is Khlyen, the father who has hidden her to protect her from the Lady. Dutch turns out to be one of Aneela's memories – a memory of herself as a child – that materializes upon being pulled out of the pool. When Dutch discovers the truth of her own origins, she must reckon with the fact that she is and is not herself. A shifting, live thing, the Green – itself the product of scientific experimentation – can materialize the past, empower individuals, or hijack identity altogether, contributing to a sense of profound disempowerment. The unpredictability of its effects enables the series to explore identity crisis, but also to highlight the inherent ambiguity of transformation. As Alena Cicholewski points out in her analysis of two adolescent literature duologies in this volume, the "liberatory potential of posthuman transformation" has its limits (132). Ripley likewise faces an identity crisis when she discovers that she is the product of a genetic experiment in *Alien Resurrection*. The very "genetics" that grant these women their extraordinary powers also prove self-destructive as they struggle to discern where the (m)other ends and their own selves begin. They survive regardless, suggesting that they are hardly cardboard cutouts of their antitheses, but rather extraordinarily human. Their humanity manifests in their resistance to oppressive forces and, in Dutch's case, her ability to bring people together to fight the oppressors. Even the alien mother and Aneela are somewhat salvaged in their respective story arcs, since the oppressive forces that wreak havoc on their respective worlds are far worse than any threat they pose. The real enemies in both series are capitalism, imperialism, and racism, which are intertwined and manifest in the monstrosity of the humanoid villains. In the end, the inhumane humans who weaponize alien biology for the purposes of destroying other humans need to be defeated. In *Alien* and *Killjoys*, patriarchal-capitalist collusion with hostile extraterrestrials backfires when tough women repurpose the alien biology forced on them. That Dutch relies on queer community to do so speaks volumes about *Killjoys'* critique of heteronormative capitalism. Embodying a uniquely post-feminist form of cross-border perversion chic, this heroine is hardly pure in her make-up but, as the multiplication of Dutch's costumes insinuate, is a composite without borders.

Killjoys, Post-feminism, and the Green

In a chapter of *Postfemininities in Popular Culture* entitled "Fighting It: The Supergirl," Stéphanie Genz describes the post-feminist action heroine precisely as "a composite character who exceeds the logic of non-contradiction" (155). She is shamelessly sexual and "garbed in the signifiers of stereotypical feminine attractiveness," but these qualities are not represented as detracting from her power (158). On the contrary, she embodies the idea of feminine sexuality as a superpower. This is made possible by her ability to demonstrate the kind of "agency, strength and self-reliance" typically associated with men (Genz 157–8). In recasting stereotypical femininity as power, she locates herself beyond the masculine/feminine binary opposition and thereby evades the charges of phallicization or figurative maleness often ascribed to heroines such as Ripley and Connor. As Genz notes, "In many ways, the feminine Supergirl is a reaction against the prevalence of the 'hardbody, hardware, hard-as-nails heroine' who dominates the action scenarios of the 1980s and early 1990s" (158). She effectively "exploits in-between spaces," contributing to an undermining of "totalizing dichotomies" (155).

Killjoys plays with what Genz calls post-feminism's signature "double gesture" (155), particularly in its depiction of Dutch. Dutch is hard-bodied, but not so much that she can be accused of looking "manly"; and while she occasionally wears baggy clothing resembling Ripley's, her typical outfit – dark pants and tight, skimpy shirts – advertises her figure. She is slender, cosmetically enhanced, and, perhaps most importantly in a TV text that features a team, smaller than her male partners. Coming in at 1.72 meters, she is the shortest of the killjoys, and her obeisance to dominant standards of feminine beauty means that despite evidence of muscularity, her limbs are slender rather than ripped. Fulfilling the post-feminist penchant for pastiche, her undercover work requires her to wear a wide range of costumes that register the various ways in which action heroines have been represented since the 1970s. This array of clothing has the added benefit of making it impossible to pin Dutch down, a welcome component in a show that seems more interested in exploring the idea of the action heroine as it has been realized throughout the twentieth and twenty-first centuries than in presenting a new one. The plot twist that enables Dutch's mirror reflection, the equally composite Aneela, de-realizes Dutch further: having been pulled out of Aneela's own pool of Green, Dutch must confront the very real question of whether she is human, or even real. She is quite literally the mirror image of Aneela's DNA. Although Aneela initially appears to be a villain, the show reveals that her actions are far more complicated. As happens to many an ill-fated character in the series, she has been infiltrated by the Green, a substance that interrupts her own agency. Despite this extraterrestrial incursion, she displays remarkable growth in moral character. The series' refusal to merely reproduce the sex/gender binary is, once again, reflected in its refusal to neatly divide characters into morally good and morally bad categories. That both Aneela's and Dutch's rebirth as compromised and composite postfeminist action heroines is made possible by the Green, however, raises the spectre of fears about networking and offers an alibi for the series' parodic upending of tired, sexist tropes.

When Johnny first encounters the Green as a liquid pool in a bronze bowl, he is excited because he quickly discovers that it is a complex network one can tap into. Because it resembles an innocuous liquid, it is, in

Johnny's opinion, a "cool" way to access information compared to the primitive screens to which he has been restricted previously. Tellingly, the owner of the pool Johnny accesses by placing his fingers inside the bowl is Khlyen, the "father" of the show's action heroine within the series' diegesis and also, when read figuratively, a signifier of the many directors who have created action heroines, oftentimes for the benefit of male spectators. Khlyen adopts Dutch after discovering that his biological daughter Aneela has created her out of her own memories. He subsequently raises her to be an assassin. Khlyen plays with this act of creation, using a fairy tale to encode messages to a now grown-up Dutch to save her life. As he tells her the tale, it is re-enacted for the benefit of the show's spectators, who finally receive a deliberately falsified version of the heroine's back story. Dutch herself is a fiction, a fragment of a memory twisted in accordance with Aneela's own desire for company in the cell where Khlyen has tucked her away. The Green itself can be here interpreted metafictionally as the entire field of pop culture from which the show itself can draw in its endless multiplication of action heroine figures. *Killjoys* is ultimately a fun-house mirror, reflecting back to spectators the very misogynist images they have grown accustomed to, but this time with a difference.

Nowhere is this mirroring more evident than in episode 6 of season 2, entitled "I Love Lucy." In this episode, the killjoys attempt to trade a vial of Green plasma with an intergalactic trader named Sam Romwell (Keon Alexander), whose asteroid ship contains ill-begotten items in a state of molecular disassembly. His possession of three titillating, vintage gynoids or fembots mark him as a figure associated with SF popular culture. While Sam's interest in the stories behind the items he collects suggests ethical engagement with other cultures, his interest in them is as self-indulgent as his interest in Dutch. In her resemblance to the tough women of SF action, she constitutes an even more titillating object than the gynoids: ironically, she is the real thing. Dutch's Blackness no doubt plays a part in Romwell's fantasies, which, like Khlyen's, can be described as Orientalist. After she shares her story, which predictably, given the series' comic reproduction of outworn tropes, leads back to the harem where her abusive father Khylen weaponized her, Sam is determined to have her. His failed attempt to take her by force compels him to ask her to stay in a bid to "make him a better man." Dutch refuses, asserting that she is not his own "personal manic pixie assassin." Her retort recalls the series' many flashbacks to her childhood, insinuating that Khlyen fetishized her in the same way Sam does. This parallel may explain the brutality of Dutch's previous attempt to murder him: she attacks him with a knife, and not without pleasure.

Sam survives thanks to his technological prowess, somewhat salvaging Dutch as a "good" heroine.

What rescues this episode from the dumpster fire of retrosexism for the feminist critic is its cutting critical edge – no pun intended. From beginning to end, it is executed with an irony that can only be fully appreciated by viewers with at least a passing familiarity with the sexist tropes deployed by the Star Trek franchise and other SF pop-culture texts. The fembots are significant, if minor, characters in this execution since they signal at once a return to, and upending of, sci-fi pop culture that panders to the kind of viewers Sam embodies. By the end of the episode, they and the asteroid are destroyed. Unlike other episodes, "I Love Lucy" announces itself most poignantly as parodic of misogynist SF. Still, there is something post-feminist about *Killjoys'* parody that does not let the series entirely off the retrosexist hook. In her defence of post-feminism as a sensibility as opposed to "an epistemological or political position," "an historical shift within feminism," or "a backlash against feminism," Gill argues that by thinking of post-feminism as a sensibility, one can acknowledge "the contradictory nature of postfeminist discourses and the entanglement of both feminist and anti-feminist themes within them" (149). If nothing else, *Killjoys* invites viewers to think about how subjectification and objectification often go hand in hand in entertainment media, not least SF film and TV. Bringing Gill's theorization of post-feminism as a sensibility into conversation with Williamson's discussion of retrosexism, one could argue that much of what passes as "feminist" representation is retrosexist in the sense that it indulges in nostalgia under the cover of irony. The pleasure *Killjoys* often takes in retrograde representation, even if it is cast as parody, makes it an extremely contradictory pop-culture text, and one difficult to salvage as a genuine example of "perversion chic," if this style is not always already a marketable brand in our neoliberal capitalist culture.

It is worth returning to the Green at this point, not simply as a symbolic embodiment of life, networking, and memory, but also as representative of the whole field of popular culture from which *Killjoys* can be seen to be drawing. This field is at once nurturing and poisonous. It is nurturing because it contains familiar and comforting narratives, but it is poisonous because many of these narratives necessarily reflect the contradictions, indifferences, and hate of a culture steeped in consumerist jingles. In its flirtation with retrosexism, its dynamic soundtrack, rapid-fire editing, and adoption of conventions associated with the western, the space opera, and dystopian fiction, *Killjoys* can easily be read "straight." It is the show's privileging of queer characters, a queered Marxism, and the brashness of its engagement with the pop-culture texts that preceded it that most recommend it as a TV text critical of post-feminism's contradictions.

One of the most alluring images of the show appears at the conclusion, when Aneela and her sidekick Delle Seyah are shown to be connected by the Green flowing through an IV tube between their bodies. Hoping to make Delle Seyah immortal, Aneela sacrifices some of her own Green. Because her gift depletes her own power, the act is a significant one. It is, moreover, dangerous given that the Green has been almost entirely eliminated from the Quad by the last episode. Only the Green in Aneela's blood remains, and no one knows what will happen if she gives some of it to Delle Seyah. Interpreted within the context of the women's playful and often combative relationship, a dynamic that reflects the show's own moral and political ambiguity, the use of IV to share the Green can be read as symbolic of medical S/M play. Such a reading would be in the spirit of the series, in which sexual inuendo is plentiful. More significantly, though, the Green's transformation from an archive to something that enables greater intimacy between two women whose own status as heroines has been compromised by the Green seems to foreclose charges of retrosexism. For this reason, one might think of the archive in this series as Alicia Fahey, drawing on Carolyn Steedman, characterizes it in her chapter in this volume, namely, as "an emergent site of world-building" (61). Aneela and Delle Sayah's privileged positioning at the end of the series suggests that viewers are expected to appreciate these characters' growth and revel in their queer love. Part of the pleasure of this scene, for this fan at least, is its provision of two heroines who have crossed over, not only from villainy to (an arguably reluctant) heroism, but also from a straight to a queer orientation. Delle Sayah's radical shift from a detestable member of the Nine to an (at least somewhat) heroic queer character is an especially pleasurable turn. If nothing else, *Killjoys* explodes the neat binary oppositions on which many critiques of Ripley as a figurative male have relied, presenting a cornucopia of intertextuality onto which viewers can project what they please. The show's use of the Green as a device is in this sense convenient, for it activates multiple subplots while evoking fears and anxieties around privacy, technology, surveillance, and artificial intelligence, issues at the forefront of political discourse today. By pulling liberally from the pool, *Killjoys* registers the difference between where we have been and where we are while also insinuating that many of the fears and anxieties of the past are our own. Dutch is not such a far cry from Ripley, after all.

Conclusion

As I pointed out in my overview of scholarly critiques of the *Alien* franchise, denunciations of Ripley as anti-feminist hinge on the extent to which she functions as a projecting screen for fears of strong women. In the twenty-first century, the tough women of entertainment media are projecting screens for ongoing misogyny, in that their status as super-skilled, super-powered, or machinic becomes an alibi for ruthless spectacles of violence against women. Examined within this context, *Killjoys'* love of the gun, though tinged with irony, seems unforgiveable even as it can be seen as mocking the gun-love south of the border, not to mention the many images of gun-toting heroes in US entertainment media. The action heroine in this series, however, is neither less contestable nor less controversial than any other. As cultural studies scholar Janice Loreck points out, notwithstanding a long history of violent women in film, viewers always appear to be surprised, and sometimes even outraged, by the latest incarnation ("Beyond"). Loreck argues that this doubtless has a lot to do with the allotted place of women as peace-loving, passive nurturers. The action heroine, violent or not, is almost always loved and hated concurrently. Ambivalence towards the action heroine is repeated offscreen, in the real-life scandals involving women perceived to have stepped outside of their allotted place as passive objects. *Killjoys* references the ways in which women function as social canvases, especially in its first season, where the action heroine appears in many different guises. While Dutch's undercover killjoy work provides the plot device that rationalizes these guises, they can also be seen as signalling play with the many forms in which the action heroine has been displayed in entertainment media. With the help of elaborate costumes, Dutch plays the roles of assassin, sex worker, socialite, warden, and many others, always with the sexy girlishness that has come to define a post-feminist aesthetic. The pleasure she offers to viewers can be likened to the pleasure the intergalactic trader Sam Romwell takes in the idea of Dutch as an exotic artefact to be collected; as with all his other artefacts, she will be "shelved" and brought out when he wants to gaze at and/or play with her. It is easy to imagine him dressing her up in whatever costume strikes his fancy, as if she is a limited-edition Barbie doll.

When Aneela enters the scene, the action heroine is doubled. This doubling has already been anticipated by the seemingly infinite series of double-Dutches. Dutch is herself doubled in her status as childhood-assassin-turned-killjoy. The variety of roles she adopts makes her a characteristically post-feminist composite heroine capable of embodying the many ways in which the female figure has been fetishized onscreen. *Killjoys* is practically a study of the action heroine. The action it features lays out the implications of fetishization, for Dutch's re-enactment of roles provokes misogynist treatments within the series' diegesis that correlate with the stereotype she embodies. The primary double to which I direct my analysis here is, of course, Ripley. Or, more accurately, Dutch, who doubles Ripley, drawing attention to the continued contestability of the action heroine and the impossibility of new, truly subversive incarnations.

NOTES

1 *Alien* is often cited as the first film to feature an action heroine, but this historicization ignores one of the most empowering action-heroine performances in American film. *Foxy Brown*, featuring Pam Grier, was released in 1974, pre-dating *Alien* by five years. Significantly, Quentin Tarantino cast Grier in his 1997 *Jackie Brown* in part as homage to the important role she played in shaping the figure of the action heroine.

2 I am indebted to Rosalind Gill for the term "post-feminist sensibility."

3 Few film theories have been as influential as Mulvey's, initially published in a 1975 issue of *Screen*, entitled "Visual Pleasure and Narrative Cinema." Many negative critiques of the *Alien* franchise have come from scholars deeply invested in Mulvey's thesis that the cinema reproduces a patriarchal unconscious in its likening of the camera to an "active" male gaze and styling of female figures as adorned objects connoting "*to-be-looked-at-ness*" (62–3). To neutralize the threat these figures may represent as fully fleshed-out human beings, they are reduced to fetish, engendering a fundamental contradiction: "the female image as a castration threat constantly endangers the unity of the diegesis and bursts through the world of illusion as an intrusive, static, one-dimensional fetish" (Mulvey 68). Yet the very notion of a "male gaze" risks reinforcing a rigid sex/gender binary and closing down possibilities for alternative viewing positions. While Mulvey's work seemed, at least to her, to make sense in the context of the 1970s, when Alfred Hitchcock and other male directors were producing films that exemplified the sadomasochistic dynamics of film viewing within a patriarchal culture, Mulvey herself stated four decades after the publication of her foundational essay that "with the advent of digital technology and the alteration of how we watch, analyse, and consume films, our relationship to these kinds of images has changed" (74).

4 I do not include the more recent films that take place in the same story world, *Prometheus* (2012) and *Alien Covenant* (2017), both directed by Ridley

Scott, or such films as *Alien vs. Predator* (2004). While it warrants extended critique, I do not discuss the most recent entry into the franchise, Fede Alvarez's *Alien: Romulus* (2024), which notably features an approximately twenty-one-year-old heroine. The effects of capitalist extraction and concomitant exploitation of miners are on full display here, with the youth of the characters drawing attention to the hopelessness of life in off-world colonies.

5 It may be worth remarking here that the episodes devoted to these two controversial figures expose systemic and profoundly gendered oppressions within the series' fictional world.

6 Stéphanie Genz and Benjamin Brabon draw on Rosalind Gill to describe *queer chic* as a trendy system of signification that "is part of an ongoing commercialization of gay and lesbian culture" (190).

WORKS CITED

Alien. Directed by Ridley Scott, performances by Sigourney Weaver, John Hurt, and Yaphet Kotto, Brandywine Productions, 1979.

Aliens. Directed by James Cameron, performances by Sigourney Weaver, Michael Biehn, and Carrie Henn, Twentieth Century Fox, 1986.

*Alien*³. Directed by David Fincher, performances by Sigourney Weaver, Charles S. Dutton, and Charles Dance, Twentieth Century Fox, 1992.

Alien Resurrection. Directed by John-Pierre Jeunet, performances by Sigourney Weaver, Winona Ryder, and Dominic Pinon, Brandywine Productions, 1997.

Alien: Romulus. Directed by Fede Alvarez, 20th Century Studios, 2024.

Banet-Weiser, Sarah, Rosalind Gill, and Catherine Rottenberg. "Postfeminism, Popular Feminism and Neoliberal Feminism? Sarah Banet-Weiser, Rosalind Gill and Catherine Rottenberg in Conversation." *Feminist Theory*, vol. 21, no. 1, 2020, pp. 3–24.

"Blame It on the Rain." *Killjoys*, season 5, episode 2, *YouTube*, uploaded by Syfy, 26 July 2019, https://www.youtube.com/watch?v=qw-Mbe3wqeQ&list=ELZVWeiPT5vfxWSFtahhiZOg&index=2.

Brown, Jeffrey. *Beyond Bombshells: The New Action Heroine in Popular Culture*. UP of Mississippi, 2015.

– *Dangerous Curves: Action Heroines, Gender, Fetishism, and Popular Culture*. UP of Mississippi, 2011.

Buffy the Vampire Slayer. Created by Joss Whedon, performance by Sarah Michelle Gellar, Mutant Enemy Productions, 1997–2001.

Cicholewski, Alena. "Posthuman Girlhoods in Canadian Young Adult Science Fiction." Roy, pp. 117–37.

Colombiana. Directed by Robert Megaton, performance by Zoe Saldana, EuropaCorp, 2011.

"Come the Rain." *Killjoys*, season 1, episode 8, *YouTube*, uploaded by Syfy, 7 Aug. 2015. https://www.youtube.com/watch?v=DH-il_0m_l4&list =EL4fZLVEPG3zCjAx2KJFvFzg&index=8.

Creed, Barbara. *The Monstrous-Feminine: Film, Feminism, Psychoanalysis.* Routledge, 1993.

Fahey, Alicia. "Speculative Archives in Novels by Thomas King and Larissa Lai: Hope in the Midst of Crisis." Roy, pp. 45–65.

Foxy Brown. Written and directed by Jack Hill, performance by Pam Grier, American International Pictures, 1974.

Gallardo C., Ximena, and C. Jason Smith. *Alien Woman: The Making of Lt. Ellen Ripley.* Continuum, 2004.

Genz, Stéphanie. *Postfemininities in Popular Culture.* Palgrave Macmillan, 2009.

Genz, Stéphanie, and Benjamin A. Brabon. *Postfeminism: Cultural Texts and Theories.* Edinburgh UP, 2018.

Gibson, Pamela Church. "'You've Been in My Life So Long I Can't Remember Anything Else': Into the Labyrinth with Ripley and the Alien." *Key Frames: Popular Cinema and Cultural Studies*, edited by Matthew Tinkcom and Amy Villarejo, Routledge, 2001, pp. 35–51.

Gill, Rosalind. "Postfeminist Media Culture: Elements of a Sensibility." *European Journal of Cultural Studies*, vol. 10, no. 2, 2007, pp. 147–66.

Girlfight. Written and directed by Karyn Kusama, performance by Michelle Rodriquez, Independent Film Channel Productions, 2000.

González, Christopher. "The Latinx Fantastic: Robert Rodriguez and the Power of His Speculative Storytelling." *Texas Studies in Literature and Language*, vol. 63, no. 2, 2021, pp. 151–72.

Hills, Elizabeth. "From 'Figurative Males' to Action Heroines: Further Thoughts on Active Women in the Cinema." *Screen*, vol. 40, no. 1, 1999, pp. 38–50.

Hutcheon, Linda. *Irony's Edge: The Theory and Politics of Irony.* Routledge, 1994.

"I Love Lucy." *Killjoys*, season 2, episode 6, *YouTube*, uploaded by Syfy, 5 Aug. 2016. https://www.youtube.com/watch?v=chrh0GcC7Rk&list=EL4mmIfr 785MfBLJGEGoH-Nw&index=6.

Inness, Sherrie A. *Tough Girls: Women Warriors and Wonder Women in Popular Culture.* U of Pennsylvania P, 1999.

Jackie Brown. Directed by Quentin Tarantino, performance by Pam Grier, Miramax Films, 1997.

Jennings, Ros. "Desire and Design: Ripley Undressed." *Immortal, Invisible: Lesbians and the Moving Image*, edited by Tamsin Wilton, Routledge, 1995, pp. 158–69.

Kaplan, Cora. "*Dirty Harriet/Blue Steel*: Feminist Theory Goes to Hollywood." *Discourse*, vol. 16, no. 1, 1993, pp. 50–70.

Loreck, Janice. "Beyond *Atomic Blonde*: Cinema's Long, Proud History of Violent Women." *The Conversation*, 29 Aug. 2017, https://theconversation.com/beyond-atomic-blonde-cinemas-long-proud-history-of-violent-women-82900.

Lovretta, Michelle, creator. *Killjoys*. Mendacity Pictures, Bell Media, and Temple Street Productions, 2015.

Morgan, Jason. "Queerly Canadian: 'Perversion Chic' Cinema and (Queer) Nationalism in English Canada." *Canadian Cultural Poesis: Essays on Canadian Culture*, edited by Garry Sherbert, Annie Gérin, and Sheila Petty, Wilfrid Laurier UP, 2006, pp. 211–25.

Mulvey, Laura. "Visual Pleasure and Narrative Cinema." *Feminist Film Theory: A Reader*, edited by Sue Thornham, Edinburgh UP, 1999, pp. 58–69.

Mulvey, Laura, Anna Backman Rogers, and Annie van den Oever. "Feminist Film Studies 40 Years after 'Visual Pleasure and Narrative Cinema,' a Triologue." *NECSUS: European Journal of Media Studies*, vol. 4, no. 1, 2015, pp. 67–79.

Roy, Wendy, editor. *ReVisions: Speculating in Literature and Film in Canada*. U of Toronto P, 2025.

Scobie, Stephen. "What's the Story, Mother?: The Mourning of the Alien." *Science Fiction Studies*, vol. 20, no. 1, 1993, pp. 80–93.

Star Trek: The Original Series. Desilu Productions and Paramount Television, 1966–9.

Star Trek: The Next Generation. Paramount Television, 1987–94.

Tasker, Yvonne. *Spectacular Bodies: Gender, Genre, and the Action Cinema*. Routledge, 1993.

The Terminator. Written and directed by James Cameron, performance by Linda Hamilton, Orion Pictures, 1984.

Thompson, William. "Climate Change and the Girl Body: Hope and the Dystopian Future in Three Novels by Monica Hughes." Roy, pp. 139–57.

Williamson, Judith. "Sexism with an Alibi." *The Guardian*, 31 May 2003, https://www.theguardian.com/media/2003/may/31/advertising.comment.

Contributors

Shelley Boyd is dean of the Faculty of Arts at Kwantlen Polytechnic University, where she is a faculty member in the Department of English. She researches food and gardens in Canadian literature. Her books include *Garden Plots: Canadian Women Writers and Their Literary Gardens* (2013), *Canadian Culinary Imaginations* (2020, co-edited with Dorothy Barenscott), and *Canadian Literary Fare* (2023, co-authored with Nathalie Cooke), which was awarded the 2024 Gabrielle Roy Prize for its contribution to Canadian literary studies.

Mabiana Camargo is a scholar from Brazil. She is a final-year PhD candidate at the University of Saskatchewan, where she is researching women's bodies and enclosed space in Margaret Atwood's speculative fiction.

Alena Cicholewski is an academic writing instructor at the University of Bremen, Germany. She also teaches at the Institute for English and American Studies at the University of Oldenburg, Germany, where she obtained a PhD in 2020. Her research focuses on connecting postcolonial approaches to the analysis of popular culture, with particular attention to graphic novels, video games, and young adult fiction.

Matthew Cormier is assistant professor of Canadian Literature at l'Université de Moncton. He is the author of *Sieve Reading Beyond the Minor* (forthcoming 2025) and co-editor of *Digital Memory Agents in Canada* (2024). His research intersects the digital humanities, memory studies, affect theory, and recent apocalyptic writing in Canada.

Gage Karahkwí:io Diabo (they/them) is a Mohawk scholar from Kahnawake and an assistant professor of Indigenous Literatures at Concordia University in Montreal. Their research focuses on decolonizing dialogue in First Peoples' literatures, and they have published essays in *Inter-Asia Cultural Studies*, *Studies in American Indian Literature*, and *Canadian Literature*. They also wrote the 2016 short documentary *Green Fees: The Evolution of the Kanawaki Lease*.

Alicia Fahey teaches in the English Department at Capilano University in North Vancouver. Her research and teaching involve Canadian literature, culture, and visual arts, as well as Indigenous storytelling in its many forms. She has recent publications in *Studies in Canadian Literature* (2023) and *English Studies in Canada* (2022).

Amy LeBlanc is a PhD candidate in English and creative writing at the University of Calgary, where she researches the intersections of Gothicism, haunted house literature, and chronic illness. She is the author of *I know something you don't know* (2020), *Unlocking* (2021), and *Homebodies* (2023). Her second poetry collection, *I used to live here*, was published by Porcupine's Quill in 2025. She was awarded a 2020 Lieutenant Governor of Alberta Emerging Artist Award and is a 2022–2024 Killam Laureate.

Cynthea Masson is an author and professor in the English Department at Vancouver Island University, where she teaches writing and literature. She is co-editor of the collection *Reading Joss Whedon* (2014). Her novels *The Alchemists' Council* (2016), *The Flaw in the Stone* (2018), and *The Amber Garden* (2020) are anchored in concepts of medieval alchemy.

Jessica McDonald (she/her) is a lecturer at the University of Saskatchewan and formerly a postdoctoral research fellow at Simon Fraser University. She researches Canadian literature in relation to social and environmental justice, and she has published on Nalo Hopkinson, Michael Crummey, and Douglas Coupland; the latter is the focus of her current book manuscript, *Complicated Geographies: Douglas Coupland's North America*.

Kai McKenzie (they/them) is an advocate for gender diversity and a lecturer in literature and gender studies. They have doctoral degrees in folklore (2004) and English literature (2024), the latter of which focuses on transgender, Two-Spirit, and other gender diverse literatures in Canada.

MacKenzie Read is an independent scholar whose main area of research is American feminist television series and films. She is a curriculum writer and educator at Saskatchewan Indian Institute of Technologies and an academic strategist with the University of Saskatchewan.

Jasmine Redford is a comics illustrator and a PhD student at the University of Saskatchewan whose academic research is on violence in Canadian comics. She has degrees in visual arts and English literature, and she is the artist for the graphic novel *Siegfried: Dragon Slayer* (2022).

Gwen Rose (she/they) is a doctoral student at the University of Saskatchewan. Her main areas of research are literary modernism and the lived experience of oppressed and marginalized peoples; these are combined in her dissertation, which examines transgender characters within modernist fiction.

Wendy Roy is professor of Canadian Literature at the University of Saskatchewan. She is the author of *Maps of Difference: Canada, Women, and Travel* (2005) and *The Next Instalment: Serials, Sequels, and Adaptations of L.M. Montgomery, Nellie L. McClung, and Mazo de la Roche* (2019), and she co-edited *Listening Up, Writing Down, and Looking Beyond: Interfaces of the Oral, Written, and Visual* (2012, with Susan Gingell). Her current research is on apocalyptic and dystopian fiction in Canada.

June Scudeler (Métis) (she/her) is associate professor of Indigenous Studies, cross-appointed with Gender, Sexuality, and Women's Studies, at Simon Fraser University. Her research includes Indigenous queer studies, Métis studies, and Indigenous horror.

Sheheryar Sheikh has published two novels, *The Still Point of the Turning World* (2017) and *Call Me Al: The Hero's Ha-Ha Journey* (2019). As Donald Hill Family Postdoctoral Fellow at Dalhousie University, he is creating a series of vignettes, short stories, and novellas to visualize a world-city on Earth in 2500–2555 CE. His first monograph, *The Post-9/11 Novel*, is forthcoming from Bloomsbury Academic in November 2025.

Heather Snell is associate professor of English at the University of Winnipeg, where she teaches children's literature, post-colonial studies, and critical theory. Her research explores young-adult climate fiction and speculative fiction from feminist, post-colonial, and ecocritical perspectives.

William Thompson is associate professor of English at McEwan University in Edmonton. He researches children's and young adult literature and culture, and he has published and presented on C.S. Lewis, J.K. Rowling, and L.M. Montgomery.

Index